New Deal Modernism

Post-Contemporary Interventions

Series Editors: Stanley Fish and Fredric Jameson

. . .

New Deal Modernism

American Literature

and the Invention of

the Welfare State

Michael Szalay

Duke University Press   *Durham & London*   **2000**

. . .

© 2000 Duke University Press

All rights reserved

Printed in the United States of America on acid-free paper ∞

Designed by C. H. Westmoreland   Typeset in Times Roman with

Monotype Twentieth-Century display by Keystone Typesetting, Inc.

Library of Congress Cataloging-in-Publication Data appear

on the last printed page of this book.

• • •

Contents

• • •

Acknowledgments

I have relied heavily on the intelligence and generosity of others while writing this book. At Johns Hopkins, Jennifer Ashton, Sharon Cameron, Jerome Christensen, J. D. Connor, Tim Dean, Graham Finlay, Michael Fried, Allen Grossman, Oren Izenberg, Dan McGee, and Mark McGurd each provided formative assistance and input. Above all, Frances Ferguson and Walter Michaels were invaluable; this project would not have been possible without their scruple for intellectual honesty. At the University of Michigan, in both the Society of Fellows and the Department of English, I benefited from the help of Sandra Gunning, Jochen Hellbeck, Andrea Henderson, Kerry Larson, Alaina Lemon, Mary Mcguire, Barbara Ryan, Rei Terada, David Thomas, and James Boyd White. Paul Anderson, Eric Guthey, and Alan Wald were especially generous with their time and learning. I also wish to thank my readers at Duke, Michael North and Fredric Jameson, both of whom offered lucid and rigorous comment during the last stages of this project. Thanks as well to Julian Koslow. Both of my readers at Duke, Michael North and Fredric Jameson, offered lucid and rigorous comment during the last stages of this project. I am also indebted to my colleagues at the New York Americanist Group: particularly generous with their input were Mary Esteve, Michael Trask, and, most especially, Sean McCann.

This project could not have been written without generous institutional support from the University of Michigan Society of Fellows and Fordham University. Very early versions of chapters 2 and 3 appeared, respectively, as "Inviolate Modernism: Hemingway, Stein, Tzara," in *Modern Language Quarterly* 56:4 (December 1995) and "Wallace Stevens and the Invention of Social Security," *Modernism/Modernity* 5:1 (January 1998). I am grateful to the publishers for their permission to reprint these essays here.

. . .

The Literature of the Welfare State

We are beginning to wipe out the line that divides the practical from the ideal, and in so doing, we are fashioning an instrument of unimagined power. — Franklin Roosevelt, Second Inaugural Address, 27 January 1937

In his State of the Union address of 1935, Franklin Roosevelt re-affirmed his commitment before Congress and the American people to make it his "first and continuing task" to provide for the "security of the men, women and children of the nation."[1] Such a commitment was necessary, he reasoned as he signed the Social Security Act into law, because "the civilization of the past hundred years, with its startling industrial changes, has tended more and more to make life insecure."[2] Acknowledging that it was impossible to "insure one hundred percent of the population against one hundred percent of the hazards and vicissitudes of life," he expressed the hope that Social Security would give "some measure of protection to the average citizen."[3] Two years after Roosevelt signed the act, Wallace Stevens embraced Social Security in "Insurance and Social Change." Surrounded by insurance agents, Stevens defended the Social Security Administration to his co-workers at the Hartford Fire and Indemnity Company by rebutting the claim that the welfare state incursion into insurance practice would fragment an already diminished market. Stressing the fact that the private industry looked to offer "insurance for everything," as op-posed to the government's "insurance for all," Stevens argued that federal insurance, far from competing with private insurance, pro-vided the precondition for the latter's efforts to "perfect" insurance coverage. "To be certain of a regular income, as in the case of social security," reasoned Stevens, "is not the same thing as to be able to repair any damage, or to meet any emergency."[4] It is only when Americans were certain of a regular income that they could afford the "insurance for everything" offered by the private industry.

Social Security was seen in this way to offer one legislative solution

• • •

to the Depression-era specter of "underconsumption," the notion — long since discredited — that the nation's economic troubles were traceable less to excessive industrial production than to the failure of Americans to consume what was produced. But "Insurance and Social Change" also suggests a more literary solution to the problem of underconsumption. According to Stevens, nothing stimulates demand more than representing a product in its perfected form. Stevens reasons that "it helps us to see [the value of] insurance in the midst of social change to imagine a world in which insurance has been made perfect" (234). He goes on to observe that H. G. Wells revitalized the field of mechanical science in this manner, coyly noting, "If Mr. Wells has preferred the machine to insurance as his field, he has only left insurance to others" (234). Thus Wallace Stevens, poet, makes his bid to be the H. G. Wells of insurance, leading Milton Bates some years later to term "Insurance and Social Change" the "prolegomenon to any future poetry of insurance."[5] And in fact, "Insurance and Social Change" does make plain that by 1937 Stevens had come to understand poetry as being importantly related to the public activities of the modern welfare state, in particular to the federal "insurance for all," Social Security, that has since emerged as the New Deal's most sacrosanct legacy. All of what follows examines the terms of this relationship between literature and the state, as those terms were imagined by both the New Deal itself and writers like James Agee, Ernest Hemingway, Robert Frost, Ayn Rand, Betty Smith, Gertrude Stein, John Steinbeck, Stevens, and Richard Wright.

Roosevelt's grandiose rhetoric is evidence enough that, in the years leading up to 1935, the modern American state had experienced a profound crisis in its social legitimacy. Unable to safeguard the security of either the working or middle classes, threatened at the poles and picket lines by elements of both, government set out to reinvent itself. The Social Security Administration was to be Roosevelt's principal contribution to this process. At bottom, Social Security made the state not an instrument of coordinated economic planning but rather a system of exchange essentially compensatory for human experience. The New Deal thus embraced actuarial models of governance that revolved around the statistical construction of population groups, the calculation of probabilities for such groups, and the varied application of these probabilities to individual persons. As I argue throughout *New Deal Modernism,* this led to a literature of liberal interdependence, as writers looked to reconcile at times conflicting impulses toward individual agency and collective affiliation, what a character in Richard Wright's *Native Son* (1940) calls the "two fundamental concepts of our civilization . . . personality and security — the conviction that the person is inviolate and that which sustains him is equally so."[6] I am not, on the other hand, concerned in what follows to characterize this literature simply as a compendium of responses to the New Deal. The writers examined below find in the specifically compensatory mechanisms of risk management not only the modern state's response to a crisis in its social legitimacy, but the framework for a response to a similar crisis facing modern literature as well. This framework changed profoundly the political valence and cultural instrumentality of existing literary conventions. Whether truly gripped by the cataclysmic anguish of the Great Depression or fearful of being seen as insensate to it, writers justified their work by situating it with respect to the legitimation crisis then facing the state. These justifications — and the extent to which they internalized the procedures of governance within literature itself — led to new accounts of how modernist concerns with form and audience might engage political and economic experience.

It might quickly be objected that Wallace Stevens was a historical anomaly, hardly a figure sufficiently representative to serve as a touchstone for the kinds of claims enumerated above. Critics on the left and the right frequently insisted that sticking with the center (not yet "vital") was a willful evasion, the kind for which Stevens was so often castigated in the radical press. And just how many writers, it might well be asked, actually took the time to comment on the New Deal? This notoriously jackbooted period, after all, quaffed its ideology undiluted; a skeptic might reason that no writer truly interested in politics would have cared overmuch about the New Deal. But writers engaged the risk management procedures of the modern state regardless of their personal relation to the political divisions often fetishized by present-day critics of the period. Literary engagements with the welfare state during the thirties and forties did not emerge simply as a function of traditionally liberal, centrist political convictions. *New Deal Modernism* insists that an ideologically diverse group of writers from the left as well as the right were active participants in the reinvention of modern governance.

Recognizing the extensive commerce between modern American

literature and the welfare state does not require pretending that the welfare state has ever inspired the kinds of heartfelt conviction elicited by either communism or fascism. Far from it: we continue to live with the welfare state at all precisely because it has proven so curiously immune to strong ideological formulation. "The welfare state does not seem able to arouse strong loyalties," writes Irving Howe. "It seems easier, if not more intelligent, to die for the Stars and Stripes, or the Proletarian Fatherland, than for unemployment insurance and social security. There are fewer subrational loyalties, and perhaps no encompassing mystique, for the welfare state to exploit." As appropriate as Howe's comments might be to the Democratic Party's abandonment of the welfare state during the 1990s, they are doubly so for the recent criticism of the 1930s. For even though Howe points out that many Marxists "see the welfare state as a mode of government designed to keep the masses quiescent with bread and circuses," it is fair to say that few on the left within the field of literary studies have been roused to treat the welfare state as an ideological formation coherent enough to be engaged at all.[7] This is true, at least in part, because the hodge-podge of often conflicting dogmas that inform the welfare state — from socialism to regulatory corporate liberalism — has not offered literary critics the kinds of antihegemonic politics they have so often wanted in the past three decades. Less subject to snappy formulation than a concept like Ernst Mandel's "late capitalism," which is often referred to in passing and described in the broadest of terms, the New Deal has baffled its critics on the left as well as the right.[8]

If the welfare state, bogged down in half-measures and compromise, has seemed to critics an uninteresting topic of analysis, then "modernism" certainly has not. We are deluged with works looking to codify yet once more this still somehow elusive period of literary history. Depending on the critic, modernism is historically explosive, containing within itself all the chaotic energies of the new, or an evasion, a project of autonomy struggling to awake from the nightmare of history; given to the streamlined and the technocratic, or to myth and the archaic; a subversion of the semiotic codes of bourgeois society or a sequence of master narratives that are the very embodiment of hegemony; awash in a stream of middle-class consciousness or a shaft into the primal imagination of the primitive unconscious; committed to the transcendent powers of the lone genius, or impersonal, steeped in the objectifying mechanisms of modern science and sociology; acutely self-conscious and metadiscursive or the very dream of a self-identical logos; pure and sanitized of generic confusion or the polyglot vanguard of multimedia society.[9] What follows does not set out to reconcile these definitions. Rather, I use the term "modernism" in an unabashedly general sense, to designate the literature of the first half of this century; within this field I have applied no acid test, no checklist of aesthetic distinction. I have, on the other hand, concentrated my examinations of modernist form almost exclusively around debates prevalent during the thirties and forties concerning what it meant for art to be considered either process or product, either an activity of creation or the artifact thus created.

The distinction between process and product was axial to the period, I maintain, because it was seen to bear directly on literature's relation as a market institution to the dire problem of underconsumption (to which Stevens addresses himself in "Insurance and Social Change"). The Depression was occasioned, many believed, because of insufficient national demand, because the American public either did not or could not purchase the goods churned out by American industry. The massive unemployment of writers and artists during the thirties suggested that the literary marketplace — subject to these same laws — had been saturated beyond its woefully limited capacity. Thus literature came to seem like the quintessential luxury good, its consumption more subject to the unpredictable equivocations of laissez-faire than practically any other. The otherwise discordant literary politics of the thirties and forties might well be united in their shared commitment to counter this trend, to depict literature as necessary a commodity as food and other daily essentials. As I show in chapter I, the New Deal assisted powerfully: its Works Progress Administration's Arts Projects proselytized tirelessly that Americans needed to consume art as surely as they needed social security itself.

But at the same time, the Arts Projects did far more than simply enhance demand for works of art. The Projects led to new ways of conceiving literary labor; in turn, a newly professionalized industry of salaried writers struggled to negotiate, in their work and in their new-found careers, the tension between liberal agency on the one hand, and collectivizing, compensatory strategies of risk management on the other. The salary paid these writers alone made clear that art was to be more than one commodity among many, regardless of how necessary it was imagined to be. Rather, the consumption of art was held to be emblematic of how the welfare state might transform the relation between markets and national community altogether. The New Deal set out to register the presence of a national community otherwise belied in aggregated acts of consumption; it placed at the core of modern welfare the conviction that markets were not the most successful means of recording and even creating American publics. So, even as enhancing the demand for art appeared representative of how the New Deal needed to prime the pump of an economy increasingly geared toward nonessential, service-oriented commodities, enhancing demand for any commodity became part of a problem that the institution of "art" — properly defined and properly paid for — was deemed uniquely able to circumvent. Of all the financial institutions regulated by the New Deal, none was held to be more emblematic of the utopian possibilities of the welfare state than the institution of art. Thus, art would become not a system of commodities at all, but an administratively coordinated process of production. Ideally, there would be no literary artifact the demand for which the state needed to enhance; instead, art would become an entirely procedural activity, a form of recreation that all might perform, regardless of their training or talent. Insofar as artists and writers did, invariably, produce objects, the New Deal Arts Projects reasoned that the consumption of these objects should approach as closely as possible the conditions of their production. In effect, art would solve the problem of underconsumption by making consumption and production one and the same process, a temporally defined activity detached as much as possible from the determining equivocations of market demand.

The New Deal's massive and often bureaucratic engagement with the consumption and production of art — at the level of policy and aesthetic theory both — makes it difficult to separate out questions of modernist form from the institutional apparatus of the state. This is the case because some of the most constitutive issues in modernist form had to do with a work's perceived relation to its audience, a concern that seemed at one and the same time a concern with a work's relation to markets and to the state's regulation of those markets. Therefore, I do not chart and catalogue formal innovation and only then set out to find its incipient politics; what follows proceeds from the premise that it is impossible to identify a set of modernist concerns as such and then build bridges between them and a more properly historical formation like the New Deal. Building such bridges has in fact played a large role in some of the most promising new work on American modernism. Alan Filreis's *Modernism from Right to Left*, for example, sets out to prove that during the thirties there were many "convergences between modernism and radicalism," and that Stevens in particular had a fuller than presumed "understanding of the rhetorical issues that gave force to the left." But recovering the influence of the literary left by focusing on a poet whose modernist credentials are imagined to be beyond question does as much to reify the coherence and autonomy of modernism as the culturally conservative writing of the New Critics and the New York Intellectuals ever did.[10] Efforts to link up modernism with the left have their corollary in similar efforts to do so with the right. Commenting on "the eagerness displayed in critically establishing a connection between modernism and fascism," Astradur Eysteinsson declares it "baffling how rarely [this connection's] further historical and formal implications are probed. First," he asks, "where does this formal-ideological nexus place modernism with regard to the prevalent capitalist-bourgeois culture of the twentieth century? Second, how, and under what conditions, can aesthetically elaborated form (*as form*) become the vehicle of a specific ideology?"[11] Such questions go to the heart of *New Deal Modernism* not because critics of modernism need to understand how form "*as form*" can be made to seem ideological — exactly what is form "*as form*"? — but because, during the thirties and forties, accounts of form did not aspire to be anything but ideological.

This conclusion is perhaps least surprising in the case of a group like the Southern Agrarians, in part because the group itself insisted on the organic interrelation of the cultural and the political. In *The World's Body* (1938), for example, John Crowe Ransom embraces T. S. Eliot's notion that "arts," "manners," and "religion" are "three institutions [that] do not rest on three foundations but one foundation."[12] To be sure, also like Eliot, Ransom insists on a fundamental difference between this singular foundation and the more instrumentalizing, "scientific" mechanisms of modern life, mechanisms Ransom associates with the workaday world of New Deal politics. On his way to proving that "aesthetic forms" are more adequate to the hazards of modern life than "economic forms," Ransom declares in his essay "Forms and Citizens" in *The World's Body* that "men become poets, or at least they read poets, in order to atone for having been hard practical men and hard theoretical scientists" (xi). But as much as he wants to hold the scientific apart from the poetic, Ransom demonstrates the distinction between them precisely by insisting that both address themselves to identical problems: he explains how rituals such as public mourning and poetry help individuals deal with loss in ways that rationalizing financial institutions cannot. Dismissing New Deal economic efforts to insulate individuals against loss, he justifies the value of the aesthetic experience in its ability to transcend these efforts. Preferring community rituals of mourning over a government check, for example, an indignant Ransom writes, "We may of course eliminate the pageantry of death from our public life, but only if we expect the widow and orphan not really to feel their loss; and to this end we may inform them that they will not find it an economic loss, since they shall be maintained in their usual standards of living by the State. It is unfortunate for the economic calculus that they are likely to feel it anyway, since probably their relation to the one dead was not more economic than it was sentimental. Sentiments, those irrational psychic formations, do not consist very well with the indifference, machine-like, with which some modern social workers would have men fitting into the perfect economic organization" (36). That Ransom was no supporter of the New Deal is hardly the point here. Far more interesting than his down-home dismissal of the social worker is his attempt to show that "aesthetic forms" offer the modern individual a more perfect form of "organization" than "economic forms," championed here by "the State." Exactly how literary objects achieved an organization unavailable to the state was a complex matter, discussed at length in chapter 2. What is immediately clear, on the other hand, is that for Ransom, truly existential loss finds no compensation in a government check.

T. S. Eliot expresses this same view one year later when he takes up insurance and its relation to the "one foundation" of "arts," "manners," and "religion." In *The Family Reunion* (1939), Eliot's chorus intones:

> We can usually avoid accidents,
> We are insured against fire,
> Against larceny and illness,
> Against defective plumbing,
> But not against the act of God.[13]

These lines are not meant to represent Eliot's views, who by the 1930s imagined his verse precisely as a transcendental insurance against acts of God, an aesthetic, quasi-secular supplement to the Anglican cosmology to which he was then so devoted. But of course Eliot's point has as much to do with the vast gulf that separates financial from spiritual compensation as it does with the supplemental relation between the poetic and the theological. Yes, poetry is a kind of compensation for acts of God, Eliot suggests, but one far more akin to religion itself than to quotidian forms of insurance.

Whereas Ransom and Eliot insisted on distinguishing between the scientific and the governmental on the one hand and the religious and the poetic on the other, the New Deal did not. The concept of social security was as valuable as it was to the welfare state because it addressed more than simply financial dislocation. By "social security" I make obvious reference to the Social Security Administration, the heart of what Roosevelt in 1935 called his "new order of things," of which "every major legislative enactment of . . . Congress," he urged, "should be a component part."[14] Almost without exception, historians bring coherence to the New Deal through what Alan Brinkley calls its "single most important contribution to the creation of the modern welfare state — the Social Security System." Linda Gordon agrees, calling Social Security "the central legislation of the U.S. welfare state," as does Alan Dawley, who writes, "If there was a watchword covering the reforms of the time, it was neither liberty nor equality, but *security*." Dawley observes that "bit by bit, [this] new ideal would be built into social policy until it was enshrined at the highest level of the state in the Social Security system in the 1930s, the cornerstone of the welfare state."[15] But even as my use of the phrase social security makes reference to the New Deal program, I am also interested in the extent to which New Deal invocations of social security were, as the epigraph from Roosevelt suggests, part of a broader state effort "to wipe out the line that divides the practical from the ideal."

In its "ideal" form, social security had as much to do with modernist alienation as it did with financial uncertainty; it was the New Deal's answer not simply to unemployment and other economic exigencies, but far more broadly, to the displacing conditions of modern life in a rapidly evolving capitalist society. In his *Quest for Security* (1934), one of the most important influences on the formation of the Social Security Administration, I. M. Rubinow writes that social insurance is "a movement, a hope, an aspiration . . . one of the most important factors for decreasing the amount of human misery."[16]

That social insurance programs understood human misery in potentially expansive terms is made clear as early as Rufus M. Potts's altogether typical "The Altruistic Utilitarianism of Insurance" (1916). Potts justifies the need for social insurance by striking a quintessentially modern, if also melodramatic, note: "When a reflective mind contemplates the career of man and considers his uncertain and transient existence, ever liable to be overwhelmed by this giant force of nature, he beholds human life stripped of all its everyday disguises and illusions; and he sees it, a puny thing, emerge from nothingness, and stand shivering a brief period on the desolate shore of infinite existence until the moment when, caught up by the ceaseless whirl of the elemental forces, it is again swept back into nonexistence like a snowflake into the surging ocean."[17] Such tremulous renderings — characteristic here not simply of insurance writing but of the recent history of American literary naturalism as well — find repeated expression during the thirties and forties. Thus, we turn to the Social Security Board's "Security for a People" (1937) and find the report insisting that "Security is more than a condition of material well being." Likewise, we find one of the program's original drafters, Edwin Witte, reasoning that "Social security is in fact more of an ideal than an institution or a group of institutions."[18]

If social security could be an ideal as much as a group of institutions, then so could government itself. The first to use the term "welfare state" (in 1936), New Deal antitrust attorney and Yale law professor Thurman Arnold agrees in *The Symbols of Government* (1935) when he declares the symbiotic coexistence of "spiritual government" and "temporal government."[19] Government, Arnold reasoned, was a multifaceted operation, as dependent on cultural factors as political ones. And in fact, much of what follows is an effort to trace the emergence of government not simply in the marbled corridors of Washington but in the byways of twentieth-century popular culture as well. The startling number of texts in the thirties and forties directly concerned with the New Deal and potentially New Deal–like governments — Sinclair Lewis's *It Can't Happen Here* (1935), Meridel Le Sueur's *The Girl* (1935–1945), John Steinbeck's *The Grapes of Wrath* (1939), John Dos Passos's *Grand Design* (1942), Ayn Rand's *The Fountainhead* (1943), and Robert Penn Warren's *All the King's Men* (1946), to name a few — indicates a substantial cultural preoccupation with what government was and what it should do. As a bewildered character muses in *All the King's Men,* "Government is committed these days to give services we never heard of growing up," and many of the texts I take up struggle to adjust themselves to this realization. But at the same time, one notes during the New Deal a consistent allegorization of the state, a series of displacements that engage it only in oblique fashion. We need only turn to a film like the *Wizard of Oz* (1939) to note such a phenomenon; "The Emerald City was the New Deal," declared lyricist E. Y. Harburg of the richly allegorical filming of L. Frank Baum's already charged political satire.[20] Having trekked to the Emerald City for help, Dorothy finds only a humbug and discovers that, all along, she has had the instrument of her own salvation (on her feet); the film's politics were as conservative as Baum's, steeped in the American tradition of small government and self-help.

But most often the New Deal is displaced during the thirties onto the private insurance company. A small but important assortment of American writers and artists — such as James M. Cain, Charles Ives, Wallace Stevens, Benjamin Whorf, and Richard Wright — actually worked for such companies. But far more strikingly, many of the remarkable number of New Deal documents concerned with insurance — Cain's *The Postman Always Rings Twice* (1934) and *Double Indemnity* (1936), Warner Brothers' *Gold Diggers of 1937,* Betty Smith's *A Tree Grows in Brooklyn* (1943), Kenneth Fearing's *The Big Clock* (1946), Jim Thompson's *Nothing More than Murder* (1949) and *A Swell Looking Babe* (1954), Wright's *The Outsider* (1953) and *Savage Holiday* (1954) — use the private insurance company to interrogate the emergent politics of welfare.

"We may well be entering into an age of insurance," Stevens declares, as he refers to the Social Security Administration as the linchpin of this emergent epoch. In a report to the National Resources Committee one year later, titled "Progress of the Insurance Idea," Alfred Manes, a German social theorist and later "Professor of Insurance" at Indiana University, confirms Stevens's perception. "The general opinion," he observes, is "that we are now living in a century of insurance." He continues in Stevens-like fashion: "There will always be enough opportunities for insurance because in no branch of it — whether fire, accident, burglary of any other kind — can 100 percent prevention point be reached. The difference between ideal and actual prevention is the field of insurance."[21] This difference is also, Manes might have added, the field of the welfare state. Long before the New Deal, the insurance company had offered the preeminent model for what would come to be called the welfare state: Oliver Wendell Holmes remarks in 1881, for instance, that the "state might conceivably make itself a mutual insurance company against accidents, and distribute the burden of its citizens' mishaps among all its members. There might be a pension for paralytics, and state aid for those who suffered in person or estate from tempest or wild beasts."[22] However fanciful this proposal might have seemed to Holmes, it usefully demonstrates how easily private insurance could be understood in public terms. By 1939, novelist Josephine Herbst refused to distinguish between private and public forms of insurance: she writes that the New Deal had entered into a "conspiracy" with the insurance company; "as long as *this government exists,*" a character exclaims in her *Rope of Gold,* "insurance is the one basic reliable investment."[23] Thurman Arnold says the same in *The Symbols of Government,* where he claims that "an enormous insurance company appears" with the passage of the Social Security bill in 1935. "The symbol of an insurance company," observes Arnold, "allows us to live at peace with our moral ideals, and still support systematically a vast class of people who are now supported in a haphazard way" (11). More recently, F. R. Ankersmit notes, "The modern welfare state considers its main task to lie in organizing the security of the citizen within a complex system of welfare facilities. What used to belong to the domain of civil society — security — has now become the very raison d'être of the state." Ankersmit observes that, on its way to guaranteeing "the citizen social, economic, and political security at a level unprecedented in the history of mankind," "the democratic state acts as an insurance company." Once akin to a "secular God," Ankersmit's state "became the state as an insurance company; and since God's gifts are free but customarily of a most doubtful status, we ordinarily have every reason to prefer the gifts of the insurance company, though unfortunately we have to pay our insurance premiums to be entitled to them."[24] It is difficult to overstate the importance of these comparisons between the state and insurance companies in the context of the New Deal, a period that quite fantastically saw the sudden emergence and almost simultaneous coded disappearance of the state as an object of representation.

Faced with the predominant displacement of the state and its security-providing functions, this study locates the New Deal not only (literally) in its policies and not only (allegorically) in insurance companies, but also in newly available discourses and structures of thought that redefined the individual's relation to the social. *New Deal Modernism* identifies as governmental often disparate forms of social organization concerned with risk management, broadly actuarial patterns of thought and practice that restructured both literary and governmental responses to instability occasioned by the Great Depression. Consequently, though I am interested in the Social Security Administration's inauguration of social insurance, I am equally interested in the methods and modes of statistical analysis that enabled such insurance in the first place. As Alain Desrosières explains in *The Politics of Large Numbers,* "The political, economic, and administrative responses" of the New Deal to the Depression "involved the construction of an entirely new public statistical system": "In the space of a few years, between 1933 and 1940, the terms of the social debate and statistical tools informing it were radically altered. The two transformations were closely connected, for the same period witnessed both the birth of a new manner of conceiving and managing the political, economic, and social imbalances of the federal American state, and a language in which to express this action. Unemployment, viewed on a national scale; inequality among classes, races, or regions; the very fact of equipping these objects with statistical tools in order to debate them — all this entered into the new language, which became commonplace in all Western countries after 1945." At the core of this new language was the first rationalized and comprehensive decennial census in 1930, the subsequent founding of the Committee on Government Statistics and Information Services (COGSIS) by the Department of Labor, the validation of random sampling techniques, and the invention of econometrics.[25] These developments were at the heart of the Social Security Administration, which was formed in close consultation with all manner of statisticians. In its original form, Social Security provided unemployment compensation, old-age benefits, federal aid to dependent children (which supported a mother's pension system and provided funds for homeless, neglected, dependent, and crippled children), and additional aid to state and local public health agencies (which involved the shoring up of the Federal Public Health Service). Each of these services required not simply raw statistical data, but actuarially organized calculations of probability. Setting up the kinds of long-term investments that would pay for Social Security, for example, required information concerning not only the number of persons then in need of assistance, but also how many persons would require such assistance in the future.

Putting matters this way suggests a nebulous boundary between the statistical and the actuarial. Establishing an individual's statistical relation to a given population group depends on identifying the risk factors that he or she shares with its members. It depends as well, however, on understanding those factors used to constitute the group in question as a coherent and distinct entity in the first place. For example, raw statistics alone went far in enabling the individual simply to grasp the staggering "reality" so often associated with the Great Depression: from 1929 to 1933 the GNP dropped by 29 percent, construction by 78 percent, investment by 98 percent; unemployment rose from 3.2 to 24.9 percent.[26] But, as Desrosières points out, the very conceptual categories here in question are inventions of the New Deal state: "Far more than before, statistics played a decisive role in giving consistency to things effected by collective action. These things — unemployment, social security, inequalities between different groups or races, national income — were henceforth formulated on the basis of their definitions and statistical measurements" (202). The unemployment rate never was and never has been a simple measurement of a stable reality: it is a discursive construction, a historically derived technology for determining why and how to consider given persons members of given population groups. What exactly makes a person count as one of the nation's unemployed, for example? That this question was particularly vexed in the case of writers and artists who previously had been "employed" only to the extent that they had been selling their work is the partial subject of my first chapter. Because it was not clear before the advent of the WPA what made a writer a "professional," it was doubly unclear how to consider the employment status of writers who had never been successful to begin with.

In what follows, I am concerned with various security practices — from the private insurance company to the WPA — that affiliated individuals with manifold population groups, heuristic constructs all. Desrosières explains, "In a time when other means of expressing collective action, such as those related to the languages of market economy or local solidarity, no longer seemed able to account for a critical situation, it became more plausible to resort to new forms of rationalism and universality as formulated in scientific, notably statistical terms, whereas this had not been plausible a few years before" (203). Kenneth Burke's *The Philosophy of Literary Form* (1941) offers one example of how these new forms of rationalism impacted on more strictly literary questions. Burke chooses to understand the problem of literary form with the aid of "one of the most 'rational' words today . . . *statistical,* as applied for instance to the thorough rationality of an actuarial table."[27] Burke likes the word statistical because it helps provide a familiar explanation of how he proposes to classify social actions as "symbolics": "Mr. Q writes a novel. He has a score to settle with the world, and he settles it on paper, symbolically. Let us suppose that his novel is about a deserving individual in conflict with an undeserving society. He writes the work from the standpoint of his unique engrossments. However, as Malcolm Cowley has pointed out, there is a whole *class* of such novels. And if we take them all together, in the lump, 'statistically,' they become about as unique as various objects all going downstream together in a flood. They are 'all doing the same' — they become 'symbolic' of something — they become 'representative' of a social trend" (18–19). The notion that Mr. Q's work is "going downstream . . . in a flood" with other works that share its generic conventions suggests a rather determined account of its genesis. It might appear, in other words, as if Burke is insisting that the "social trend" with which Mr. Q's book correlates is what most completely accounts for the work. Mr. Q's novel, for example, might be understood in terms of a long history of alienated Romantic literature, in which case the critic is interested in the antagonism Mr. Q insists on between the individual and society. But the novel might also be understood in terms of a 1930s "social trend," say an obsession with the relation between the individual and the collective, in which case the critic is interested not only in the antagonism imagined between the self and society, but in the specific terms by which "society" is understood.

The important point for Burke is that both lines of analysis can be taken up in a rationalized fashion even in the absence of what seems a direct authorial mandate to do so: the statistical enables Burke to explain why literary criticism that recognizes multiple symbolic or statistical relations in texts come "about as near to the use of objective, empirical evidence as even the physical sciences. For though there must be purely theoretical grounds for selecting some interrelationships rather than others as more significant, the interrelationships themselves can be show *by citation* to be there" (21). The actuarial table provides such a fruitful model to Burke because it enables him to reconcile scientific objectivity to methods of analysis that are not immediately concerned with authorial intention. Burke reasons that with a statistical system "there is no need to 'supply' motives" for a writer's work: "The motivation out of which he writes is synonymous with the structural way in which he puts events and values together when he writes; and however consciously he may go about such work, there is a kind of generalization about these interrelations that he could not have been conscious of, since the generalizations could be made by the kind of inspection that is possible only *after the completion of the work*" (20). Burke does not provide an account of what determines the symbolic interrelations of a given literary text, nor does he suggest (as Stevens does) that meaning is simply a readerly construction. Rather, he makes an essentially actuarial observation about how literary texts, like social actions and individuals, can be classified along more than one axis, even as these classifications retain their absolutely objective character.

Burke's *Literary Form* suggests further that even in the absence of declared allegiances, individuals also can be considered part of more than one classification group, a point that returns us to the issue with which we began, namely, what it means to take up the literary politics of the welfare state in the first place. Aided by his sense that texts and individual actions can meaningfully speak to any number of analytical contexts, Burke emphasizes, *"In this complex world, one is never a member of merely one 'corporation.' The individual is composed of many 'corporate identities.' Sometimes they are concentric, sometimes they are in conflict"* (307). Following Burke, I identify a series of financial or financially inspired exchanges between the governmental and the literary that bear no obvious relation to political dogma as it was espoused by parties and groups of the time. Without doubt, the most impressive new scholarship on the thirties and forties — from Alan Wald's *The Revolutionary Imagination* (1983), through Cary Nelson's *Repression and Recovery* (1989), Paula Rabinowitz's *Labor and Desire* (1991), James Bloom's *Left Letters* (1992), Barbara Foley's *Radical Representations* (1993), Alan Filreis's *Modernism from Right to Left* (1994), and Constance Coiner's *Better Red* (1995) to Michael Denning's *Cultural Front* (1997) — has explored comprehensively the often conflicted corporate identities that operated on the left of the period. These critics have tended to understand literary politics by mobilizing increasingly refined distinctions between conservative and radical, Stalinist and Trotskyist, fellow traveler and Popular Front moderate, and, most recently, between a "cultural front" and mainstream communism and liberalism. Understanding the politics of the era through impressively involved research, this body of scholarship faithfully reproduces and negotiates the often agonized constellation of political identities available to the radical writer of the time. Yet precisely because of the scruple for historical detail these critics have brought to their work, their otherwise excellent scholarship has operated within some very discernible parameters. In part because the distinctions among different political groups of the era seem crucial to these critics, their work has tended — with one exception, we will see — to "recover" the traditional protocols of literary biography as much as the literature of heretofore neglected writers. Hoping to compensate for a tradition of cold war criticism that whitewashed the impact of thirties radicalism, most of these critics believe that the most intelligent political accounts of the literature of the thirties and forties were made during the thirties and forties.

As Filreis has amply demonstrated in *Modernism from Right to Left,* for example, Stevens himself made any number of comments with respect to the left. "I hope I am headed left," Stevens anxiously confesses to his editor in 1935, "but there are lefts and lefts."[28] Invariably concerned to show himself both progressive and cautious, Stevens writes one year later, "For my own part, I believe in social reform and not in social revolution" (309). Flaunting his support for such reform in the middle of his most aggressive defense of autonomous art, "The Noble Rider and the Sound of Words" (1941), Stevens sees fit to defend the income tax. Admitting his own reluctance to pay the tax, he goes on to laud "the blanks [on the forms] as mathematical prose. They titillate the instinct for self-preservation in a class in which that instinct has been forgotten. Virginia Woolf thought that the income tax, if it continued, would benefit poets by enlarging their vocabularies, and I dare say that she was right."[29] But what exactly does such a statement tell us about Stevens's movements across Filreis's right-left continuum, save that Stevens was far more astute in poetical than in political analysis? It is hard to imagine an American upper middle class ever stripped of its instinct for self-preservation; on the other hand, it is well worth asking (as I do in chapter 3) how it is that for Stevens money can take on the status of mathematical prose. Granting the critically neglected commerce between Stevens and the left that Filreis so lucidly points out, when all is said and done we are still left with a wealthy, conservative Democrat who understood his own politics with exactly the kind of level-headed, bourgeois rationality we would expect from the vice president of a major insurance corporation.

It would be easy to stop here, and nuance Stevens's relation to social security only insofar as his letters and writings speak directly to the New Deal itself. This eminently prudent line of reasoning might further suggest that Stevens made no definitive defenses of the nascent welfare state (on the few occasions that he mentioned it at all) for good reason. Why go to the trouble to claim that writers engaged a form of government for which they did not proclaim great fervor? But essentially biographical scholarship of the kind that has often characterized the new studies of the thirties invariably remains insufficient precisely because the newly forming welfare state apparatus did not jump out at contemporaries in anything like a full-blown, totalized form. But then again, ideology rarely does present itself color-coded and ready-made for consumption. Quite the contrary: "In this age of statistics," reasoned Max Horkheimer and Theodor Adorno in 1944, "ideology conceals itself in the calculation of probabilities."[30] So concealed, ideology does not always lie waiting to be unearthed in the marginalized, previously unheard voice, or in some further special collection of unpublished papers. For even if the bulk of Stevens's papers written at the Hartford had not been destroyed after his death, there is little likelihood that we would have discovered there a cache of material declaring the poet's allegiance to the welfarist government then being wrought by the New Deal. The term welfare state itself would not become popularized until well after the thirties, and there is little reason to believe that even the most fiscally minded of writers would have found in the New Deal the kind of coherence I will attempt to give it after the fact. As I have maintained throughout, the welfare state is an omnipresent but at the same time poorly mapped political category throughout the thirties and forties just as surely as it is in our own.

As much as we need biographical scholarship, we need a vocabulary with which to interrogate the political and economic status of literary form in a period when the very meaning of the political and the economic was changing in massive but still insufficiently theorized ways. The absence of this vocabulary gives way to schematic mappings of left, right, and center as well as to utterly familiar rehearsals of academic politics. Here I am thinking of a cultural studies project that has at moments become more concerned with reinvigorating the left politics of the academy than with interrogating what it means to produce literary-political analysis in the first place. In this regard, Michael Denning's *The Cultural Front* is exemplary. Denning's term "cultural front" identifies artists and cultural artifacts united in generally Marxist responses to the Great Depression. Above all, the term describes the artistic and intellectual flowering of the Popular Front, which was announced at the Seventh World Congress of the Soviet Comintern in the summer of 1935 and was intended to forge an alliance of working-class and liberal-capitalist parties against the growing forces of fascism. For Denning, however, the "cultural front" is more a principle than an actual historical bloc; the term is interchangeable with the Popular Front, save for the crucial fact that it encompasses radical factions — such as Trotskyists and die-hard Stalinists — that did not consider themselves part of any united movement.

"The heart of the Popular Front as a social movement," Denning explains of the cultural front, "lay among those who were non-Communist socialists and independent leftists, working with Communists and liberals, but marking out a culture that was neither a Party nor a liberal New Deal culture."[31] But how is it, one might ask, that a coalition so capaciously conceived can with such precision be set against communism on the one hand, and the New Deal on the other? Surely we are witnessing with Denning a politically safe reinvention of American radicalism, one in which the current academic left gets to discard two twinned versions of statism: the troubled legacy of Stalinism on the one hand, and the presumably hegemonic, mainstream liberalism of the New Deal on the other. As Denning confesses, he invents the idea of a cultural front in order to produce a genealogy for "an emancipatory cultural studies" (425). And as any New Left intellectual will tell you, the state, almost by definition, cannot be an instrument of emancipation. No doubt, it is difficult not to be attracted by Denning's version of American radicalism; his cultural front is a repository of virtually every value championed by the academic left in the past twenty years, from antiracism to anti-capitalism. My point is not to question these values — far from it — but rather to point out the extent to which Denning imagines himself needing to purify them of any association with the modern state. New Deal culture, Denning argues, was "official [and] mainstream" (126), hardly ingredients for the emancipatory.

To be fair, it is tempting to endorse Denning's aversion to the New Deal, especially when we observe how paltry if not irrelevant its programs have come to seem in the face of the corporate feudalism that now passes for modern democracy. But at stake in his unabashed jettisoning of the state is a set of defining issues that have become particularly vexed since the close of the cold war and the re-emergence of "big government" as a site of national self-loathing. If there has in fact been an end of history, if, cradled in the arms of liberal governance, this nation has slept through the death of non-capitalist ideology, then we need to trace our slumbers back to the New Deal, when the welfare state, visible in its newness perhaps only for a moment, becomes all too quickly the signpost of bankrupt political compromise. If nothing else, reclaiming the interventionist state as an object of cultural analysis might help us to negotiate between revolutionary politics and more seemingly prosaic debates over congressional funding and appropriation. It is crucial, I believe, that literary historians begin to close this gap by exploring how important the politics and exigencies of funding have been to the cultural production of this century. Taking cultural capital literally might further generate interest in a topic that, inexplicably, has proven to be of next to no interest to politically motivated critics: the quite staggering extent to which contemporary culture is under-written — financially and otherwise — not by government agencies but by a small cartel of media conglomerates. Failing to take these cultural fundings and appropriations seriously, we concede the field to the modern multinational.

Now more than ever, confident dismissals of New Deal liberalism simply will not do. For surely, as Raymond Williams never tired of pointing out, it is possible to understand even the most radical of commitments as expressions of an undeniably liberal tradition. And just as surely, it is important to understand the ways in which liberalism can and has operated with far more complexity and ambivalence

than has been accorded it by literary critics eager to distance them-
selves from "the official and the mainstream." As it is, Michael
Denning finds in the New Deal a simplistic center against whose
Frank Capraesque pieties he sets the cultural front, which was not, he
reiterates, "simply New Deal liberalism" (xvii). Similarly, Michael
North, one of our most intelligent commentators on the diverse poli-
tics of modernism, is least compelling when he glosses liberalism in
The Political Aesthetic of Yeats, Eliot, and Pound:

> Modern, liberal conceptions of freedom . . . are subjective and per-
> sonal. Freedom means the absence of external constraint. This differ-
> ence in the concept of freedom, of the proper relationship between the
> individual and society implies a new definition of the two terms of the
> relationship. But this new definition is in a sense no definition at all,
> because the individual who is to be free of constraint must also be
> independent of all the influence and prior to all purpose. This theoret-
> ical individual has no particular character, no goals, no inclinations
> except the fulfillment of a self that seems to lack anything specific to
> fill. Like this individual, the community defined by liberal theory is a
> neutral arena in which different goods contend according to certain
> rules. Separating the individual from the community thus results in
> the removal of particular social or moral values from the realm of
> politics.[32]

North is in good company. Some of the most substantial refutations of
liberal philosophy — Michael Sandel's *Liberalism and the Limits of
Justice* (1982), most famously — make precisely this critique, focusing on a tendency within liberalism to imagine abstract persons whose
very nonspecificity masks a world of hegemonic norms and values. It
cannot be gainsaid that the idea of a transcendental, universal human
subject has been and continues to be imagined for such purposes. As I
explain in chapters 4 and 5, the Social Security Administration in
particular provided its primary assistance almost solely to White,
male wage earners. Farmers, African Americans, and women were
aided only indirectly by the program, despite the fact that "welfare"
as we now know it (dispensed by Aid to Families with Dependent
Children) grew from a clause in the original provisions of the Social
Security Administration. But if anything, welfare as we now know it,
as it is reinvented daily in the nation's presses, has nothing to do with
the abstract liberal subject. To the contrary, we have succeeded as a

nation in imagining that the welfare state exists only for those who have failed to become disembodied liberal abstractions. In an amazingly unselfconscious instance of this phenomenon, Edward Berkowitz's *America's Welfare State* (1991) begins with the confession, "When we think of welfare, we envision a black woman, who lives in a sinister section of the city, miles from the suburbs in which many of us grew up, taking care of her illegitimate children and government checks."[33] Given this common propensity to relegate the welfare state to the marginalized, it might not be so harmful after all to theorize an abstract welfare subject.

During and immediately after the New Deal, however, Americans often felt most marginalized when they went unnoticed by the state. After working on the Illinois Writers' Project, Nelson Algren would turn in *Nonconformity* (1950–53) to the overlooked underbelly of the American state, to the "wanderer untroubled by names and numbers: unregistered, unattached, uncounted and unbereaved in the files of the American Century." Algren's wanderer seems so fatally forgotten precisely because she is never processed by the instruments of modern governance. "There are no insurance policies to bereave her," he laments, "no bankbook to grieve her, no driver's license nor visa, no hospitalization plan nor social security number to say, the day after the nameless burial, what her true name was."[34] Seen from this point of view, it is not surprising that Algren's colleague on the Illinois Project, Richard Wright, should identify "the glorious Rooseveltian experiment — the liberalism of the Roosevelt era" as a vehicle for making "the Negro . . . a more or less free agent." As I argue in my last chapter, Wright identified "the reality of the state" as the only mechanism for securing the Black body from the abrasions of history. Of course, it is easy, looking back, to fault Wright for embracing the universalizing mythologies of either the New Deal or the Old Left. But the fact that the "abstract subject" would later become the hallmark of all that was wrong with a White, homogenizing mass society had less to do with liberal philosophy writ large than with the counterculture's studied antagonism toward the New Deal. An early expression of that counterculture, Norman Mailer's landmark essay "The White Negro" (1957) would describe a generation of malcontents fleeing from the bourgeois stability so desired during the Great Depression, a generation for whom "security [was] boredom and therefore sickness." If the Black American had never quite been granted the privilege of becoming an abstraction, then Mailer's hipster too would resist with all his considerable energy becoming "a cipher in some vast statistical operation." Attuned only to the immediate demands of his body, stuck within "the perpetual climax of the present," the hipster — a violent psychopath, but relentlessly cool nonetheless — launches himself against "the collective violence of the state."[35] It remained to James Baldwin to chastise this "thin" and "diluted" vicarious identification. "The world is not interested in anyone's identity," Baldwin informed Mailer, don't you be too interested in ours; Black Americans lived in their bodies because they had to; they embraced abstraction when and where they could find it.[36]

I glance past the New Deal, however fitfully, not to suggest that there is any particularly emancipatory politics to be had either in embracing or rejecting New Deal identity politics. I do so simply to suggest that little is gained and much is lost when we let a scorn for liberalism occlude the often nuanced and conflicted work performed by political abstractions. This, I take it, is the virtue of Fredric Jameson's insistence that even the most ideological of forms are at one and the same time utopian: false promises, however insidious, carefully mark out the possibility conditions of resolutely historical ideals. With this in mind, I have chosen to focus less on the extent to which the New Deal consistently failed to realize some of its most socially progressive promises than on how, from the start, even its most utopian ambitions marked a considerable reconfiguration of the kind of liberalism North describes above. As Roosevelt put it in his "Message to Congress on Social Security" on 17 January 1935, "The establishment of sound means toward greater future economic security of the American people is dictated by a prudent consideration of the hazards involved in our national life. No one can guarantee this country against the dangers of future depressions." And no one actually lived unmarked by history. What the state could do, he countered, was "provide the means of mitigating . . . results" (*Essential FDR,* 93).

Chapter One

"The Whole Question of What Writing Is"

Jack London, the Literary Left, and

the Federal Writers' Project

Living with three tenant families in rural Alabama during the summer of 1936, gathering material for what would become *Let Us Now Praise Famous Men* (1941), James Agee expresses profound misgivings about the fact that he is in some sense exploiting his hosts. Despite all the compassion he feels for the families whose hardships and daily lives he records, he cannot escape the fact that his writing makes money only for his employer, Luce Industries. "I have no right, here," he intones to himself, "I have no real right." A despondent Agee recalls, "[I] wished to god that I was dead."[1] Agee does do his best to distance himself and Walker Evans from the institutions — *Fortune Magazine* and the New Deal's Farm Securities Administration — that paid the two to make their book. He depicts the two of them as undercover defenders of what he calls the "individual, antiauthorative human consciousness" (xlvi): "It seems to me curious, not to say obscene and thoroughly terrifying, that it could occur to an association of human beings drawn together through need and chance and for profit into a company, an organ of journalism, to pry intimately into the lives of an undefended and appallingly damaged group of human beings. . . . It seems curious, further, that the assignment of this work should have fallen to persons having so extremely different a form of respect for the subject, and responsibility toward it, that from the first and inevitably they counted their employers, and that Government likewise to which one of them was bonded, among their most dangerous enemies, acted as spies" (7). Self-proclaimed enemies of corporation and government, Agee and Evans don the mantle of the radical conspirators. But persistently, despite these and similar efforts to imagine himself and Evans at odds with their employers, Agee is stuck with the fact that he is spying on his hosts

• • •

more than his employers. He finds it "obscene, terrifying, and unfathomably mysterious" that, "realizing the corruptness and difficulty of the circumstances," he and Evans "accepted the work in the first place" (8).

In his response to a 1939 *Partisan Review* questionnaire that was never published by the journal, but that he includes in *Let Us Now Praise Famous Men,* Agee makes clear that, as an artist, he should under no circumstances enjoy the economic security his tenant families so noticeably do not. Fielding the *Review*'s question— "Do you think there is any place in our present economic system for literature as a profession?" —Agee responds firmly in the negative. "A good artist," he declares, "is a deadly enemy of society; and the most dangerous thing that can happen to an enemy, no matter how cynical, is to become a beneficiary. No society, no matter how good, could be mature enough to support a real artist without mortal danger to that artist" (355). But Agee is also concerned that the mundane realities of his employment, however morally and politically dubious, have rather serious consequences for his work. Radical artists seem least oppositional to him, least likely to break with the middle class and capitalism, when they are salaried employees of corporations, universities, or governments. "Communist by sympathy and conviction" (249), the Catholic humanist *cum* anarchist avers that it is next to impossible to protest the institutions of bourgeois society from inside their pockets. This is the case, Agee suggests, because "beneficiaries" cannot but produce reactionary, status quo art.[2]

Nothing relegated art to this kind of irrelevance quite so much as its own objecthood. Agee insists of his work, "This is a book only by necessity" (xlviii). Were he not bonded to the world of necessity, there would be no book. For the journalist equates being a "good artist," a "real enemy of society," with an embrace of the aesthetics of "Performance, in which the whole fate and terror rests" (16). Agee urges from the start, "Above all else: in God's name, don't think of this as Art" (15). "It is simply impossible," he later explains, "for anyone, no matter how high he may place it, to do art the simple but total honor of accepting and believing it in the terms in which he accepts and honors breathing, lovemaking, the look of a newspaper, the street he walks through" (240). Consequently, "anything set forth within an art form, 'true' as it may be in art terms, is hermetically sealed away from identification with everyday 'reality' "

(240). Agee's desire to break this seal — like his wistful regret that he cannot include in his text "fragments of cloth, bits of cotton, lumps of earth, records of speech, pieces of wood and iron, phials of odors, plates of food and excrement" (13) — leads him back once more to his commitment to performance. Agee warns of his tendency to lose sight of what he calls "the actual" (244); generalizing from the particular without keeping an eye on the quotidian, he declares, is "artifacting" (245). Again, he urges "that you should so far as possible forget that this is a book" (246). Agee struggled to do the same: John Hersey reports in his introduction to *Let Us Now Praise Famous Men* that its author initially urged Houghton Mifflin to publish it on low-grade paper, not simply so tenant families could afford it but so that, fifty years hence, nothing of it would remain (xxiv).[3]

At stake in Agee's willful amnesia is more than simply an avant-garde desire to collapse art into the everyday; forgetting that his writing constituted a book, Agee struggles to forget that he is not just a literary producer, as Walter Benjamin had recently put it, but an owner as well. A salaried journalist researching his story, Agee was pointedly not an owner; initially, he had no rights over his material. Returning from his sojourn in Alabama, Agee found that the already conservative *Fortune Magazine* had taken a still sharper turn to the right. Suddenly, his gushingly sympathetic portraits of rural labor were no longer desirable to the journal. But because the magazine had paid Agee a wage while he researched and wrote, it would not at first release its rights to the material that Agee then wanted to publish independently, as a book. Agee did eventually secure the rights to his material. But it is worth pointing out that the "necessity" Agee speaks of when he observes "this is a book by necessity" was his own, not *Fortune*'s. To be sure, Agee's necessity was real. Novelist, historian, and first head of the Office of War Information, Elmer Davis might have been speaking for the perennially broke writer when, lecturing in 1940 at the New York Public Library on "Some Aspects of the Economics of Authorship," he suggested that writers and sharecroppers were equally victimized by their employers. Davis quoted at length from a recent piece in the *Saturday Review* by David Cohn: "He is a cotton sharecropper, I am a literary sharecropper. Each of us, by virtue of the system, has a certain amount of economic security, even if it is at a low level. His employer, the planter, and my employer, the publisher, must keep us alive so that we may create cotton and books by the sales of which they earn their livelihood. If he gets an advance of $15 a month so he can eat and clothe himself while he is making a crop, I get a lump sum advance so that I can eat and clothe myself while I am writing a book. In both cases, whether by calculation or by coincidence, the advance always seems to be just short enough to keep body and soul within hailing distance of each other."[4] Though Cohn's analogy usefully registers how writers like Agee imagined themselves exploited by the publishing industry, some obvious problems remain. As much as both writer and cotton sharecropper are paid in anticipation of an eventual market income, the sharecropper is forever denied actual ownership over the land he tills. Conversely, Cohn's writer at some point sells his work to his publisher; unlike the sharecropper, he owns and controls his own means of production. Likewise, Agee did eventually secure the rights for his work; he and not Luce Industries ended up owning and selling his now classic volume. Fulminations to the contrary aside, *Let Us Now Praise Famous Men* is in the end a book; Agee is in the end a capitalist.

It is precisely because of its imprecision, on the other hand, that Cohn's analogy explains why Agee opposes himself so strongly to what he calls "artifacting." Awash in middle-class self-loathing, intent on identifying with his host families as best as he is able, Agee embraces an aesthetics of performance that makes him seem more like a sharecropper than a landowner. For Agee, writing is a form of labor rather than a marketed commodity; in this light, his commitment to performance disavows his control of the means of production that sustain him. In what follows, I will have occasion to view similar celebrations of performance as representative of a "performative aesthetic" that played a similar role in the changing dimensions of bourgeois literary patronage.[5] This aesthetic was given strongest formulation by Harry Alsberg, director of the Federal Writers' Project, who described writing as an activity subject to public regulation rather than an artifact for which one received a profit. Producing "books" was most assuredly not a "necessity," Alsberg reasoned, when writers were paid for their efforts. "Nothing like it, to my knowledge, has ever been in history," declared Edward Bruce, painter and government official. "The very method of payment is democratic. The artist is paid the highest craftsman's wage allowed under existing conditions and the product of his work becomes the property of government."[6] The sheer number of writers who took advantage of this craftsman's wage on the WPA's Federal Writers' Projects after 1935 — well over ten thousand — begins to suggest the impact of these performative commitments. "More than any other literary form in the thirties," declared Alfred Kazin in 1942, "the WPA writers' project, by illustrating how much so many collective skills could do to uncover the collective history of the country, set the tone of the period."[7] But the project provided something more important than a utopian vision of collective agency: the Federal Writers' Project provided its workers with a method of payment meant to accommodate its performative view of art. Offering a wage for the labor of creation, but no dividends from an artifact over whose marketing and consumption a worker had no control and for which he or she was never cited as author, the Federal Writers' Project assimilated working-class politics, wage labor, and a performative aesthetic each to the other. The WPA was thus the first of many subsequent commitments the federal government would make to a performative aesthetic that — in the hands of NEA-funded Performance Artists from Robert Ashley and Laurie Anderson to the recently embattled Karen Finley — would seem like an assault on the middle class only to the most hostile of conservatives.

Agee is thus just one of a broad contingent of radical writers — including those, like Agee, never themselves "clients" of the Writers' Project — who responded to the rise of salaried patronage by theorizing the relation between the specific modes of support used to enable writing and the aesthetic criteria used to justify that support. In their commitment to literary labor, and in the concomitant polemics they offered against the aesthetics of literary objecthood, these writers assimilated themselves to an emergent professional-managerial class in a way that belied the often radical content of their writing. Looking back on the Project in 1954, Malcolm Cowley reasoned that this "democratic" method of payment had taken the radical writer, initially allied with the working class, and turned him into "the salaried writer . . . a new figure in American society." During the thirties, Cowley explains, this figure worked most visibly for the WPA, Hollywood studios, and universities' rapidly expanding creative writing and English departments. After the depression, Cowley's salaried writer found employment even farther afield from the literary. Where Agee and Evans "acted as spies" against the corporate interests that paid them — preserving in this way some residual loyalty to political and aesthetic commitments untenable to their employers — Cowley's writer, embracing camouflage of a different sort, maintained a more profound fealty to what would soon be called the establishment. The critic whispers that his new breed of salaried writers "might be disguised as a businessman, hired by a corporation to act as its spokesman or to edit and contribute articles to its house organ. Sometimes his disguise might be a military or naval uniform. . . . The writer might also be employed by other branches of the federal government, which, in addition to its many other functions, was the largest American publishing house."[8]

1.

And what is this "hazardous occupation"? Why
> that's where you're liable to break your neck
> or get smashed on the job so you're no good
> on that job any more and that's why you
> can't get any regular life insurance so long as
> you're on that job.

— Carl Sandburg, *The People, Yes* (1936)

More than any other American literary figure, Jack London provided writers of the Depression era with an idealized image of the proletarian literary "professional" who succeeds by virtue of a maniacal work ethic, by working at writing as if it were a physical discipline. London was widely recognized as one of the notable predecessors in America's socialist tradition of letters; Michael Gold and Joseph Freeman both insisted that he was the significant forebear of the Depression-era radical writer.[9] Jim Thompson makes this debt particularly clear in his working-class novel, *Now and on Earth* (1942). Barely able to support a large family with his job at a military aircraft factory, Thompson's protagonist, the emotionally and physically spent James Dillon, begs his family to let him strike out on his own so that he can get back into freelance writing. His mother and wife immediately refuse. "Of course, this isn't the best place in the world to write," his mother explains, "but you can't always have things just like you want them. Now look at the way Jack London did."[10] Dillon interrupts her, declaring that he is not Jack London. "No, you're not Jack London," his mother replies. "Jack London didn't give up just because he didn't have everything right like he wanted it. He wrote on fishing boats and in lumber camps and — " (236). Dillon interrupts again and quickly lists his credentials: "Yes, and I wrote in caddie houses and hotel locker rooms and out on the pipeline; I wrote between orders of scrambled eggs and hot beef sandwiches; I wrote in the checkroom of a dance hall; I wrote in my car while I was chasing down deadbeats and skips; I wrote while I was chopping dough in a bakery. I held five different jobs at one time and I went to school, and I wrote. I wrote a story every day for thirty days" (237). Being a literary as well as a manual laborer, Dillon insists, is no solution at all. "You didn't read your London far enough," he tells his mother. "He began slipping off the deep end when he was thirty" (237).

The relevant text here is London's *Martin Eden* (1909), which tells the story of a working-class seaman who struggles through all manner of hardship to become a writer.[11] Eden literalizes Dillon's metaphor: having left the working classes and won the middle-class approbation he once dreamed of, the now wealthy writer slips quietly into the deep end of the Pacific Ocean. And this *after* he has achieved literary and financial success. His success notwithstanding, Eden's rather lethal embourgeoisement suggests some specific limitations in Progressive-era literary professionalism. For starters, Eden professes a great disdain for the bourgeois lifestyle epitomized by what his refined companion Ruth calls "the position." His decidedly naturalist literary ambitions are in marked contrast to Ruth's constraining morality, the novel's preeminent Bildungsbürger. "Their highest concept of right conduct," notes Eden of Ruth and her family, "was to get a job" (402). Eden wants a job himself, but for entirely different reasons. "Martin is after career, not culture," states one of the characters in the novel. "It just happens that culture, in his case, is incidental to career" (155). Eden puts this simply: "I seek to do what men have done before me — to write and to live by my writing" (329).

But Eden does not want simply to live by writing: he is obsessed with the particular mechanisms through which he makes his money. He muses to himself that "he must earn money" (159). He tells his sister that he came by what money he already has "more honestly than if I'd won it in a lottery. I earned it" (419). For Eden, earned money is had through a strict accounting of time spent writing, and comes only in the form of a "good salary" (236). At first he diligently records the number of hours spent on each piece of writing and calculates all of his anticipated royalties as wages based on that time (276). Yet, when the magazines to which he has been fruitlessly sending his work suddenly decide to publish the same writing that they had been rejecting for years, and when the reading public inexplicably decides to consume that writing voraciously, Eden is confounded by the lack of any logical relation between his income and labor: "Martin could not puzzle out what strange whim animated them to this general acceptance of the things they had persistently rejected for two years. . . . It was sheer jugglery of fate." "Fawn or fang," he concludes, "it was all a matter of chance" (442). And nothing is more repugnant to Eden than chance: "Under the bludgeoning of Chance / My head is bloody but unbowed," he drones (339). If "it was accidental," he reasons, "there was no merit in it" (59).

Unfortunately for Eden, as William Dean Howells had already observed in "The Man of Letters as a Man of Business" (1893), "a book sells itself, or it does not sell at all." Authors can never themselves sell their books, Howells reasons, for "the secret" of the literary marketplace "is in the awful keeping of fate, and we can only hope to survive it by some lucky chance. To plan a surprise of it, to aim a book at the public favor, is the most hopeless of all endeavors."[12] Eden cannot earn his money "more honestly than if [he'd] won it in a lottery" because, as Howells points out, the literary marketplace is as random as any lottery. Eden likens his literary efforts to gambling because, he reasons, publishing houses are "like slot machines wherein one dropped pennies" (110). Though Eden wants to be paid for what he calls "work performed," he is instead paid for an artifact that seems increasingly to have no relation to himself or to the labor that went into it. As Eden learns, markets never pay wages.

Having learned this lesson, Eden comes to view the laborer who writes his stories as different from a capitalist alter ego, who then sells this same material: "His thoughts went ever around and around in a circle. The center of that circle was 'work performed.' He drove along the path of relentless logic to the conclusion that he was nobody, nothing. Mart Eden, the hoodlum, and Mart Eden, the sailor, had been real, had been he; but Martin Eden! the famous writer, did not exist. Martin Eden had arisen in the mob mind and by the mob mind had been thrust into the corporeal being of Mart Eden, the hoodlum and sailor" (454). I will have more to say about such moments of doubling in the final chapter, where I take up at length the penchant of New Deal writers to produce similarly schizophrenic representations of their own professional agency. Here, however, Richard Poirier's comments on what he calls the "performing self" of the modern writer are apropos: "The gap between the completed work, which is supposed to constitute the writer's vision, and the multiple acts of performance that went into it is an image of the gap between the artist's self as he discovered it in performance and the self, altogether less grimy, discovered afterward in the final shape and the world's reception of it."[13] For Poirier, different methods of valuing the literary enterprise invariably provide an author with different accounts of his identity. So too for London: because worker Eden does not get his wage, he is replaced by Eden the phantasmagoric capitalist, who receives unearned royalties by selling what worker Eden has already produced. Eden's "relentless logic" points out the inability of worker Eden to cause, as an effect of his own actions, the popular success enjoyed by capitalist Eden, who, paradoxically, exploits his proletarian half. It is easy to see how a salary might counteract this ghostly bifurcation of agency. Whereas writing can be sold twice, and worth two different amounts of money to the fickle mob of readers, labor time can only be sold once.

Such a reading might suggest that Eden desires modes of valuation amenable to the concrete labor time he puts into each piece. Perhaps he seeks a strictly Marxist alternative to exchange value, a labor theory of value grounded in the specificity of his labors and the concrete and unique nature of his artifact.[14] This aspiration is expressed by Ezra Pound, for example, when he insists that "In a Station of the Metro," a two-line poem completed in 1911, took him "well over a year" to compose. In this instance, stressing the labor that "goes into" the poem still means stressing the poem (and not labor itself) as the locus of value. Pound imagines that a labor theory of value is absolutely consonant with his Objectivism, with what William Carlos Williams called "the presentation of . . . new objects." As Louis Menand puts it, for Pound, "the poem is an object to be looked at, and the response it produces is therefore owed to the hard work of the person who made it."[15] London, on the other hand, insists that what looks like a crisis posed by exchange value is in fact a crisis in agency that is altogether inimical to *any* effort to value the literary object. Caught between what seem purely random windfalls and fictitious structures of wage labor (derived backwards from those windfalls), Eden takes his life, unable to answer for himself how a professional writer earns money in a market in which all work, as London puts it, is "handled precisely like merchandise."[16]

Like his character, London insistently converted into wages all income associated with the artifact that was *Martin Eden.* He did so by imagining himself as something of a capitalist. During the sale of *Martin Eden* to Macmillan, London insists on maintaining a strict accounting of costs that figures all income associated with the book in terms of hourly wages. He angrily corrects one of his agents who imagines she has received a $100 commission for helping sell the book. London reasons, "When I take a schooner, pay all expenses of said schooner, supply it with food and diving suits and boats, and hire divers at a monthly salary, and go to a pearl lagoon and one of my divers finds an unusually large pearl, he does not get any commission on that pearl." What is true for a pearl goes doubly for a literary artifact. The $100, London insists, was not a commission, but a "voluntary increase in salary." He argues that "the $100 had to be looked upon as perquisite of your office. . . . If I should string that $100 out through this year, it would come to $8.50 a month. Adding this to the $30 dollars a month salary you are receiving, we get $38.50 a month. And if this is not enough, if you feel that I am overworking you and underpaying you, why it is up to you to do what I have told you to do from the beginning — to set your own price upon your time" (*Letters,* 760). Money is earned, London insists, by imagining it as local payment for what Eden calls "work performed." Wages in this way establish a clear structure of agency in which financial outcomes are understood in terms of the labor that produces them. For London, the worker must never concern herself with the products of her actions, even when these actions bring to light an artifact such as a pearl. Therefore, though literary employees can earn a salary, there is for London no way that they can earn a commission garnered from the capital London produces by selling *Martin Eden,* even if their wages do directly reflect the sale of that book.

London thus endorses what Henry James had just recently advocated in his preface to the New York edition of *The Portrait of a Lady*

(1906). A writer, James argues, must "have schooled himself, from the first, to work but for a 'living wage.'" James reasons that anything beyond that wage is an "occasional charming tip," "a gratuity 'thrown in.'" Whereas writers can always claim their wages, they cannot, according to James, claim any form of payment that requires the validation of a fickle public, for that validation, the "miraculous windfall, is the fruit of a tree [the writer] may not pretend to have shaken."[17] For James, miraculous windfalls cannot be earned; by definition, like accidents, they happen to one and are beyond the limits of personal agency. And for both James and London, the wage is the only form of payment that confirms the fact that actions cause, that is to say earn, their outcomes. Still, the fact that London's employees can set their own salary, and the fact that that salary does indirectly reflect the sale of *Martin Eden,* suggests that they share more with an emergent white-collar, professional-managerial class than with proletarian workers. And it is central to *Martin Eden* that Eden himself is unable to appropriate such a professional identity. As it is, Eden's popular success alienates him from both the working and the middle classes: "The gang could not understand him, as his own family could not understand him, as the bourgeoisie could not understand him" (429). In the end, Eden dies a wealthy writer unable to find a mode of employment that might suture wage labor to a middle-class identity.

Howells concludes "The Man of Letters as Man of Business" at a similar impasse, by musing that "perhaps [the artist] will never be at home anywhere in the world as long as there are masses whom he ought to consort with, and [upper] classes whom he cannot consort with" (35). Howells makes clear that the writer *should* be consorting with the masses, stating that he is "allied to the great mass of wage-workers who are paid for the labor they have put into the things done or the thing made; who live by doing or making a thing, and not by marketing a thing after some other man has done it or made it" (33). Howells himself had already invented a mechanism for providing the author with such an income. In *A Hazard of New Fortunes* (1890), Basil March, soon-to-be editor of a periodical put out by an insurance company, is wooed by a Mr. Fulkerson, who is looking to set up an innovative literary journal. Fulkerson starts the novel by telling March, "What you want to do is get out of the insurance business, anyway . . . it's killing you. You ain't an insurance man by nature, you're a natural-born literary man. I don't say you're going to make your everlasting fortune, but I'll give you a living salary, and if the thing succeeds, you'll share in its success." [18] The irony is unmistakable: for Howells, there should be no real distinction between the insurance man and the literary man. Fulkerson's literary journal (originally titled *The Mutual*) treats writers as part of a "collective" and is run on the principle of "co-operation" (17). Banding freelance writers together, the magazine's salary insulates them against unpredictable market vicissitudes.

It is difficult to imagine such a middle-class endeavor helping matters in *Martin Eden.* Recipient of Eden's scorn, the dyspeptic clerk, Mr. Butler, might well have been an insurance salesman. Likewise, everything about Eden's embattled relation to Ruth and the genteel, middle-class culture she represents suggests that he is meant to embody an assault on the white-collar professionalism offered by Basil March's journal. He rages that Ruth's family does not understand art simply because they are part of the bourgeoisie (311, 346). He declares that he is against traders and merchants (384), and is increasingly drawn to writing that offends its readers (356). These sentiments would seem to fly in the face of Eden's desired wage. But if nothing else, *Martin Eden* makes clear why the salary offers a perfect fit with hostility toward the bourgeoisie. What Eden does not want — what he learns to distrust — is public approbation. Success on the market means success with a middle-class readership, success with precisely those Eden learns to revile. Paid for his time, on the other hand, Eden would be sequestered from this same public and, most of all, from the capricious vicissitudes of its consumption patterns. *Martin Eden* is striking, then, because it imagines a literary professionalism — one in which an author can earn his or her living the way dentists or lawyers earn their livings — valuable precisely in its ability to provide for an avant-garde hostile to professional-managerial classes. [19] In the end, however, there is no way for Eden to participate in the evolution of white-collar professionalism; there is no way for Eden to imagine himself part of the service sector, given the fact that, lacking the mediation offered by Fulkerson's literary journal, his success depends less on a service than on an artifact.

The 1930s would offer a considerably wider range of options for aspiring Jack Londons. In Thompson's *Now and on Earth,* for example, the insurance offered writers in Basil March's weekly is about to take on vast proportions: the novel is written under the shadow of the Social Security Administration, which first began dispensing benefits in 1942, the year Thompson's novel is published. Dillon is eagerly awaiting these benefits: he asks his wife and his mother for permission to quit his job at the aircraft factory because, he says, " 'I've got about a month to go before I'm eligible for unemployment compensation' " (228). Dillon reasons that, with help from Social Security, he can write and support his family at the same time, by retiring from his job and sending his family his government benefits. But it is the WPA's Federal Writers' Project and not Social Security toward which Dillon most wistfully looks. Like Thompson himself, Dillon once drew a salary from the Writers' Project. Indeed, Dillon's eventual employment at a plant manufacturing fighter planes for the war symbolizes the passing of the WPA's Federal Writers' Project altogether, for the project was being dissolved into the War Services subdivision of the WPA as Thompson wrote his novel. Dillon thus ends his argument with his mother over Jack London by proudly invoking his accomplishments on the project. "I've written three times as much as London wrote," he tells her. Asked to "skip" reciting his resume, he thunders, "You skip it! Skip through fifteen million words for the Writers' Project" (237). Only there, he suggests, can one read London to the end.

2.

What can the bourgeois writer write or think of, where can
he find passion, if the worker of the capitalist countries is not
sure of his tomorrow, does not know whether he will have work, if
the peasant does not know whether he will be working on his bit
of land or thrown on the scrap heap by a capitalist crisis, if the
working intellectual is out of work today and does not
know whether he will have work tomorrow?
— Andrei Zhdanov, First All Union Congress of Soviet Writers,
1934[20]

Wanting to "accelerate the destruction of capitalism and the establishment of a worker's government," writers gathered in the Mecca

Temple in New York City for the first American Writers Congress to found the League of American Writers.[21] At 8:15 P.M., on 26 April 1935, 216 delegates from 26 states, as well as another 150 from Mexico, Germany, Cuba, Japan, and other nations, stood before a cheering audience of over four thousand.[22] By virtually any account, the congress was a foundational moment for the literature of the period. John Howard Lawson found the congress "so memorable that it stands amidst all the clamor and controversy of the thirties as the decade's central cultural event — the first congress of its kind ever held in the United States, and the first collective statement of an American declaration of a revolution in the arts."[23]

Organized by cultural workers of the Communist Party and conceived as a replacement for the recently disbanded John Reed Clubs, the League embraced working-class radicalism from the start.[24] Henry Hart, editor in chief of G. P. Putnam's Sons and on the pre-planning committee of the congress, characterized those in attendance as "creative men and women who did not need to be convinced of the decay of capitalism, of the inevitability of revolution" (*First American Writers Congress,* 9). Counted among this group were Nelson Algren, Jack Conroy, Malcolm Cowley, Theodore Dreiser, James T. Farrell, Michael Gold, Lillian Hellman, Josephine Herbst, Langston Hughes, Meridel Le Sueur, Clifford Odets, Tillie Olsen, and Richard Wright. "Within the last five years," explains Hart in his introduction to the proceedings, "those whose function is to describe and interpret human life — in novel, story, poem, essay, play — have been increasingly sure that their interests and the interests of the property-less and oppressed, are inseparable" (9).

Participants at the congress described these shared interests most often in economic terms. In his introduction to the volume *Proletarian Literature* (1935), released in conjunction with the Writers Congress, Joseph Freeman writes, "It does not require much imagination to see why workers and intellectuals sympathetic to the working class — and themselves victims of the general social-economic crisis — should be more interested in unemployment, strikes, the fight against war and fascism, revolution, and counter-revolution than in nightingales, the stream of middle-class unconscious, or love in Greenwich Village."[25] Writers, Freeman reasoned, were suffering through the same social and economic degradations as workers; both were out of work, and both needed jobs. Not surprising, then, that

1. Federal writers on strike in 1937. *(Courtesy Photofest/Icon)*

Malcolm Cowley, literary editor of *The New Republic* and another member of the League's preplanning committee, declared in his talk to the congress, "What the Revolutionary Movement Can Do for a Writer," that "literature and revolution are united not only by their common aim of liberating the human, but also by immediate bonds of interest." Writers, he claimed, "if they approach the revolutionary movement without pride or illusion or servility, will receive certain practical benefits" (*First American Writers Congress,* 65). Cowley reasoned that the writer would "profit" from an alliance with "a class that is rising, instead of . . . [a] futile and decaying class" (65). The working class, Cowley maintained, offered him a "whole new range of subject matter" (62) and, most important, a "responsive audience" for his writing (61).

If the working classes did not in the end consume proletarian novels in sufficient number to sustain the radical writer, they did offer these same writers an opportunity for the kind of solidarity so fatally missed by Martin Eden. Recalling the response of fellow writers to the Depression years, Orrick Johns, one-time head of the New York Writers' Project and a member of the League's preplanning committee, recalls that "most of the people I knew had been hit hard by the Depression. They were beginning to see that their professional lives depended upon forms of organizations. They were joining artists' unions and writers' unions, picketing in strikes of publishers and newspapers, and even walking in the ranks of department store strikers"[26] (see fig. 1). Emulating workers who had organized so recently from the San Joaquin Valley to the Carolina Piedmont, Johns's writers understood themselves to constitute a working-class group, source material perhaps for James T. Farrell's satirical retelling of the Writers Congress, *Yet Other Waters* (1952), in which a Communist writer stands before a crowd of picketing workers and declares, "Writers and intellectuals, fellow workers of the brain have come here to seal the unity of workers of hand and brain on the picket line, in front of the class struggle. Intellectuals and writers who are not living in ivory towers, who are not living far away from you in clouds of hot air that is called beauty instead of being called what it really is — the hot air of cowardice — they are here to march with you, side by side, shoulder to shoulder."[27]

For a Marxist like Granville Hicks, literary editor of *New Masses* and in attendance at the congress, walking in picket lines was only the start of the radical writer's would-be affiliation with the working class. In his influential essay "The Crisis in American Criticism" (1933), he reasons, "Inasmuch as literature grows out of the author's entire personality, his identification with the proletariat should be as complete as possible. He should not merely believe in the cause of the proletariat; he should be, or should try to make himself, a member of the proletariat."[28] Hicks argues that becoming directly involved in labor struggles, even to the point of temporarily giving up writing, assists in the revolutionary struggle and confers authenticity on the aspiring proletarian writer. Others at the congress felt that writers need not be proletarians to produce proletarian literature. Edwin Seaver declared that anything written "from the standpoint and in the interest of the proletariat" was in effect proletarian (*First American Writers Congress,* 165). A version of this view is confirmed by Freeman in his introduction to *Proletarian Literature.* Here, Freeman suggests that though the proletarian writer often "is not himself a worker," he becomes identical to workers in the process of representing them. Driven "into the ranks of the proletariat," the middle-class writer produces art in which his personal experience "becomes contiguous to or identical with that of the working class; they see their former life, and the experience of everyone around them with new eyes; their grasp of experience is conditioned by the class to which they have now attached themselves" (13).

In many respects, debates over what constituted proletarian literature proper turned out to be academic. This is the case partly because, at least in the estimation of Walter Rideout, the form had peaked in sales by 1935.[29] But more immediately, imperatives like Hicks's to join the working class took a back seat to the occupational concerns of those in attendance at the congress. The call to the congress made clear that "the problems of effective political action" needed to be understood within the context of "the problems peculiar to us as writers" (*First American Writers Congress,* 10). While writers at the congress ostensibly embraced what Waldo Frank, chairman of the League, called "accelerating the destruction of capitalism," few were interested in participating in overtly revolutionary activities with the proletariat. By their own admission, most at the congress were committed to being radical writers before they were committed to being proletarians. Merle Colby disparaged the idea of becoming involved in labor struggles when he declared that "a writer should write." He continued, "Several times at this Congress I have asked about so-and-so, who was a remarkable writer. I was told that he has changed his name, that he has grown a mustache, and that he is organizing a trade union" (179). This same sentiment had motivated the call to the congress; though the call endorsed a wide range of proto–Popular Front platforms — "the struggle against war, the preservation of civil liberties, and the destruction of fascist tendencies everywhere" (11) among them — it concluded with the simple assertion that the congress intended to "reveal, through collective discussion, the most effective ways in which writers, as writers, can function in the rapidly developing crisis" (11).

The desire of those at the congress to assist the working classes "as writers" required taking up a question that one participant at the second congress, held two years later, put very simply: "Who are really writers?"[30] This question was particularly pressing for the League of American Writers, whose initial membership of 125 was meant to come in well below the number of those who had attended the first congress. As Isidor Schneider reported of the League's efforts to remain selective, "Applications for membership flow in, but the standard is kept high, membership is granted only to creative writers whose published work entitles them to a professional status."[31] But for John Dos Passos, writing in to the first congress, this nebulous invocation of standards granted too much sway to the private publishing industry in determining who the "professional" writers were: "Anybody who can put words down on paper is a writer in one sense, but being able to write no more makes a man a professional writer than the fact that he can scratch up the ground and plant seeds in it makes him a farmer, or that he can trail a handline makes him a fisherman. That is fairly obvious. The difficulty begins when you try to work out what really distinguishes professional writing from the average man's letters to his family and friends. . . . The whole question of what writing is has become particularly tangled in these years during which the industry of the printed word has reached its high point in profusion and wealth, and, to a certain extent, in power" (*First American Writers Congress,* 278). A representative of "the industry of the printed word," Hart had opened the congress by stating of those before him, "These writers are all professionals. They make their living by writing" (15). But for Dos Passos, neither Hart's capacious characterization of the writer as one who "describes and interprets human life" nor his recognizable definition of the professional writer as one who makes a living by writing was of much help. For one of the problems repeatedly discussed was that almost no writer could eke out a living at the hands of the Depression-era publishing industry.

By 1933, the combined revenue of American publishers had dropped by more than 50 percent since 1929. Whereas 214 million new books were sold in 1929, only 111 million were sold four years later.[32] In fact, there were only fifteen authors in the United States in 1934 who sold more than 50,000 copies of their books. Royalties of well-established writers, whose books customarily sold over 10,000 copies, had by 1935 dropped 50 percent below their 1929 levels.[33] The *Partisan Review*'s 1939 survey of the decade's most prominent writers was conducted with just this problem in mind. James Agee, Wallace Stevens, William Carlos Williams, John Dos Passos, Gertrude Stein, Henry Miller, Lionel Trilling, Robert Penn Warren, and R. P. Blackmur were among "the representative list of American writers" who were asked, in addition to other questions, "Have you found it possible to make a living by writing the sort of thing you want to, and without the aid of such crutches as teaching and editorial work? Do you think there is any place in our present economic system for literature as a profession?" The vast majority (thirteen of fifteen) said that they had never been able to make their living exclusively by writing, and that laissez-faire literary patronage was not then, and never had been, able to support literature as a profession.[34]

American writers had organized against this problem for at least twenty years. The leadership of the American League of Authors (ALA) — crucial to the eventual formation of the WPA Writers' Project — had proposed a merger with the American Federation of Labor (AFL) in 1916, hoping that the 2.5 million-strong trade organization might use its economic clout to help writers secure more advantageous rights from what Dos Passos would call the "industry of the printed word." Imagining writers as workers and publishers as capitalist bosses, the ALA looked to the AFL for assistance in what some of its members cast as a classic labor struggle. Membership in the AFL promised resolution to Dos Passos's "whole question of what writing is": "Authorship is labor" one member in favor of the union argued.[35] But affiliation with the AFL was soundly rejected by the ALA, for most felt that the cultural aspirations of literature were compromised by its association with labor, imagined as a demeaning form of bodily hardship. Arthur Stirling, the poet-protagonist of Upton Sinclair's *The Journal of Arthur Stirling* (1903), might have spoken for the ALA when he exclaimed, "There is nothing that brings me down like physical toil." As Christopher Wilson argues, Stirling expresses a late-romantic naturalist aesthetic that rigidly opposed art to both industry and physical exertion.[36] Dominated as it was by the associations forged in that still genteel crucible, the ALA was in the end committed to denying the claim that authorship is labor. However much writers might want to professionalize, writing was deemed an art, something categorically different from what Hamlin Garland, disparaging the arts and crafts movement, called the "trade."[37]

By 1935, however, American writers like Michael Gold, coeditor with Joseph Freeman of *New Masses,* glamorized the withering nature of proletarian work. Floyd Dell once asked, if there was "any validity in Gold's preference for Strength and Steam and Steel and Noise and Dirt, then 'why abolish capitalism?' "[38] Why indeed? Gold's romance with physical labor helped revolutionary writers reconcile their commitment to the working class with their commitment to the literary. Refusing more often than not to distinguish between concrete and abstract labor, locating salvation in alienation, embracing with gusto those exploitative structures to which he was most violently opposed, Gold imagined sweat-soaked writers drinking in the harsh conditions of their techne. For Gold, a writer was a "professional" to the extent that he stoically, if not eagerly, embraced the physically bruising nature of his calling. This apparently was what Merle Colby had in mind when he proudly noted that writing, like digging ditches or loading docks, "was the worst sort of grueling work" (*First American Writers Congress,* 179).

But, as many at the congress pointed out, stressing the physical nature of proletarian labor made it difficult to recruit the middle class to the revolutionary cause. As it was, the fact that each class depended more and more on essentially exploitative forms of wage labor suggested the emergence of a new common ground between the two classes. In *The Crisis of the Middle Class* (1935), Lewis Corey maintained that new forms of economic "collectivism" had led to "the creation of a new 'class' of dependent salaried employees who perform economically useful functions."[39] For Corey, the middle class was more like the proletariat than ever before. He stressed that *"Both the proletariat of wage-workers and the 'new' middle class of salaried employees are the creation of collective forms of economic activity"* (180; emphasis in original). Although the difference between "blue-" and "white-" collar labor might depend on the degree to which each was physically strenuous, this difference was not itself economically salient; both kinds of labor, in other words, could be exploited in the same manner. As Corey pointed out, "Four out of five professionals are salaried employees" (183). This suggested to Corey that the modern professional class had a great deal in common with the working class. As was the case with the proletariat, whose survival depended on the eventual emergence of collective self-consciousness, the future of the professional class was "bound up with collectivism" (181). "The heart of Corey's book," explains Richard Pells, "was his assertion that the 'new' middle class was being rapidly 'proletarianized,' that their economic and psychological problems were no different from those of the workers. . . . Corey reminded his readers that salaried employees held no property, could never hope to own the means of production, and had to sell their labor power on an open market unprotected by labor unions."[40] In this context, the last thing the League wanted was to stress the bruising nature of proletarian work; Corey realized that the working class was in danger of becoming an atavism to the degree that it based its identity on the physical difficulty of the work it performed.

The 1930s did in fact see the culmination of radical transformations in American capitalism during which, according to James Livingston, "relations of production no longer seemed to regulate or describe the content of social relations, and in which the question of class relations could therefore be reopened."[41] For Livingston, the first forty years of the twentieth century saw "the accelerating separation of ownership and control within the legal organization of the corporate economy." This separation, he reasons, "created new social strata — and the demand for new institutions — that stood between, or at the periphery of, labor and capital and thus complicated or displaced the more transparent class relations of the nineteenth century. . . . The class relation of capital and labor was now occluded by the insertion and expansion of a social stratum whose political position could not be deduced from or traced to its occupational and functional profile" (177). Livingston locates the source of this schism in the diminished role manual labor was coming to play under the aegis of corporate capitalism: "In short, the secular increase in the capital-output ratio that had characterized the growth pattern of industrialization, especially after 1880, was halted or reversed between 1910 and 1920. . . . In the 1920's, therefore, the number of industrial workers, and the total labor time required to increase capacity and output in manufacturing by about 64 percent, declined absolutely" (179). In this light, the radical writer's tendency to identify with manual laborers seemed almost willfully nostalgic, not because there was no longer a substantial class of alienated manual laborers that needed defending (there was), but rather because reorganizations in the national economy meant that increasing numbers of workers were coming to understand their status within that economy as having less and less to do with distinctions between manual and mental labor. Considering oneself part of "Labor," in other words, was coming to demand more than simply a sense of how physically demanding certain kinds of work were.

The welfare state's commitment to social security, particularly in the form of immediate relief, insisted still further on the divorce between labor time and social value that Livingston indicates. From programs like the Federal Emergency Relief Administration (which administered unearned "doles" to recipients) to Social Security itself (which provided individuals with "earned" money when they were not working), the New Deal enabled citizens to be consumers while they were not actively producing value in the market. As Livingston points out, "In view of the New Deal's net contribution to consumer demand out of federal deficits it would also be difficult or impossible to think of consumers' income as a simple function of employment in the private sector or, again, as the derivative of private investment" (117). Committing to the working class, then, was a complicated proposition for the radical intellectual; the intellectual needed to specify the terms by which labor might be preserved as a meaningful category of economic analysis if his or her identification with the working class was ever to involve more than the codes of sympathy.

Thus, Joseph Freeman very adroitly explained in discussion at the congress that invoking the shared difficulty of literary and physical labor did little to advance the writer's affiliation with the proletariat: "The proletarian is not simply someone who works. An English journalist told me the other day that the Prince of Wales is getting a nervous breakdown. He works too hard. As a matter of fact the Prince of Wales does work hard — and we know what he is working for. But this does not make him a proletarian. The proletarian is the man who has nothing to sell but his labor power. He not only works, but depends upon his labor solely for his existence. That is why he is the most exploited and oppressed man in capitalist society; that is why he is the only one in a position to break with that society completely" (*First American Writers Congress,* 169). For Freeman, wage labor alone made one working class, even, *pace* Lewis Corey, as it promised to make the middle class more proletarian. Freeman argued that despite the commendable sympathy offered by the congress to the working class, actual membership in the proletariat remained a formal category determined solely by modes of payment. Hart's definition of the professional as one who makes his or her living writing was in this way doubly inadequate to Freeman. Whether or not writers made a living evaded the fact that they "could never lead the fight for the new world," because they had their "own vested interests in the old" (169). Paramount among those interests was the writer's ownership of the literary artifact. Whereas workers sold only their labor power, writers sold the commodity their labor power produced.

Freeman's comments occur virtually concurrent with Walter Benjamin's "The Author as Producer" (delivered in 1934; published in 1937), in which Benjamin writes, "Rather than asking: what is the *attitude* of a work to the relations of production of its time? I should ask: what is its *position* in them? This question directly concerns the function the work has within the literary relations of production of its time."[42] To the degree that the left wanted to embrace a revolutionary "position" as well as a revolutionary "attitude," Dos Passos's "whole question of what writing is" led inexorably to one very specific answer; as members at the congress consistently proclaimed, radical writing was a form of labor not primarily or necessarily productive of an artifact. Hart had claimed that the interests of writers and the "property-less" were inseparable. To the extent that left-wing writers were committed to this proposition, they had to imagine their writing valuable, not as an object (as potential property) but as a form of labor, what Waldo Frank called "an activity." Writing was decidedly not the physical thing William Carlos Williams had in mind when he stated "the poem, like every other form of art, is an object."[43] Rather, the radical writer restructured the definition of "what writing is" such that the "activity" of writing took precedence over the objects that activity produced. But writing could not simply be labor: it had to be labor sold a particular way. Hence the radical poet Louis Zukofsky went to great lengths to distinguish his interest in "rested totality" — "the apprehension satisfied completely as to the appearance of the art form as an object" — from Williams's and Pound's Objectivism.[44] As Michael Davidson points out, "Zukofsky's actual practice exposes the object status of the poem as a delusion, a stoppage of what is, in reality, a dynamic process" (522). A furious Zukofsky would reply to Pound's assertion that "A commodity is a material thing or substance," by insisting that "*labor* is the *basic commodity*" (538). Labor is the basic commodity, that is, not when performed by the Prince of Wales, but when sold by a worker and then sold again in the commodities he or she produces.

Zukofsky's agonized exchange with Pound usefully illustrates why so many on the left took their commitment to literary labor to be directly at odds with certain strains of modernism. Radical writers aggressively castigated the ostensibly hermetic formalisms of Pound, Stein, and Joyce principally on the grounds that a fascination with form as such was tantamount to a solipsistic refusal of the hardship occasioned by the Depression. But the left's critique of modernism was often grounded in more than this. Any interest in "art for art's sake," Diego Rivera had explained in 1932, "serves to limit the use of art as a revolutionary weapon." Such an interest, he said, "serves, moreover, to limit the possessors of art, to make art into a kind of stock exchange commodity manufactured by the artist, bought and sold on the stock exchange, subject to the speculative rise and fall which any commercialized thing is subject to in stock exchange manipulations."[45] Dada had declared, "No more cubism. It's nothing but commercial speculation!"[46] Following comments like these, radical writers often associated what they took to be a modernist investment in form with an investment in the unpredictable nature of laissez-faire economics. Intent on producing singular, autonomous, and ultimately salable objects, formalists like Stein and Joyce (it was reasoned) embraced the speculative excess of the twenties that had brought the art market to a boiling point.

The left's attitude toward modernism would seem from this vantage to make them part of what Peter Bürger terms the "historical avant-garde" in *Theory of the Avant-Garde*. Focusing primarily on anti-modernist European art movements grouped around Dada and surrealism, Bürger characterizes the avant-garde in terms of its hostility toward the "concept of art as an institution." This concept, he notes, "refers to the productive and distributive apparatus and also to the ideas about art that prevail at a given time and that determine the reception of works. The avant-garde turns against both — the distribution apparatus on which the work of art depends and the status of art in bourgeois society as defined by the concept of autonomy."[47] These terms do in fact apply to writers on the American left, most of whom were hostile both to the idea of "art for art's sake" and to the middle-class market that had emerged during the twenties to support this idea. Recalling this period, Cowley writes in *Exile's Return* (1934) that "The literary business was booming like General Motors."[48] The stock market, he declares, "was slowly rising toward dizzier heights; and American literature, too, was entering a period of excitement and inflation. . . . There was an appalling overproduction of genius" (185).

At the same time, Bürger defines the avant-garde in its commitment to an aesthetics of "risk," "chance," and the "accidental." These aesthetic tenets, Bürger reasons, were inseparable from the avant-garde's antibourgeois politics.[49] Given its opposition to "means-ends rationality as such," Bürger's avant-garde commits itself to "chance, which subjects men to the totally heteronomous [and] can thus seem a symbol of freedom."[50] But almost no one on the American left equated chance with emancipation. For Cowley, "risk" and "chance" are the hallmarks of a reactionary commitment to precisely the laissez-faire institution of art that Bürger's avant-garde was supposed to revile. As it is, Bürger does not look too closely at the stated political positions of the groups he takes up. Dada may not have endorsed art as a bourgeois institution, but neither did it spend much energy supporting the working class. Far from it: Berlin Dadaists, for example, demanded "the introduction of progressive unemployment through comprehensive mechanization of every field of activity," because "only by unemployment does it become possible for the individual to achieve certainty as to the truth of life and finally become accustomed to experience."[51] James Agee's celebration of chance seems at moments just as indifferent to working-class politics. Writing for a Luce Industry publication, *Fortune,* whose very name played coyly, tantalizingly, on the potentially random nature of wealth (with the Luck in Luce), a salaried employee like Agee was safely insulated from the accidental. "Are things 'beautiful' which are not intended as such, but which are created in convergences of chance?" Agee could afford blithely to query his readers.[52] He confirms "that matters of 'chance' and 'nonintention' can be and are beautiful and are a whole universe to themselves" (204).

The vast majority of Depression-era American writers felt otherwise. As Carl Sandburg put it in his popular epic, *The People, Yes* (1936):

> And in the air a decree: life is a gamble; take a
> > chance; you pick a number and see what you
> > get: anything can happen in this sweepstakes:
> > around the corner may be prosperity or the
> > worst depression yet: who knows? nobody:
> > you pick a number, you draw a card, you
> > shoot the bones.[53]

Unaffiliated with the left, Sandburg spends close to three hundred pages insisting that a culture of gambling is not in anyone's best interest. Writers affiliated with the left had a still lower tolerance for risk culture. Kenneth Fearing, radical poet and soon-to-be employee of the Federal Writers' Project, could thus write in "Dirge" (1930–1935):

> Denouement to denouement, he took personal pride in the
> > certain, certain way he lived his own, private life.
> But nevertheless, they shut off his gas; nevertheless, the bank
> > foreclosed; nevertheless, the landlord called; nevertheless,
> > the radio broke.[54]

Far from embracing the aesthetics of uncertainty, writers on the American left linked it with life under capitalism and, more pointedly, with modernism. In Josephine Herbst's *The Executioner Waits* (1934), for example, an investment in literary modernism is in some sense already an investment in speculative market economics. Herbst's fictional writer, Jonathan Chance, is on the brink of a long-awaited success at the end of the twenties. Possessed of a natural gift for moving merchandise, Chance sails "into a fine salesman job for a publishing house" at the same time that he discovers *The Waste Land,* Gertrude Stein, and Kurt Schwitters.[55] Secretly repulsed by his father, a stock speculator, and the capitalist world he represents,

Chance is particularly captivated by Eliot's poem, for he finds in its celebration of "dying things" the last gasp of "the life his father was holding out to him" (282). But Chance gets Eliot profoundly wrong; Herbst insists that Eliot and his ilk exemplify capitalism more than they announce its demise. Immediately after joining the publishing house, Chance's own work "had finally got to Paris, was in with a group who were the vanguard, so he said. They had printed a piece Jonathan had sent with selections from Gertrude Stein, Joyce, any number of people to be proud of" (300). Imagining himself suddenly freed from middle-class drudgery, Chance quits his salaried job selling books at the publishing house in the hope that he might make a living selling his own merchandise. In doing so, however, he casts himself onto the rocks of the ostensibly dying world of *The Waste Land*. Seduced by modernism, Chance passes up a salaried job and actually embraces the hazard captured in his patronymic: "The uncomfortable and doubtful future of the kind of writer he wished to be, didn't bother him" (308). Misguided bravado: in Herbst's sequel to *The Executioner Waits, The Rope of Gold* (1939), we find Chance overwhelmed and impoverished, foolishly holding on to his financial insecurity. For the Chance clan — Chance Sr. the stock speculator included — "insurance was the bedrock of their lives; if insurance went, what was left?"[56] But Jonathan Chance, modernist aspirant, abjures. "I don't carry insurance" (25), declares the writer in a moment of hubris, just before he suffers through the first years of Depression-era misery. Having alienated his father and family, Chance has nowhere to turn when he decides finally that he needs certainty in his life. "He proposes that I get a steady job," says Jonathan of his father, "if only I could" (60).

Robert Browning Hurley, the struggling writer in Jack Conroy's proletarian novel, *A World to Win* (1935), is caught in the same bind: unable to pay the bills with his writing alone, he asks his editor, "What do you expect me to do, work at writing like punching a clock?"[57] Hurley finds such an idea distasteful, invested as he is in the effete "little magazines" of modernism. But his editor suggests that the idea is not so implausible, particularly because "the lightning strikes [only] a few books each season." Such strikes "bring their authors big money," but seem to do so at fantastically infrequent and unpredictable intervals. "Each year since '29 it's been getting worse" (271–72), he explains. In his first novel, *Disinherited* (1933), Conroy uses the metaphor of lightning striking to suggest that an individual's class identity is beyond personal control. A fellow worker tells the protagonist, "You might get t' be a foreman. That pays higher than most white collar jobs you'd likely wait years for. I know you got ambitious ideas, kid, but it'll only ever be an accident if you get out of your class. You might as well make up your mind you're a workin stiff and that you'll stay one unless lightning happens to strike you."[58] Here, lightning striking accentuates the irrelevance of agency in escaping the working class: no amount of earned money as a foreman will free you from your class the way a white-collar job will; unfortunately, such jobs are available to workers only through miraculous windfalls, unaccountable twists of fate. In *A World to Win,* however, the random nature of lightning striking is offered to a different audience: if in 1933 the metaphor is meant to convince a worker to stick to his class, in 1935 it is meant to convince a writer to defect from the middle class and join the proletariat. An ostensibly white-collar job like writing, Conroy reasons, is victimized by chance because it is impossible to predict what kind of writing will sell. Consequently, Hurley's editor argues that, although "writing is work, and hard work," "there is never a whistle to tell you when you can knock off and forget about it till it blows again" (*World to Win,* 273). Hurley, he argues, should blow his own whistle, should implement his own workmanlike discipline; thus, "punching a clock" emerges as an alternative to those mercurial consumption patterns attendant on literary modernism.

Hurley eventually breaks with modernism. Turning his back on the little magazines and the wealthy wife who once supported him, Hurley joins his half brother in the revolutionary movement. Writing in the *New Masses* in 1932, Sherwood Anderson provided terms that might seem to explain Hurley's actions: "If it be necessary that in order to bring about the end of a money civilization and set up something new, healthy and strong, we of the so called artist class have to be submerged, let us be submerged. . . . We will in the long run be healthier and better if we get it in the neck now along with the workers," Anderson concludes.[59] But Hurley does not "submerge" himself when he joins the workers; although there is no indication that Hurley remains concerned to sell his writing, there is nothing in *A World to Win* to suggest that he stops writing. To the contrary, Conroy insists that joining the revolutionary movement is desirable for exactly the same reasons that punching a clock is desirable. Hurley's class defection, we are meant to presume, affords him a way of understanding writing as if it were a form of salaried labor valuable in and of itself. Hurley does not give up writing so much as he gives up his readership.

Like Zukofsky's desire to produce poetic objects that reveal writing to be a "dynamic process," Hurley's commitment to literary labor is primarily symbolic. For unlike Conroy himself, who wrote for the Federal Writers' Project, Hurley does not find an institution that actually pays him to "work at writing like punching a clock." Counterfactually or not, however, myriad writers on the left understood their writing in performative terms. A colleague of Conroy's on the Illinois Project, Richard Wright argued at the Second American Writers' Congress in 1937 against "the tendency of writers going into labor work and trying to escape their writer's personality" (*Writer in a Changing World,* 226). Nonetheless, he explains in his essay "How 'Bigger' Was Born" (1940) that the labor movement crucially enabled him to understand Bigger Thomas and to write *Native Son* (1940). He notes, "Just as a man rises in the morning to dig ditches for his bread, so I'd work daily [writing *Native Son*]."[60] And "How 'Bigger' Was Born" does more than describe "the deep fun of the job" of that writing; it concludes that the act of writing the book, what Wright calls "a kind of significant living," is more meaningful than the putative quality of the book his writing produced. Wright concludes, "I don't know if *Native Son* is a good book or a bad book. And I don't know if the book I am working on now will be a good book or a bad book. And I really don't care. The mere writing of it will be more fun and a deeper satisfaction than any praise or blame from anybody" (881).

Of course, writers, however proletarian their sympathies, produced objects. And Freeman's logic insisted that if a writer owned those objects, that writer was not working class. But few were as unforgiving and thorough as Freeman. Hart claimed that the publisher was in essence the original owner of the literary artifact.[61] Hart's publisher was "one of the most astonishing caricatures of the human being that capitalism has ever twisted out of shape" (*Writer in a Changing World,* 109, 110). Perched atop Dos Passos's "industry of the printed word," he appeared the capitalist owner of the literary commodity. In this somewhat contrived disenfranchising, the writer ignores the fact that he is the original owner and seller of his writing, conflating his first and most stringent market (the market of publishers) with a coercive extortion that is imagined to transcend markets altogether.

At the second congress, Clifton Fadiman defended publishers against Hart by invoking the aesthetic criteria Wright would later dismiss. For Fadiman, the opposition between amateur and professional took shape as a distinction between "authors" and "writers." He noted "that most of the authors I have known, and I have known about ten thousand of them, are not writers" (*Writer in a Changing World,* 229). Writers distinguished themselves from authors by producing exceptional artifacts, the publisher reasoned, and the existence of just "a few good books" on the contemporary literary scene proved to him that most authors were not writers. Books were "commodities just like sugar, steel, pins" (231), and he determined who was and was not a writer based on the nature of the commodity one produced, if not in literal terms (that it existed), then in aesthetic terms (how it existed). These criteria could not be assimilated to Wright's valorization of the "job" of writing, for the answer to Fadiman's question "Who are really writers?" required recognizing that "most of us are not cut out to be writers" (230).

But this conclusion only accentuated the fact that for Hart and others, questions of professionalism had nothing to do with the artifact writing produced. Hart maintained that the reason there were so few authentic professional writers for Fadiman was because "the emphasis is placed upon the thing Fadiman has accepted" (*Writer in a Changing World,* 231). While Fadiman suggested that "most of those who devote their lives to becoming writers would do better to become plumbers," Hart wanted it otherwise, and imagined, with the assistance of a change in "emphasis," that writing differed from plumbing only as one form of labor differed from another. Also responding to Fadiman, Alexander Godin noted, "I have known people who could easily have been advised to become plumbers but who, like Jack London, practically killed themselves in order to survive as writers" (233). But valorizations of the physically strenuous aside, Freeman's commitment to what Nicos Poulantzas calls "structural class determination" made clear that literary professionalism, like class identity, needed to be grounded in exclusively formal criteria, and not in the codified designations of expertise that separated the amateur from what Burton Bledstein has termed the "culture of professionalism."[62] A worker was no less a proletarian if he or she produced poor steel or steel that did not sell. In fact, it was precisely the lack of any direct relation between the worker and the social production of his or her artifact's value that made the worker proletarian. Therefore, the difference between the amateur and the professional writer could never depend on the characteristics of the artifact a writer did produce.

Any single-minded appeal to the quality of the artifact was distasteful because it reinscribed the middle-class standards and tastes that a revolutionary movement ostensibly was designed to combat. Choosing the artifact in this sense meant recommitting oneself to those bourgeois ideologies one hoped to transcend. But on a more general level, the recourse to evaluative criteria was suspect not because the criteria at hand were wrong or distasteful, but because the existence of any criteria mistakenly associated professional identity and artistic value with the product of artistic labor, and not with the labor itself. In a paper entitled "The Economic Status of the Artist Today," delivered in 1936 at the American Artists Congress, a congress inspired by the Writers Congress of 1935, Ralph Pearson objected to a capitalist vision of art that made it possible to promote art "without promoting the artist."[63] Pearson argued that the modern art market conceived of art as "a concrete thing existing in a finished product with a measurable value established by the average taste over a long period of time" (57). Modern art patronage got things backwards, Pearson claimed, not simply because art's "measurable value" was invariably incorrect, but because that value, be it economic or aesthetic, located the value of art in an object and not a practice.

Cowley was right, then, in suggesting at the First American Writers Congress that a writer's affiliation with the working classes would in some sense release him or her from dependence on a fickle middle-class audience. Affiliation with the working classes went far in providing the radical writer with a means of understanding his or her work, not as a "measurable value" to be sold on an open market, but as a continuous process of labor. But putting matters this way only suggests how ultimately mistaken Cowley was to presume that a working-class audience would have offered the radical writer any more "practical benefits" than a middle-class audience. For the issue most at stake to writers in attendance at the first two Writers Congresses was not the particular tastes and predilections of middle-class audiences, but the extent to which depending on the tastes of any audience reduced the "measurable value" of writing to the responses readers had to it. What matter, then, that most radical novels did not find a wide audience in the working classes? (Sales were poor for the majority of those seventy novels Walter Rideout counts as "pro-letarian.") Radical novels were truly avant-garde to the extent that their authors imagined them opposed not to success with a middle-class audience per se but to the idea of audience altogether. "Official acceptance," James Agee declares in one of his more avant-garde moments in *Let Us Now Praise Famous Men,* "is the one unmistak-able symptom that salvation has been beaten again, and is the one surest sign of fatal misunderstanding, and is the kiss of Judas" (15). But American writers from Jack London to Jack Conroy had already realized that acceptance was not necessarily any more loathsome than obscurity; each condition mattered only to the extent that writers made the mistake of basing their professional identity on the unpre-dictable behaviors of their audience.

Seen from this perspective, the refusal to validate literary labor by appealing to the artifact it produces might seem as pure a desire for self-sufficiency as any motivating the kinds of "autonomous" art examined in the next chapter. Refusing evaluative criteria external to itself, performative writing starts to seem as autotelic as any well-wrought object. In such cases, it might seem as if autonomy has simply changed registers, from the artifactual to the temporal. But the performative aesthetic outlined above, steeped in Protestant and working-class ethics of "work," was not a proto-postmodern version of nonteleological "play." If, as we will see in the next chapter, artifactual art anchors its autonomy in claims about its own ontology, then the New Deal performative anchors itself in the regulative func-tion of a wage. At bottom, the New Deal performative was com-mitted to buttressing the agency of the artist, to shoring up her ability to cause, as a result of her own actions, a specific outcome. Ra-tionalized and guaranteed, this outcome, in its most utopian form, was a government wage.

3.

No culture can develop without a social basis,
without a source of stable income.
— Clement Greenberg, "Avant-Garde and Kitsch" (1939)

In 1932, Franklin Delano Roosevelt accepted the nomination of the Democratic National Convention to run for president by pledging "a new deal for the American people."[64] Borrowing from John Baer's political cartoon of 1 January 1931, which depicted a "farmer," a "worker," and "honest business" demanding a "new deal" in a poker game being played between a "speculator," "big biz," and a "crooked politician," Roosevelt appropriated a gambling trope only to rail against all that gambling represented. For in the New Deal imagination, gambling epitomized laissez-faire economics. According to John Dewey, "The psychology and morale of business are based on trading in insecurity. They are criticized by serious moralists as if the animating spirit were that of acquisition. The accusations do not reach the mark. . . . It is the excitement of the game which counts. . . . We hunt the dollar, but hunting is hunting, not dollars." Stuart Chase explained Dewey's remarks in his pro-Roosevelt bestseller, A New Deal (1933): "The element of gambling enters into even the soberest and most orthodox of financial calculations. Profit is the reward of *risk,* the classical economists tell us. When the market is not rigged in advance, this is often true. Risk means something not sure, upon which one takes a chance, in short, a game."[65]

Roosevelt believed the American people were tired of games. "What do the people of America want more than anything else?" the president asked. "To my mind they want two things: work, with all the moral and spiritual values that go with it; and with work, a reasonable measure of security. . . . Work and security — these are more than words. They are more than facts. They are the spiritual values, the true goals towards which our efforts of reconstruction should lead" (*Public Papers,* 1:657).[66] If work and security were "spiritual" values, they were to replace baser ideals: "Let us be frank in acknowledgment of the truth," Roosevelt argued, "that many amongst us have made obeisance to Mammon, that the profits of speculation, the easy road without toil, have lured us from the old barricades. To return to higher standards we must abandon the false prophets" (1:658).

When he opposed work and security to the profits of speculation, Roosevelt tapped into a theoretical distinction between the earned wage and the always unearned market windfall that had taken on wide cultural force in the years leading up to the Depression, as the existence of *Martin Eden* suggests.[67] It is not surprising that in the first and most difficult years of the Depression this distinction came under scrutiny as economic hardship placed a premium on getting by in any way possible. In the film *Corsair* (Warner Brothers, 1931), for example, the main character attempts to convince his girlfriend that his profession as a pirate is identical to her father's profession as a stockbroker. "It doesn't matter how you make your money," he claims, "it's how much you have when you quit."[68] But Warner Brothers would soon after show that it did in fact matter how one made money, not so much by distinguishing the stockbroker from the gangster or pirate as by showing that they were all in fact the same: pirates, stockbrokers, gangsters, and gamblers all received unearned, "miraculous" windfalls. "Doing its part" for the New Deal in 1935, Warner Brothers transformed gangsters into government employees. In fact, the studio recast actors such as James Cagney and Edward G. Robinson (once "Public Enemy" and "Little Caesar," respectively) as federal and state agents ridding America of the gangsters they had originally immortalized. In *G-Men* (1935), Warner Brothers' revised economic morality enables a character to claim that rackets "don't pay off, except in dough" (see fig. 2). In Warner Brothers' *Bullets or Ballots* (1936), Edward G. Robinson is told by a gangster, "I could do more for you in a year than you could earn in a lifetime on the force." Robinson replies, "Maybe I like to make my money the hard way." Maybe, that is, he likes to earn his money. "How anxious everybody was to *earn* the money he received," recalls an employee of the WPA's Federal Writers' Project in Jack Balch's *Lamps at High Noon* (1941).[69]

Ira Wolfort's *Tucker's People* (1943) — about the rise and fall of the organized "policy" racket in Depression-era New York — also insists that money does not in and of itself provide security. For brothers Joe and Leo Minch, two key players in the numbers game, "poverty was their cultural heritage, the endless chain of life by which the past manacles itself to the future."[70] Joe struggles with "what it mean[s] to be a human mind robbed of security"; his brother's "only need was to keep his insecurity under control" (26, 43). But simply making money turns out not to help either brother. Neither "had ever found anything in their work but aggravation of the insecurity into which they had been born. Joe had found insecurity in failure and Leo had discovered that success did not end insecurity" (48). Like Martin Eden, Leo therefore aspires to nothing so much as a middle-class professional identity. He muses, "Money was not enough to keep his feelings of insecurity under control. He did need money. His

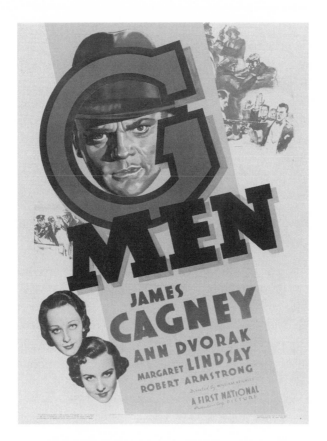

2. James Cagney: From public enemy to federal agent.
(Courtesy Photofest)

mind needed money to breathe, exactly as his lungs needed air. But money itself was insecure. He required 'position,' too, a commendable place in society, one in which he need not feel vulnerable to his enemies. Money was only the first need. 'Position' was to make survival endurable" (11).

During his first inaugural address in 1933, Roosevelt declared, "Happiness lies not in the mere possession of money; it lies in the joy of achievement, in the thrill of creative effort."[71] What better way to concretize the professionalist ambitions of the New Deal than to turn the "thrill of creative effort" itself into what Eden and Minch both call a "position"? Participant at the First Writers Congress and advisor to both the Federal Art and Writers' Projects, Harold Rosenberg explains that this was the principal goal of the New Deal's sponsorship of the arts. During the thirties, "income" became translated into "job," and the artist was no longer a gentleman, or bohemian pseudo-gentleman, but a socially employed expert. It seemed easy to raise painting to the level of a profession when members of most professions had nothing to do; an artist who cannot sell his painting is not substantially different from a lawyer without clients. In its lack of earning capacity, art also took on the aspect of a trade whose practitioners were out of work. The Depression brought forth the novel idea of the unemployed artist — a radical revision of the traditional conception, for it implied that it was normal for artists to be hired for wages or fees and that in the absence of commissions they were idle.

In this new version of his relation to his products, the artist was bidden to cease thinking of himself as an adventurer of genius and to believe that what he wanted most was to be put to work. He was no longer to desire freedom through an income . . . he was to seek the assurance of a professional rate of pay.[72]

For Rosenberg, the artist's quest for a rate of pay had far-reaching consequences. "The effort during the Depression to establish art as a profession," he declares, "was the chief interest of art in the thirties" (197). This led, he suggests, to "an atmosphere of giddiness," in which artists advanced "dreamlike demands, such as the right to remake the world and be paid for doing so" (195).

Designers of the Project had more recognizably bourgeois goals in mind when they decided to pay artists by the hour. Rates of pay were assuring, advisors to various New Deal arts programs pointed out, not simply because they could be relied on but because they gave artists the opportunity truly to "earn" their money. Thus Forbes Watson, a prominent art critic and the principal advisor to the Public Works of Art Project (PWAP), the New Deal's first federally funded art project, brought Roosevelt's distinction between work and speculation to bear on the world of art. Watson believed that before the government stepped in and transformed laissez-faire into New Deal welfare capitalism, the problem with the art market was that the artist existed in it as "a speculator in his own work," as one who " 'found' the money for his student days" and "again 'found' the money for his materials and his studio."[73] In an essay titled "The Chance in a Thousand," Watson explains that because "the number who attempt to become artists have no discernible ratio to the demand for art," the artist knows "what the ordinary business man never knows. He knows the mocking hollowness of an intensive competitive system which at no point offers a basis on which future results can be measured." Unable to predict future responses to their work, artists can never earn success; at best, they can fortuitously "find" their living as speculators find their profits.[74]

artist as
self-speculator

Hart had maintained that the writer suffered at the hands of publishers because he was by trade "a writer and not a stock gambler" (*Writer in a Changing World,* 116). For Watson, the problem with the art market did not lie in the fact that artists were victims of exploitative payment structures. Quite the contrary: the sale of art represented a paradigmatic instance of market capitalism, a parody of the mercurial market speculation at the heart of stock gambling. To Watson, artists were not the victims of laissez-faire capitalism so much as they were — like pirates, gamblers, and stockbrokers — its purest practitioners. Watson's artist-as-capitalist can never, through the sale of his artifact, be said to earn, to cause directly, the income he receives from it. Artists needed federal aid not simply because they were out of work but because their employment epitomized precisely the kind of speculative breakdown in agency that New Deal programs hoped to plan away.[75]

Like writers on the left, the belligerently populist Watson associated the speculative art market with modernism. In "The Artist Becomes a Citizen," Watson writes that during the twenties "the age of publicity and the age of speculation had together brought to its highest peak the age of snobbery. The artist was living in a dream of material profits unfit for the true development of his art. Too often he was not living like an artist; too often he was living like a stockbroker." With its "orgy of theorizing and aesthetic revivalism . . . 'Modernism' had fallen into a final series of academic formulae."[76] As part of his antimodernist crusade, Watson advocated wage payment for all artists on the newly created government arts projects in order to keep them from living like stockbrokers. He notes in his 1934 essay, "A Steady Job": "A moment's thought will show the difference, in the spirit of the worker, between producing on speculation and producing under the terms of a steady job. It may sound dull and bourgeois to remove the artist from the high plane of romantic finances, which never freed him from worry or kept his feet on solid ground, down to the lower work-a-day plane. On the contrary, knowing what is going to happen to him materially has freed his imagination from the irritating interruptions certain to enter into the working life of a man who does not know how he is going to pay rent, his bills for materials, and the grocer" (168). Merely paying for rent and grocery bills is one matter. "Knowing how" you are going to pay rent, generally "knowing what is going to happen" because you are going to make it happen as a result of your own actions, is quite another.

At the outset of what many historians have called the "second" New Deal in 1935, Roosevelt transformed Watson's steady job into a comprehensive WPA program designed to provide "work and security" for an unprecedented number of unemployed American artists. Watson's distinction between earned and speculative money formed the core of Roosevelt's characterization of the WPA. Selling the work-relief program to Congress, Roosevelt declared that direct relief was "a narcotic, a subtle destroyer of the human spirit." "I am not willing," he said, "that the vitality of our people be further sapped by the giving of cash, of market baskets, of a few hours of weekly work cutting grass, raking leaves or picking up papers in the public parks" (*Public Papers,* 4:20). The federal provision of funds as dole without work, or as payment for essentially "made" work, robbed workers of their capacity for autonomous agency: unable to wed their actions to their financial outcomes, dole recipients passively received a windfall unrelated to their labor. According to Harry Hopkins, administrator of the WPA, direct relief took from people "their sense of independence, their sense of individual destiny."[77] To reinforce the worker's sense of individual destiny, the WPA professionalized relief, rigorously distinguishing between made work and work that fit the specialized capacities of each worker. Whereas doles or programs of direct relief provided the worker with either a gratuity or undifferentiated work, Hopkins noted that "the purpose of the Works Progress Administration [is] to provide useful work for particular groups of people in their particular skills."[78] The WPA in this way imagined that each worker's unique skill was an extension of his or her "only true capital," and that he or she could earn money only by tapping into that particular skill.[79]

Hopkins's belief in the worker's "only true capital" would seem to have found its purest expression in the unprecedented federal commitment to the arts made by the WPA. Being an authentic artist, after all, presupposed the almost genetic talent implicit in the suggestion that workers had one true capital (this is what Fadiman implied when he claimed that "most of us are not cut out to be writers"). Accordingly, the WPA's Federal Arts Projects — designated Federal One and comprising the Federal Theater Project (FTP), the Federal Arts Project (FAP), the Federal Music Project (FMP), and the Federal Writers' Project (FWP) — were perhaps the most exclusive of the WPA projects. Federal One was likewise but a small part of an enormous relief effort. Out of the almost $5 billion allotted the WPA in its first year, Federal One received just over $27 million. The initial six-month budget of the Writers' Project in particular came in just under $6,288,000 for an estimated 6,500 writers. During the course of its eight-year existence, an average of 4,500 to 5,200 people were at work for the FWP, as compared with the 2,060,000 workers who drew salaries each month from the WPA in general. On 25 July 1935, Henry Alsberg received his official appointment as national director of the Federal Writers' Project. On 12 September, the Projects received their final executive approval.

Former journalist, translator, and activist on behalf of Russian dissidents and political prisoners, Alsberg initially claimed that only "professional" writers qualified to work on the project. The impressive list of writers at one time employed by the Project suggests that Alsberg did just this: Conrad Aiken, Nelson Algren, Saul Bellow, Maxwell Bodenheim, Arna Bontemps, John Cheever, Edward Dahlberg, Floyd Dell, Ralph Ellison, Kenneth Fearing, Zora Neale Hurston, Claude McKay, Tillie Olsen, Kenneth Rexroth, Philip Rahv, Meridel Le Sueur, Margaret Walker, Richard Wright, Frank Yerby, and Anzia Yezierska, to name just a few. But Federal One ended up granting professional status to a broad range of talent, making clear, ultimately, that a Writers' Project wage alone made one a professional writer. In September 1935, Alsberg wrote that those eligible for the program included not only "writers and research people but librarians, architects, reporters, lawyers, and others whose classification indicates education that would make them useful to us."[80]

Alsberg was able to accommodate such a diverse if distinctively educated group of workers because the value of the project itself was not deemed reducible to the caliber of the writing it turned out. The principal undertaking of the Writers' Project, *The American Guide Series,* had its obvious attractions. The series was a vast compilation of the history, folklore, and cultural and natural resources of each of the forty-eight states, and Hopkins had every intention of using the series as a spur to domestic tourism. Nevertheless, defenses of Federal One resisted justifying the projects with any such explanation of their potential financial benefits. In fact, the Writers' Project was forbidden by law to make money from the publication of *The American Guide Series,* the distribution of which was farmed out to private presses. And though FAP workers punched clocks while working on canvases that remained the property of the United States, the government never made an effort to capitalize on the work of what would become the next generation's avant-garde.[81] (*Life* magazine reported in 1944 that a junkman had recently purchased bales of WPA canvases from the Chicago Project for 4 cents a pound. The bales contained three pieces by Jackson Pollock, several by Mark Rothko, and others by Adolph Gottlieb and Ben Benn. They were eventually purchased by an astute framer for roughly $5 each.[82]) In the words of George Biddle, a painter and friend of Roosevelt's who had conceived the idea for the PWAP, the Projects did not intend "to discover Michaelangelos, but to put needy artists intelligently to work."[83]

The fact that the Projects refused to sell the artifacts it did produce did not in and of itself mean that the projects were not useful to the government. There were any number of ways that Washington derived cultural capital from its sponsorship of the arts. The photographic documentary project on Rexford Tugwell's Farm Securities Administration (FSA), for example, was established during the Depression primarily to sell to the nation the severity of the hardship the New Deal intended to redress. The purpose of the project, argues Terry Smith, was to evoke popular sympathy for, in Walker Evans's case, " 'distressed' peasants . . . temporarily beyond the pale of 'all the people of America.' "[84] Similarly, *The American Guide Series* stressed the urgent need for the New Deal that funded it. "The creative forces of the nation were being mustered," declares an employee of the project in Balch's *Lamps at High Noon,* "to produce The Story of America. Not just the history, not merely the politics, the economics, the village folklore, the literature, but the whole thing. Think of it, to tell the story of AMERICA! What a huge job this was!" (35).[85] Huge indeed, for the series — a comprehensive account of each state aimed at tourists and amateur historians alike — was to be no simple compendium of great achievements, no adoring paean to the self-possessed agents who had taken each state into the twentieth century. *The American Guide Series* was instead committed to depicting the arbitrary nature of progress, the ways in which fortuity and failure had laid the foundations for both local and national community in the United States. "Optimists look only for climaxes in history," declares the *Key West Guide,* "and so they deal almost entirely in the past and the future; but this is the Age of the Anti-Climax, in which realists are at home."[86]

To a realist like Robert Cantwell, writing in the *New Republic* in 1939, the series drove home the unplanned and haphazard nature of American progress. The series, claimed Cantwell, offered "a slightly alarming picture, largely because of the impression it gives that carelessness and accident bulk so large in American history." Cantwell was nevertheless impressed. "How has it happened," he asked, "that nobody ever thought before to trace the careers of the vast majority who guessed wrong—the leading bankers who put their money in canals in 1840 and in Maine shipyards in 1856, who plunged on slaves in 1859?" He observed that the guidebooks provided "a grand, melancholy, formless, democratic anthology of frustration and idiosyncrasy, a majestic roll call of national failure, a terrible and yet engaging corrective to the success stories that dominate our literature. These financiers and prostitutes who went broke, these prophets whose positive predictions were so badly mistaken, these skilled engineers and technicians whose machines never worked . . . all of these combine in the American Guides to make the country's past seem simpler than we could have imagined it, and to make some of the horrors of its present less difficult to endure."[87] This knowledge made the Depression easier to endure, one suspects, because it spoke well of the government that conveyed it; readers could rest assured that the New Deal was out working to correct the entropic tendencies its series depicted.[88] Just as the photographic division of the FSA worked to justify New Deal agricultural policy, *The American Guide Series* justified the New Deal's more general alleviation of the nation's economic insecurity. Representing "the chaotic march of history" perfectly suited an administration committed to regulating laissez-faire, to aggressively mitigating what Roosevelt called the "insecure" nature of the modern, industrial world. The New Deal therefore coded its administration's interventions in the economy not as the logical culmination of liberal progress (as "the end of history"), but as the overcoming of a certain kind of American history; this, because the accidents that characterized that history were now more than ever impossible to bear.

Form was as urgent a matter as content in the *Guide Series*. In Alexander Williams's Popular Front depiction of the Writers' Project, *Murder on the WPA* (1937), "Administrative procedure was an extremely personal matter, a fighting and killing matter. Men lived, died, and were reborn over the placement of a comma."[89] More pointedly, in Norman Macleod's *You Get What You Ask For* (1939), a forlorn project writer asks a more general question: "What does a poem signify at this present time, or a novel?"[90] The answer was unmistakable. Federal One would avoid the mistakes of the "financiers" and "speculators" described with such distaste by Cantwell and Watson by insisting that even poems and novels were forms of social work more than they were material repositories of value. It was important to George Biddle that Federal One's "emphasis and its criterion of success are not so much a high standard of art as the social value of the work to the community."[91] Archibald MacLeish, the first librarian at the Library of Congress, later agreed: "I doubt that [Roosevelt] expected the projects to produce paintings or plays or books or records of the first importance. Certainly it was with no such purpose in mind that the projects were established."[92]

Holger Cahill, director of the FAP, made this clear: "The organization of the Project has proceeded on the principle that it is not the solitary genius but a sound general movement which maintains art as a vital functioning part of any cultural scheme. Art is not a matter of rare occasional masterpieces. The emphasis upon masterpieces is a nineteenth-century phenomenon. It is primarily a collector's idea and has little relation to an art movement."[93] Of the four project heads, Cahill was perhaps the most influential on the overall aesthetic philosophy of Federal One. Cahill had been a student of John Dewey before assuming his post at the Art Project, and, not surprisingly, the director's views on art strongly echoed those laid out by his mentor in *Art as Experience* (1934). At first pass, Dewey's text provides some fairly run-of-the-mill explanations concerning what it meant for art to be "a vital functioning part of any cultural scheme." Using words that Roosevelt and project administrators would recycle time and again, the philosopher holds that "The political and economic arts that may furnish security and competency are no warrants of a rich and abundant human life save as they are attended by the flourishing of the arts that determine culture."[94] But Dewey does not imagine that art should simply replicate then dominant modes of production; far from it, he insists on the difference between quotidian and artistic labor: "The mechanical stands at the opposite pole to that of the aesthetic, and production of goods is now mechanical. The liberty of choice allowed to the craftsman who worked by hand has almost vanished with the general use of the machine. Production of objects enjoyed in direct experience by those who possess, to some extent, the capacity to produce useful commodities expressing individual values, has become a specialized matter apart from the general run of production. This fact is probably the most important factor in the status of art in the present civilization" (341). Drawing heavily from fin de siècle arts and crafts movements, Dewey suggests that artistic labor offers something like a last holdout against industrialization and the alienation of human labor precisely because, as some on the left insisted, it was a physical activity.

But *Art as Experience* is interested more in what the idea of labor means to art in general than in how artistic labor compares to industrial labor. "Art denotes a process of doing or making," explains Dewey (47). "It is no linguistic accident that 'building,' 'construction,' 'work,' designate both a process and its finished product. Without the meaning of the verb that of the noun remains blank" (51). Cahill thus follows Dewey closely when he insists that art is not a question of "masterpieces." In fact, Dewey suggests we make something of a mistake when we use the term "work of art" in any but a transitive sense: "Art is a quality of doing and of what is done. Only outwardly, then, can it be designated by a noun substantive. Since it adheres to the manner and content of doing, it is adjectival in nature. When we say that tennis-playing, singing, acting, and a multitude of other activities are arts, we engage in an elliptical way of saying that there is art *in* the conduct of these activities, and that this art so qualifies what is done and made as to induce activities in those who perceive them in which there is also art. The *product* of art — temple, painting, statue, poem — is not the *work* of art" (214). "The fundamental mistake," he continues, "is the confusion of the physical product with the esthetic object, which is that which is perceived. Physically, a statue is a block of marble, nothing more. . . . But to identify the physical lump with the statue that is a work of art and to identify pigments on a canvas with a picture is absurd" (219).[95] Instead, Dewey insists that the consumer of a given work of art understand himself or herself as a consumer of a particular experience. And this experience recurs to nothing less than the labor that goes into the construction of a given work of art in the first place. "We lay hold of the full import of a work of art," Dewey declares, "only as we go through in our own vital processes the processes the artist went through in producing the work. It is the critic's privilege to share in the promotion of this active process. His condemnation is that he so often arrests it" (325). Art is so much a temporal process, Dewey concludes, so much a finite performance, that in appreciating even the most artifactual of forms we engage vicariously in its moment of creation.

For Richard Poirier, this moment of identification stands at the core of what he has termed Emersonian pragmatism. In *The Performing Self,* Poirier exhorts literary critics to "cultivate the protean reader" (78) by "feeling . . . the power, still generating in . . . works, of the retraceable acts of writing, composition, performance" (84). Likening the performance of literary composition to art scene "happenings" in the volume's title essay, Poirier defines reading as a restaging of the dramatic energies that constructed a given text in the first place. The masterworks of American pragmatism collapse the difference between their consumption and production, Poirier suggests, by understanding both as processes equally absorbed within the immediate constraints of physical labor. "It seems to me," Poirier offers, "that one way literature can and should be taught is in conjunction with other kinds of performance — with dance, music, film, sports. . . . We must begin to begin again with the most elementary and therefore the toughest questions: what must it have felt like to do this — not to mean anything, but to do it. I think anyway that that's where the glory lies" (111). Poirier would spend the next twenty-odd years making clear that this form of glory was a particularly American discovery. *Poetry and Pragmatism,* for example, is an extended meditation on the subsequent influence on American pragmatism of Emerson's claim that "The only path of escape known in all the worlds of God is performance" (33). "Coming as close as possible, while we read, to duplicating the actions which went into the writing — actions inevitably of cultural resistance as well as of conformity — readers will discover, as Thoreau, in anticipation of Dewey, puts it in his Journal for January 7, 1844, that 'Writing may be either the record of a deed or a deed. It is nobler when it is a deed.' Or, to return to Emerson's 'Art,' we look to writing not for meanings but for 'signs of power,' 'tokens of the everlasting effort to produce' " (99).

Peter Bürger would no doubt find in Dewey's and Poirier's desire to collapse the difference between making and experiencing art less a testament to Emersonian pragmatism than a quintessentially avant-garde gesture. Bürger explains that "given the avant-gardiste intention to do away with art as a sphere that is separate from the praxis of life, it is logical to eliminate the antithesis between producer and recipient."[96] At the same time, Bürger does not imagine that government might eliminate this antithesis. When he schematizes the history of art patronage — from "sacral" to "courtly" to "bourgeois" — he avoids any mention of state patronage for the arts. This omission is striking not simply because it casually glosses almost two centuries of uneven development with the term "bourgeois," but because the New Deal Arts Projects were fundamentally in accord with what Bürger considers to be the principal tenets of the avant-garde: unqualified hostility toward the individual production and reception of art as well as toward the distribution of art through laissez-faire markets and institutions. The WPA understood performative art in particular as a self-sufficient, regulated activity that produced no outcome by which it might be judged: the advantage of the salary form in particular, writers came to realize, was that it made the writer's ability to perform his or her work no longer dependent on the public's response to what that labor did in fact produce.

For Federal One, art aspired to the fusion of production and consumption, a fusion that elided audience members as consumers of art by enshrining them as producers of the very same art. The Federal Theater and Writers' Projects, for example, went to great lengths to incorporate American citizens into the productive process. According to one historian, both worked "closely with the common publics they saw as their main audience. For the FTP, this took a number of courses, the most superficial of which was canvassing audience opinion after each performance. . . . The most profound attempt at audience collaboration was the FTP's program to produce plays by local writers immersed in the life and problems of farm-worker or immigrant, working-class communities."[97] Ideally, Waldo Frank's "activity" or Wright's "significant kind of living" applied equally to the artist and community alike. Echoing Cahill and Dewey, Alsberg repeatedly reminded his state directors that "our projects themselves, no matter how important and interesting, come second" to the fact that writers were producing literary performances in which local citizens could feel themselves involved.[98] Federal One proposed that art might thus fuse the nation's producers and consumers in a way that markets themselves never could. As a national institution, "Art" was never reducible to art objects. "Occasional masterpieces" might represent Art, but Art itself was more than the sum of any list of artifacts, however catholic that list might be. Rather, Federal One served a community best when that community learned for itself to perform art in the process of consuming it. Educational institutions supported by the WPA Projects consequently focused on instructing local communities in the thrill of what it called the "creative experience." The guidebooks put out by the FWP thus insisted that " 'housewives, blacksmiths, potters, carpenters, itinerant portrait painters" were always themselves in the process of making "a genuine indigenous art."[99]

Just as Federal One suggested that every act of artistic consumption was itself an act of production, the fact that the bulk of the art celebrated by Federal One was indigenous further suggested that the Arts Projects were vehicles for conveying forms of culture to the American public that, properly speaking, it already possessed. An enthusiast of the WPA thus pauses in Balch's *Lamps at High Noon* when he compares the legacy of the WPA's construction projects to its Writers' Project: " 'America will have, for always, things now that it could never afford: Hospitals, schools, roads, books, theater, most of all, a research, a consciousness and a possession of culture of—' he broke off. 'Paradoxical, isn't it? In the midst of a depression we are allowed to hand ourselves riches we could never *afford*' " (229). But of course, the Writers' Project handed to Americans the "consciousness and possession of a culture" that they already had. Providing art education, setting up free exhibitions, and in general demonstrating that Art need not be owned in the form of artifacts to be engaged, Federal One maintained that the only thing that separated the amateur from the professional artist was a wage itself.

4.

Writing must be such a nice profession.
Fill in the coupon. How do you know? Maybe you can be a
   writer, too.
— Kenneth Fearing, "Literary" (1935–1938)

When Richard Wright, then a member of the Writers' Project, introduced Alsberg at the Second American Writers Congress in 1937, he dubbed him "a man who has been associated with one of the most interesting experiments in the history of America" (*Writer in a Changing World,* 241). Wright's glowing words did not fall on deaf ears, for Alsberg brought to the gathering a vision of artistic labor very similar to its own. The League was already predisposed to Alsberg's message. Frank Folsom recalls that "support for the WPA Federal Writers' Project engaged the League from the beginning to the end of that very fruitful enterprise."[100] In fact, leftist writers' groups had been instrumental in pushing Roosevelt to institute the FWP to begin with.[101] Wright was walking proof of this intimacy between the radical aspirations of the left and the professionalizing impetus of the WPA. "Negro writers should seek through the medium of their craft to play as meaningful a role in the affairs of men as do other professionals," Wright wrote the same year he so glowingly introduced Alsberg to the League. "Writing," he reasoned, "should complement other professions."[102]

Writers on the left did not necessarily see in the New Deal anything like an acceptable long-term solution to the Depression.[103] "For most Americans," wrote Robert Warshow in 1947, the atmosphere of the thirties "was expressed most clearly in the personality of President Roosevelt and the social-intellectual-political climate of the New Deal. For the intellectual, however, the Communist movement was the fact of central importance; the New Deal remained an external phenomenon, part of that 'larger' world of American public life from which he had long separated himself — he might 'support' the New Deal (as later on, perhaps, he 'supported' the war), but he never identified himself with it. One way or another, he did identify himself with the Communist movement."[104] Malcolm Cowley agrees: "We were, at the time, so dismayed by the jackbooted march of the fascists in Europe that, once more, we paid less than the proper attention to events in Washington."[105] And before 1935, attention paid to Washington by the left was as hostile as not. In 1934, the preplanning committee of the First American Writers Congress wanted the nascent League of American Writers to "strike a blow at the growing fascist enemy, the rapidly developing white guard and fascist criticism, and the Roosevelt-fostered national-chauvinist art."[106]

By May 1935, however, all such traces of anti–New Deal sentiment had vanished from the congress, which was criticized in turn by die-hard Stalinists for "making too many concessions to the petty bourgeois element and to the 'hobo bohemians.' "[107] In all likelihood, these concessions were made in anticipation of the Popular Front, announced just months after the congress, which made it easy for writers to reconcile their radical commitments to the New Deal. At the Seventh Congress of the Communist International that declared the Popular Front, Georgi Dimitrov, general secretary of the Comintern, thus rebuked his American comrades for their attacks on the New Deal, reminding them that Roosevelt was a victim of "the most reactionary circles of American finance capital," those that "represent first and foremost the very force which is stimulating and organizing the fascist movement in the United States."[108] Two years later, Earl Browder, head of CPUSA, called Roosevelt's government "progressive, liberal, and democratic in character"; there were, he claimed, only two possible political parties, the New Deal Party and the Anti–New Deal Party.[109]

Some members of the left reconciled themselves to the New Deal so completely that by the end of the decade it was common to find radical writers defending the WPA projects at the expense of the Communist Party. In Norman Macleod's *You Get What You Ask For,* for example, Communist Party member and aspiring writer Gordon Graham, like Macleod himself, eventually gets what he needs from the New Deal and not the Party. Paralyzed by "the uncertainty of the future," Graham muses that "there was hardly any market anymore for the stories he wrote. The magazine and publishing market had shrunk almost out of sight" (14, 15). The left had no solution; Graham complains that "The depression had made it difficult to land a job with the movement as with anything else. He had distributed leaflets, joined hunger marches and got socked plenty by the cops. All this was very well, but it didn't land him a job" (21). Indeed, Graham feels exploited by the movement: "How many revolutionary magazines were there in America that paid for the material used?" he asks. "Practically none" (34). As a result, "Chance stood out as the arbiter of his days"; "insecurity had plagued him all his life" (25, 69). Hoping to escape this quagmire, Graham lobbies urgently for the creation of the Federal Writers' Project, which, once instituted, gives him "a chance, in time, to reorganize his life" (128).

Loathe to force radical writers to choose between party and project,

Alsberg, who appears as something of a saint in Macleod's novel, introduced his Project members to the League of American Writers in 1937 by declaring, "These are your comrades" (*Writer in a Changing World,* 246). After admitting the flaws in the Project, he presented the government to the League as the logical and necessary extension of its own aesthetic and professional commitments. "Not concerned with the theoretical side, which isn't my business here really" (245), Alsberg offered the U.S. government as the institution uniquely capable of sustaining and sanctioning the League's vision of literary professionalism. Whereas Hart's shift in "emphasis" away from the literary "thing" might seem a disingenuous elision of the author's actual ownership of his or her writing, the Writers' Project offered to take that writing, not to extract surplus value from it, but to facilitate the writer's transformation into a professional. Wanting to construct an "alliance between the artists and writers and the working class," the League could do nothing so much as affirm the centrality, indeed the desirability, of the economic structures that accounted for class, principally, the ways in which workers could sell only their labor power. Wanting to put out-of-work writers to work, on the other hand, the Writers' Project asserted the centrality of the government, not simply in its ability to support writers, but in its ability to provide the right kind of literary work for writers, work that neither exploited labor nor derived its social, aesthetic, or economic value backwards from the mercurial marketplace.[110]

"No decent career was ever founded on a public," F. Scott Fitzgerald had written dejectedly the year before the Second Congress.[111] Alsberg had a similar notion in mind when he acknowledged to the League that "Newspapers and magazines are taking things again." For he qualified his enthusiasm by observing that these media did not always pay for writing "properly" (*Writer in a Changing World,* 243). Newspapers and magazines could only ever pay writers for other people's responses to their work (directly if the writer received a share of market royalties, indirectly if the writer's flat fee anticipated those royalties). The project made the alternative clear: "Actually to be paid for writing . . . why that was a wonderful thing," recalled Ralph Ellison, a member of the project.[112] A wonderful thing not because Ellison wanted to "get it in the neck" like Anderson's artist and not because he wanted his artifact to be valued for the time spent producing it, but because anywhere else but on the Projects his artifact was going to be valued as the definitive receptacle of literary value. Describing his early ideas of writing, before he joined the FWP, an embarrassed Ellison recalls, "It was not then the *process* of writing which initially claimed my attention, but the finished creations, the artifacts — poems, plays, novels. The act of learning writing technique was, therefore, an amusing investigation of what seemed at best a secondary talent, and exploration, like dabbling in sculpture, of one's potentialities as a 'renaissance' man."[113]

Alsberg offered the League what it wanted perhaps more than anything else: a notion of literary professionalism freed from the constraints of aesthetic hierarchy. He declared to the congress, "We must get over the idea that every writer must be an artist of the first class, and that the artist of the second or third class has no function" (*Writer in a Changing World,* 245), suggesting instead that all writers equally realized their importance when working for the government. To be sure, such equality came with its price. "The craftsmen who worked on the cathedrals were anonymous," Alsberg told the congress, and so were all Project members (245), particularly those at work on the *Guide Series,* who, as a rule, did not receive individual credit for the material they contributed. Some grumbled, but head of the Writers' Project folklore division Benjamin Botkin touted this impersonal form of authorship as one of the Project's most laudable attributes.[114] Echoing T. S. Eliot's "Tradition and the Individual Talent" (1919) Botkin maintained in "The Folk and the Individual: Their Creative Reciprocity" (1937) that the federal writer must "live the life of the people he writes about . . . so that when he writes about them he becomes not merely an interpreter but a voice — their voice, which is now his own." Botkin goes on to claim that a writer should be eager to accept the "loss of sense of authorship" if he understands that "it did not mean extinction, but extension and integration of personality, through identification with his audience and complete submergence in his materials."[115] Submerged in his materials, fused with his audience, the Project writer becomes indistinguishable from his subject matter and his readers. No doubt ex-Project writer Meridel Le Sueur had this in mind when, in her afterword to *The Girl* (1935–1945), she observed that her book, "a memorial to the great and heroic women of the depression was really written by them." "This should be the function of the so-called writer," she adds, "to mirror back the beauty of the people, to urge and nourish *their* vital expression and *their* social vision."[116]

Burton Bledstein suggests that by the turn of the century, "the culture of professionalism incarnated the radical idea of the independent democrat, a liberated person . . . a self-governing individual exercising his trained judgment in an open society." "Most importantly," Bledstein notes, "the professional person absolutely protected his precious autonomy against all assailants." "The professional resisted all corporate encroachments and regulations upon his independence, whether from government bureaucrats, university trustees, business administrations, public laymen, or even his own professional associations."[117] But nothing could be farther from the case with respect to the literary professionalism promulgated by the FWP; the *Guide Series* in particular had no intention of expressing the individuals who created it. As Biddle put it, "America is realizing herself anew. And in proportion as the realization is not something forced by conflict from without but grown out of a struggle within, it is taking the form not of a crude, complacent patriotism, but of a critical, rather restless self-determination. The Federal Writers' Project at once expresses and seeks in some measure to direct that self-determination, to restore America to herself."[118] Facilitating the "self-expression" of an impersonal, national abstraction in a performative representational act, the Project writer was simply a catalyst in the linguistic self-incarnation of America. He was a professional writer and a client of the state, but decidedly not an author. For, as Harry Hopkins put it, the principal goal of the FWP was to have the government "appear in the role of an author" in a way that "would have been considered fantastic a few years ago."[119]

Chapter Two

The Politics of Textual Integrity

Ayn Rand, Gertrude Stein, and Ernest Hemingway

Where then does security lie? What protection can you invent that has not already been thought of? It is hopeless to think of security: there is none. The man who looks for security, even in the mind, is like a man who would chop off his limbs in order to have artificial ones which will give him no pain or trouble. — Henry Miller, *Sexus: The Rosy Crucifixion* (1950)

"Art should resemble a tree rather than a machine," declares William Slater Brown to Malcolm Cowley in Cowley's *Exile's Return*. "The perfect machine is one to which any added part is useless and from which no part can be subtracted without impairing its efficiency. Trees, on the other hand, have any number of excess branches; and art should resemble them, should have a higher factor of safety than the machine."[1] Cowley remembers that, shocked and in disbelief, he disagreed at the time "so vehemently that [he] slipped and plunged head foremost into a snow bank" (207). Cowley says little about his friend's comment and even less to explain his fervent response to it, though we are left to understand that his response has something to do with the automatic writing exercise that he and Brown complete immediately preceding their discussion on aesthetics. Writing "at top speed, for three hours by the clock," the two try for the first time a literary experiment "in the manner of our Dada friends, with whom the exercise was popular" (206–7). "Disappointed with the results" (207), disillusioned with Dada in general, Cowley objects to his friend's notion that any work of art should celebrate the extraneous.

Just pages later, Cowley describes an epiphany he experiences during his visit with Brown, an epiphany that sheds light on both his friend's metaphor and his generation's transition from bohemian aestheticism to hard-minded radicalism, which *Exile's Return* sets out to chronicle. Overwhelmed by the distractions of New York, Cowley

• • •

writes a letter to himself in which he proclaims, "You must confine yourself to essentials. . . . You must arrange your life against interruptions; you must sleep, exercise, earn your living and pass the other moments beneath a lamp or talking" (210). Cowley imagines that similarly stoic lifestyles helped ease repatriating writers into the social responsibility and class consciousness of the thirties. But more than this, he imagines that, confined to essentials such as earning a living, returning exiles became better writers. Disencumbered of the extraneous in their lives, they produced writing that was likewise pared down to the core. "Once the returning exiles had been stripped of their ambitions," Cowley declares, they began "to write poems worth the trouble of reading. . . . Modestly, they were rebelling once more. They hadn't time to be very unhappy; most of their hours were given over to the simple business of earning a living" (213, 214). So if Cowley's hostile response to Brown's metaphor suggests that a work of art should be as reduced to essentials as a machine, Cowley's response to the economic plight of the writer in the thirties suggests further that literary lives reduced wholly to the professional — to earning a living — were most able to produce such intrinsically unified art.

But despite his encouragement of "modest rebellion," Cowley ends up lionizing precisely the kind of art most celebrated on the right. While Cowley's colleagues at the first two American Writers' Congresses were insisting that writing made most sense as a form of labor (like a timed Dada experiment), Southern Agrarians Cleanth Brooks and Robert Penn Warren were proselytizing on behalf of whole, unified works of art. What is more, Brooks and Warren did so in *Understanding Poetry* (1938) precisely by championing the salaried poet devoted only to earning his or her living. Singling out Robert Frost as the exemplary "professional" writer of the time (the university employee, they reason, appreciates "the pathos and horror of the unreasonable and unpredictable end that at any moment may come to life"), Brooks and Warren teach "amateurs" to appreciate the kinds of unified, organic art that, ostensibly, only the trained few could produce.[2] But for Brooks and Warren, living forms and not machines were the most pared to essentials. The textbook analogizes poetry to living organisms not to claim, like Slater Brown, that a part of a poem "can be subtracted without impairing its overall efficiency" but to insist on just the opposite, that poems are self-sustaining wholes that very much need each of their constitutive parts. "If we should compare a poem to the makeup of some physical object," the conservative poet-scholars explain, that object would be "something organic, like a plant" (19). There is nothing remotely redundant in an object in which every component serves an invaluable function, they claim: "A poem should always be treated as an organic system of relationships, and the poetic quality should never be understood as inhering in one or more factors taken in isolation" (ix). This ideal of self-integration lays the ground for what would later become the "heresy of paraphrase." Poems are unique to and immanent in their original form, the authors conclude, because two different forms could "hardly be exactly the same any more than the personalities of two different people could be exactly the same or the features of two men" (370).

Needless to say, analogies between human and artistic forms predate the 1930s. The Romantic conception of organic form in particular had insisted that works of art were recognizable as such by virtue of resembling natural organisms in their wholeness and completeness. A large contingent of broadly modernist critics seemingly took up this belief intact: looking back over the history of abstract art, Clement Greenberg described the postcubist painting as "an entity belonging to the same order and space as our bodies."[3] Taken with I. A. Richards's talismanic pronouncement (so influential on Brooks and Warren) that "it is never what a poem says which matters but what it *is*," such a claim makes reference to the kind of identity expressed in human bodies and other living organisms. In this context, giving a text what Gertrude Stein will call its "complete existence" might mean rendering it as "whole and solid" a form as the human body. And yet, the comparisons between bodies and texts taken up below — in Ayn Rand and Gertrude Stein briefly, and then in Ernest Hemingway at length — do not make the phenomenological and empirical assertion that texts are like bodies because both are of "the same order and space." Instead, these comparisons are above all concerned with the relation between parts and wholes. Preoccupied with finding strategies of organization that perfectly achieve completion and unity, writers as diverse as Cowley, Rand, Stein, and Hemingway ask how literary and governmental forms differently safeguard what they aim to represent. Far from somehow refusing history, this often conservative preoccupation with organic wholeness, what

Astradur Eysteinsson identifies as "the center of the revolutionary *formal* awareness and emphasis that most critics detect in modernist works,"[4] was instead concerned to refuse the idea that organic works of art were directed at or even had an audience. In the eyes of the New Deal modernists I identify below, works of art were threatened with the kinds of dangerous incompletion that faced the human body to the degree that these works acknowledged their prospective consumers.

1.

Samuel Taylor Coleridge's *Biographia Literaria* (which stands behind Richards, and so much of the New Criticism of Brooks and Warren) characterizes the ideal poem as a union of parts and whole so complete that every stanza, line, and word is fundamentally necessary where and as it is. For Coleridge, the poem's organic body remains incomplete without this unity: "All the parts of an organized whole must be assimilated to the more *important* and *essential* parts."[5] In producing his opposition between trees and machines, Cowley's interlocutor suggests that a tree has "a higher factor of safety than the machine" because its integrity is not necessarily impaired by the removal of individual parts from the whole. Trees are safe in a way machines are not, he reasons, because they survive alteration, because they can continue to function after they are diminished. Brandishing Aristotle's dictum that poetry "avoids all accident," Coleridge imagines his texts "safe" in an entirely different manner: so pared down that only the essential and necessary remain, they refuse contingency in their very constitution (72).

Given such rarefied terms, however, the organic text begins to move beyond those living organisms (trees, human beings, etc.) on which it bases itself, becoming, in the end, more like William Slater Brown's machine than any human form. In Ayn Rand's *The Fountainhead,* for example, Howard Roark proclaims that he wants to make buildings "living" because "every living thing is integrated. . . . Whole, pure, complete, unbroken."[6] But at the same time, Roark is the only character in the novel who even comes close to sustaining this kind of integrated existence. Roark's staunchest supporters make plain that the architect's ideals are not organic at all, for they offer a vision of formal integrity unavailable to living things. "Do you know what you're actually in love with?" beseeches Roark's lover, Dominique Francon: "Integrity. The impossible. The clean, consistent, reasonable, self-faithful, all-of-one-style, like a work of art. That's the only field where it can be found — art. But you want it in the flesh" (496).

This belief that art can improve on and change the rules of quotidian reality finds its most powerful critical expressions in Theodor Adorno's *Aesthetic Theory* (1970), where Adorno explains that "Artworks detach themselves from the empirical world and bring forth another world."[7] This second world, Adorno makes clear, has a "higher factor of safety" than the one inhabited by artists themselves. Writing in the mid-1950s, he champions the kind of organically conceived art pursued by figures such as Stein and Hemingway in part because he imagines that such art mitigates against the accidental. Rebuking those on the left who, eager to integrate life and art, reviled "autonomous" art in the early decades of the century, Adorno observes, "Only by virtue of separation from empirical reality, which sanctions art to model the relation of the whole and the part according to the work's own need, does the artwork achieve a heightened order of existence. . . . The emphasis on the artifactual element in art concerns less the fact that it is manufactured than its own inner constitution. Artworks are alive in that they speak in a fashion that is denied to natural objects and the subjects who make them. Thus they come into contrast with the arbitrariness of what simply exists" (4–5). For Brooks and Warren, organic unity provides "calculation" in place of the "unthinking" (440). Uneasy that "the truth of the new . . . is situated in the intentionless" (26), consistently suspicious of aesthetic movements such as Dada and surrealism that seemed to wallow in the accidental, Adorno finds a similar haven for human agency in organic wholes.

Adorno associates the accidental, intention-killing techniques of the avant-garde with exactly the celebrations of process discussed in the previous chapter. He observes that early in the twentieth century there "arose the pleasure of substituting for the artworks the process of their own production. Today every work is virtually what Joyce declared *Finnegans Wake* to be before he published the whole: *work in progress.*" Like Bürger after him, Adorno understands this substitution in terms of its commitment to chance: "What provokes protest in works of the past is precisely what was arranged and calculated." Conversely, "Progress in art as the process of making . . . has been accompanied by a tendency toward absolute involuntariness" (26).[8] This last is bitingly ironic, for Adorno is invariably scathing concerning the modern celebration of the arbitrary. In the *Dialectic of Enlightenment* (1944), he and Max Horkheimer describe a cultural industry under whose aegis "chance and planning become one and the same thing, because, given such equality, individual success and failure — right up to the top — lose any economic meaning."[9] The two declare that "chance itself is planned" not by any literal set of individuals, but by an economic system in which "any person signifies only those attributes by which he can replace everybody else: he is interchangeable, a copy" (145). In this context, autonomous art appeals to Adorno because it is able to particularize human intention and realize it in concrete form: "In contrast to the semblance of inevitability that characterizes . . . forms in empirical reality, art's control over them and their relation to materials makes their arbitrariness in the empirical world evident" (*Aesthetic Theory,* 138). In fact, Adorno reasons that even the most ostensibly radical protests against the totally administered society end up producing the effect of the planned: "Today artists would like to do away with unity altogether," he reasons, "though with the irony that those works that are supposedly open and incomplete necessarily regain something comparable to unity insofar as this openness is planned" (141).

Hence Fredric Jameson observes not simply that Adorno treats writing as "a poetic object," but also that Adorno's notion of objecthood is inseparable from his engagement with the modernist "*planification* of the work of art, whether in Joyce or Schoenberg: the absolute conscious control which modern artists seek to establish over the last remains of free-floating contingency."[10] Cynical statements concerning the culture industry's fusion of chance and planning aside, Adorno held that art could achieve this eradication of contingency in a unique manner. He declares in *Aesthetic Theory,* "Artworks organized by the subject are capable *tant bien que mal* of what a society not organized by a subject does not allow: city planning necessarily lags far behind the planning of a major, purposeless, artwork" (33). Works of art order and plan their tertia in a way that governments cannot; it is easier to organize a literary text, Adorno suggests, than an interventionist state. The fact that art secures the capacity to plan more effectively and meaningfully than a city, or society writ large, provides Adorno with the ultimate justification for autonomous art. One of the failures of avant-garde art, he suggests, is that there is no compelling reason to integrate life and art when capitalist society can realize in art what it cannot in life.

But this is only half the story, for a crucial component to *Aesthetic Theory* is its insistence that, in the end, serious art does not achieve the perfect unity toward which it strives. Adorno's thought traces out a negative as opposed to a positive dialectic precisely because it imagines critical or serious art refusing the aesthetic unity toward which it nonetheless importantly gestures. Jameson notes that in Adorno's dialectical method, "for a fleeting instant we catch a glimpse of a unified world, of a universe in which discontinuous realities are nonetheless somehow implicated with each other and intertwined, no matter how remote they may at first have seemed; in which the reign of chance briefly refocuses into a network of cross-relationships wherever the eye can reach, contingency temporarily transmuted into necessity."[11] That this utopian eradication of chance reveals itself only in a fleeting glimpse turns out to be crucial, for Adorno insists that autonomous art cannot sustain its perfection of the quotidian. Jameson again: "The contradictions of the age reenter the microcosm of the work of art and condemn it to ultimate failure" (37); thus, Adorno's "negative dialectic has no choice but to affirm the notion and value of an ultimate synthesis, while negating its possibility and reality in every concrete case that comes before it" (56). Striving for unity, gesturing to its own ability as artistic form to eradicate chance, autonomous art instead fails in the manner that social reality itself fails. Autonomous art in this manner manifests and then rejects its ability to transcend the empirical.

The reversals Adorno effects between the necessary and the contingent, it needs noting, are as much a product of the aesthetic traditions he examines as of a dialectical method. Where Adorno imagines that all representations of unity grounded in a capitalist reality devolve into accidental as opposed to necessary component parts, the avant-garde tradition to which he was responding had been fascinated with just the opposite, with how representations of the accidental ended up, ineluctably, reintroducing order and meaning.[12] At least since Dada, avant-garde art had been interested in how representations of contingency and chance ended up simply displacing as opposed to eradicating criteria for unity and coherence. As one art historian notes, "The Dada artists who gathered in Zurich just after World War I seized on the principle of chance as a mechanism for liberating their paintings and performances from the conventions of art and the restrictions of speculative thought that had been governing Western art for centuries. By giving over rational control of their work to 'spontaneous acts,' they hoped to gain access to the subconscious and reveal its 'primitive coherence.' "[13] In this version of Dada, spontaneous acts take on coherence as the artist redefines his or her source of intention: unplanned and ostensibly accidental actions take on necessary and understandable form when examined at the level of the unconscious. Working so fast, he claimed, that he did not have time to stop and think, Jackson Pollock would declare "I don't use the accident — 'cause I deny the accident."[14] According to Alan Kaprow, his "Happenings" also attempted to negotiate this fine line between the necessary and the accidental. Chance, he declares, "is a deliberately employed mode of operating. . . . It is the vehicle of the spontaneous. And it is the clue to understanding how control (setting up of chance techniques) can effectively produce the opposite quality of the unplanned and apparently uncontrolled. I think it can be demonstrated that much contemporary art, which counts upon inspiration to yield that admittedly desirable verve or sense of the unconscious, is by now getting results which appear planned and academic."[15]

But whereas even the most performative art can in this manner "appear" always on the verge of becoming organic and whole, New Deal modernists such as Rand, Stein, and Hemingway base their analogies between art and government on necessarily intentional criteria for coherence. As we will see in the next chapter, Wallace Stevens's performative aesthetics holds that no account of authorial intention can ever sufficiently speak to the meaning of a poem; for Stevens, government and poetry both continually compensate for their respective failures to achieve the ideal of social planning. Conversely, Rand, Stein, and Hemingway hold that organic art can in fact be planned in ways that government actions and structures cannot. Working within a tradition of comparing the state to the human body — from Plato's "Gorgias" through Hobbes's *Leviathan* to Hegel's *Philosophy of Right* — Hemingway in particular points to the relative organizational superiority of the literary text over the human body as one stage of an argument that, ultimately, lionizes the literary text as more successfully organized than American government itself. This sequence of comparisons is quintessentially New Deal modernist even given its ultimate rejection of the New Deal; Hemingway's organic form thoroughly engages the modern state even in its adamant withdrawal from it. His New Deal modernism stems not from his refusal of the state but rather from the comparisons he makes between literary and political theory that sustain this refusal.

None of what follows suggests that either Rand, Stein, or Hemingway produced what Adorno would have considered legitimately critical art. That each of these American writers is content instead to retreat into the literary and away from the empirical is, no doubt, in part a function of their political convictions: Rand, Stein, and Hemingway valorize the literary over the governmental because they are each, to different degrees, conservative, socially reactionary writers. But at the same time, the particular kind of engaged retreat we find in these writers is not reactionary in anything like the manner usually associated with such writers as T. S. Eliot, Wyndham Lewis, W. B. Yeats, and Ezra Pound. At first pass, the two groups seem very similar. Michael North describes the aesthetic commitments of generally fascist modernists in *The Political Aesthetic of Yeats, Eliot, and Pound* principally in terms of their commitment to organic art: "At least since Schiller, the aesthetic object has enjoyed the peculiar privilege of being 'a whole in itself,' which gives it the power to harmonize faculties that are in conflict outside it. The attempt to rejoin subject and object, individual and community, fact and value is therefore inevitably aesthetic. From I. A. Richards on, twentieth-century criticism has taken the reconciliation of such opposites as the preeminent task of literature."[16] North reasons that his figures take up this aesthetic as part of an antiliberal crusade meant to install a reactionary, equally organic polity: "Claims that modernists like Yeats, Eliot, and Pound offer aesthetic resolutions of the tension between part and whole, fact and myth, personality and impersonality are inseparable from the claim that they also offer social reconciliations of unity and difference" (16). He continues: "As Pound's case shows more clearly than any, the writers of the right shared with Lukács the temptation to believe that the antagonisms of modernity had been overcome by an actual political system. This temptation is evident as well in the dream of a form that would balance fragment and totality, immediate experience and abstract form, personal voice and impersonal construct" (19). In this model, then, organic art—imagined as a vanguard for still more profound reconstructions of the social—prefigures and ushers in those reactionary organic political systems on which it is modeled.

But President Franklin Roosevelt also surely described the New Deal as a perfectly integrated, necessary whole. Early in his first term, Roosevelt averred that his legislation had "not been just a collection of haphazard schemes, but rather the orderly component parts of a connected and logical whole."[17] Two years later, on 28 April 1935, he confidently declared in a "Fireside Chat" that "the administration and the Congress are not proceeding in any haphazard fashion in this task of government. Each of our steps has had a definite relationship to every other step. The job of creating a program for the nation's welfare is, in some respects, like the building of a ship." Later in this speech he adds, "More and more people, because of clear thinking and a better understanding, are considering the whole rather than a mere part relating to one section, or to one crop, or to one industry, or to an individual private occupation" (*Essential FDR,* 95). It is this latter, specifically New Deal vision of a national, symbiotic interconnectedness that Rand, Stein, and Hemingway each reject.

But if these authors refrain from escapism (they make no Paterian claim that human beings can somehow live in a world of art), neither do they couple their art to alternative organic political systems. Relentlessly excoriating the New Deal, consistently fetishizing the autonomy of the literary, they are adamant that art refrains from the instrumentality of human life, however organized. From this perspective, we can begin to see just how inadequate the quick equation of autonomous art and the right can be, and here I am thinking not of North's intelligent analysis, but of Peter Bürger's still influential sense that virtually all autonomous art militates toward an undifferentiated reactionary social agenda. For whereas Yeats, Eliot, and Pound base their poetic systems on a utopian integration of the individual and community, Hemingway and Stein reject the proposition that individual life can be organized at all: organic art does not, for them, prefigure an ideal polis so much as it signals a desire to escape from political organization altogether. If North's poets can be united in their antiliberalism, then New Deal writers like Stein and Hemingway cleave to classical, laissez-faire liberalism. "What you wanted," recommends a character in one of Hemingway's short stories, "was a minimum of government, always less government."[18]

2.

Professional art critic and university professor Ellsworth Toohey is the mouthpiece of Depression-era mass politics in Rand's libertarian manifesto *The Fountainhead*. Educated at Harvard with funds drawn from his mother's life insurance policy, Toohey champions the forces of "collectivism" against which the Übermensch architect Roark heroically struggles. Speaking at a rally held in support of striking newspaper workers, Toohey intones, "The lesson to be learned from our tragic struggle is the lesson of unity. We shall unite or we shall be defeated. Our will—the will of the disinherited, the forgotten, the oppressed—shall weld us into a solid bulwark, with a common faith and a common goal. . . . Let us listen to the call. Let us organize, my brothers. Let us organize. Let us organize. Let us organize" (109). Echoing the last words of the martyred Joe Hill, and speaking at the third American Writers Congress just two years before Rand's novel was published, Dorothy Parker called out, "Don't mourn, organize!"[19] No less fervent, Toohey personally oversees the consolidation of left-minded artists into labor guilds: "The Council of American Builders, the Council of American Writers, the Council of American Artists. He had organized them all" (305). His social conscience extends farther still. Bequeathed a large sum of money, Toohey gives it "to the 'Workshop of Social Study,' a progressive institute of learning where he held the post of lecturer on 'Art as a Social Symptom' " (221).

In this capacity, Toohey orates strenuously against the self-interested laissez-faire mentality he sees embodied in Roark's buildings. But Toohey imagines Roark a threat to collectivist political organization not simply because Roark is a solitary artist who refuses to partake in any "common goal." In addition, the critic faults Roark because the "organization" of the architect's work sets itself apart from the economic and political conditions of the Depression, because Roark's buildings embody "unity" in a way that political and economic forms of representation cannot. In her notes to the novel, Rand explains: "Let us decide once and for all what is a unit and what is to be only a part of the unit, subordinated to it. A building is a unit. . . . Also—man is a unit, not Society. So that man cannot be considered as only a subordinate part to be ruled by and to fit into the ensemble of society. . . . Much of the confusion in 'collectivism' and 'individualism' could be cleared up if men were clear on what constitutes a unit, what is to be regarded as such" (*Fountainhead*, 703). Toohey's call to "organize" socially in the name of "unity" is thus doomed to failure, and *The Fountainhead* is meant to show how judiciously laissez-faire economics brings this about. The architects in Rand's novel are frightened that "business, as they had known it, was finished, that government would take over whether they liked it or not, that . . . the government would soon be the sole builder" (565). But in the end, Roark's buildings sell, despite Toohey, and more particularly, despite a New Deal eager to become an architect just as surely as it was, in the words of Harry Hopkins, eager to "appear in the role of an author." *The Fountainhead* is striking, then, not for its adolescently conceived battle between the forces of conformity and the lone individualist, and certainly not for its draconian commitment to laissez-faire liberalism. Rather, the novel is as pure an example as there is of how fluidly the New Deal imagination moved between formal interests in how to organize works of art and more explicitly political interests in how to do the same for groups of individuals. Roark's desire to produce what he calls a "logical whole" (170) is meant to stand in marked contrast to a welfare state unable to do so.[20]

Whether they were reactionary or radical, it no doubt struck those who read her as unfortunate that Rand so starkly opposed an investment in form to collective action. Writers associated with the Trotskyist *Partisan Review* — such as James Farrell, Philip Rahv, Meyer Shapiro, and Clement Greenberg — had by 1943 gone out of their way to combat the Communist Party's sense that concern with form necessarily indicated a reactionary investment in the status quo. Indeed, even the veritable reactionary John Crowe Ransom, scandalized by the breakneck pace of American industrialization in *The World's Body* (1938), maintained that art was crucial in facilitating a community's self-awareness as a collective entity. Still, Rand was not the first or last New Deal writer to oppose the organization of the modernist work of art to the organization of economies and persons. However unlikely it might at first appear, Stein and Hemingway are the significant forebears of her efforts to theorize the "unit" in both literary and political terms.

Rand would not have viewed Stein as an influence of any kind. In fact, a writer very similar to Stein is an object of considerable parody in *The Fountainhead*, which associates experimental linguistics

with the radical left. Toohey's "Council of American Writers" —
dedicated to the idea that "writers were servants of the proletariat" — "included a woman who never used capitals in her books, and
a man who never used commas; a youth who had written a thousand
page novel without a single letter o, and another who wrote poems
that neither rhymed nor scanned" (306). Here, Rand seems to recall
not the American Writers Congresses of the thirties (which for the
most part disavowed experimental form), but an earlier era of radical
politics in her place of birth, the Soviet Union. Soon after the revolution, futurist poets like Kruchonykh and Maiakovskii sought to forge
a communistic sensibility with hypermodern linguistic forms. Thus,
for example, the "New Orthography" decreed in 1918 excised the
hard sign (*tverdij znak*) from the "Language of Lenin" because it
was seen to reflect the ossification of tsarist Russia.[21] That Rand is
also spoofing Stein, however, is made clear by Rand's depiction of
the head of the council, Lois Cook, who is described by Toohey as
being "so much above the heads of the middle-class who love the
obvious" (231). "It's so commonplace to be understood by everybody" (240), drones Cook. "For an author who did not sell," one
character muses of Cook, she was "strangely famous and honored.
She was the standard bearer of a vanguard of intellect and revolt.
Only it was not quite clear . . . exactly what the revolt was against"
(241). The object of revolt was clear to Rand. In a letter dated 8 June
1941, Rand identifies Stein as the epitome of all those who were out
to ruin contemporary writing: "Our literature, our theater and all our
arts are now one gigantic conspiracy against the mind. Not even
merely against the great mind, but against any mind, against the mind
as such. Down with thought and up with emotions. When thought is
destroyed — anything goes. . . . Look at such a phenomenon as Gertrude Stein. She is being published, discussed and given more publicity than any real writer. Why? There's no financial profit in it. Just
as a joke? I don't think so. It is done — in the main probably quite
subconsciously to destroy the mind in literature."[22]

Not that Rand actually read Stein, whose *Geographical History of
the United States, or, The Relation of Human Nature to the Human
Mind* (1936) explains at length how, unlike human nature — simply a
variant of the same abilities and proclivities possessed by animals —
"the human mind" — associated by Stein with language, literary
"master-pieces," and money — separates human from animal. More-

over, Stein was hardly a darling of the left as Rand implies; Stein was consistently rebuked by Michael Gold, editor of *New Masses*. She was, according to Gold, a "literary idiot." In fact, Gold sounds a lot like Rand in *Change the World* (1936), when he declares that Stein had "destroyed the common use of language," and explains that her writing took place "in the vacuum of private income" where "you can write as you please."[23] The simple fact is, Stein's politics were as conservative as Rand's. "That organization business is a funny story," notes Stein during her lecture tour of the United States in 1934–1935. "Organization is a failure and everywhere the world over everybody has to begin again."[24] If this particular critique of the New Deal seemed too oblique, Stein insisted on her American tour that Republicans "are the only natural rulers" in the United States. "When a Democrat gets [elected], he only does so because of the singular seductiveness which he possesses." "People have a peculiar attitude toward being governed," she explains in 1936, "in that they allow themselves to be governed not by people who think but by people who never have thought in their lives."[25]

"What is the use of Franklin Roosevelt being like the third Napoleon?" she asks that same year in *The Geographical History*.[26] Here, and in a series of nationally syndicated magazine articles published one year earlier, Stein takes aim at Roosevelt's tax-and-spend economics. Her essays — titled "Money," "More about Money," "Still More about Money," "All about Money," and "My Last about Money" — savagely lampoon what she took to be the president's penchant for spending more than the nation had:

> Everybody now just has to make up their mind. Is money money or isn't money money. Everybody who earns it and spends it every day in order to live knows that money is money, anybody who votes it to be gathered in as taxes knows money is not money. That is what makes everybody go crazy. . . .
>
> When you earn money and spend money every day anybody can know the difference between a million and three. But when you vote money away there really is not any difference between a million and three. And so everybody has to make up their mind is money money for everybody or is it not. (*How Writing Is Written*, 116)

If at times Stein singles out Roosevelt as the problem, she is just as willing to turn on Congress: "In America, where, ever since George

Washington, nobody can imagine a king, who is to stop congress from spending too much money. . . . They will not stop themselves, that is certain. Everybody has to think about that now. Who is to stop them" (108). Stein favored a more patriarchal model; she declared that "until everybody who votes public money remembers how he feels as a father of a family, when he says no, when anybody in a family wants money, until that time comes, there is going to be a lot of trouble and some years later everybody is going to be very unhappy" (107).

Invoking the specter of an insurmountable deficit crippling the future, Stein, fiscal and social conservative, urges American voters to just say no to the New Deal.[27] But at the same time, her interest in money had as much to do with literary form as with conservative politics. In *The Geographical History of America,* she explains how it is that these interests are related. "I cannot begin too often begin to wonder what money is," she declares (435). Her conclusion: "Money is what words are. Words are what money is" (461). Surprisingly enough, this brings her back to the New Deal and its heedlessly irresponsible spending: "Perhaps Franklin Roosevelt wants to get rid of money by making it a thing having no meaning but most likely not most likely it is only electioneering" (480). Rand's paranoia that writers like Stein were trying to evacuate the English language of meaning emerges in Stein, ironically enough, as the paranoia that Roosevelt was trying to evacuate money of meaning. Stein's conspiracy theory is far more comprehensive than Rand's, however, for it has less to do with Roosevelt than with the system over which he presides. As Stein explains earlier, government per se "has nothing to do with money and the human mind nothing to do with money and the human mind" (423). Whereas money compels Stein, government — an attribute of human nature — does not. "You see the only thing about government and governing that is interesting is money," she explains. "Everything else in governing and propaganda is human nature and as such is not interesting. Everything else has time and identity which is human nature and that is not at all interesting. No it can be completely understood that the only thing that is interesting in governing and government is money. Money has no time and no identity and no human nature, because of course it has not" (462). But if government is not in and of itself interesting to Stein, what she calls the literary master-piece is profoundly so, for it exists in a manner unavailable both to human bodies and to the elected bodies that govern them.

Stein had laid the groundwork for her extraordinary if dizzying analogies between literary and governmental acts in *Four in America* (finished in 1933), where she asks, "If Ulysses S. Grant had been a religious leader who was to become a saint what would he have done. If the Wright brothers had been artists that is painters what would they have done. If Henry James had been a general what would he have had to do. If George Washington had been a writer that is a novelist what would he do."[28] The purpose of *Four in America* is to inquire whether or not it makes sense to compare what seem to be unlike cultural activities. Not only does she insist that it makes sense, Stein further contends that each of the figures she takes up would be performing the identical activities even were they to change the outward nature of their pursuits. Washington the novelist, Stein concludes, would have performed actions identical to Washington the general. In fact, Stein reasons that Washington was a novelist in being a general: "I can say what I have to say. George Washington did not write a play. He wrote a novel every day. He who was the father of his country" (168). The same is true in the reverse for Henry James; his writing, she insists, might well have been generaling: "Remember that there are two ways of writing and Henry James being a general selected both, any general has selected both otherwise he is not a general and Henry James is a general and he has selected both" (138). And so on: "If Wilbur Wright had been a painter, just like there are painters American painters would he have been different from what he was. Not at all" (86).

Stein does not suggest that James would have made a good general or that Grant would have made a good novelist; rather, she means simply to point out that James's actions would have possessed the same attributes had they been acts of writing or war. Distinguishing between acts of writing is the purpose of *Lectures in America* (1935) and "What Are Master-pieces and Why Are There So Few of Them" (1936), a companion piece to *The Geographical History of America*. In "What Are Master-pieces," Stein announces that a master-piece is not an "identity," but an "entity."[29] Master-pieces "do not exist because of their identity, that is what anyone remembering then remembered then, they do not exist by human nature because everybody always knows everything there is to know about human nature, they exist because they came to be something that is an end in itself and in that respect it is opposed to the business of living which is relation and necessity. That is what a master-piece is not although it may easily be what a master-piece talks about" (358). Proclaiming the advent of "twentieth century literature" — embodied in her own work particularly and in American literature more generally — "What Is English Literature" anticipates Stein's faith in the "end in itself" when it praises British literature for being as self-contained as England itself: "When anybody at any time comes to read English literature it is not at all necessary that they need to know that England is an island, what they need to know and that in reading any real piece of English literature they do know is that the thing written is completely contained within itself." English literature, Stein reasons, "has existed each piece of it inside itself in a perfectly extraordinary degree compared with other literatures that is other modern literatures."[30] The advantage to this kind of writing is that it offers clearly demarcated boundaries between itself and the rest of the world. Organic form is compelling, then, because "What was outside was outside and what was inside was inside" (201).

Elizabethan writing ("in a kind of way more connected" with American literature than any other ["What Is English Literature," 220]) represents for Stein the best model for how to produce such autotelic artifacts. She observes that "there was then at this period constant choice constant decision and the words have the liveliness of being constantly chosen" ("What Are Master-pieces," 204). And again: "As they chose so early and often so late and often as they were everlastingly choosing and choosing was a lively occupation you have an infinite variety of length and shortness of words chosen of vowels and consonants of words chosen and that is the important thing it was the specific word next to the specific word next it chosen to be next it that was the important thing. That made the glory that culminated in what was called the Elizabethan" (207). "Everlastingly choosing . . . the specific word next to the specific word" guarantees in turn the production of what Stein alternately calls a "completed thing" and a "whole thing" (215, 216). These objectifying acts provide an almost tautological answer to Stein's initial question "What is English literature": English literature is literature that *is* — "choosing and choosing," Stein reasons, gives what she will call a literary entity "its complete solidity . . . its complete existence" (198).

Unlike entities, on the other hand, governments and individuals are imprecated in networks of relation that have no natural endpoint; also unlike entities, they do not have a complete existence. For like individuals, governments can never become perfect wholes. This leads Stein to the fantastic conclusion that, as entirely self-sufficient entities, literary master-pieces embody all that government wants to be but cannot: "If there was no identity no one could be governed. But everybody is governed by everybody and that is why they make no master-pieces, and also why governing has nothing to do with master-pieces it has completely to do with identity but it has nothing to do with master-pieces. And that is why governing is occupying but not interesting, governments are occupying but not interesting because master-pieces are exactly what they are not" ("What Are Master-pieces," 363).

Stein's analogies between government and writing make an even finer point. Not only are governments not master-pieces, they militate against writers in their employ ever producing master-pieces. This is a claim crucial to *The Fountainhead,* which culminates with Roark's dynamiting a government housing project built from one of his designs but altered at the last minute. The New Deal corrupts Roark's vision, which the architect prefers destroyed rather than realized in bastardized form. Rand suggests that this corruption is due in part to the method of payment used to fund those affiliated with the housing project. Whereas the WPA insisted that artists and workers could earn money only through a salary, and never directly from speculative markets, Rand maintained that money is earned only when it comes, unmediated, directly from the market. Salaried artists, she decides, are absolutely unable to produce what she calls a "unit." Thus, Roark refuses jobs that are offered him at architectural firms. "It's your insurance," declares a bewildered prospective employer. "You don't want to break loose just yet. Commissions won't fall into your lap like this" (129). But for Roark, "architecture is not a business, and not a career" (80). Later, he explains that he "earns" what little money he does only because his buildings are "real and living" (579), because "every part" of one of his buildings "is there because the house needs it" (136).

As with Rand, so with Stein, who had much to say about the work-relief philosophy of the WPA. "All Americans," Stein claims in "The Capital and the Capitals of the United States of America" (1936), "have always felt that they were not employed but that they were hired which was an entirely different thing" (*How Writing Is Written*, 75). Stein links this vision of transitory employment, which romantically recalls the self-indentured laborer of preindustrial America, to a vision of "small" or "invisible" government. "There is nothing," she states, "that makes any one know more quickly that they are employees that is that they are employed and not on their own or a hired man than when the government is where everybody always knows about it" (75). "This country," she reasons, "does not need any of its capitals and likes them to be tucked away so that they won't know where they are" (74). But most of all, the country did not need federal unemployment programs: "One of the funny things is that when there is a great deal of unemployment you can never get any one to do any work. It was true in England it is true in America and it is now true in France. Once unemployment is recognized as unemployment and organized as unemployment nobody starts to work" (109). "The more everybody wanted to be organized and the more they were organized the more everybody liked the slavery of being in an organization." She concludes, "That is the inevitable end of too much organization" (III).

In "What Is English Literature," Stein suggests that such inept governmental organization leads to inept literary organization. She does so by distinguishing the writer who "earns" money from those who simply make it. Strikingly, she uses exactly the terms Roosevelt used in his introduction of the WPA that same year: a writer earns money by serving "God," she writes, and makes money by serving "mammon." "Let us be frank in acknowledgment of the truth," Roosevelt had argued, "that many amongst us have made obeisance to Mammon, that the profits of speculation, the easy road without toil, have lured us from the old barricades. To return to higher standards we must abandon the false prophets."[31] But whereas Roosevelt's "spiritual values" were to replace those of Mammon by insisting on the importance of regulated, salaried labor over that of speculative market economics, Stein claims that serving God necessitates not salaried labor but the completion of an organically unified artifact, the entity described in "What Are Master-pieces."[32] As we have seen, earning money, serving God, and producing "entities" requires committing to the significance of every word in a text, as well as to their relation to each other.

3.

In an unpublished and undated short story, Ernest Hemingway spoofs John Baer's political cartoon of 1 January 1931 that coined the term "New Deal." In Baer's cartoon, a "farmer," a "worker," and "honest business" demand a "new deal" in a poker game being played by a "speculator," "big biz," and a "crooked politician." Hemingway's scenario is decidedly less populist. Walking through a surreal wonderland, Alice comes upon "four tramps" playing poker: Baer's porcine representatives of moneyed interest are replaced by a mechanic, a bookkeeper, a salesman, and a farmer. "What are you doing?" she asks the players. "Redistributing the wealth," they answer. As it turns out, the four are playing with a "fifty-two ace deck." Satirizing Roosevelt's academic "brain trust" as well as his famous "forgotten man" radio address, a "professor" declares, "This is the new thing, the really scientific deck which we have worked out to solve the forgotten man problem." After each hand with the rigged deck, they all throw in their cards with excited shivers, showing their five aces. "Who won?" asks Alice. "Nobody," cries the salesman. "It's a new deal." "If anybody ever won," asks the salesman, "what would become of our code of fair competition?"[33]

A consistent anti–New Dealer, and a particularly vicious maligner of the WPA in particular, Hemingway was adamant that there be no rules of fair competition in his own profession. Writers, he suggested, should never count on an income. In a letter to Paul Romaine on 9 August 1932, Hemingway bragged, "I could make my living, without capital, *in these times,* in at least three other ways than by selling what I write." Three and a half years later he would brag again: "I've made my living since I was fifteen and there are several things I can do well enough beside my writing to make a living at so I do not get that despair personally."[34] It was precisely because he was financially independent, Hemingway reasoned, that his work had not been compromised by the substantial income it was then beginning to generate; his work had what he called a "complete existence" because he did not depend on writing to make a living. Using Stein's adjectives, Hemingway explained that his writing did not describe reality but "made up" something "round and whole and solid."[35] This complete existence, however, did more than just add to the reality that Hemingway's texts apparently did not describe. Textual identity registered itself in its difference from the quotidian; the writer, Hemingway repeatedly declared, made "truer things than can be true."[36] This comment went beyond the "realism" of Hemingway's representations to explore the unique nature of textual identity. Hemingway produced complex analogies between human bodies and textual artifacts that interrogated the different response each had to alteration. Pursuing Stein's commitment to "the specific word next to the specific word" in the context of the amputation and destruction of human body parts, Hemingway imagined a textual identity impervious to the wounding that so often beset human identity. For Hemingway, literary texts are "whole, pure, and complete" in a way that actual living organisms can never be.[37] Pressing the Romantic analogy between bodies and texts to an entirely new conclusion, Hemingway contrasts bodies that can continually absorb replacement parts to texts for which every word counts as a vital organ. He claims in this way to produce safe, unwoundable identities that respond to violation more distinctly and adequately than any human body. His texts may be altered, but never wounded; once changed, his texts are gone.

Critics have almost single-mindedly read Hemingway's writing through the wounding he received in World War I. Philip Young believed in 1952 that Hemingway "had spent his whole life as a writer composing variations on the story of the physically crippled 'sick man' in 'Big Two-Hearted River'"; ten years later, Mark Schorer argued that Hemingway's injury in Italy dictated the course of his entire writing career, noting that "nothing more important than this wounding was ever to happen to him."[38] Such criticism is useful in identifying an undeniable intimacy between Hemingway's physical wounds and his writing but depends on therapeutic assumptions that imagine Hemingway's writing to be an endless "acting out" of a real or imagined trauma from which he never recovered.[39] In this model writing is significant as an activity or labor that reflects and expresses anxieties and neuroses that are always elsewhere and never specific to the text in question. But although it is true that the wound remains a central category in Hemingway's writing, the wound is a threat that writing is meant to alleviate as a surrogate identity, not as an endless process that metonymically extends the failings of human identity. Hemingway's stories involve not an ongoing labor to represent, reproduce, or displace the wounded body but an attempt to create forms that are superior alternatives to that body. For Hemingway, texts do not reinscribe human limitations so much as they transcend them. Responding to George Plimpton's "fundamental question," "What do you think is the function of your art?," Hemingway declares, "You make something through your invention that is not a representation but a whole new thing truer than anything true and alive, and you make it alive, and if you make it well enough, you give it immortality. That is why you write and for no other reason that you know of" ("Interview," 136).

Given such a hyperbolic commitment to the redemptive possibilities of literary creation, it is not surprising that Hemingway's letters to his editors obsessively detail the importance of preserving his writing in exactly the form he gives it. At times, this seemed to require recognition of what Greenberg called the "order and space" occupied by a work of art. Writing to Maxwell Perkins in 1938 about the advertising of *The Fifth Column and Four Stories of the Spanish Civil War,* for example, Hemingway urged him to "emphasize the size and number of words in the book," seeming to suggest that only an appreciation of the sheer quantity of the writing would lure prospective consumers (*Letters,* 474). Yet, in the context of Hemingway's lifelong fascination with textual identity, such a quantitative emphasis is revealing not because it accentuates the palpability of the text's physical presence but because it specifies a formal configuration that Hemingway insists has to be unique to each text. In one of many similar pleas made on behalf of such textual specificity, Hemingway demanded that Perkins spare his texts any alteration: "I imagine we are in accord about the use of certain words and I never use a word without first considering if it is replaceable" (*Letters,* 211). Hemingway likewise made Horace Liveright in 1925 legally agree never to alter a word on his own: "As the contract only mentions excisions it is understood of course that no alteration of words shall be made without my approval. . . . the stories are written so tight and so hard that the alteration of a word can throw an entire story out of key. . . . There is nothing in the book that has not a definite place in its organization and if I at any time seem to repeat myself I have good reason for doing so" (*Letters,* 154). According to Hemingway, the alteration of any one word means that the whole story is altered, reinforcing the idea that every word is irreplaceable and fundamentally necessary to a text's identity.

Roark makes similar claims in *The Fountainhead:* "Every piece of it is there," he claims of one of his buildings, "because the house needs it" (136). Roark goes on to declare that "an honest building, like an honest man, had to be of one piece and one faith; what constituted the life source, the idea in any existing creature, and why — if one smallest part committed treason to that idea — the thing of the creature was dead" (196). But the bodies in Hemingway's writing (invariably male) continually commit this kind of treason, and do not die. This is particularly striking in *To Have and Have Not* (1937) and "The Snows of Kilimanjaro" (1935). Not everything is as irreplaceable as a word, and a person's identity appears in these works to be less dependent on the body than a text's identity is on its words. Harry Morgan, the central character in *To Have and Have Not,* gets angry when his companion Albert attributes Morgan's dissatisfaction with the government's New Deal economic programs to the fact that he has lost his arm. "The hell with my arm," Morgan argues. "You lose an arm you lose an arm. There's worse things than lose an arm. You've got two arms and you've got two of something else. And a man's still a man with one arm or with one of those."[40] If the "size and number" of words in a text determine its identity, the size and number of arms or testicles a man has do not determine his. That an entirely intact male body is not necessary to sustain male identity makes clear that the body is distinct from the identity that is, at least ostensibly, housed within it. Of course, Morgan does argue that one arm and one testicle are necessary to human identity, though not one particular arm or testicle. "The body," then, does not itself constitute the identity in question; human identity and the body constitute two distinct terms for Hemingway. The fact that Morgan needs an arm, and not one specific arm, means that the arm of which he speaks is an enabling condition for an identity not itself determined by that arm. Textual identity is dependent on each of its constitutive units; human identity is not.

This discrepancy seems to imagine for the person a certain resiliency unavailable to the text. After all, persons, unlike texts, are not destroyed by the alteration of any part of their form. But seen from a different perspective, this resiliency must be understood as the susceptibility of the male body to being wounded, for if altering the male body does not entail destroying it, one is left with an identity that lives through physical mutilation. And it is the vulnerability to continued alteration implicit in the wound that Hemingway's textual organicism is meant to circumvent, for nothing is more characteristic of Hemingway than the physically mutilated character who survives his debilitating injuries. One recalls the grotesquely scarred fighter in "The Battler" (1925) and the hospitalized soldiers from "In Another Country" (1927), who try vainly to rehabilitate their broken bodies. There is the incapacitated Jake Barnes and then the racially caricatured Native American cripples from *The Torrents of Spring* (1926), whose prosthetic arms and legs refuse to stay attached. In "The Snows of Kilimanjaro," Harry recalls an evening when a wounded bombing officer, Williamson, *"very brave,"* came into camp *"with his bowels spilled out"* and who *"begged every one to kill him." "Shoot me, Harry. For Christ sake, shoot me. They had had an argument one time about our Lord never sending you anything you could not bear and some one's theory had been that meant that at a certain time the pain passed you out automatically. But he had always remembered Williamson, that night. Nothing passed out Williamson"* (*Complete Short Stories,* 53). Similarly, in *For Whom the Bell Tolls* (1940), a communist guerrilla tells the story of a comrade who "made us promise to shoot him in case he were wounded. . . . He had a great fear of being tortured" (21). The guerrilla Pilar concurs in her treatment of enemies: "Kill him, yes. Curse him, yes. But wound him, no" (89). Conversely, the homeless war veterans in *To Have and Have Not* spend their evenings cruelly assaulting each other in drunken stupors; they are walking corpses referred to as "poor bastards [who] won't die" (206). Finally, there is the baffled observation of the doctor in that book, who cannot explain why the internally bleeding, amputated Harry Morgan has lasted so long. The wounded and unconscious Morgan is "alive, that's all you can say" (247).

Morgan would seem in this way to embody the epigraph from Petronius's *Satyricon* provided by T. S. Eliot at the start of *The Waste Land* (1922): "For indeed I myself have seen, with my own eyes, the Sibyl hanging in a bottle at Cumae, and when those boys would say to her: 'Sibyl, what do you want?' she would reply, 'I want to die.' " Immortal but subject to the withering of age, the Sibyl heralds in a poem similarly concerned with the continually frustrated desire for cleansing, eschatological endings. From the poetry of William Butler Yeats and Hart Crane through Freud's *Civilization and Its Discontents* (1931) to Richard Wright's *Native Son,* modernist writers were fascinated in a general sense with the allure of definitive endings and new beginnings promised in death. But Hemingway worked through this promise with a detail unparalleled in modern literature. Bodily damage is endemic to Hemingway's work; his most striking and contested legacy is the hard-boiled masculine ethos adopted by characters as they endure their wounds and look hopefully toward death. The limbo of excruciating and incremental change that the wound visits on Hemingway's characters is attributable to the fact that these characters outlive, in mutilated form, the alteration of their bodies. Because of this inability to die, to change categorically from alteration, it is pain, and not death itself, that emerges in Hemingway as the most enfeebling attribute of human identity. Harry from "The Snows of Kilimanjaro," for example, is concerned less about death than about the possibility of being "broken" by his suffering: the "one thing he had always dreaded was the pain" (*Complete Short Stories*, 53). Convalescing after his own legs were shot up in 1918 at the Italian front, Hemingway similarly notes the "227 wounds" he could count on his body and sardonically writes, "I wouldn't really be comfortable now unless I had some pain" (*Letters*, 14, 15). The pain that Harry dreads, and the impossible "comfortable" pain ironically referred to by Hemingway, designate, both metaphorically and literally, the vexing indeterminacy between the human body and a human identity that is embedded in but never completely separable from or reducible to the body. Consequently, existential pain and physical pain rarely can be differentiated in Hemingway; Lieutenant Henry's mantra in *A Farewell to Arms* (1929), "The bastards break you," has a useful generality precisely because Hemingway leaves little ground for distinguishing one's identity from a body that literally bleeds into that identity.

So, if personal identity is in some sense stronger than textual identity (one can lose an arm and remain the same person), its strength is indistinguishable from a certain vulnerability, of which, readers of Hemingway have long recognized, the wound is emblematic. Responding to this vulnerability, a wounded Italian major from "In Another Country" urges the narrator to look for his salvation somewhere else than in a body that can never be healed. He suggests that the narrator might overcome his state of irreparable deformity by finding, external to himself, "things he cannot lose" (*Complete Short Stories*, 209). The major insists not on an impregnable identity (for no such identity exists in Hemingway's writings) but on an identity that cannot tolerate or survive a loss that might itself be inevitable. The worst loss, he suggests, is one that you can afford, one that will not kill you. The major in turn suggests that grammar itself provides a paradigm for things that cannot be lost; as the two work listlessly at physical therapies that offer no real hope of repairing their broken bodies, the major proceeds to instruct the wounded American on the fine points of Italian. Already able to understand his companion, the major insists — in high-Hemingway fashion — that the narrator express himself with perfect syntax; he is committed not to the content of what the two communicate, but to the correctness of its form. The stark simplicity of grammar offers the major an all-or-nothing clarity: his pupil's sentences are either right or wrong. Hemingway's conception of textual identity expresses just such a commitment to a logic of formal arrangement whose rules cannot be compromised. Rather than representing a brittle version of the human, then, textual identity, like grammar, represents an escape from human vulnerability. For speaking correctly, like fashioning fully organic texts, is a means of producing forms invulnerable to the wounds that beset the body and personal identity.

Insofar as they are about male bodies, Hemingway's texts are meant to replace those bodies, not as new vessels for human identity but as exemplars of an invulnerable identity entirely unavailable to persons. For after the conclusion of editorial negotiations over the status of specific words, there is no problem locating the identity of a Hemingway text. A literary text "is" itself: it is the aggregation of a specified set of words and the stipulation that this set of words is a unique identity. Because the identity of such a text is embedded in each and every word, the loss of any one of its words makes it not a lesser version of the original but something categorically different from it. Inviolate, this text is not subject to pain, because once altered "it" is a different form unrelated to the original. As Hemingway informs Perkins about *For Whom the Bell Tolls* in 1940, "Every damned word and action in this book depends upon every other word and action" (*Letters,* 514). Editing out one such word or action destroys the book, he writes to Charles Scribner: "This book is one whole thing; not just a lot of parts. You start taking out parts put there for a purpose and the next thing you haven't any whole" (*Letters,* 509).

This is not meant to suggest that Hemingway's texts are somehow immune to physical danger; one can imagine numerous compelling ways to damage one of his novels. Rather, Hemingway imagines the damage to be significant only when altering a word is seen to alter more than the form that word takes on the page. In *For Whom the Bell Tolls,* for example, the generic labels "unprintable" and "unnamable" replace those words Perkins and Scribner's refused to include. On first observation, this compromise seems to jeopardize Hemingway's claim that the text's integrity necessitates all of its words. The reader experiences the blatant excision of a word integral to the text, and the logic of Hemingway's aesthetic suggests that such a "wounded" text is not in any sense the text Hemingway intended to count as *For Whom the Bell Tolls.* But the novel's excisions are patently explicit, and it might reasonably be asked why Hemingway did not leave out the words completely and change the constitutive conditions of the text, deciding, as he often did, that the text's identity no longer required such words. For Hemingway, however, labels such as "unprintable" and "unnamable" are meant to indicate that the words in question are still present — not literally, but theoretically, as requirements of identity. Hemingway confirmed as much when recollecting his agreement with Perkins concerning words that "were not then publishable" (the "then" recording the historicity of an absence not meant to impinge on the text's imagined identity): Hemingway notes that in place of labels, often "blanks were left." He adds that "anyone who knew the words would know what they were," making clear that such words exist as part of the text even if they are not there on the page. Anyone "who knew the words would know" that they were, in an important sense, still part of the text ("Interview," 127).

Paralyzed by the idea of variation, Hemingway did often insist on the significance of material form itself. Pursuing the kind of analogy between writing and manual labor so often invoked by the radical left, he mused, "You know that fiction, prose rather, is possibly the roughest trade of all in writing. You do not have the reference, the old important reference. You have the sheet of blank paper, the pencil and the obligation to invent truer things than can be true. You have to take what is not palpable, and make it completely palpable" (*Letters,* 837). Here, prose writing appears to collude with its most palpable, empirical attributes. But Hemingway just as quickly makes clear that his version of textual identity — "not a representation but a whole new thing" — depends less on a distinction between the material and the ideal than it does on stipulated formal relationships.[41] This is why his texts — "The Snows of Kilimanjaro," *To Have and Have Not,* and *For Whom the Bell Tolls* — do not offer new material forms, new bodies for the corroded human bodies they represent. Rather, their putative invulnerability confounds any body-identity distinction at all.[42]

4.

Centrally concerned with the textual reconfiguration of bodily identity, "The Snows of Kilimanjaro" juxtaposes the gangrenous leg infection of Harry with his abandoned writing career. Dying on the plains of Africa, Harry manages most to regret that he long ago stopped writing. At first glance, Harry seems to imagine the writing he might have written as a lost form of physical therapy, a means of improving the body, for writing "work[s] the fat off [the] soul" in the same way that a boxer "burn[s] it out of his body" (*Collected Short Stories,* 44). But Harry misses less a therapeutic process than the object such activity might have produced. Recalling those memories of his that were never written down, he asks his wife if she takes dictation and on her negative reply thinks, "There wasn't time, of course, although it seemed as though it telescoped so that you might put it all into one paragraph if you could get it right" (50). From within the italicized section of the story — sections, we are meant to presume, indicative of the writing Harry wishes he had done — he makes a distinction between those memories that can be dictated and those that cannot: *"You could not dictate the Place Contrescarpe where the flower sellers dyed their flowers in the street"* (51). Harry's puzzling distinction between what can and cannot be dictated makes clear that we should not confuse Harry's memories with his idealized "one paragraph." This is the point of there being italics at all: set off from the roman type of the rest of the story, the italics differentiate those sheltering and wistful memories Harry recalls and wishes he had himself produced as writing; they draw our attention to the form of the story at hand as something existing independent of Harry. As it is, the story's third person comes tantalizingly close to a first person, particularly when we read unmediated, internal dialogues in which Harry addresses himself with the pronoun "you": "It seemed as though it telescoped so that you might put it into one paragraph."

During one italicized section, the narration even slips into the first person, calling attention to the unstable intimacy between the story's omniscient, free-indirect third person and Harry's failed aspiration to have communicated his experiences in an autonomous form different from the story at hand.

In this respect the italics present themselves as a wounded representation, a form of print that underscores its own insufficiency. His body dissolving, his stories never written, Harry wants new material forms. Harry's final dream — during which he imagines himself rescued by Compie, a pilot — offers him only a temporary escape from the constraints of his rotting flesh. As Harry dreams he soars above the African landscape on his way to safety, Hemingway effects a remarkable collapse of Harry's gangrenous leg and the terrain he and Compie transcend. Early in the story, Harry remarks, "I'm rotted half way up my thigh now" (49). As he gains altitude in the plane, he continues to observe the lethal, seemingly northward progress of his infection, suddenly collapsed with the fauna he spies marching across the ground below: "The zebra, small rounded backs now, and the wildebeeste [sic], big-headed dots seeming to climb as they moved in long fingers across the plain . . . and then another plain, hot now, and purple brown, bumpy with heat" (55). Witnessing himself spread out on the surface of the earth, his infected skin seeming to cover the world, Harry's pathetic fallacy works toward breathtaking conclusion as the plane carries him higher and higher above the ground. Burning purple and brown flesh now suffused in a gauze-like, flesh-colored mist, herds of zebra and wildebeest now transformed into a swarm of voraciously consuming locusts, Harry talks himself through his own death: "Looking down he saw a pink sifting cloud, moving over the ground, and in the air, like the first snow in a blizzard, that comes from nowhere, and he knew the locusts were coming up from the South. Then they began to climb and they were going to the East it seemed, and then it darkened and they were in a storm, the rain so thick it seemed like flying through a waterfall, and then they were out and Compie turned his head and grinned and pointed and there, ahead, all he could see, as wide as all the world, great, high, and unbelievably white in the sun, was the square top of Kilimanjaro. And then he knew that there was where he was going" (56).

But exactly where is Harry going? We find out in the very next sentence that Harry lies dead in his cot, having expired, presumably, during the almost religious transcendence he undergoes witness-ing Kilimanjaro. But what are we to make of this moment of self-transcendence, during which Harry seems to rise above his corrod-ing form and find in its place a sublime, square, whiteness? Given Harry's principal regret — that he never wrote as he wished he had — it might be helpful to recall Hemingway's comment, "You know that fiction, prose rather, is possibly the roughest trade of all in writing. You do not have the reference, the old important reference. You have the sheet of blank paper . . . and the obligation to invent truer things than can be true." Confronted with a self-transcendence that, at least in secular terms, is truer than any death could ever be true, we might imagine that Harry dies into something like a blank page, whose square and empty whiteness signifies all that Harry did not write. But whether the referent here is Eliot's *The Waste Land* — "I was neither / Living nor dead, and I knew nothing / Looking into the heart of light, the silence" — or Frost's "Desert Places" — "A blanker whiteness of benighted snow / With no expression, nothing to express" — the un-diluted white of Kilimanjaro signals that, his best stories unwritten, Harry's own page will remain forever blank.

What seems paramount, however, is the sudden disappearance of what Hemingway calls "the old important reference," here figured as Harry himself. For if Harry's dream releases him from physical trauma, it also marks the definitive elision of his consciousness and the story's free-indirect style. Harry's final dream is not in italics, and although this is in part explicable as a stylistic suspension of the reality of his dream (we assume the events are actually unfolding until the last paragraph of the story), it is also the case that the story's final refusal of italics indicates a collapse of the distinction made earlier between Harry and text. The story conflates Harry's con-sciousness with its own form of reference during a death the reader never actually witnesses, erasing Harry's consciousness into its own newly unified form. Seen from this perspective, the uninterrupted roman type of the final dream marks the text's refusal to serve as a self-consciously material vehicle for the wounded and insistently self-representing Harry. Instead, in a moment of textually contrived euphoria, Harry is released from the pain and wounding he has been experiencing.

It is tempting to view Harry's death as a change different in degree but not kind from the kinds of transformations he has imagined himself undergoing throughout his life. "The Snows of Kilimanjaro" is preoccupied with the possibility that endings are never recognized as such, that, in a kind of existential wounding, individuals live through their own deaths. Harry worries about somehow living through his own natural demise. He describes himself as having "traded away what remained of his old life" (46) to take his place at his wealthy lover's side: "When he went to her he was already over. . . . He had had his life and it was over and then he went on living it again with different people and more money" (44). But Harry's death at the close of the story is not a continuation of this process of incremental decay so much as its long awaited culmination. Harry does in fact die; at the close of "The Snows of Kilimanjaro," no human subject remains to be eased of its pain.

5.

Lending condemnation to his claim that Hemingway's prose apes the process of commodification, Richard Godden notes that the wounds most often found in that prose "derive . . . conclusively from the market."[43] Although the remark goes largely unexplained, it bears closer analysis, for in both *To Have and Have Not* and "The Snows of Kilimanjaro," explicitly economic terms do code instances of physical wounding. "Buy me that, Papa," one Key West tourist says regarding the armless Harry Morgan, suggesting that Harry's wounds are themselves inseparable from the labile consumption of the visiting tourists (*To Have,* 130). But it is not Morgan's lost arm that most effectively relates economic to bodily damage. Before he finally dies, Morgan lingers for days with a hemorrhaging stomach that literally bleeds away his insides. His eventual death in turn leaves his wife Marie impoverished, wondering if "you get over being dead inside" (257). Being "empty like an empty house" (257), as Marie puts it, serves as the central metaphor for wounding in the novel. Hemingway tells us that most children at Key West "have their bellies hurt" (96); some "started starving when they were born" (148).

However, *To Have and Have Not* targets political responses to the economic rather than the economic per se. Most of the wounds derive less from "the market" than they do from attempts to mitigate the admittedly devastating effects of laissez-faire. When Harry is shot in the stomach by Cuban Marxists, we are meant to understand this wound in the context of the "left" activism that pervades the novel, an activism that associates Cuban revolutionaries, the New Deal, and Richard Gordon. A middle-class "proletarian" American novelist modeled after John Dos Passos, Gordon self-righteously sets out to represent the beleaguered Conchs of Key West, but does them as little good as the radical politics with which Hemingway associates him. But then why, it might reasonably be asked, does Morgan declare just before he dies that "one man alone ain't got. No man alone now. . . . No matter how a man alone ain't got no bloody fucking chance" (225)? Unusual fare from an unflinchingly libertarian author who would boldly declare to a friend at this time, "Everyone tries to frighten you now by saying or writing that if one does not become a communist or have a Marxian viewpoint one will have no friends and will be alone. They seem to think that to be alone is something dreadful; or that to not have friends is to be feared."[44]

To Have and Have Not is not really a departure from these sentiments, for though Morgan's parting lines would seem to suggest some form of activism, some mode of protective affiliation, nothing in the novel is adequate to this demand. The radical Cuban revolutionaries, like Gordon, are immediately suspect: "The hell with his revolution," thinks Morgan (168). The New Deal fares no better, as Hemingway was stridently hostile to its programs and social ambitions. Morgan refuses to work for a government wage, and mocks his friend Albert, who does go to work for the WPA. Morgan has his boat taken from him by a pompous and maniacal New Deal official, a "government man" (84) who claims to be one of the three most important men in the country. Most significantly, the wounded vets in the novel are meant to recall some four hundred war veterans who in 1934 lost their lives in a hurricane while working for the Federal Emergency Relief Administration (FERA) in Key West. In an issue of *New Masses* just weeks after the hurricane, Hemingway's article "Who Murdered the Vets?" blasts the government for having sent the men down to work in Key West during hurricane season without making any preparations for their evacuation. "Who is responsible for their death?" he asks. "The writer of this article lives a long way from Washington and would not know the answers to these questions. But he does know that wealthy people, yachtsmen, fishermen such as President Hoover and President Roosevelt, do not come to the Florida Keys in the hurricane months."[45] Concerned with the gulf that separated the experiences of the haves and the have-nots, *To Have and Have Not* shows these vets — "poor bastards [who] won't die" — degraded and isolated even before they are lost in the hurricane, condemning in the process the New Deal's inability actually to organize its clients, to provide anything like the "relief" it promised.[46]

Hemingway's text provides for itself a mode of organization that radical politics and New Deal economics cannot provide actual individuals. In fact, *To Have and Have Not* replaces Harry just as "The Snows of Kilimanjaro" replaces its own Harry. His first novel to use the third person, *To Have and Have Not* is also Hemingway's last novel to use the first person; specifically, Harry's first person and Albert's first person are replaced with the third-person narration that follows each man's death. A competition between the first-person representation of a wounded identity other than the text's and the text's own identity results, as it did in "Snows," in the instantiation of the text's dominant and unified form. Absorbing the dead Morgan in the same way that "Snows" absorbs Harry and his italicized first-person narration, the novel substitutes itself for the wounded autonomy of "one man alone," responding analogically to Morgan's wounds with its own inviolate identity.[47] Apparently, Hemingway took this alternative seriously. Gordon's wife expresses her disgust for her husband with the simple dismissal, "you writer." Gordon's failure is disappointing to the degree that his writing might have produced something beyond the pain inflicted on all in the novel. Gordon's failure passes up a truly separate peace: "If you were just a good writer," she concludes, "I could stand for all the rest of it maybe" (186). Such resignation leaves little in the way of party politics; just how little is made clear in Hemingway's next novel, *For Whom the Bell Tolls,* which follows directly on the heels of Morgan's concluding remark, that "No man alone now. . . . No matter how a man alone ain't got no bloody fucking chance."

During the thirties, Morgan's faltering rejection of the kind of self-sufficient autonomy so often associated with Hemingway might well have seemed an endorsement of the popular Depression-era claim that American citizens were, and needed to be, profoundly interdependent and interconnected. For writers on the left and the right, the individual was never isolate: invariably, he or she was either secured or put at risk by the very existence of others. In *The Fountainhead,* Dominique Francon derides this belief when she mockingly declares, "Everything has strings leading to everything else. We're all so tied together. We're all in a net, the net is waiting" (143). For Rand, this "net" is objectified in the social consciousness of the New Deal, which Roark refuses most decisively when he blows up the government housing project he designed. In *Let Us Now Praise Famous Men,* James Agee celebrates the interconnection that Roark so despises by invoking the organic connectedness of humanity itself, suggesting that individual experience is necessarily collective because all people are part of the same whole: "Each is intimately connected with the bottom and the extremist reach of time. Each is composed of substances identical with the substance of all that surrounds him, both the common objects of his disregard, and the hot center of stars: All that each person is, and experiences, and shall never experience, in body and in mind, all the things are differing expressions of himself and of one root, and are identical: and not one of these things nor one of these persons is ever quite to be duplicated, nor replaced, nor has it ever had precedent: but each is a new and incommunicably tender life, wounded in every breath, and almost as hardly killed as easily wounded."[48] For Agee, this paradigmatically Hemingwayesque combination of the fragility of form and the resiliency of life is proof of the need for concerted social action: already "intimately connected" in profound theological registers, individuals realize themselves only by understanding their relation to others.

When Hemingway begins *For Whom the Bell Tolls* with John Donne, and informs the reader that "no man is an island," it might seem as if he has suddenly embraced this vision of interpersonal connection. Religious or otherwise, it appears at the start of the novel as if Hemingway has found the form of organization that Morgan goes to his death wanting. But *For Whom the Bell Tolls* is quite hostile to left politics. Hemingway makes clear that Robert Jordan's support is for Spain and the Republic, not for any particular left ideology. Thus Jordan wryly toys with fellow Loyalists by asserting that, like them, he grew up in a staunchly "Republican" tradition. "My grandfather was on the Republican national committee," Jordan observes. "The United States is a country full of republicans. They don't shoot you for being a republican there" (66). The humor is pointed, for Jordan will come to realize that as committed to the cause as he might be, he is nonetheless more of an American republican than a Marxist: his primary concern is to free individuals from tyranny, to leave them unyoked by any form of statism. "You're not a real Marxist and you know it," Jordan tells himself. "You believe in Liberty, Equality, and Fraternity. You believe in Life, Liberty, and the Pursuit of Happiness. Don't ever kid yourself with too much dialectics" (305). Jordan's eventual endorsement of American republican politics is in turn associated with the dangers of social security. For Hemingway's opus is an extended discourse on the evils of feeling too secure during times of political crisis. Thus Pablo is dangerous to his guerrilla group because he has begun to fear death. "Safety," his wife Pilar chastises him. "There is no such thing as safety. There are so many seeking safety here now that they make a great danger. In seeking safety now you lose all" (54). Jordan agrees: "My obligation is the bridge and to fulfill that, I must take no useless risks of myself until I complete that duty." However perversely, Jordan reasons that, ultimately, opening oneself up to risk offers a kind of security: "It is sometimes more of a risk not to accept chances which are necessary to take" (63).

But in *For Whom the Bell Tolls,* collective forms of political organization present characters with the gravest danger, for they promise to magnify the interminable wounding that Hemingway characters long to escape in death. In this novel concerned primarily with blowing up bridges and other ligatures of human connection, personal loss is experienced by every person associated with the afflicted. Here the social polity enacts the failures of human identity on a grand scale — "any man's death diminishes me," reads the Donne epigraph, making plain that human interconnectedness results in an organic form that suffers from every loss, from every alteration of its composition. This much Roosevelt himself had made clear: in his speech at Boulder Dam on 30 September 1935, for example, the president declared that Americans "know that poverty or distress in a community two thousand miles away may affect them, and equally that prosperity and higher standards of living across a whole continent will help them back home" (*Essential FDR,* 110). By 1940, this kind of organic connectedness seemed to promise agony more than anything else. The assertion "never send to know for whom the bell tolls; it tolls for thee," then, is hardly a plea for concerted political action. Granting the New Deal premise that persons are unavoidably interconnected, *For Whom the Bell Tolls* is a plea not to exacerbate this already excruciating condition, and suggests that political action amplifies the extent to which individuals experience others' deaths as personal losses, private wounds.

Written after the Loyalist cause in Spain had already been lost, Hemingway's novel continually returns to the desire, indeed the need, for repressing and displacing the political. It is not clear what the contemporary reader is meant to do with the suggestion that he or she is diminished by Robert Jordan's death in Spain. At the very least, Donne's injunction "never send to know" urges the kind of political repression that underwrites Hemingway's entire aesthetic. This is a novel, after all, whose protagonist remains focused on his task only by refusing to dwell on the certainty of his own impending death. "It is better not to know," declares the Soviet general who gives Jordan his orders to blow up the bridge. "Many times I wish I did not know myself" (7).

"For what are we born if not to aid one another?" asks a Loyalist in the novel. Jordan has no idea, save the fact that he disagrees. "All people should be left alone and you should interfere with no one," he thinks to himself. "So he believed that, did he? Yes, he believed that. And what about a planned society and the rest of it? That was for the others to do" (163). In a by now familiar pattern, Jordan finds salvation in a more personal calling. For though he imagines leaving "a planned society and the rest of it" for the others, he does covet Pilar's ability to tell stories. "If only that woman could write," he exclaims. "He would try to write it and if he had luck and could remember it perhaps he could get it down as she told it. God, how she could tell a story. . . . I wish I could write well enough to write that story, he thought" (134). "What were his politics then?" Jordan asks. "He had none now, he told himself. But do not tell anyone else that, he thought. Don't ever admit that. And what are you going to do afterwards? I am going back . . . and I am going to write a true book" (163). There perhaps he will be able to realize the kind of organization dreamed of in a planned society.

6.

During one italicized moment of recollection in "The Snows of Kilimanjaro," Harry recalls "that American poet with a pile of saucers in front of him and a stupid look on his potato face talking about the Dada movement with a Romanian who said his name was Tristan Tzara, who always wore a monocle and had a headache" (*Complete Short Stories*, 49). Hemingway knew and disliked Tzara, the founder of Dada, from his days in Paris, where he came into contact with Tzara through Ford Madox Ford and the *Transatlantic Review*. Concerning the magazine, Hemingway believed that Ford ran "the whole damn thing as a compromise [because] . . . anything Ford will take and publish can be took and published in Century, Harpers etc." (*Letters*, 116). The venture was for Hemingway insufficiently committed to the organic singularity required of textual identity; the notion that one piece could be published in two different formats by two different magazines without compromising that piece's identity was to him absurd. He felt threatened not by a change between two different typefaces but by the contamination that might result from moving the text from one set of relationships into another.[49] Seeing the magazine itself as a kind of text, Hemingway imagines that his story is as integral to that text as words are to his stories. Indeed, Ford once published one of Hemingway's pieces adjacent to one of Tzara's poems in the *Transatlantic Review*, which to Hemingway was an infraction of the organic identity both together comprised. Hemingway responded with a scathing dismissal of Dada, likening it to a corpselike child that refused to die and sustained itself by teething at Tzara's monocle.[50]

This image of a parasitic and lingering child is curious if only because of the echo it establishes with Dada's sense of itself. In his "History of Dada," George Ribemont-Dessaignes suggests that Tzara's performance art was born from the desire to leave behind no such vulnerable physical body: "Either the mind must consent to die by belying the aim it had set for itself or it must kill itself in advance. That is to say, either Dada would have to become crystallized in an activity perpetually the same [or] . . . it would have to destroy itself."[51] Cowley strikes a similar note in *Exile's Return*: "One might say that Dada died by principle: it committed suicide" (165). These notions are distinctly Hemingway; both Ribemont-Dessaignes and Cowley suggest that Dada was obsessed with putting itself out of its misery. On the one hand, Dada's interest in performance art set it against Hemingway's commitment to whole artifacts. The avant-garde's famed interest in performance, Peter Bürger reminds us, aimed "to negate . . . the relation between the part and whole that characterizes the organic work of art."[52] Hence Cowley's timed automatic writing exercise, performed "in the manner of our Dada friends," was an attractive idea to members on the left because it suggested a way that writing could become a form of nonproductive, regulated labor. On the other hand, Dada's fascination with performance was motivated by the same anxieties concerning alteration and mutability so prevalent in Hemingway. Killing itself in advance, a Dada performance leaves nothing behind; performance art can never belie its aim because nothing exists in difference from that aim.

In "An Introduction to Dada," Tzara explained that Dada's commitment to performance needed to be understood in the context of the potential mutability of the artifact:

> When in 1919 Picabia, at a gathering sponsored by Litterature, exhibited a drawing which he executed on a blackboard and erased as he went along; when I myself, on some pretext which I no longer remember, read a newspaper article while an electric bell drowned out my voice; when, a little later, under the title of Suicide, Aragon published the alphabet in the form of a poem in Cannibale; when in the same magazine Breton published an extract from the telephone book under the title Psst. . . . Must we not interpret these activities as a statement that the poetic work is without static value, that the poem is not the aim of poetry, since poetry can very well exist elsewhere? What better explanation can I offer of my instructions for the manufacture of a Dadaist poem (draw words at random out of a hat)?[53]

Dada solved the problem of wounding through the massive repetition and performance of formal suicide, repeatedly negating the physical expression of identity in the service of absolving it from change. Dada wished to "destroy poetry with its own weapons" (404), and Tzara's paradigm of composing a poem by drawing words from a hat (words that Tzara elsewhere suggests should be cut from a printed article) uses print to assert interchangeability as a product of materiality: the choice of words, as well as their ordering, does not affect the identity of the literary artifact. Publishing the alphabet and extracts from the telephone book likewise reduces published print to a physical form lacking particular content. Aragon and Breton destroyed publishing "with its own weapons": they performed publishing or, rather, published literal instances of printed matter such that their materiality signified their complete interchangeability and non-specific content.[54]

Amidst all the besieged rhetoric (the mind killing itself in advance, Dada itself committing suicide), it seems reasonable to ask what Dada was guarding itself against. "Mistakes have always been made," declared Tzara, "but the greatest mistakes are the poems that have been written" (87). But exactly why was writing poems such a mistake? Poems should not be written, Tzara maintained, to spare them debasement at the hands of their readers. As committed as Dada was to performance, it nonetheless railed against the idea that art was made for an audience in the first place. In the "Dada Manifesto 1918," Tzara declares, *There is a literature that does not reach the voracious mass. It is the work of creators, issued from a real necessity in the author, produced for himself"* (Motherwell, *Dada Painters and Poets,* 78). Ideally, literary producers were their own consumers. In this context, reaching a market at all signaled compromise. "Art is a private affair," Tzara declared, "the artist produces it for himself; an intelligible work is the product of a journalist. . . . The artist, the poet rejoice at the venom of the masses condensed into a section chief of this industry, he is happy to be insulted: it is a proof of his immutability. When a writer or artist is praised by the newspapers, it is proof of the intelligibility of his work: wretched lining of a coat for public use" (80). Dada held the public in such low esteem that it was more often than not openly hostile to its audience. Recalling that Dada would hurl "insults and obscenities" at those attending its events, Ribemont-Dessaignes's "History of Dada" reproduces a notice "TO THE PUBLIC" posted by members of Dada that warns their audience, "Before going down among you to pull out your decaying teeth, your running ears, your tongues full of sores, Before breaking your putrid bones, Before opening your cholera-infested belly and taking out for use as fertilizer your too fatted liver" (109). Were they possessed by *"real necessity,"* members of Dada would never have stood up before an audience in the first place.

Hemingway evinces this same disdain when he criticizes his contemporaries who believe that "to be alone is something dreadful." In fact, Richard Gordon in *To Have and Have Not* is made to look as pathetic as he does principally because he obsessively ingratiates himself with his reading public. Gordon's wife does not think him a "good writer" because, she says, "I've seen you bitter, jealous, changing your politics to suit the fashion, sucking up to people's faces and talking about them behind their backs" (186). This kind of fickleness is fatuous, Hemingway suggests, not just because it indicates shallow political commitment. Gordon's efforts to please are in vain because no two people in the novel have the same politics. Gordon struggles to keep up with political fashion, but can't seem to anticipate his readers. When he meets a devoted fan of his in a bar, he finds out that the reader loves his novels not because of their avid politics but rather because they offer him a distraction from "real" politics. Reading proletarian fiction such as Gordon's, the reader explains, is "the only way to be happy in times like these. What do I care what Douglas Aircraft does? What do I care what A. T. and T. does? They can't touch me. I just pick up one of your books . . . and I'm happy" (197). Later that evening, Gordon finds himself with a group of war vets drinking themselves into oblivion. As the gnarled and hardened men break out into political disagreement and then proceed to tear each other to pieces, Gordon shuttles between them buying drinks, trying to reconcile one to the other.

Clearly, these are not acts of diplomacy for which the mercurial and antagonistic Tzara would have been well suited. But Hemingway was savvy enough to realize that even in his aggressive disgust for his audiences, Tzara was nonetheless oriented toward them in an unabashedly theatrical manner, to borrow a notion from Michael Fried. The affect Tzara brought to his audience was in the end less important to Hemingway than the fact that he was engaged with them at all; Hemingway tended more toward the absorbed ideal. Thus Hemingway leaves Tzara with what Gordon leaves his wife: aborted children. Anxious that children of his own will take time from his social activism, Gordon insists that his wife perform an abortion against her will. "Love is ergoapiol pills to make me come around because you were afraid to have a baby," she yells at him. "Love is my insides all messed up. It's half catheters and half whirling douches" (186). As we will see in chapter 5, Gordon's fear of children prefigures not simply the many men in John Steinbeck's *The Grapes of Wrath* (1939), but Steinbeck himself, who felt his civic obligations to "the people" threatened by his own wife's pregnancy. For Steinbeck, this stand against children suggested an aesthetic every bit as performative and "nonreproductive" as Dada's: both babies and books, he suggested, were reminders that writers were capitalists more than they were laborers.

Hemingway was himself transfixed by the relation between success and quality. In *Green Hills of Africa* (1935), he lists the ways "we destroy" our writers: "First," he declares, we do so "economically. They make money. . . . Then our writers increase their standard of living and they are caught . . . they write slop."[55] As we have seen, "The Snows of Kilimanjaro" is meant to exemplify this statement: Harry attributes his failed writing career to having grown too comfortable with his wife's money. What is most striking about this short story, on the other hand, is the distinction it insists on between its ability to communicate a given set of information to the reader and Harry's ability himself to have written the story. The story is remarkably uninterested in what the reader does or does not know; the pathos from Harry's demise derives almost entirely from the story's ability to divorce the production of his memories from their consumption. When Harry mourns his failure to have written about a given episode in his life, we read all about that episode. But of course, "The Snows of Kilimanjaro" does nothing if not insist on the insignificance to Harry of what we read. All that matters is that Harry did not write down the memories for himself; "Snows" suggests, in other words, that these memories are never published or read, as, in fact, they are.

But perhaps it is wrong after all to say that "The Snows of Kilimanjaro" is indifferent to its own consumption. To what is the Hemingway text inviolate in the end if not to its readers, or to their minions, overzealous editors too eager to cater to the whims of a middle-class public? The kind of organic autonomy so dear to Hemingway, after all, is more often than not conceived as a defense against what Tzara called "the wretched" condition of "public use." Railing against a mode of musical consumerism that "blatantly snatches the reified bits and pieces out of their context and sets them up as a potpourri," Theodor Adorno offers a similar set of terms in "On the Fetish Character of Music and the Regression of Listening" (1938)[56] Responding to the degradations faced by art at the hand of the instrumentalizing financial institutions of the culture industry and the poorly educated public to which they pander, this essay rigidly opposes a text's organic form to its public consumption. Unfortunately, he declares, formal unity is next to impossible with modes of production and consumption that fetishize parts as opposed to wholes.[57] And audiences, he reasons, tend to ruin autonomous art by consuming it not as a whole but in bits and pieces. "The emancipation of the parts from their cohesion," he explains, "and from all moments which extend beyond their immediate present, introduces the diversion of musical interest to the particular sensory pleasure" (278). Adorno goes on:

> Marx defines the fetish character of the commodity as the veneration of the thing made by oneself which, as exchange value, simultaneously alienates itself from producer to consumer — "human beings." "A commodity is therefore a mysterious thing, simply because in it the social character of men's labor appears to them as an objective character stamped upon the product of that labor; because the relation of the producers to the sum total of their own labor is presented to them as a social relation, existing not between themselves, but between the products of their labor." This is the real secret of success. It is the mere reflection of what one pays in the market for the product. The consumer is really worshipping the money that he himself has paid for the ticket to the Toscanini concert. He has literally "made" the success which he reifies and accepts as an objective criterion, without recognizing himself in it. But he has not "made" it by liking the concert, but rather by buying the ticket. To be sure, exchange value exerts itself in a special way in the world of cultural goods. For in the world of commodities this realm appears to be exempted from the power of exchange, to be in an immediate relationship with the goods, and it is this appearance alone which in turn gives cultural goods their exchange value. But they nevertheless simultaneously fall completely into the world of commodities, are produced for the market, and are aimed at the market. (278–79)

Adorno's primary anxiety is that American and German strategies of producing and consuming music invest the consumer with the very real power of being able somehow to compose or author music in paying for it. Consequently, his claim that consumers "literally" make music by paying for it condemns not simply "regressed" listening, but Dada and surrealism as well, both of which, he felt, embraced the fracturing of formal unity. Adorno's essay is written as a response to Walter Benjamin's "The Work of Art in the Age of Its

Technical Reproducibility": nothing displayed the degradations of capital more successfully, Adorno claims, than the fractured aura of a work of art — precisely the partialized, fragmentary consumption of art lionized by Benjamin as potentially emancipatory.

The fear that consuming publics might compromise formal unity is at the core of Gertrude Stein's literary theory as well, and is particularly evident one year before Adorno's essay, in *Everybody's Autobiography* (1937). Here, Stein meditates on the effect the attribution of monetary value to a text has on its identity: "Before one is successful that is before any one is ready to pay money for anything you do then you are certain that every word you have written is an important word to have written and that any word you have written is as important as any other word and you keep everything you have written with great care. And then it happens sometimes sooner and sometimes later that it has a money value . . . when something began having a commercial value it was upsetting. . . . Before anything you write had commercial value you could not change anything that you had written but once it had commercial value well then changing or not changing was not so important."[58] The attribution of a money value to a text somehow causes the author of that text to forsake an earlier belief that "you could not change anything," that identity was "so much a thing that it could never be any other thing." This is why serving God necessitates producing entities. The moment the criteria that influence formal composition become financial, a writer serves Mammon. For Stein, monetary value threatens the most basic level of textual identity, for it produces the possibility of an infinite interchangeability in which "changing or not changing [is] not so important." Being paid for her writing does not produce for Stein a simple mistake, a problem in which market value is incommensurate with aesthetic identity, so much as it precipitates a crisis in which the very terms that initially constitute identity change. She worries that the attribution of a monetary value somehow competes with and destroys the capacity a finite set of words once had to designate an entity: "Somehow if my writing was worth money then it was not what it had been" (84).

Stein's concerns over the relation between money and textual identity, however, are just part of a broader fascination with what she terms in "What Are Master-pieces" the "question of a writer to his audience" (356). A writer bent on producing master-pieces can never, she maintains, orient his work toward its audience. "I am I because my little dog knows me," she confesses, "but, creatively speaking the little dog knowing that you are you and your recognising that he knows, that is what destroys creation" (355). It is one thing to have people consume your work, quite another for the work to anticipate its eventual consumption. Stein makes clear that the simple fact of others finding her work valuable is not in and of itself a problem. In *Everybody's Autobiography* she writes, "Picasso and I used to dream of the pleasure if a burglar came to steal something he would steal his painting or my writing in place of silver and money" (90). If this fantasy endows the work with a value beyond money, it does so by suggesting that artistic objects come by whatever value to others they might have only clandestinely, serendipitously. Theft is appealing because it is unexpected, because the stolen works could not have anticipated in their form the burglar that eventually enjoys them.

"The question of a writer to his audience" turns on whether the writer's text establishes theatrical relations with its audience. This might at first seem only to repeat the tired literary cliché that good writing never tries too hard to please, never tries too hard to anticipate its audience's tastes and desires. But Stein is concerned less with how craven writing becomes in gesturing to an audience and more with how any orientation between a text and its audience disables the text from being concerned only with itself. For Stein, the literary master-piece needs to be entirely self-contained. These entities are unlike governments and persons, she holds, because they represent finite and coherent sets of relations. Insofar as an entity represents "an end in itself . . . opposed to the business of living which is relation and necessity," it can have relations with nothing beyond its borders, least of all an audience. This last point provides Stein with terms for distinguishing between literary genres. She writes in "What Are Master-pieces": "One of the things that I discovered in lecturing was that gradually one ceased to hear what one said one hears what the audience hears one say, that is the reason that oratory is practically never a master-piece very rarely. . . . It is very interesting that letter writing has the same difficulty, the letter writes what the other person is to hear and so entity does not exist there are two present instead of one and so again creation breaks down. I once wrote in *The Making of Americans* I write for myself and strangers but that was merely a literary formalism for if I did write for myself and strangers if I did I would not really be writing because already then identity would take the place of entity" (357). If oratory and letter writing produce unacceptably theatrical relations between the writer and his or her audience, then so did the actual theater. Stein notes in her essay "Plays," "The fact that your emotional time as an audience is not the same as the emotional time of the play is what makes one endlessly troubled about a play."[59] Stein is troubled because "the business of Art" as she "tried to explain in Composition as Explanation is to live in the actual present" (251). Theater can never exist in the actual present, she reasons, because of the discrepancy between its performance and the audience's experience of that performance; insofar as she writes plays herself, Stein explains, she does so in an effort to solve this problem.

The important point for Stein is that any literary genre not committed to organic form might become inappropriately theatrical. Nineteenth-century English literature represents a falling off from Elizabethan literature, she reasons, in part because its self-consciousness is so theatrical. "They thought about what they were thinking," Stein says of writers of this period, "and if you think about what you are thinking you are bound to think in phrases, because if you think about what you are thinking you are not thinking about a whole thing." Nineteenth-century literature betrays its wholeness in an almost identical manner, in its commitment to what Stein calls "explanation": "If you are explaining, the same thing is true, you cannot explain a whole thing because if it is a whole thing it does not need explaining, it merely needs stating" ("What Is English Literature," 216). She declares that "if a thing is a completed thing then it does not need explanation" (215). The reasoning here is twofold: completed things eschew explanation because explanation addresses itself to an audience and also because, as I. A. Richards might have pointed out, true works of art endeavor to be, not to mean. Here, being an entity militates against the instrumentality of linguistic communication as such. As Tzara might have pointed out, nothing testified to "the wretched" state of "public use" quite so much as "intelligibility." Stein might well have agreed: insofar as literary objects were self-conscious enough to require explanation, they failed "to live in the actual present," which, she reminded us, is the very "business of Art."

Chapter Three

Wallace Stevens and the Invention of Social Security

When many millions of people all over the world demand
security and a state that must guarantee it, that's one thing. But
when bowlers or batsmen, responsible for an activity essentially
artistic and individual, are dominated by the same principles,
then the result is what we have. — C. L. R. James, "The Welfare
State of Mind"

First delivered as a public lecture during the heated primaries for the
1932 presidential election, Robert Frost's "Build Soil" might well be
the first work of art to figure the question of artistic autonomy in
unmistakably New Deal terms. Expounding the same performative
philosophy later embraced by the Federal Writers' Project, Tityrus,
the poem's central figure, declares, "Thought product and food product are to me / nothing compared to the producing of them."[1] These
views were very much Frost's own. As the poet would later put it, "I
look upon a poem as a performance."[2]

"Poems by Frost," Richard Poirier explains, manage to "make the
forms and processes of actual work into a version of literary archeol-
ogy. The implication in all of them is that careful and intense ordinary
labor, when applied to the things of this world, can gradually dissolve
their commodity values into mythological ones. And this is just what
any intense literary labor does, so it is suggested, when it digs into
and transfigures words. Frost's worker thereby *becomes* a poet by
virtue of his labor."[3] "As a result of such work," Poirier continues,
the reader comes to realize that "physical objects which before
seemed obdurate, or texts that seemed definitive, are in fact transi-
tional, fluid, and indiscrete" (91). Poirier understands Frost's fascination with literary labor in terms of a broadly Emersonian dispensation given to performative aesthetics. In the poetic and philosophical
texts of this tradition (exemplified for Poirier in the writings of Emer-

• • •

son, William James, John Dewey, Stein, Wallace Stevens, and Frost), "the correspondence between physical work and mental work, between manual labor and writing (which is no less an operation of the hands), is expressed with an eagerness that effectively blurs the social and cultural distinctions known to exist between these different kinds of activity" (81). Despite these perceived correspondences, Poirier refuses to situate Frost's commitments to labor in political or economic terms. Stevens, Stein, and Frost, he asserts, "never bother . . . fully to puzzle out the literary, much less the social consequences of their inferable linguistic theories" (92). "Frost, Stein, and Stevens in their shared distaste for social and economic theory," Poirier adds, never ask "why the inescapable hardness of life needs to be exacerbated by practices of economic and political organizations and networks" (119). As the previous chapter makes clear, this claim is patently false in the case of Stein, who persistently analogized literary and governmental acts of organization. Here, I will show that this claim is equally mistaken in the case of a poet like Stevens who, as I suggest in the introduction, was absorbed during the thirties and forties with how poetry (imagined in terms every bit as performative as Frost's) could become a kind of "perfect insurance," something like a transcendental supplement to the New Deal's Social Security Administration.

Modeled on Virgil's "First Eclogue," Frost's "Build Soil" is itself an explicitly political poem: it takes as its subject the social obligations incurred by the kind of literary patronage offered by the Federal Writers' Project. Should the salaried Tityrus, the poem asks, somehow address in his poetry the impoverishment of his peer Meliboeus, a struggling self-employed farmer? Unlike Meliboeus, both Virgil's and Frost's Tityrus draw their respective wages from public institutions meant to secure them from the market: Virgil's from the Roman state, and Frost's from a university poets-in-residence program (presumably like the one at which Frost himself was then employed). In fact, Frost's Tityrus insists there is no real difference between working for the state and working for the university: he tells Meliboeus to "Join the United States and join the family — / But not much in between unless a college" (325). "I keep my eye on Congress, Meliboeus," notes Tityrus. "They're in the best position of us all / To know" (317).

In both Virgil's and Frost's pastorals, Tityrus is asked for help by the farmer Meliboeus; in both he refuses the plea for assistance. In "Build Soil," however, Tityrus explains his refusal as a rejection of collectivism per se. He avers that the only revolution available is a "one-man revolution":

> . . . inside in is where we've got to get.
> My friends all know I'm interpersonal.
> But long before I'm interpersonal,
> Away way down inside I'm personal. (320)

Thus, even though Frost seems to champion something like Social Security when he writes in "Provide, Provide" that it is

> Better to go down dignified
> With boughten friendship at your side
> Than none at all,

Tityrus claims that poetry is most valuable in its ability to counterbalance the forms of interpersonal association that programs like Social Security demanded.[4] "We're too unseparate out among each other" insists Tityrus, and we are meant to believe that poetry, imagined as a form of nonmarketed labor, compensates for this fact (324). Of course, it is not at all clear how this advice helps Meliboeus, particularly because Tityrus's refusal to take his thought product to market is not private in any clear sense. On the contrary, his embrace of "producing" over "product" is underwritten by a salary unavailable to Meliboeus.

But Tityrus is unmoved by his friend's plight; as is the case with many of Frost's poetic narrators in *A Further Range* (1936), in which "Build Soil" is collected, he is indifferent that conditions had "reached a depth / Of desperation that would warrant poetry's / Leaving love's alterations" (317). Tityrus confesses this indifference most explicitly when he explains that he does not "dare / Name names and tell you who by name is wicked":

> I prefer to sing safely in the realm
> Of types, composite and imagined people:
> To affirm there is such a thing as evil
> Personified, but ask to be excused
> From saying to a jury "Here's the guilty." (317)

Faced with such a decidedly pastoral refusal to treat the details of the political scene, Meliboeus concludes the poem with an ironic paraphrase of Tityrus's incoherence, stating that "going home / From company means coming to our senses" (325). If a reassuring poetic retreat from a threatening reality is a familiar theme in pastoral, then so is the pronominal oscillation that here confuses the isolate with the collective.[5] What does it mean, for instance, that "we" come to "our" senses only when "we" are most alone? For what kind of "composite and imagined people" would this be the case? At the very least, the often conflicted movement to collective pronouns that marks pastoral generally and Frost's poem specifically throws doubt on Tityrus's claim that simply "producing" poetry as opposed to marketing it somehow protects against the erosion of private and autonomous experience.

Poirier's protestations to the contrary, these questions are literary and political at one and the same time. For perhaps at no point in American history prior to the Depression had the simple pronoun "we" seemed so freighted with significance. In his 1936 memoir *American Testament,* for example, Joseph Freeman, editor of *New Masses,* discovers that "*we* replaced *I,* and to speak of your own life . . . was to speak of the life of mankind in whose development you found your whole undivided being."[6] "We feel threatened," Stevens notes at his first public lecture that same year; "We look from an uncertain present toward a more uncertain future. One feels the desire to collect oneself against all this in poetry as well as in politics."[7] The New Deal was already in the process of collecting against the future in a strictly economic sense: "We must begin now to make provisions for the future," Roosevelt declared during a "Fireside Chat" on 28 April 1935.[8] But if collecting money seemed a relatively simple affair, collecting the interests, needs, and desires of collectivities into coherent wholes was not, and remained a perplexing subject for writer and policymaker alike during the Depression.

Poets and politicians most typically represented groups — national, economic, racial, and otherwise — as if they were self-coherent individuals. Thus "Doc" in John Steinbeck's *In Dubious Battle* (1936) describes the "Group-men" that a body of strikers often becomes by mobilizing the rhetoric of organicism discussed in the previous chapter: "They seem to me to be a new individual, not at all like single men. A man in a group isn't himself at all; he's a cell in an organism that isn't like him any more than the cells in your body are like you. I want to watch the group, and see what it's like. People have said, 'mobs are crazy, you can't tell what they'll do.' Why don't people look at mobs not as men, but as mobs? A mob nearly always seems to act reasonably, for a mob."[9] Roosevelt was hardly immune from the appeal of such metaphors. "A real economic cure," he declared in his "Forgotten Man" radio address of 7 April 1932, "must go to the killing of the bacteria in the system rather than to the treatment of external symptoms" (*Essential FDR,* 14). Roosevelt would continually humanize government in just this manner. In his speech before the 1936 Democratic National Convention on 27 June 1936, he declared, "We seek not merely to make government a mechanical implement, but to give it the vibrant personal character that is the very embodiment of human charity" (*Essential FDR,* 118). Here, the president embodies government in the name of a "we" that refers at once to his public audience and to the administrative machinery he represents. Roosevelt's pleonastic recourse to this particular pronoun bordered on the obsessive. Thus, while Frost's Meliboeus points out the seemingly incomprehensible project of "going home" to discover collective "senses," Roosevelt's rhetoric of inclusion invariably encoded conflicts of interest between literal persons and what Tityrus calls "composite and imagined people." On 9 December 1935, for example, the president declared, "We are regaining a more fair balance among the groups that constitute the Nation, and we must look to the factors that will make that balance stable. The thing that we are all seeking is justice."[10] Impossibly, Roosevelt's "we" sets itself above the groups between which he claims to adjudicate. His encompassing "we" cannot as a whole achieve the kind of justice he imagines it is after: "regaining a more fair balance among the groups that constitute the Nation" necessitated, of course, taking from one group and giving to another. Roosevelt had made this clear himself on more than one occasion, as in his first Annual Message to Congress on 3 January 1934: "Now that we are definitely in the process of recovery, lines have been rightly drawn between those to whom this recovery means a return to old methods — and the number of these people is small — and those for whom recovery means a reform of many old methods, a permanent readjustment of many of our ways of thinking and therefore of many of our social and economic arrangements" (*Essential FDR,* 73).

The Depression-era fascination with Tityrus's "composite and imagined people" — rooted deeply in the poetical and political imagination of the United States, from Tocqueville to Whitman — finds Stevens inventing "Major Man" in "Notes Toward a Supreme Fiction" (1942):

The major abstraction is the idea of man
And major man is its exponent, abler
In the abstract than in his singular

More fecund as principle than particle
Happy fecundity, flor-abundant force,
In being more than an exception, part,

Though an heroic part, of the commonal.
The major abstraction is the commonal,
The inanimate, difficult visage. Who is it?[11]

In one respect, Stevens's lingering question "Who is it?" has a simple answer: according to Harold Bloom, major man (transmogrified later in the poem into one "MacCallough") personifies "a hardheaded clan, producing eminent political economists, geologists, and even the American Secretary of the Treasury when Stevens was a student at Harvard."[12] But as suggestive as this proves to be, Stevens himself insisted that major man was nothing more or less than a principle of humanism, a mobile placeholder for the idea of collective man. Society itself (or "himself," more accurately), major man is what the poem calls an "abstraction blooded," what Stevens describes as a "possibly more than human human, a composite human."[13] As Stevens writes later in the poem of one of the many embodiments of major man (this time a statue of one General Du Puy), "There never had been, never could be, such / A man" (391). Thus Stevens's "Who is it?" inquires into the potentially problematic nature of personification itself. As such, the question has notable precedent in the query that drives "The Idea of Order at Key West" (1934) — "Whose spirit is this?" — asked by two men standing before a woman apparently churning a sea with her song.[14] Taken up at length below, "The Idea of Order" asks its question as part of an inquiry into the origin of phenomena — such as collectivities, economies and, Stevens will suggest, poems — that cannot be understood as having, or being the product of, an individual mind.

In "Notes Toward a Supreme Fiction," Stevens is absorbed with the problematic manner in which poetical and political acts of representation mistakenly endow abstract collectivities with the attributes of the human mind. Stevens follows his definition of major man in "Notes" with an account of a fastidiously organized "President," whose method of rule seems as improbable, as "fictive" as major man himself. Taking off from Bernard Mandeville's laissez-faire classic *The Fable of the Bees* (1714), Stevens's "President ordains the bee to be / Immortal." Dripping scorn, the poet adds, "The President ordains" (390). If the private vices of Mandeville's bees lead, *tout court,* to fortuitously organized public benefits, Stevens's poem parodies the President's efforts to shape the body politic by simple decree. The poet suggests that we partake in the fantasy of major man to the extent that we believe in such forms of presidential power. In one respect, this seems to place Stevens in the camp of Ayn Rand, whose right Hegelianism conflates the unbowed body of Howard Roark with the ultimate good of a laissez-faire community, that figures like Roark — left alone, Atlas-like — ultimately carry on their shoulders. Roark benefits others only to the extent that his actions are private and, like his art, self-sufficient, uncoerced by others. Also like Rand, Stevens eschews political models of central planning that begin from the assumption that collectivities can rationalize and intend the economies they constitute. His defense of the Social Security Administration, we will see, depends on a previous rejection of early New Deal attempts to formulate a collective plan that might direct the course of the economy.

But crucially unlike Rand (and Stein and Hemingway, for that matter), Stevens does not displace his skepticism of collective planning onto an ideal of organic art. Rather, Stevens's poetry, his "perfect insurance," emerges from the ashes of what Fredric Jameson calls the "plannification" of art.[15] Devoted to the same performative aesthetic as Tityrus, Stevens takes up the trope of ceaseless monetary circulation to celebrate poems and economies that, he claims, can never be organized into intention-bearing wholes. The one thing a collectivity cannot have, he adds, is a conscious mind. Idealizing the autonomy and perfection of literary creations, Stein and Hemingway understand their own writings as shrines of the intentional, as embodiments of the kind of organized and concerted planning that no state or collectivity could ever effect. More committed to a performative conception of the literary than his two contemporaries, Stevens does not exempt his own admittedly autonomous art from his critique of collective planning. Quite the opposite: he imagines that, like economies and governments, his own poems are testaments to the insufficiency of even the most individuated instances of intentional agency. It is just as impossible to plan a poem, the poet maintains, as to plan the stock market itself. Here is one reason, then, why "Insurance and Social Change" so productively compares poetry to insurance, why Stevens declares that "Poetry and surety claims are not as unlikely a combination as they may seem."[16] This is the case, the poet imagines, because insurance and poetry both supervene at the limits of intentional agency; in his conception of both insurance and poetry, the objectification of social relationships intrinsic to both practices compensates for the fact that no premeditated plan — in either poetic or political tertia — can ever make the future sufficiently secure.

1.

All forms of insurance — private or public, poetic or political — aggregate social relationships and experiences. In particular, the individual's imagined experience of and susceptibility to "risk" serves as the principal means by which actuarial science situates persons within population groups. At its heart, risk identifies the frequency with which a given outcome will occur in a given target group. As a measure of probability, risk is not predictive for the individual per se. For though it might make sense to say, based on past calculations, that 30 percent of all adult males in a given test group will be in at least one automobile accident before they are forty years old, it does not make sense to say that there is a 30 percent risk that a given adult male within that group will have an automobile accident before that age. "Risk is collective," explains François Ewald. "Whereas an accident, as damage, misfortune and suffering, is always individual, striking at one and not another, a risk of accident affects a population. Strictly speaking, there is no such thing as an individual risk."[17] Insurance orders and systematizes what seem to be random events by studying those events as they occur in population groups; the population group alone is the subject of statistical analysis. Only the most faulty leaps of deductive faith lead an individual to conclude that probabilities apply to him or her the same way they do a population. No individual is major man; no single person can embody probability.

James Farrell explains just this in his attack on the allegedly reductive literary criticism of Granville Hicks and the *New Masses, A*

Note on Literary Criticism (1936): "If one takes a large number of people about whom a sufficient number of data are known, it is possible to predict statistically how the component parts of such a number will react to a given and fairly familiar situation or stimulus. It can be predicted with a fair degree of accuracy how many of this number will (say) react in one pattern, and how many in another. It cannot, however, be predicted how any single individual of that number will react. In other words, in every individual there is an aspect of uniqueness and intractability, and this makes him not completely predictable in every potential situation."[18] In Farrell's fictional retelling of the First American Writers Congress, *Yet Other Waters,* Bernard Carr reiterates this point: "I'm talking about prediction and probability. In predicting what human beings will do, you can predict with some confidence if you have a large mass of them and are predicting what they might do in given situations."[19] "That's Marxism," interrupts a friend of Carr's. "It predicts what masses and classes will do." Carr replies, "But you can't predict what any single individual will do. The riskiest prediction of all is to predict about an individual" (48). For Carr as well as for Farrell himself, this gulf between probability as it is derived from the population and probability as it can only mistakenly be applied to individual persons provides a singular opportunity for the literary, which Farrell imagines is best suited to mediate between the material determinants of class identity and the irreducibly unique nature of individual behavior. "The novelist is concerned not merely with either the similarities or the differences [between classes and individuals], but with both of them," reasons Farrell in *A Note on Literary Criticism* (111). Likening writers to actuaries — both, he suggests, attempt to predict hypothetical futures — Farrell participates in the New Deal invention of social security not by embracing the New Deal itself, but by taking up the actuarial to understand the individual's relation to the group, and, moreover, by using actuarial terms as a way of understanding the social functions of the literary.

Still, Farrell's sense that the literary mediates between the objective and the subjective is in many respects out of step with the striking "impersonality" of New Deal modernist form, which in many cases militates against the subjective per se. The thirties and forties upped the ante considerably on T. S. Eliot's famous dictum in "Tradition and the Individual Talent" (1919) that "the progress of the artist is . . . a continual extinction of the personality."[20] Federal writers on the WPA, for example, were encouraged to find security in the absorption of their creative abilities by a collective, national project. Thus Henry Alsberg, director of the Federal Writers' Project, proudly declared that his project provided writers with a form of collective and impersonal artistic labor unavailable since the late Middle Ages, when artists laboring on cathedrals would seek union with God more than expressions of their own individuality. Impersonality would loom large in Stevens's work as well; he declares in "Adagia" that "Poetry is not a personal matter."[21] This said, Stevens uses the idea of insurance to understand the ways in which the statistical objectification of social relationships enables rather than threatens the sanctity and security of the individual, both in poetry and business. Both insurance and Stevens's poetry might be said to authenticate experience precisely in the process of making it reproducible.[22]

Stevens underwrites what "Insurance and Social Change" calls "a world in which nothing unpleasant can happen" not by somehow cordoning private experience off from public reality, but by relocating the social significance of experience from the private and the subjective to the public and the transferable. Frost's phrase "boughten friendship" is useful here, for it exemplifies how insurance transforms relations once thought to be the product of private proclivity into generalized economic relations newly dependent on the "interpersonal" nexus Frost's Tityrus so despises. Stevens avoids the accidental by focusing on objectifications of the social never reducible to any one person's experience. As it is, the accidental is only a coherent concept as it is defined in relation to a given unit of perception or identity. As we saw in chapter 2, "accidents" in a work of art are defined as they exceed the stipulated requirements of wholeness for a given work. The same criteria are readily applied to the human imagination. "Relatively to a given human being," reasons Oliver Wendell Holmes in *The Common Law,* "anything is accident[al] which he could not fairly have been accepted to contemplate as possible."[23] Accidents have meaning, Holmes makes clear, only to the extent that they mark a transgression of an individual's imaginative capacities, his ability to predict or foresee future states. In this context, it is hardly surprising that a poet as concerned with the imagination as Stevens would work in close orbit of a financial technology committed to providing for unimagined, often unimaginable futures.

Stevens takes up the relationship between the imagination and the accidental directly in his claim that "The Idea of Order at Key West" is somehow devoid of contingency. Reviewing Stevens's *Ideas of Order* in a 1935 issue of *New Masses,* Stanley Burnshaw claimed that in "The Idea of Order at Key West" "contradictory notions" produce a poem in which "uncertainties are unavoidable."[24] As if in response to Burnshaw, Stevens insists to his editor just after this review that "in 'The Idea of Order at Key West' life has ceased to be a matter of chance" (*Letters,* 293). Stevens explains his comment by noting, "It may be that every man introduces his own order into the life about him and that the idea of order is simply what Bishop Berkeley might have called a fortuitous concourse of personal orders. But still there is order" (293).

It is not immediately clear what it means for chance to be replaced by a "*fortuitous* concourse of personal orders." If the elimination of chance is "fortuitous" — and not the result of the personal agency gestured to in the phrase "every man introduces" — then in what respect has chance been eliminated? Stevens's comment, however, makes perfect sense in the context of the actuarial science just discussed. What appears fortuitous to one person is, from a more totalized perspective, part of a predictable pattern; as one economist explains of insurance, whereas "individuals may face uncertainty . . . society can face approximate certainty."[25] As I will demonstrate shortly, "The Idea of Order at Key West" depends on this move from the isolated individual to the population group, which is why Stevens can explain the elimination of chance in this poem with the simple but authoritative assertion, "But still there is order": chance becomes probability — becomes calculable — the moment a set of what at first seem to be discrete accidental events takes on a recognizable pattern. Paradoxically, life becomes a matter of risk when it "ceases to be a matter of chance." Stevens's desire to collect himself against uncertainty consequently emerges here with a literal force: uncertainty is eliminated when individuals are "collected" into population groups impersonal enough to turn chance into probability, impersonal enough to warrant the emergence of Stevens's vastly inclusive "our" in the final stanza of "The Idea of Order at Key West." That Frost, committed as he was to the inviolate privacy of the poetic experience, should write to Burnshaw at this time that "it was chance when the right subject matter and the right words came together" is in this context not surprising: looking "inside in," a poetic devoted to the private will invariably experience as accidental those events that, seen from a totalizing perspective, constitute the most perfect of orders.[26]

2.

English playwright and social reformer George Bernard Shaw champions social insurance in "The Vice of Gambling and the Virtue of Insurance" (1944). "How is it possible to budget for solvency in dealing with matters of chance?" he asks. "The answer is that when dealt with in sufficient numbers, matters of chance become matters of certainty."[27] As Shaw goes on to explain, insurance is used to account for events in their most public and totalized form, and as such, is relatively uninterested in the irreducibly private dimensions of personal experience. "A million persons organized as a state can do things that cannot be dared by private individuals," Shaw gleefully adds, things that "no private company can do" (109, 114). Some fifty years later, Michel Foucault heartily agreed, though with considerably less enthusiasm. Admittedly ambivalent over the prospect of rendering French Social Security more comprehensive than it already was, Foucault saw private and public versions of insurance as too insistently collective and therefore potentially coercive. Eager to support a system that provided for the financial autonomy of the modern subject, Foucault nevertheless identified social insurance as a principal mechanism through which the modern state "managed" population groups.[28] Social insurance was, he reasoned, one element in the para-institutional forces of "governmentality," defined as "a triangle, sovereignty-discipline-government, which has as its primary target the population and as its essential mechanism the apparatuses of security."[29]

But as much as social security might in some sense construct the modern subject (Foucault is notably vague in this regard), there are empirical limits to what social insurance can in fact accomplish. Far from testifying to an Orwellian State, an agency such as the Social Security Administration might be said to symbolize all that the modern state cannot (or refuses to) accomplish. "A million persons organized as a state" may well, as Shaw suggests, accomplish "things that cannot be dared by private individuals." But all told, the modern state has been remarkably unambitious in deciding what kinds of socially progressive policy it has wanted to accomplish. In the United States, Social Security has been the limit case of macroeconomic, progressive governmentality in both the best and the worse senses: if on the one hand it stands out as the most egalitarian correction to date made by the welfare state to laissez-faire capitalism, it is on the other hand the outer marker of what the welfare state has been willing to do. In fact, we might say that Social Security looks to naturalize the impossibility of collective action as such; it stands as the United States' most singular refusal to anticipate and actively control future conditions of the national economy. Despite the comforting image of the "safety net," invoked so frequently to describe the aspirations of the modern welfare state, it is worth noting what the necessity for such a net implies. If the need for "boughten friendship" speaks to "the hazards and vicissitudes of modern life," it also, and perhaps more importantly, institutionalizes the impossibility of there being any immediate political remedy to these hazards. If modern life leaves the individual unable to plan or effect her future, the very existence of social insurance stands as an acknowledgment that the state too is thus incapacitated.

In the years leading up to the establishment of the Social Security Administration and the WPA, it seemed briefly, and however quixotically, that an interventionist state might do more than simply provide security. At first, the widespread acknowledgment occasioned by the Depression that the individual in capitalism is for the most part unable to cause or even foresee the conditions of his economic existence led to the hope that government might plan such conditions. During what is often termed the "first" New Deal (1933–1935), public opinion overwhelmingly supported the pooling of more than financial resources, supported, that is, a form of national planning that located in government the very capacity for intentional agency that the uncertainty of modern life was seen to threaten. The desire for economic centralization — which, ideally, would give the state the power not to ameliorate the effects of economic downturns but to direct the course of the economy such that there would be no downturns — resulted in what Frank Warren has called "an apotheosis of the idea of planning, in which planning became almost synonymous with liberalism."[30]

Soviet and German economies — both committed to national planning—had by this time already turned to increasingly authoritarian centrisms, in which national plans were drawn up by a finite group of individuals. New Deal national planning, on the other hand, orchestrated by the National Recovery Administration (NRA), was sold as the culmination of democratic representation.[31] "There is nothing complicated about it," Roosevelt declared of the NRA during a "Fireside Chat" on 24 July 1933. "It goes back to the basic idea of society and of the nation itself that people acting in a group can accomplish things which no individual acting alone could even hope to bring about" (*Essential FDR*, 65). But the NRA was seen to articulate and organize more than collective accomplishments, more even than collective hopes. "The social will," noted Rexford Tugwell while presenting his case for what would shortly thereafter become the NRA, "is a vague and elusive thing, difficult to apprehend, more difficult to pin down to specific issues." However, governments, "presumably, are expressions of [the] social will. That is their excuse for being."[32] Accordingly, Tugwell urged that the plans formulated by the NRA be sold as the invention of this social will. Following Tugwell, Roosevelt described the NRA as a brain trust of macroeconomic, national proportions. This, he suggested, made the New Deal "the public's government" (*Essential FDR*, 128).

Of course the NRA was no such thing. Constructing a corporate-liberal alliance with big business, the government board at the core of the administration looked to stabilize the market by eliminating wasteful competition, ultimately allowing the president to endorse and supervise the cartelization of private industry. Declared unconstitutional in 1935, the NRA convinced no one that its plans were the product of the public's will. But this was not the only problem confronting a "democratic" version of national planning. According to Walter Lippmann, any endeavor like the NRA was doomed from the start not because business interests and government boards invariably ignored the public will, but because the public did not have a will at all. Responding in large part to then Secretary of Commerce Herbert Hoover's repeated corporate-liberal invocations of the public interest, Lippmann's *The Phantom Public* (1927) insists that a public is not a person, and that there is no meaningful sense in which a public can be said to have interests, let alone intentional agency. Updating "Occam's razor," Lippmann argues persuasively that intentional agency dissolves during the move from the individual to the collective; there is, he claims, only a virtual and impersonal public, one that by definition cannot formulate designs. "A mere phantom," "an abstraction," the public is not "a fixed body of individuals," and therefore could never "direct . . . the course of events."[33]

Lippmann's core argument was recast as a central criticism of the welfare state in the hands of a laissez-faire conservative like Ayn Rand. In *Atlas Shrugged*, (1957) her libertarian übermensch John Galt hijacks a radio broadcast from a band of aging New Dealers and speaks to a captive audience: "The good, say the mystics of muscle, is Society — a thing which they define as an organism that possesses no physical form, a super-being embodied in no one in particular and everyone in general except yourself."[34] But as Rand would insist again and again, "Mankind is not an entity, an organism, or a coral bush."[35] There was no sense in which one could attribute intention of any kind to a collective. Howard Roark puts this most simply during the trial at the close of *The Fountainhead*. Roark stands accused of blowing up a government housing project that he designed but that has been altered by the state. "The mind is an attribute of the individual," he explains. "There is no such thing as a collective brain. There is no such thing as a collective thought. An agreement reached by a group of men is only a compromise or an average drawn upon many individual thoughts. The primary act — the process of reason — must be performed alone. . . . No man can use his brain to think for another. All the functions of body and spirit are private. They cannot be shared or transferred."[36] For Roark, as well as for Rand, the welfare state rested on the faulty premise that public, collective groups could perform those functions reserved for private, necessarily singular persons.

As was often the case with Rand's characterizations of the contemporary scene, however, she was mistaken in her belief that the New Deal was exclusively interested in producing a collective brain. To be fair, a thinker as serious as Talcott Parsons was at the time asking, "Was 'society' only a conventional abstraction referring to the interaction of concrete individuals who are the sole real components of social existence, or was society a substantive reality to itself — *sui generis* — apart from the constituent individuals?"[37] On the other hand, the vastly influential New Deal antitrust attorney Thurman Arnold shared Lippmann's impatience with the postulation and personification of collective desires and beliefs. "Governments can act in no other way than in accordance with the popular ideals of what great abstract personalities should do," he complains in *The Symbols of Government*.[38] Two years later, in his landmark *The Folklore of Capitalism,* Arnold notes, "It is impossible to conduct debate on political or economic questions today without assuming some sort of group free will. . . . Therefore an abstract man is created who has the ability to understand sound principles and the free will to follow them. All public debate is supposed to be addressed to him."[39] The problem, he continues, is that "These particular ceremonies are fundamental to our present disunited industrial feudalism. They are the most important psychological factors which are now hampering the growth of organizations with a definite public responsibility" (347).

John Dewey's *Liberalism and Social Action* (1935) — the philosopher's defense of the "organized social control of economic forces" — would seem to exemplify the kind of problem Arnold points to when it claims that the state "has to assume the responsibility for making it clear that intelligence is a social asset, and is clothed with a function as public as its origin."[40] But Dewey imagines that social intelligence — embodied in technocratic, administrative expertise — is a resource for the public, not an attribute or expression of it. By 1935 he was well aware of the conservative critique of the personified public; in fact, he had responded directly to Lippmann's *The Phantom Public* in *The Public and Its Problems* (1927), where he insists, "The state must always be rediscovered" precisely because of the ontological ambiguity at the heart of the "public" it was said to represent.[41] "The problem of discovering the state," he avers, "is not a problem for theoretical inquirers engaged solely in surveying institutions which already exist" (32). Instead, he suggests that the state includes "all modes of associated behavior . . . [that] have exclusive and enduring consequences which involve others beyond those directly engaged in" (27). The philosopher adds, "Indirect, extensive, enduring and serious consequences of conjoint and interacting behavior call a public into existence having a common interest in controlling these consequences" (126).

The problem was that both the public and the state were equally elusive, abstract entities, and *The Public and Its Problems* is often caught in circular efforts to ground one term with the other. Dewey points out that "the machine age has so enormously expanded, multiplied, intensified and complicated the scope of . . . indirect consequences, has formed such immense and consolidated unions in action, on an impersonal rather than a community basis, that the resultant public cannot identify and distinguish itself" (126). But the state itself seemed just as hard to distinguish: "The state is not created as a direct result of organic contacts as offspring are conceived in the womb, nor by direct conscious intent as a machine is created, nor by some brooding indwelling spirit, whether a personal deity or a metaphysical absolute will. When we seek for the origin of states in such sources as these, a realistic regard for facts compels us to conclude in the end that we find nothing but singular persons, you, they, me. We shall then be driven, unless we have recourse to mysticism, to decide that the public is born in a myth and is sustained by superstition" (37–38). Dewey is quick to point out that the state's most important and salient characteristics, namely its social functions, have little to do with the theoretical problems of collective personification. When he lists "the questions of concern at the present," such as matters of "public health, healthful and adequate housing, transportation, planning of cities, . . . [and the] scientific adjustment of taxation," Dewey consequently asks, "What has counting heads, decision by majority and the whole apparatus of traditional government to do with such things? Given such considerations, the public and its organization for political ends is not only a ghost, but a ghost which walks and talks, and obscures, confuses and misleads governmental action in a disastrous way" (124–25).

But even as Dewey tries to render Lippmann's critique something of an unnecessary hindrance to the practical, workaday requirements the state needed to perform, he returns time and again to Lippmann's spectral language: "The ties which hold men together in action are numerous, tough and subtle. But they are invisible and intangible. We have the physical tools of communication as never before. The thoughts and aspirations congruent with them are not communicated, and hence are not common. Without such communication the public will remain shadowy and formless, seeking spasmodically for itself, but seizing and holding its shadow rather than its substance" (142). Substituting "tough and subtle" ties for Lippmann's more phantasmagoric identifications, Dewey nonetheless concludes that the public remained perplexingly "invisible and intangible." He does suggest that the public sidestep Lippmann's critique by articulating itself through debate and display, through the sustained implementation of all the startlingly new "physical tools of communication" that modernity had to offer. Formulating a proto-Habermasian commitment to the salutary effects of communicative action, Dewey imagines that the public comes into being as it witnesses itself debating itself. This implicitly performative invocation of the public — had, Dewey suggests, through the staging of mass events — is meant to produce self-consciousness in an otherwise abstract entity, in much the same way that Marx and others looked to foster "class consciousness" in the working class.[42]

Dewey is noticeably short on details in describing the contours of such debate in *The Public and Its Problems*. It is not until *Art as Experience* that he explains just how a public might bring itself out from Lippmann's shadows. Here Dewey suggests, in high New Deal fashion, that the right kind of aesthetic experience might provide individual citizens with a form of imaginary participation in national politics that, according to Lippmann, they could never have in substantive form. Citing Shelley's conviction that poets are "the founders of civil society," *Art as Experience* reasons that an understanding of aesthetic experience as fundamentally performative might supplement the public-minded social policy of the New Deal. "The labor and employment problem of which we are so acutely aware," he avers, "cannot be solved by mere changes in wage, hours or work and sanitary conditions."[43] Dewey reasons that, in addition, changes in the perceived relation between artistic production and consumption — of the kind discussed in chapter I — had profound implications for public government. Thus, when Dewey maintains that "As long as art is in the beauty parlor of civilization, neither art nor civilization is secure" (344), he invokes the economic and political connotations of the word "secure." He continues: "The political and economic arts that may furnish security and competency are no warrants of a rich and abundant life save as they are attended by the flourishing of the arts that determine culture" (345). For Dewey, the WPA's Federal One constituted just such a flourishing, one that took art out of the beauty parlor and handed it, as a form of experience, to tens of thousands of laboring Americans.

John Maynard Keynes's writings of the mid-thirties would trace a trajectory almost identical to the one we find in Dewey, away from issues of collective representation and toward issues of public art. Like Dewey, Keynes held that modern citizens could in their consumption of art experience forms of public franchise unavailable to them in more traditionally civic forms. Keynes's *General Theory of Employment, Interest, and Money* (1936), perhaps the most important influence on the future of the American welfare state, made clear that intelligence was not a social asset, particularly in the case of nationally planned economies.[44] National planning, Keynes reasoned, embraced the faulty proposition that the state's involvement in the economy needed to proceed by refining technologies of representation, by deciding how successfully to personify collective agency, by deciding how a board, a president, or even an entire government might think and plan for the larger totalities they represented. Keynes, however, argued that these views were based on "a fundamental misunderstanding of how . . . the economy in which we live actually works," and maintained that personifying groups did not address the fact that there was no way for groups, or the persons they were made to resemble, to intend the economies they constituted.[45]

Keynes argued as early as 1936 that government spending on the arts was an ideal way to redress this situation. Like Dewey, Keynes believed that the right kind of economic organization could do more than simply pay for the arts. More strongly, he believed that the arts should be made to supplement modern welfare government. Keynes was in fact the first head of Britain's Council for the Encouragement of Music and Arts, established in 1941, and later founded and ran the British Arts Council. Like the New Deal's Arts Projects, both organizations would work to implement his claim, made in 1936, that the performative arts in particular were ideal recipients of government spending. In "Art and the State," Keynes reasons that "Even more important than the permanent monuments of dignity and beauty in which each generation should express its spirit to stand for it in the procession of time are the ephemeral ceremonies, shows and entertainments in which the common man can take delight . . . and which can make him feel, as nothing else can, that he is one with, and part of, a community, finer, more gifted, more splendid, more care-free, than he can be by himself."[46] It is of course the aim of Keynesian economics to demonstrate that this hypothetical common man could not meaningfully imagine himself part of a community able to effect the economy. But if collective agency was dead, the common man might receive art in its stead. The artist, Keynes reasons, in need of "economic security and enough income," would thus become the "servant of the public" (372). As such, he would express what by his own account Keynes held to be a mostly fictive "spirit" (374). Indeed, Keynes reasoned that the artist was most expressive when his art was at its most "ephemeral" (374). Artists, as well as "architects and engineers," might in this way "embody the various imagination . . . of peaceful and satisfied spirits" (374). With Dewey, Keynes reasons that the reflexive moment of performance is "an immortal function of the state, an art of government regarded at most times as essential" (373).[47]

Keynes sided with Lippmann, on the other hand, in maintaining that national planning could never be a similarly immortal function of the state. From Keynes's perspective, national planning picked up on a faulty premise central to classical economics, namely, that personified collectivities directed the course of the economy by entering into contracts with each other. Whereas classical economy was based on the idea that individual agents could never control the consequences of their actions on the economy as a whole, it had nonetheless relocated their agency to abstractions seen to possess the contract-making potential of persons. Thus, though individual workers, and even individual unions, might never have the power to set their own wage levels, classical economy maintained that there was a source of collective and intentional agency implicit in an aggregate of individual actions. "Labor" did in fact determine its wages, for the actions of every worker and union constituted the contract into which the abstract personification "labor" was invariably seen to enter. Keynes argued that there was no way to exert this kind of agency in the economy, however the agents themselves were conceived. He insisted that "there may exist no expedient by which labour as a whole can reduce its *real* wage to a given figure by making revised *money* bargains with the entrepreneurs" (*Collected Writings,* 7: 13). Alan Brinkley explains that the introduction of this Keynesian tenet into the New Deal led to the belief that "the industrial economy was too large, too complex, too diverse; no single plan could encompass it all."[48] Robert E. Goddin generalizes this claim when he notes that the Keynesian welfare state emerges most clearly in its contrast with the planned economy: "The point of welfare state interventions is to remedy unplanned and unwelcome outcomes. The welfare state strives to produce a post-fisc[al] distribution of certain goods and services that is preferable to the pre-fisc[al] one. In a planned economy, by contrast, all outcomes are the outcomes of planning. Not all are necessarily intended or welcome outcomes, to be sure. But correcting planning errors is surely qualitatively different from correcting the market's unplanned perversities."[49]

Keynes maintained that, like individual persons and collectivities, government had no significant intentional agency in matters of economy. The overwrought complexity of economies meant that no government plan, however comprehensive, could anticipate or account for economic contingencies as they developed. Drawing from his earlier studies in probability, he averred that no traditional actuarial calculus could accurately measure probability in questions of macroeconomics; the government, for example, could never foresee exactly how many unemployed would need to claim unemployment benefits each month from the Social Security Administration.[50] Keynes's reasoning in turn helped explain why an ailing nation needed social as opposed to private forms of insurance. In one sense, the necessity for social as opposed to private insurance is rather straightforward. As Goddin explains, "If participation in the insurance scheme were voluntary, and if individuals had better information concerning their own true risks than did underwriters, then those with better-than-average risks would opt out of the scheme (preferring to self-insure) and only bad risks would be left in it. Premiums would have to rise to cover the above-average level of claims from those now left in the pool. As they did so, more and more people would find it to their advantage to opt out. Eventually, only the very worst risks would remain in the pool, and the whole scheme would collapse."[51] But Keynes's early work on probability as well as his insistence that national economies were not self-inclosed, stable systems led to a second argument as well, namely, that only the state was in a position to insure against certain risks. Again Goddin:

> The financial integrity of mutual insurance schemes in the private market presupposes that each person's risks are, to a very large extent, statistically independent of everyone else's. Only under that assumption will the law of large numbers guarantee that the actuarially expected pattern of outcomes will actually occur. . . . Where risks are interdependent, no such guarantee can be given. Consider the example of unemployment insurance. The probability that any given individual will be employed is not just a function of trends within his or

her own firm or industry. It is also a function of the state of the national economy in general. Under such circumstances, it would be impossible to guarantee the financial integrity of any mutual insurance scheme. The problem is not just that actuaries are unable to set the right rate for premiums. What is worse, with interdependent risks there can be no guarantee (as there can, through the law of large numbers, with independent risks) that premiums from "winners" (those still in work) will suffice to cover claims from "losers" (those out of work) *whatever* the rate that is set. (27–28)

In the case of interdependent risks, then, only the government has any hope of remaining solvent as an insurance provider, in part because only the government can coerce total participation in an insurance scheme, but more important, because only the government has any hope of addressing those macroeconomic, interdependent risks that produce a phenomenon like massive unemployment in the first place.

To reiterate, Keynes insisted that government planning was futile in the case of interdependent risks. Instead, he believed that, as a supplement to social insurance schemes, only the continual regulation of fiscal and monetary policy could be adequate in the face of modern, international economies, principally because no single government could ever anticipate or stabilize the contexts in which it would execute its plans. In this respect, then, Keynes saw the controlled circulation of money as the consummate means of addressing the inherently uncertain nature of increasingly postindustrial economies, writing with emphasis that *"the importance of money essentially flows from its being a link between the present and the future"* (*Collected Writings*, 7: 293). Thus, although governments did not necessarily know what was done with the money they regulated, money remained one of the only traceable lineaments connecting governmental actions and their outcomes. If the state could not provide specific representations of the future, it could nonetheless regulate access to the language of private actors who, eventually, would. That language, New Deal modernists were quick to recognize, was money. If the public could not actually come to know itself by debating itself—if the imagination remained a private affair—perhaps there was a sense in which individuals could come to understand their interrelations simply through the movement of the money that bound them together.[52]

3.

The legislators of the world, acknowledged and unacknowledged both, were retrenching, and doing so hand in hand. Thus Stevens endorses "up to date capitalism" in the same letter that he describes his own performative poetic, by asserting, "The only possible order of life is one in which all order is incessantly changing" (*Letters,* 291–92). This fantastical confluence of the poetic and the economic might begin to explain his famously cryptic proclamation "money is a kind of poetry" ("Adagia," 191).[53] As the example of Gertrude Stein in the previous chapter makes clear, Stevens was by no means the only modernist to be fascinated with money. No fan of bourgeois writers like Stein, whose writing he said took place "in the vacuum of private income," Michael Gold beseeched his revolutionary muses to "send a strong poet who loves the masses, and their future. Send someone who doesn't give a damn about money."[54] As it happened, Gold received no such poet. Instead, he found himself amidst a sea of bards who, like Stein, were more interested in the idea of money than in making it per se. Carl Sandburg's *The People, Yes,* for example, is entirely absorbed with the question, "The public *has* a mind?"[55] Just as Stein unites language, the literary master-piece, and money under the rubric of "the human mind," so Sandburg links his interrogation of the public mind with choruslike apostrophes demanding,

> Tell us what is money.
> For we are ignorant of money, its ways and
> meanings,
> Each a child in a dark storm where people
> cry for money. (167)

Like Stein, Sandburg is interested in money as a kind of language. When the poet notes that "money is talk bigger than talk talk" (167), he refers not simply to the fact that moneyed interests invariably win the day but also to the idea that money is itself a form of language, possessed of its own, oftentimes inscrutable and cabalistic "meanings."

Gripped by the quirky theories of British economist C. H. Douglas, Ezra Pound is perhaps the poet who most famously engaged the idea of money during the thirties. He declares in 1935, "Every honest man in my time who has started thinking about the nature of money has seen a need to reform the present system of control of it. What is money? how does it get there? who makes it?"[56] In "The Individual and His Milieu," published the same year, he observes that Henry James "perceived the *Anagke* of the modern world to be money." The poet confirms: "The *Anagke* of our time is money" (*Selected Prose,* 242). "The question for our time is: 'What is money?' After reading and writing and before arithmetic, or even before reading and writing, the first human instruction, in our time, should lie in this query" (244). Here is Pound with equal vigor four years later, in the essay "What Is Money For?": "We will never see an end of ructions, we will never have a sane and steady administration until we gain an absolutely clear conception of money. I mean an absolutely not an approximately clear conception" (*Selected Prose,* 260). William Carlos Williams figures prominently among the many American poets, influenced by Pound, who tried to formulate this clear conception. Like Pound, he turned his fascination with money into an assault on the New Deal and its legacy. In book 1 of *Paterson* (1946) he declares, "My doors are bolted forever (I hope forever) against all public welfare workers, professional do-gooders and the like."[57] A prose section in the middle of book 2 (1948) reads, "The Federal Reserve System is a private enterprise . . . [with power] given to it by a spineless Congress." Williams continues, "They create money from nothing and lend it to private business (the same money over and over again at a high rate of interest), and also to the government whenever it needs money in war and peace; for which we, the people, representing the Government (in this instance at any rate) must pay interest to the banks in the form of high taxes" (73).[58] The solution to this state of affairs, the prose section of Williams's poem suggests, is drastically curtailing government spending: "In all our great bond issues the interest is always greater than the principal. All of the great public works cost more than twice the actual cost, on that account. Under the present system of doing business we SIMPLY ADD 120 to 150 per cent to the stated cost. The people must pay anyway; why should they be compelled to pay twice?" (74).[59]

Stevens shared little with the left localism of Williams, and even less with the right corporatism of Pound. Rather, and in this respect he is like Stein and Sandburg, Stevens was absorbed by the formal properties of money, its ability to function as its own self-sufficient system. Pound wanted the state to keep money "moving, circulating, going out the front door and coming in the tax window" (*Selected Prose,* 267). Stevens wanted just to trace and capture this motion itself. For he saw in money a profound, connective fungibility, the same that Keynes identifies when he notes that *"the importance of money essentially flows from its being a link between the present and the future."* "More fecund as principle than particle," money is for Stevens analogous to the possibility conditions of communication as such. Seen from this vantage, Stevens's poetic interest in money cleaves rather closely to Jean-François Lyotard's definition of "performativity" in *The Postmodern Condition*: "the optimization of the global relationship between input and output."[60] Prominently citing Talcott Parsons's work — written, Lyotard notes, "under the aegis of a moderate welfare state" — he claims that a technically rationalized, performative society fundamentally changes the criteria through which knowledge is generated and then subject to critical evaluation. Above all, he insists, performativity refrains from evaluating the truth or falsity of a given statement based on a governing "master narrative" such as intention. "The fact remains," he says, "that since performativity increases the ability to produce proof, it also increases the ability to be right" (46). Under a postmodern regime of knowledge, "The question (overt or implied) now asked by the professionalist student, the state, or institutions of higher education is no longer 'Is it true?' but 'What use is it?' " (51).[61] Here, Lyotard simply retools J. L. Austin's sense of the linguistic performative, first formulated in *How to Do Things with Words* (1962), to fit a more explicitly socioeconomic context. For as Barbara Johnson, Jacques Derrida, and Stanley Fish have all suggested, Austin's performative utterance — not meant to make claims about the world, but to effect an action within it — is meant to bracket the category of intention altogether; as Derrida notes, Austin's performative "has no referent in the form of a thing or of a prior or exterior state of things."[62]

Not only would Stevens repeatedly insist on the essentially performative nature of poetic language, he would use the metaphor of money to do so. "I do not think there is any secret to the merit of a poem," he muses to his editor late in 1935. "I mean by this that it is not a question of accuracy of conception or of expression. It might be, and then it might be something quite different. There is no more secret to this sort of thing than there is, say, to the stock market. There are too many influences at work; there are too many people subject to influence" (*Letters,* 299–300).[63] Three years later, Cleanth Brooks and Robert Penn Warren argue in *Understanding Poetry* that poetic effects are never reducible to any given amount of knowledge, such as, they suggest, the kind of knowledge one might get from perusing reports on the stock market.[64] Imagining both poems and stock markets as self-sustaining systems whose motions can be traced and experienced, but never adequately planned or reduced to any one propositional statement — to a "secret" — Stevens directly anticipates Brooks and Warren's notion of the heresy of paraphrase. "People sometimes say," the poet-scholars write in *Understanding Poetry,* " 'But the poet couldn't have been thinking of all of this when he wrote the poem.' And in the sense in which they are using the term 'thinking' they are right. The poet certainly did not draw up an analysis of his intention, a kind of blueprint, and then write the poem to specification. But it is only a very superficial view of how the mind works that would cast the question into those terms" (480).[65] More invested in "up to date capitalism" than the Southern critics, Stevens endows the stock market with the same elusive performativity as a poem, and understands both poem and market in decidedly Keynesian terms. But whereas Brooks and Warren tend toward endorsing the organically whole, unified work of art, Stevens celebrates the purely procedural nature of poetry.

This aesthetic theory finds most precise performative formulation in poems like "The Pleasures of Merely Circulating" — where the notion that "things go round and again go round" is meant to embody the poetic experience as such — and "Mr. Burnshaw and the Statue" in *Owl's Clover* (1936), where the injunction "To live incessantly in change" comes with the command "turn / Your backs upon the vivid statue."[66] As Douglas Mao puts it, the Hartford poet consistently "stressed art's immersion in life as against the repose of an artifact that never fails to gesture to its own gratuitousness."[67] Stevens takes this opposition — between "life," figured in fluid and temporal terms, and the artistic artifact — into the concluding cantos of "Notes Toward a Supreme Fiction," where he contrasts the civic aggressions of an architect and sculptor who "builds capitols" and "establishes statues of reasonable men" to the intrinsically poetic song of a robin (403). Whereas the sculptor attempts to impose an artifactual order of his own making on a public world, the robin produces art in the simple process of singing. In this way, the public circulation of money that funds the sculptor is transformed into a poetic commitment to circulation as such, for the robin's songs

> . . . at least comprise
> An occupation, an exercise, a work,
>
> A thing final in itself and, therefore, good:
> One of the vast repetitions final in
> Themselves and, therefore, good, the going round
>
> And round and round, the merely going round,
> Until merely going round is a final good . . . (405)

Here, then, is one context in which to understand the poem's edict "It Must Change" (389). Poetry — like an act of establishing, but unlike the statue that finally is established — is conceived as "an occupation, an exercise, a work" as fluid as the money that funds it.

The idea that circulation could itself become an aesthetic value was far from the mind of Anzia Yezierska when she declared of her experience on the Federal Writers' Project that "every day it became harder to blind ourselves to the cold fact that we, like the privy-builders and road-makers of other public projects, were being paid, not for what we did, but to put money into circulation."[68] Yezierska refused to imagine herself a wage laborer. Stevens, however, would cannily suggest that the commitment to the literary artifact (as opposed simply to producing it) opened one up to precisely the uncertainty both he and the Writers' Project were committed to protecting against. *Owl's Clover,* for example, does more than simply relocate poetic value from the artifact to a process of making: it associates the fixity of the statue with the inevitable uncertainty of how others respond to it. As we saw in the first chapter, Richard Wright, veteran of the Writers' Project, claimed that he didn't care whether critics or consumers deemed *Native Son* "a good book or a bad book" because "the mere writing of it will be more fun and a deeper satisfaction than any praise or blame from anybody."[69] Dubbing writing "a significant kind of living" (535), Wright divorces writing from the unpredictability of consumption in much the same way that Keynesian theory, committed to the ongoing regulation of monetary and fiscal policy, divorces governments from having to anticipate future economic contingencies. Neither author nor government could anticipate the whims of the consumer. So, whereas the second stanza of "The Old Woman and the Statue" in *Owl's Clover* begins "So much the sculptor had foreseen," the third stanza represents a consumer of the statue that the sculptor "had not foreseen" (75, 76). This consumer, *Owl's Clover* suggests again and again, is the very embodiment of contingency, the locus of uncertainty against which poetry needed to guard itself. Who does consume poems? asks "Mr. Burnshaw and the Statue." "Who knows?" the narrator answers (80).

4.

In "I Came Near Being a Fascist," published in the *Partisan Review* in the fall of 1934, Ramon Fernandez describes the process through which, living in Paris, he came to understand "the spirit of the Left"; *Partisan Review* adds that, in turning to the left, Fernandez, "until very recently a humanist . . . illustrates the rapid radicalization of the French intellectuals." It was the vitriolic reaction of his friends to his own tentative forays into radical thought, the converted critic explains, that convinced him of the self-interested and ultimately fascistic leanings of the intellectual class. Addressing this class, Fernandez concludes, "There is possible an economic system which, freeing mankind from want, shall lift real humanity to the plane of real power; yet you are so blinded by self-interest, by indolence and fear, that you see in all this humanity's downfall. So much the worse for you, Ladies and Gentlemen. You are throttling us, and in return, you bring us nothing."[70] As Fernandez would explain in a different venue that same year, radical intellectuals needed to do all they could to counter the tendency toward self-interest among their less committed peers: "The task is to win over the intellectuals to the working class by making them aware of the identity of their spiritual enterprises and of their conditions as producers."[71] Appearing as the epigraph to Walter Benjamin's "The Author as Producer," first delivered in 1934, these lines offer Benjamin a springboard for exploring the economic and sociological status of literary production within bourgeois society. Fernandez makes still another appearance in 1934, in Stevens's "The Idea of Order at Key West." If Fernandez offers Benjamin a means of insisting that authors consider themselves producers, he serves Stevens as a prop for exploring the origin of a natural phenomenon that seems well in excess of any one individual's productive capacities. "Whose spirit is this?" asks the speaker of the poem, as he and "Ramon Fernandez" observe a singing woman walking by the side of a raging sea and become interested in the relation between her song and the sea's motions (129). Does the singer orchestrate the sea with her voice, or is she a more passive poetic device, an objective correlative meant to "embody the various imagination . . . of peaceful and satisfied spirits" (as Keynes puts it), or is the raging sea an entirely natural force, beyond the control of any imagination?

Even before the poem sets out to answer these questions, it is evident that its relentless quest to locate the origins of order as well as its opposition of the natural and the social — fundamental to political theory since Rousseau — speaks in potentially expansive registers. Still, there is ample evidence to specify the scope of Stevens's concerns. "Order has to be created," Keynes insisted. "It is not natural."[72] There was, the economist maintained, no systemic genius; laissez-faire could in the end lead only to what "The Idea of Order at Key West," developing Stevens's analogy between poetry and the stock market, calls "meaningless plungings" (129). Stevens himself raises the possibility of such analogies between the poetic and the economic when he notes on the jacket cover of *Ideas of Order,* "We think of changes occurring today as economic changes, involving political and social changes. Such changes raise questions of political and social order. . . . [I]t is inevitable" he continues, "that a poet should be concerned with such questions."[73] Following Stevens, Douglas Mao notes that "in *Ideas* Stevens staked much on the parallel between natural disorder and the political disorder."[74] These parallels would hardly have needed mentioning to a Depression-era reader. As Michael Denning notes, "Metaphors of natural disaster were deeply embedded in popular discourses about the depression. Edmund Wilson had written that the slump 'was like a flood or an earthquake,' and the terrible Mississippi floods served both blues singers and novelists as an emblem of economic and social crisis."[75] Though we do not know when in 1934 Stevens wrote his poem, we do know that in September of that year, thousands of veterans had been, at least according to Ernest Hemingway, left to die at the hands of a hurricane by an inexcusably negligent Federal Emergency Relief Administration (FERA). Could Stevens's singer, planted precariously on the crepuscule between land and raging sea, seeming at times to master nature and at others to be so mastered, speak any more directly to the New Deal's response to the Depression?

But even without the specter of the hurricane haunting the island, Key West was a markedly political topography. The year Stevens wrote the poem, 1934, saw the high-water mark in a federal and state publicity campaign that held Key West up as the perfect encapsulation of the early New Deal. The Roosevelt administration lauded the island as "an illustration" and "model" of the goals of its work-relief programs; its town was declared "New Deal Town" as newspapers across the country followed Roosevelt's lead in associating Key West with the possibilities of a federally orchestrated economic recovery.[76] The WPA's *American Guide Series* concurs when it notes that federal efforts to revitalize the island, "hailed as one of the Nation's most interesting experiments in community planning, made the city a proving ground for Government-sponsored cultural projects."[77] Liberal intellectuals were just as sanguine. "In that isolated microcosm you could study the whole issue of disinterested collective planning versus interested private enterprise," wrote Elmer Davis of Key West in 1935. This led him to conclude with grandeur that Key West had become nothing less than "the New Deal in miniature."[78] This was the case, Davis reasoned, because "City and county had surrendered their powers, via the Governor, to experts from Washington backed by Federal funds" in their efforts to rebuild Key West after it was devastated by a hurricane in 1934 (641). By July 1934, Julius Stone, the ranking FERA officer in Florida, had assumed control of the town and begun disbursing the $935,000 FERA would spend on the now-stranded island in its first year alone.

But for Davis, federal relief had done more than save Key West; it had transformed it into something of an intellectual hothouse: "It was Greenwich Village, Montparnasse, Provincetown—on a little tropical island" (648). The hot topics, however, were not those that had characterized earlier centers of modernist bohemia; Davis claims that "groups of men and women" would sit up "till two A.M. discussing problems of administrative technique, and having as good a time as they would have had at the nightclubs" (649). "The dominant interest," Davis explains of these discussions, was "the application—however hampered and unsuccessful—of the trained and disinterested intelligence to the problems of collective welfare" (649).

At the same time, Davis's celebration of "administrative technique" and those whose "disinterested intelligences" would perfect it is cause for suspicion as well as for marvel, for Davis laments that if the New Deal "had got started earlier, the rehabilitation of Key West would have been a really collective enterprise; now it cannot help looking to many people like something imposed by outside authority" (650). Thus we are left, Davis concludes, with "a picture of a group of intelligent men and women applying their intelligence (under whatever handicaps, with however limited success) to the problems of a community which could not save itself" (652).

The imposition of order "by outside authority" on a "community which could not save itself" speaks readily enough to the organizing question of "The Idea of Order at Key West": "Whose spirit is this?" But it is the opposition Davis sets up between the civic planning of administrative experts and a planning that might "have been a really collective enterprise" that speaks most directly to the poem, which is meant precisely to moot the opposition between these two alternatives, both of which presume that human agents impose order on the world through constructive imaginative acts. Key West was the New Deal in miniature for Stevens as well as for Davis. But the insurance executive saw what the future head of the Office of War Information did not, namely, that welfare government would be felt most powerfully not in the worlds it built, but in the provisions it made for its inevitable failure to secure those worlds from the hazards of the unforeseen.

"The Idea of Order" is most explicitly about the difficulty of discerning, let alone controlling, the causes of events. The lines of influence between woman and sea are next to impossible to discern; the speaker is bemused that "The song and water were not medleyed sound / Even if what she sang was what she heard, / Since what she sang was uttered word by word" (128). Amid the qualification, the words seem to utter themselves, lending force to the ambiguous phrase at the beginning of the stanza, "No more was she" (128). But if this phrase suggests the potential irrelevance of individual agency, the speaker returns to his desire to understand the subject of his question "Whose spirit is this?" in human terms. The relentless personification in the poem is perhaps the most telling sign of the speaker's efforts to locate this agency. The sea is produced as a personification ("the ever-hooded, tragic gestured sea" has a "genius," a "body," "sleeves," and a "dark voice" [128–29]) precisely so the speaker can treat it as a potentially intentional agent equal to the singer. The reader is given pause, however, by Stevens's insistence that genius and body are not interchangeable aspects of personhood; rather, the poet suggests, the former designates the capacity to control and direct the latter. Thus the sea is least like an intentional agent when the speaker notes that "the water never formed to mind or voice, / Like a body wholly body" (128).

Similar mind-body dualisms pervade Stevens's writing; the possibility that a genius or spirit — like Lippmann's phantom or Rand's "organism that possesses no physical form" — might transcend and intend an otherwise inhibiting physical world is perfectly consonant with the utopic vision in "Insurance and Social Change" of a "perfect insurance" under whose aegis all wishes instantly become reality. More specifically, in "Surety and Fidelity Claims" (1938), his only other surviving essay on insurance, Stevens imagines an insurance agent whose body vanishes into his work as a result of his ability to guarantee plans: the surety agent, who provides bonds guaranteeing the fulfillment of contracts, "finds it difficult sometimes to distinguish himself from the papers he handles and comes almost to believe that he and his papers constitute a single creature, consisting principally of hands and eyes: lots of hands and lots of eyes."[79] As pure interpersonal, communicative facility (with hands, eyes, and a body of text), Stevens's agent guarantees the elimination of chance and the fulfillment of contact by dispossessing himself of the bulk of his body. This is the panacea of national planning: a vision of the private imagination gone public, the beginnings of a truly collective agency enabled by minds acting and thinking together in spite of all physical demarcation.

Stevens would appear to gesture to this utopia in "Insurance and Social Change" as well, when he asks that we "Compare the man who, as an individual, insures his dwelling against fire with that personality of the first plane who, at a stroke, insures all dwellings against fire; and who, without stopping to think about it, insures not only the lives of all those that live in the dwellings, but insures all people against all happenings."[80] The identity of Stevens's "personality of the first plane" is left resolutely nebulous; he seems at once Roosevelt, God, and a messianic poet turned insurance provider. But whoever or whatever it is, Stevens's personality is in many respects not like a person at all. The office this personality performs seems public precisely because it is opposed to thought of any kind. And in fact, Stevens's poetic corpus of the 1930s and early 1940s opposes "stopping to think" to public action in just this manner. The poet declares in "A Duck for Dinner" (1936), for example, "As the man the state, not as the state the man."[81] But as is the case with major man, we are dealing here with an idea of man utterly unattainable in the quotidian; as Stevens says of General Du Puy in "Notes Toward a Supreme Fiction," "There never had been, never could be, such / A man." Writing to his editor to explain the line in "Duck for Dinner" that describes poetry as "this base of every future," Stevens reasons that if poetry "is to be identified with the imagination, then the imagination is the base of every future. If so, the application of the imagination to the future (to think of the future) is a thing, and, considering the sort of thing it is, it is genius itself. . . . Briefly, he that imagines the future and, by imagining it, creates it, is a creator of genius and stands on enormous pedestals" (*Letters,* 372). This would be clear enough, were it not for the fact that earlier in this same letter, Stevens cautions that this self-same genius should be "superhuman," a "prodigy capable of measuring sun and moon, some one who, if he is to dictate our fates, had better be inhuman, so that he shall know he is without any of our weaknesses and cannot fail" (371–72).

Such fantasies aside — the kind of fantasy, no doubt, that led the poet to declare and then soon after retract his support for Benito Mussolini — Stevens most often takes up the task of representing a world deprived of the superhuman. As a result, Stevens's poetry persistently stages the substitution of thought with the "impersonal" representation of social relationships; hence his aphorism in "Adagia," "People take the place of thoughts" (198). "The Idea of Order" is a case study in this transition. The fourth stanza in particular indicates that the difficulty of the question "Whose spirit is this?" is that bodies and voices designate the only recognizable markers of human identity and agency. Lippmann's public and Keynes's "spirits" are in the end impotently passive precisely because they are abstract entities. Likewise for Stevens, if spirit is completely disembodied, it becomes invisible and potentially manifold, difficult to identify and understand as a coherent intentional force. In the fourth stanza the speaker is thus unable to locate any origin for the cacophony of voices he hears — without any one body, spirit seems to transcend the sum of its sources:

If it was only the dark voice of the sea
That rose, or even colored by many waves;
If it was only the outer voice of sky
And cloud, of the sunken coral water-walled,
However clear, it would have been deep air,
The heaving speech of air, a summer sound
Repeated in a summer without end
And sound alone. But it was more than that . . . (129)

What first promised to be a poetic event caused by one intentional agent goes on to emerge as a sublime and agentless natural event; "meaningless plungings" and "bronze shadows heaped / On high horizons" (129) overcome the speaker in all their accidental grandeur, overwhelming his efforts to imagine one mind capable of serving as a cause for the tumult before him.

What follows seems at first a typical compensatory gesture designed to consolidate the autonomy and cognitive powers of the isolate and intentional mind. Almost inexplicably, the speaker now appears to accord the singer her constructive powers:

It was her voice that made
The sky acutest at its vanishing.
She measured to the hour its solitude.
She was the single artificer of the world
In which she sang. And when she sang, the sea,
Whatever self it had, became the self
That was her song, for she was the maker. Then we,
As we beheld her striding there alone,
Knew that there never was a world for her
Except the one she sang and, singing, made. (129–30)

At first glance, these assertions seem successfully to mitigate the sublime excess to which the speaker just bore witness. Yet this is at best an ambivalent moment of compensation, for it insists on the necessarily hermetic nature of the imaginative powers conceded the singer. The seemingly definitive claim "She was the single artificer of the world" is qualified by the enjambed phrase "In which she sang," suggesting that the world in which the singer sings is not necessarily the same as the world in which the speaker moves. Burnshaw was suspicious of the poem for exactly this reason, and notes that before he wrote his infamous review he began to wonder "which world" it was that the singer actually made.[82] The claim made in the stanza's final two lines does little to clarify this confusion, for it similarly allows a world-organizing agency at the moment that it signals the singer's potential alienation from the social. Indeed, the qualifying "for her" looms large in the stanza's penultimate line, which sets off the singer's world-making powers from the social "we" speaking the poem: "Then *we*, / As *we* beheld her striding there alone, / Knew" (emphasis added).

In William Wordsworth's "The Solitary Reaper" (1807), very much behind "The Idea of Order," the speaker stops to marvel at a woman singing in a field. When he departs, he takes the song with him: "The music in my heart I bore, / Long after it was heard no more."[83] In one respect, it seems that Stevens's two men similarly take the woman's song with them back to town. Following this line of thought, we might imagine that the two men do not so much grant the woman her ability to form the physical world to her voice as they acknowledge the extent to which her song organizes and makes that world available to her in a particular manner. As they return to town, suddenly wondering why it is that this space seems fortuitously "ordered," we might imagine that the two men have internalized the woman's song so that it makes their world available to them as her song does to her. In one respect, this reading jibes loosely with the notion that, for Stevens, the "imagination" is invariably privileged over "reality," such that the former essentially dictates to and forms the latter. The problem here is that while the speaker has no better sense of who or what makes the order in the town, the order characterizing the town stands in marked contrast to the natural setting of the first half of the poem. The singer having concluded her song, the speaker asks his companion to

> tell me, if you know,
> Why, when the singing ended and we turned
> Toward the town, tell why the glassy lights,
> The lights in the fishing boats at anchor there,
> As the night descended, tilting in the air,
> Mastered the night and portioned out the sea,
> Fixing emblazoned zones and fiery poles,
> Arranging, deepening, enchanting night. (130)

This request is as plaintive as it is precisely because it refers to "The Solitary Reaper," precisely because, in other words, it seeks to reconcile the world-organizing power of song with the fact that not all worlds are organized in the same manner. As I observed in the introduction, this is precisely the dilemma to which Kenneth Burke imagines the "actuarial" responding: use of actuarial, or statistical methods, he reasons, allows literary criticism to come "about as near to the use of objective, empirical evidence as even the physical sciences. For though there must be purely theoretical grounds for selecting some interrelationships rather than others as more significant, the interrelationships themselves can be shown *by citation* to be there."[84] Even though, in other words, the poem would seem to suggest that the physical world is apprehensible only through the ordering mechanisms of sensibility — like song, poetry, and, we will see in the next section, language itself — the physical world nonetheless seems to change in objectively verifiable fashion. This, I take it, is the reason there are two male observers in this poem and not one: as a community of observers, the speaker and Ramon Fernandez are in a position objectively to specify the limits of the Romantic (here Wordsworthian) postulate that song or poetry might shape the world around it.

Still searching for an agent — still, that is, unable to answer the question "Whose spirit is this?" — the speaker responds to the fact that, whether or not the singer's song lingers in his mind, the world before him seems rationalized in a way it previously did not. The speaker now tentatively attributes agency to synthetic as opposed to natural phenomena, such that "the lights in the fishing boats" have "Mastered the night and portioned out the sea." This rationalized civic space, then, displaces an expressive privacy that stands in striking opposition to the public of two that observes the singer. What gets displaced, however, is less the ability to sense and apprehend the world than the desire to shape or mold it. When the speaker muses that there "never was a world for her / Except the one she sang and, singing, made," he grants less the singer's ability to shape the objective world, and less even her ability successfully to inhabit a subjective world of her own imagination. Rather, before turning to town, the speaker turns toward the extent to which mechanisms of sensation and apprehension need continually to adjust themselves to changing physical realities that seem always, however nebulously, to show through the technologies that perceive them.

Throughout the 1930s Stevens would dissociate the intending, world-shaping mind (as opposed to the sensing, apprehending mind) from both public and poetic order. He writes in "Adagia" that "the poet represents the mind in the act of defending *us* against itself" (199; emphasis added). After noting that "the mind is not equal to the demands of oratory, poetry etc." (200), he goes on to declare that "poetry is a cure of the mind" (201). Hence the prevalent critical conviction that the mind is most suspect in Stevens's poetry when it seeks to realize itself in a publicly apprehensible reality.[85] Poetry does not, as Frost's Tityrus suggests it should, rescue the private imagination from the public sphere so much as it rescues collective groups of persons existing in a public sphere from their commitment to the private imagination, and from their corollary belief that they could make life secure by somehow realizing in a social domain the worlds they collectively imagined.

The penultimate stanza of "The Idea of Order at Key West" concludes by confirming the incompatibility of the singer's song with the world to which the speaker and his companion return in the last stanza of the poem, a public world in which lights on fishing boats are the only identifiable traces of an agency that now, more than ever, seems to have no identifiable source. "Turn[ing]," in what looks to promise a quintessentially modernist act of poetic conversion, "toward the town," the speaker turns toward a public sphere dominated by bodies open to experience but unable to direct the course of their world. Rather than getting rid of bodies, Stevens gets rid of minds; here too, "people take the place of thoughts."

5.

In his landmark essay "The Relation of Habitual Thought and Language to Behavior" (1939), the linguist Benjamin Whorf proposes that hearing is the most notable of those "nonspatial" perceptions that are rendered "spatial" by "linguistic metaphorical system[s]."[86] This linguistic production of order is at times a risky business, for it contributes to "behavior evincing a false sense of security or an assumption that all will always go smoothly, and a lack of foreseeing and protecting ourselves against hazards" (154). The "indifference to the unexpectedness of life" (154) built into Standard Average

European language groups motivates the essay, committed as it is to demonstrating that specified language patterns form the bedrock on which individuals build their perceptual abilities and ultimately their behavior.

Citing his mentor Edward Sapir, Whorf claims that "the cue to a certain line of behavior is often given by the analogies of the linguistic formula in which the situation is spoken of, and by which to some degree it is analyzed, classified, and allotted its place in that world which is 'to a large extent unconsciously built up on the language habits of the group' " (136). This claim would find its way into college textbooks during the second half of the century, as anthropologists and psychologists debated the validity of a debased "Whorfian Hypothesis," most often simplified into the claim that Eskimos could see distinctions among different kinds of snow that English-language speakers could not, because Eskimos used more words to describe snow. Hence the notoriously poststructuralist conclusion always lurking in Whorf's work: reality is in the end simply a linguistic construct. In its most simplified version, then, the Whorfian Hypothesis suggests a striking similarity to a simplified but nonetheless critically popular version of Stevens, one that sees the poet committed to the proposition that reality, far from being a fixed constant, is instead constructed by imaginative paradigms hammered out in the forge of poetry.

Whorf's first ideas on this topic were formed, he claimed, while working "in a field usually considered remote from linguistics" (135). That field was insurance, and the insurance company for which Whorf worked was Stevens's, the Hartford Fire and Indemnity Company. Whorf consequently published the findings that formed the basis for "The Relation of Habitual Behavior and Language to Thought" in *The Hartford Agent,* the house journal that first carried Stevens's "Insurance and Social Change." In fact, it was while Stevens was vice president of the Hartford that Whorf conducted experiments in how different phrases on fire-warning labels enabled individuals to perceive danger. Individuals anticipated future danger, Whorf insisted, through language, specifically through highly specified language patterns. Correctly phrased labels, reasoned Whorf, might thus key the individual into a perceptual mode adequate to the situation at hand, a mode meant to register the ghostly presence of risks that are themselves only fictions of the potential, inductions from past events. The warning label, then, functions in a manner strikingly similar to how the insurance company's proliferation of risk groups key individuals into potential dangers of which they were previously unaware; ideally, a warning label attunes individual perception to the potential risk producers at hand in the same way that a person informed he or she is part of a given risk group discovers danger in actions and behaviors once thought to be harmless. Needless to say, as discursive a category as risk is, it remains "real"; although intelligently phrased warning labels might tune individuals into dangers of which they were unaware, they do not themselves alter the objective existence of the danger. A lit match remains dangerous in a room crowded with propane regardless of the warning labels.

If warning labels represented one way specialized language systems enabled individuals to discover (as opposed to create, or eliminate) hazard in the world around them, Whorf reasoned that poetry was another (260). Still Whorf's boss when the linguist made this suggestion, Stevens was himself concerned throughout his poetic career with how poetic language enabled individuals to refine their perceptions of an impersonal world they could not control. "Notes Toward a Supreme Fiction" finds Stevens fascinated with "The fluctuations of certainty, the change / Of degrees of perception" (221). "Esthétique du Mal" (1944) is an attempt to generate an apparatus of perception for danger and pain in a world that has come to think of both in abstract and impersonal terms. "Life is a bitter aspic," the poem insists. "We are not at the center of a diamond."[87] Thus the third-person conditional claim in the poem, "That he might suffer or that / He might die" (322), is met with the compensatory suggestion that poetry might do more than simply smooth the edges of looming suffering and death. Poetry, Stevens would claim in poem after poem, addressed the reality of pain and suffering by enhancing empirical perception; it was, he claimed in "The Man with the Blue Guitar (1937)," "a composing of senses."[88]

"The Idea of Order at Key West" ends with just such a composing of senses, with the cryptic emergence of "ghostlier demarcations, keener sounds" from "The maker's rage to order words of the sea" (130). That the poem's demarcations have been ghostly throughout hardly needs reinforcing; moving from sea to town, the speaker remains unable to distinguish cause from effect even as his physical surroundings present him with radically different orders. What is significant, however, is his insistence that "keener sounds" emerge precisely in his inability to distinguish cause from effect in either world. Only in giving up the search for the origin and source of effects, the line suggests, do individuals begin to experience these same effects with heightened acuity, with an enhanced ability to distinguish, to refine, to classify. "Keener sounds" is in this respect the poem's true compensatory offering, a tendering of Whorfian logic — that poems, like all language systems, guard against chance by enabling the sensations of risks — in the wake of the speaker's inability to locate the ultimate source of any order, either natural or synthetic.

But then who creates the order that does organize the town at the close of "The Idea of Order at Key West"? Who is the maker of which the final stanza speaks? Is he or she what Stevens calls in "The Creation of Sounds" (1944) "a separate author, a different poet, / An accretion from ourselves, intelligent / Beyond intelligence, an artificial man"?[89] Perhaps the "superhuman" from "A Duck for Dinner"? Or the "personality of the first plane" Stevens speaks of in "Insurance and Social Change"? Or major man himself? Down the hall at the Hartford, Whorf was finding it equally difficult to personify the "mass mind" through which linguistic orders seemed to him to legislate the actions of individuals. "It is as if the personal mind," he argued, "which selects words but is largely oblivious to pattern, were in the grip of a higher, far more intellectual mind, which has very little notion of houses and beds and soup kettles, but can systematize and mathematize on a scale and scope that no mathematician of the schools ever remotely approached" ("Relation," 257). What matters most in "The Idea of Order," however, is the simple fact that no human being within the poem can be this "far more intellectual mind," a "personality of the first plane." Most of all, the author of the poem itself does not qualify. "[T]here are words / Better without an author, without a poet," Stevens writes in "The Creation of Sounds" (310). Throughout his career Stevens would suggest that, like the solitary singer who cannot definitively be said to order her world, not even the poet could experience the meaning of the poem as willed or intended. Stevens notes in "Adagia" at this time that "a poem is like a natural object" (205) and that "it is not every day that the world arranges itself in a poem" (191). Thus Stevens invents the quintessential mystification of poetic authority, a mystification that formal-izes the refusal of intentional agency thematized in "The Idea of Order" itself. "Poetry has to be something more than a conception of the mind," he writes in "Adagia"; "It has to be a revelation of nature" (191).[90]

By the seventh stanza of "The Idea of Order," then, the frames collapse even the poet into an all-inclusive population marked by the impotency of the mind: "the maker's rage to order words of the sea" offers knowledge "of ourselves and of our origins" (130) at the precise moment that the referent for "ourselves" and "maker" is expansively inclusive. The speaker, like those around him, like the poet himself, does not personally intend or otherwise cause the aggregation of this collectivity. In the process of rejecting public statuary in favor of continuous song, Stevens explains in "Notes Toward a Supreme Fiction" that this is the gift of public experience, "To discover an order . . . to find, / Not to impose, not to have reasoned at all" (404). Membership in this population group is defined by all those things individuals *cannot* impose on the future, and by these criteria, the reader, like the author, is as much a member as any character in the poem.

But what exactly does it mean to claim that the poem itself has no maker? Stevens's poetry after the New Deal, as well as New Critical theory more generally, would answer this question head-on. His poems staged the incapacity of intentional agency, and he maintained that their making and reception rehearsed the same: "The basis of criticism is not . . . the hidden intention of the writer" (*Letters,* 390), he writes in 1941. It would remain for the New Critics to codify this quintessentially New Deal disavowal: "The poem is not the critic's own and not the author's," note W. K. Wimsatt and Monroe C. Beardsley in "The Intentional Fallacy"; "it is detached from the author at birth and goes about the world beyond his power to intend about it or control it."[91] Here again we see the insistence that poetry and criticism address themselves to the abdication of control, to the fatuity of the intentional.[92] Control and intention certainly are not recouped in Wimsatt and Beardsley's "The Intentional Fallacy," where the two make clear that the reader does not determine or cause the poem any more than does the poet or critic. This seems to leave a vacuum: exactly who does intend or control the poem; exactly who is the maker of a poem? Having disqualified all the individual sources of agency that might make claim to that office, Wimsatt and Beardsley move, in a by now familiar fashion, to the necessarily impersonal mechanism of the public itself, claiming that "the poem belongs to the public."[93] What that public could finally be, and how a poem could actually belong to it, remain concerns, questions of literary theory on the one hand, and federal funding for the arts on the other.

Chapter Four

The Vanishing American Father

Sentiment and Labor in *The Grapes of Wrath*

and *A Tree Grows in Brooklyn*

The bad conscience is an illness, there is no doubt about that,
but an illness as pregnancy is an illness. — Friedrich Nietzsche,
On the Genealogy of Morals

As she treks westward with the rest of the Joads in John Steinbeck's
The Grapes of Wrath (1939), Rose of Sharon grows with child. But,
curiously, as Rose's body becomes more visibly pregnant, it becomes
less available to the family around her. Steinbeck mourns that her
"plump body, full soft breasts and stomach, hard hips and buttocks
that had swung so freely and provocatively as to invite slapping and
stroking—had become demure and serious."[1] This turning inward
terrifies Rose's nineteen-year-old husband Connie, who "had mar-
ried a plump, passionate hoyden, [and] was . . . frightened and bewildered at the change in her" (130). Appalled by Rose's new de-
meanor, he flees the Joads. The departed husband, Tom Joad later
guesses, is "prob'ly studyin' to be President of the United States"
(459). As improbable as it is, the joke is worth taking seriously, for
Connie's departure perfectly captures how, throughout *The Grapes
of Wrath,* men become principals of social sympathy and public
policy by absenting themselves from women and from local family
needs. In fact, Connie would seem to disappear into precisely the
civic world discovered in Wallace Stevens's "The Idea of Order at
Key West."

Comparisons between high modernism's premier poet of thought
and the liberal left's most popular sentimentalist are admittedly unlikely. The two contemporaries seem to epitomize the opposing poles
of what T. S. Eliot termed the modern "dissociation of sensibility";
measured cerebrations and deep emotion are rarely united in either

• • •

Stevens or Steinbeck. Nonetheless, the men in *The Grapes of Wrath* flee from women even as they search for precisely the disembodied, seemingly sourceless order celebrated at the conclusion of Stevens's poem. Importantly, both authors suggest that admission to this order demands turning away not simply from the female body, but also from the agency symbolized by that body. Steinbeck's hapless and unemployed men see themselves belonging to a New Deal community only by giving up what Stevens calls "words of ourselves and of our origins," as those words offer, simultaneously, accounts of both the laboring maternal body and its insufficiently sympathetic relation to the needs of others. Effective public policy, the author reasons, like effective writing, requires a gendered abstraction, a disavowal not simply of laboring women but of the embodied and self-interested relation to sentiment that they symbolize.

We find this same gendered abstraction in Betty Smith's sentimental classic *A Tree Grows in Brooklyn* (1943), a novel whose fathers flee their families even as they espouse liberal social policy. Here, as in so many New Deal texts, men fulfill their domestic responsibilities only with the help of their life insurance policies. Insurance is an absolute necessity for the Nolans, even though the family just barely manages to provide for basic necessities. Katie Nolan muses, "Sometimes after the rent is paid and the insurance there is hardly enough left for food."[2] The insurance that the Nolans contribute to is markedly pre–New Deal. The friendly agent who comes to the Nolans' door once a month collecting their premiums bears little resemblance to the calculating representatives of corporate America who would begin to appear in James Cain's *The Postman Always Rings Twice* (1934) and *Double Indemnity* (1935–1937). "I insured your father and mother and all you Rommely girls and your husbands and children," the neighborhood collector tells Katie, "and, I don't know, but I carried so many messages back and forth among you about birth, sickness, and death that I feel like part of the family" (265). The family collector is so much an ally to Katie that he helps maximize her benefits when her husband Johnny dies. Not until the end of the novel does Katie glimpse the changes looming on the horizon. Talking to her family agent, she is amazed to discover that there exist forms of coverage in which "you don't have to die to collect" (389). "Oh my, first a doctor and a hospital to give birth, then college insurance. What next?" asks the old-world mom. The question is Smith's sly wink to her readers, any one of whom would have known that the New Deal itself was next. *A Tree Grows in Brooklyn* prepares Katie's daughter Francie for the New Deal; it takes her beyond her mother and in the process rewrites the family in strikingly impersonal terms.

As it is, the fact that the Nolan family collects from Johnny's death links it to a distinctly New Deal fascination with the translation — via insurance — of male wage earners into capital for the women they leave behind them in death. Cain's *Double Indemnity,* in which the aggressively sexual femme fatale Phyllis Nirdlinger kills her husband for his insurance money, offers the locus classicus of this fascination. As the hardboiled narrator explains, "There's many a man walking around today that's worth more to his loved ones dead than alive, only they don't know it yet."[3] Frank Capra's *It's a Wonderful Life* (1946) finds Jimmy Stewart ready to plunge from a bridge because he imagines that he is worth more to his family dead than alive. "A man has got to add up to something," agrees Willie Loman three years later in Arthur Miller's *Death of a Salesman.* This just moments before killing himself with car fumes in the hope that his family will collect on his $20,000 life insurance policy. Kenneth Fearing was likewise absorbed with how insurance presided over the translation of the living into the financial. His "Sunday to Sunday" in *Poems* (1930–1935) figures this translation in gendered terms:

> Unknown to Mabel, who works as a cook for the rich and snobbish
> >Aldergates
> The insured, by subway suicide, provides for a widow and three
> >sons;
> Picked from the tracks, scraped from the wheels, identified, this
> >happy ending restores the nation to its heritage: A Hearst
> >cartoon.
>
> Meanwhile it is infant welfare week, milk prices up, child clinics
> >closed, relief curtailed.[4]

The working-class Mabel "restores the nation to its heritage" because her recently deceased husband is insured and can therefore meet his financial obligations even after his death. The restoration is a Hearst cartoon because this national heritage seems unmistakably laissez-faire: Mabel will be using her insurance money, it appears, to pay for services recently adumbrated by the welfare state.

Richard Wright might well have read these Fearing poems before he wrote *The Outsider* (1954), discussed in the next chapter. Cross Damon is incorrectly presumed dead in a subway accident: he is mistaken for another whose remains, quite literally, are picked from the tracks. With $800 in his pocket, borrowed against his Social Security benefits, Damon seizes on this opportunity to flee his pregnant girlfriend and his own hungry family, with whom he leaves his life insurance money. Wandering the earth as a specter of the postwar, downsized New Deal, Damon vainly struggles to theorize a "third way" between fascism and communism. That Damon leaves his wife and family in the lurch, taking from them even his Social Security benefits, in no way impedes his theorizing. Far from it: like Connie before him, Damon's quest for what Wright will call "the reality of the state" is premised on both his increasing disembodiment and his refusal of family obligations.

The crucial point in these texts is that death, real or imagined, is not a subject of pathos so much as it is an opportunity for a transcendent political experience. The terms of this experience are specified in the next chapter; here it is enough to note that each of these texts imagines life insurance as a device for facilitating precisely the ascension to the abstract achieved by public-minded men like Tom Joad at the end of *The Grapes of Wrath*. Johnny Nolan, Willie Loman, and Cross Damon die into their insurance policies, instruments of translation that, quite literally, convert their suddenly superfluous male bodies into capital. But whereas these men remain with their families only as money, Tom, fast on the heels of Connie, leaves no lucre behind him. Instead, he leaves in his wake an entirely new form of sentiment.

1.

Broken and resigned, at the end of a long road that has done little to improve the family's financial prospects, Ma Joad gives her favorite, Tom, the bulk of the family's negligent savings just before he leaves to enlist himself in the public struggles of his fellow men. "A fella ain't got a soul of his own, but on'y a piece of a big one" (572), Tom expounds to his heartbroken mother. That grand Emersonian soul, the novel has by this point made clear, is "the people's," not the biologically defined family's. But how will I know where you are? asks Ma Joad. "Wherever they's a fight so hungry people can eat, I'll be there. Wherever they's a cop beatin' up a guy, I'll be there. . . . I'll be in the way kids laugh when they're hungry an' they know supper's ready" (572). Steinbeck thus casts Tom's ascension to the abstract as an evolution of family intimacy; his presence to her will henceforth be mediated by abstractions, by "people," "a guy," and "the way kids laugh." Leaving his family behind, Tom, like Connie before him, enters the impersonal ether of the New Deal public; leaving his body behind, he becomes what Steinbeck calls a "spirit."

It is not at all clear what exactly Tom will do for the groups for which he says he will be fighting. What seems important is that he find himself in the grip of something beyond himself, emotionally compelled by a cause that, invariably, is distant and ill defined. Ill defined because *The Grapes of Wrath* shares little with the working-class fiction of its time; its populist sentiment, its moral indignation in the face of privation and want, is detached from anything like a coherent critique of capitalism. Whoever or whatever is responsible for the Joads' unemployment remains as obscure in *The Grapes of Wrath* as "ghostlier demarcations, keener sounds" do in "The Idea of Order at Key West." Steinbeck does little to span the comforting distance he places between cause and effect, between capital and its human agents. Moreover, time and again the novel subordinates the details of political and economic action to the sentiments surrounding them. Describing those who wrest farms from tenant families, Steinbeck writes, "Some of the owner men were kind because they hated what they had to do, and some of them were angry because they hated to be cruel, and some of them were cold because they had long ago found that one could not be an owner unless one were cold. And all of them were caught in something larger than themselves" (42). Steinbeck here reduces the novel's seminal act of economic alienation to sentimental terms. Even capitalists, it would seem, are alienated, if only because they feel bad about their jobs. And feelings do matter, Steinbeck consoles his reader. He explains that the banks will fail to profit from their actions because they cannot be "proud" of their work. If they cannot be proud, Steinbeck reasons, they cannot love the land, in which case the land dies, "for it was not loved or hated, it had not prayers or curses" (49).

Such sentiment goes a long way in explaining the gender politics in *The Grapes of Wrath,* a novel that locates political agency only in how men feel about abstractions over which they can exert no control. From Mikhail Bakhtin to Ann Douglas and Philip Fisher, critics have observed that the sentimental novel draws much of its power from such studied helplessness; Fisher notes that the "questionable politics" of the sentimental novel derive from the fact that "feeling and empathy are deepest where the capacity to act has been suspended."[5] Persistently compared by critics to Harriet Beecher Stowe's *Uncle Tom's Cabin* (1852), *The Grapes of Wrath* is in fact a high-water mark in twentieth-century American sentimentalism. Although Steinbeck's best-selling novel is certainly not "written by, for, and about women" — Jane Tompkins's definition of sentimental fiction — it is unabashedly sentimental in its morally didactic use of a child's death, and in its mobilization of suffering and deep feeling to change hearts and minds.[6] More specifically, the novel's desire to extend what Pa Joad calls "kin bonds" to complete strangers finds perfect expression in a sentimental tradition that, according to Fisher, "is democratic in that it experiments with the extension of full and complete humanity to classes of figures for whom it has been socially withheld."[7]

In sentimental fiction, Elizabeth Barnes adds, "to read sympathetically becomes synonymous with reading like an American. . . . sociopolitical issues are cast as family dramas, a maneuver that ultimately renders public policy an essentially private matter. The conversion of the political into the personal, or the public into the private, is a distinctive trait of sentimentalism . . . [for] *family* stands as the model for social and political affiliations."[8] *The Grapes of Wrath* reverses this trajectory: for Steinbeck, private matters are made into questions of public policy. Although Steinbeck borrows shamelessly from sentimentalist fiction, he tailors it to a very different end, celebrating detachment and impersonal charity rather than attachment and affective interpersonal identification. If *Uncle Tom's Cabin* is about the translation of abstract social and economic bonds into concrete human ones, then *The Grapes of Wrath* mobilizes sympathy principally for detached, impersonal objects. Rather than making real and palpable the otherwise unnoticed and forgotten — the project of the documentary realist aesthetic so often ascribed to his work — Steinbeck's novels do just the opposite: they are technologies of invisibility, designed to disembody and render abstract the most pressing of human needs. Rendered spiritual in his commitments, Tom is perhaps the novel's preeminent agent of abstraction; ultimately, he will insist that the most needy are always elsewhere, beyond the immediate horizons of lived experience.

But even as Steinbeck's vanishing men become avatars of a New Deal social justice, they continue to require the female body, in an unabashedly disciplinary sense.[9] Left only with feelings for an environment they can neither understand nor effect, the men in Steinbeck's novel turn toward the immediate: they exert themselves not over the economic conditions responsible for their unemployment, but, in displaced form, over intimates whose laboring maternal bodies are reminders of lost forms of wage labor. While men like Connie and Tom depart to engage abstract public collectives, women like Ma Joad experience the quotidian responsibilities these men leave behind with less than utopian force. Thus there is far more at stake in Rose's moral development than in her brother Tom's, whose disappearance at the close of the novel perfectly epitomizes Steinbeck's sense that men remain salient agents only to the extent that they vanish. While Tom Joad dispossesses himself of his body, Rose is castigated for removing her body from public circulation. "Demure and serious," Rose's pregnant body is insufficiently theatrical. Whereas once it invited "slapping and stroking," her body becomes instead closed off, hermetic, inhospitable to public participation. "Her whole thought and action," we are told, "were directed inward toward the baby. She balanced on her toes now for the baby's sake. And the world was pregnant to her; she thought only in terms of reproduction and of motherhood" (130). The self-absorbed Rose is castigated even by her mother for her decision to look inward and not outward. "Forget that baby for a minute," an angry Ma Joad tells her daughter. "He'll take care of hisself" (178). Rose is instructed how to adjudicate between her potentially selfish desire to guard her pregnancy and her more civic obligations to entertain — and, ultimately, to nourish — increasingly large constituencies.

For Steinbeck, the interactive, public codes of sympathy consistently militate against the solipsistic, biological requirements of pregnancy. Hence, *The Grapes of Wrath* allows its women to engage in sympathetic identifications only after robbing them of their children. Within Weedpatch Campsite, Rose of Sharon is accosted by "Jesus lovers" who inform her that she will lose her child if she participates in the activities sponsored by the Entertainment Committee. One of the zealots whispers, "Ever' Sat'dy night when that there strang ban' starts up an' should be a-playin' hymnody, they're a-reelin' — yes, sir, a-reelin' " (422). She "paused for emphasis and then said, in a hoarse whisper, 'They do more. They give a stage play' " (422). Unforgivably, this entails "Struttin' an' paradin' and speakin' like they're somebody they ain't" (422). Steinbeck's contempt for these objections would seem to be thinly veiled. The dance put on by the committee appears to offer campers self-respect, all the more precious a commodity because most of those in the camp cannot find work. As one camper puts it, "These here dances done funny things. Our people got nothing, but jes' because they can ast their frien's to come here to the dance, sets 'em up and makes 'em proud. An' the folks respects 'em 'count of these here dances. Fella got a little place where I was a-workin.' He comes to a dance here. I ast him myself, an' he come. Says we got the only decent dance in the country, where a man can take his girl and his wife" (464). And while the dance enables workers to meet their past employers on an equal, and importantly theatrical footing, it also provides them with the only opportunity they will have to defeat those who would not employ them. Looking to close the camp down, the local farmers' alliance enlists thugs to precipitate a riot at the dance and thereby give the police an excuse to invade. Tipped off in advance, the Weedpatch community rounds up the potential instigators and wisks them out of the camp before any trouble can begin. The campers do so from the dance floor itself, as the strangers attempt to break in on dancing couples, bringing home what is implicit in the dance from the start, namely, that "play actin' " (424) — a vision of unalienated labor understood at the level of theater and performance — enables what the workplace cannot.

But even as he scorns the Jesus-lovers, everything about *The Grapes of Wrath* supports their warnings that certain kinds of theatrical behavior might cause (or require) a mother to lose her child. As we have already seen, Steinbeck opposes the private requirements of pregnancy to the public offices of sympathy. And the camp's "play actin' " seems to emblematize the very process of producing sympathetic identifications among the campers. In this respect, the intense theatricality sponsored by the Entertainment Committee constitutes the very stuff of interpersonal identification, what Steinbeck calls "the beginning — from 'I' to 'we' " (206). That Steinbeck's migrant workers might consolidate their feelings of sympathy (and hence responsibility) for each other in this theatrical, performative manner is hardly surprising. As David Marshall reminds us in *The Surprising Effects of Sympathy,* "the experience of sympathy" has long been considered "both a figure for and a paradigmatic example of theatrical relations."[10] Marshall points out that, "For [Adam] Smith, acts of sympathy are structured by theatrical dynamics that (because of the impossibility of really knowing or entering into someone else's sentiments) depend on people's ability to represent themselves as tableaux, spectacles, and texts before others" (5). He continues, "The experience of sympathy may be presented as a figure for the ideal experience of (for example) reading a novel; but sympathy itself finally must be seen as a theatrical relation formed between a spectacle and a spectator, enacted in the realm of mimesis and representation. . . . not only must works of art touch or move their readers or beholders; people in the world must regard each other as spectators and spectacles, readers and representations. At the same time that the experience of novels and plays and paintings is transported into the realm of affect, sentiment, and sympathy, the experience of sympathy itself seems to be uncomfortably like the experience of watching a play" (26–27). Given this historical identification between sympathy and theater, and given what I have been suggesting is Steinbeck's rigorous opposition between sympathy and pregnancy, it is no surprise that, ultimately, Rose is made by her mother to sit out the dance. Rose needs to remain a spectator of the performances around her so that she is not herself taken as an object of another's sympathy. Pregnancy is as threatening as it is in *The Grapes of Wrath* because, above all, it makes women recipients of sympathy when they should instead be experiencing it for others. Insofar as women do not offer participation to the men around them — and pregnant, they cannot be slapped, stroked, or otherwise engaged — they need to be sanctified and made into agents of public aid.

Rose becomes just such an agent when she does lose her baby. That the child does not in fact take care of itself, that it dies stillborn at the end of the novel is not, in this respect, the result of anything like neglect. Rose is not punished for forgetting her baby, even for a minute; rather, Rose's baby dies because she cannot ignore it, and because Steinbeck would have his readers themselves forget about the child. The point of his novel is not to teach Rose how to be a good mother, but rather to reinvent motherhood itself. And this, of course, is the lesson so famously inscribed in the concluding scene of *The Grapes of Wrath,* the scene that Steinbeck guarded so jealously from skeptical editors at Viking, the one scene that did not make it into John Ford's film of the novel. The scene begins with Rose's delivery of her child, stillborn. Far from being ascribed to human agency, Rose's miscarriage is rendered as an unavoidable natural disaster. Her water breaks at the moment that floodwaters burst through a bank wall protecting the Joads and a small band of migrants. This monstrous objective correlative proceeds to wreak havoc in the camp; the men struggle to overcome the rising wall of water even as they struggle to overcome the terror they feel listening to Rose's cries of pain.

But Rose recovers almost immediately from her miscarriage; she does not mourn but turns instead to a stranger in need, an old, dying man, and suckles him at her breast. It is "huge and symbolic," Steinbeck proclaimed of Rose's action, "toward which the whole story moves."[11] As huge and symbolic as it may be, Rose's decision to nurse a dying stranger is not brought about because she has learned through her own pregnancy how to care for others. Quite the contrary, Rose is offered a dying man as an alternative to her own recently dead child and to the narcissistic attention she paid him while pregnant. "It is a survival symbol," Steinbeck cries, "not a love symbol, it must be an accident, it must be a stranger, and it must be quick."[12] What survives, I suggest, is not so much the dying man, but, in altered form, the functions of sympathy and sentiment in New Deal literature. For the once virtuous and compassionate heroine of the nineteenth-century sentimental novel emerges in Steinbeck as a symbol of the contested intersection between private interest and public aid, a pedagogical subject in need of moral reeducation. *The Grapes of Wrath* in this way collapses the difference between the private and the public, the familial and the national referents of the phrase "domestic economy."[13] In one respect, Steinbeck's quick and accidental substitution of stranger for child is the apotheosis of a nineteenth-century sentimental tradition that often figured newborns as "little strangers" intruding into the smooth operation of a household's economic and sexual arrangements. But the fact that Steinbeck literally replaces Rose's child with a stranger also situates *The Grapes of Wrath* in the context of broadly welfarist, New Deal concerns about the operation of a resolutely national domestic economy. From the start of the novel, the Joads have been exiled from the domestic, dispossessed of their house and farm. Struggling to sustain on the road the values and divisions of labor once attendant on their possession of a home, the Joads develop a domestic economy that is less a sanctuary from the market and more an emblem of how both markets and families were being reinvented by the welfare state.[14] The advent of massive unemployment during the Great Depression; the concomitant erosion of the traditional home as men joined women at home, as men left home, and as both men and women lost their homes; and finally the New Deal's incursions into laissez-faire labor markets brought with it new socioeconomic functions for sentimental writing.

Most significantly, the sentimental novel would evolve hand in hand with New Deal social policy committed to extending sympathetic identifications beyond the family, beyond the citizen's immediate horizon of experience, the same social policy that Ralph Flanders's *The American Century* (1950) would later deride as "emotional" or "sentimental liberalism."[15] Literary critics have frequently suggested that the sentimental novel grew up in the orbit of laissez-faire. Ann Douglas in particular has written forcefully on what she takes to be the politically complacent stance of nineteenth-century American sentimentalism. "The sentimentalization of theological and secular culture," she reasons, "was an inevitable part of the self-evasion of a society both committed to laissez-faire industrial expansion and disturbed by its consequences." Douglas concludes, "Sentimentalism provided the inevitable rationalization of [a laissez-faire] economic order."[16] If so, later sentimentalisms provided the rationalization for a reappraisal, however modest, of one of laissez-faire's most constitutive ideologies; during the thirties and forties, the sentimental form responded directly to the falterings of separate spheres.

2.

President Roosevelt maintained that reading sympathetically was an intrinsically American trait. Indeed, the impulse to charity that, ideally, followed on the heels of such readings was nothing less than a hallmark of the national experience. In his "Address to the Conference on the Mobilization of Resources for Human Needs" on 28 September 1934, he reasoned:

If we go back to our own history to those earliest days of the white man in America, with those first winters of suffering in Jamestown and at Plymouth, we know it has been the American habit from that time on continuously to render aid to those who need it. Through the centuries, as the first struggling villages developed into communities and cities and counties and states, destitution and want of every description have been cared for, in the first instance by community help, and in the last instance as well.

With the enormous growth of population we have had, with the complexities of the past generation, community efforts have now been supplemented by the formation of great national organizations.[17]

Enormous population growth did not alter the fact that the family was to remain the bedrock unit of American civilization, the principal object of national sentiment. Roosevelt reasoned, "It is right, I think, for us to emphasize that the American family must be the unit which engages our greatest interest and concern. With this we must stress once more the task of each community to assist in maintaining and building up that family unit." All the same, local communities could no longer themselves maintain the family's integrity; communities needed, Roosevelt maintained, to pass their "great and humane task on to [a] central body at the seat of federal government" (80).

The Social Security Administration was to be this central body. As one of the principal draftsmen of the Social Security Act confessed, "social security . . . is oriented toward family and individual welfare rather than the functioning of the economic system."[18] The Eighth Annual Report of the Social Security Board in 1943 concurred: "The purpose of a comprehensive program of social security" is "to enable the working population to maintain economic independence throughout the cycle of family life" (487). The cycle of family life that Social Security maintained, historians such as Linda Gordon have pointed out, was decidedly traditional: the New Deal shored up divisions of labor between male productive labor and female reproductive labor. "The form of the welfare state — bureaucratized provision for strangers — is public," Gordon points out, "but its content — individual family 'independence' and women's responsibility for child raising and domestic work — is private."[19] The New Deal, concurs Nancy Fraser, "was centered on the ideal of the family wage. In this world, people were supposed to be organized into heterosexual, male-headed nuclear families, which lived principally from the man's labor-market earnings. The male head of the household would be paid a family wage, sufficient to support children and a full-time wife-and-mother, who performed domestic labor without pay."[20] No coincidence, then, that in his "Second Annual Message to Congress" on 4 January 1935, Roosevelt vowed to throw the weight of government behind "the ambition of the individual to obtain for *him and his* a proper security, a reasonable leisure, and a decent living throughout life" (*Essential FDR,* 83; emphasis added).[21]

We find these same values at work in *The Grapes of Wrath,* in the Weedpatch Campsite that figures so prominently in the novel. The New Deal camp—"the United States," Steinbeck writes, "not California" (456)—provides the Joads the one safe haven on their odyssey. Most important, the camp sponsors the theatrical pastimes—the "play actin' "—that Steinbeck links to the offices of sympathy and indirectly opposes to Rose's pregnancy. More generally, the camp manager responsible for these activities, Jim Rawley, embodies the kind of caring state patriarchy that Talcott Parsons would so influentially describe in the following decades, one in which state-provided experts negotiated citizens through the unfeeling corridors of an increasingly rationalized economy. *The Grapes of Wrath* is in fact dedicated to one such expert, Tom Collins, a Farm Securities Administration official who granted Steinbeck domain over numerous sketches and stories derived from his experience as a New Deal administrator, and who then took the author on an extended tour of New Deal emergency relief camps in California's Central Valley. In the novel, Rawley, modeled on Collins, protects his campers from the aggressions of the local farmers' alliance and offers sanitary living conditions and a child care program to boot. "If your ma isn't working," the benevolent Rawley tells Tom Joad, "she'll look after kids for the ones that is working, an' when she gets a job—why, they'll be others" (392).[22] The women in the camp have their particular tasks carefully laid out for them, and like the New Deal itself, Weedpatch is committed to the separate spheres ideology of the traditional family. Tom marvels at how fluidly a mother in the camp works and at the same time nurses her child; her task involves cooking for men who leave the camp to engage in wage labor. The women remain within the camp, to assist with the housekeeping and to nurse men back into the workforce.[23]

The only trouble with this federal utopia is that the preponderance of the men in the camp cannot find work. Men want wage labor in *The Grapes of Wrath,* but almost never get it. Instead, they stay at home, which profoundly alters the divisions of labor at the heart of the traditional nuclear family. Inhabiting spaces at once public and private — campsites and rest stops that seem to blur the boundaries between families, as well as between work and leisure — Steinbeck's men amble aimlessly about. In the process, Steinbeck reinvents the family as much as he does the polity to which, in sentimental fiction, it usually corresponds. Conflating the private and the public, the political and the biological, Steinbeck's families grow inexorably larger. He writes with utopian zeal of migrant communities from all corners of the nation in which "twenty families became one family, the children were the children of all" (264). He notes, "The rights of the pregnant and the sick transcend all other rights" (264) in these collectives. This is a world, he declares, "hungry for security and yet sensing its disappearance from the earth" (211). From this desiderata, "There grew up governments. . . . And a kind of insurance developed. . . . A man with food fed a hungry man, and thus insured himself against hunger. And when a baby died a pile of silver coins grew at the door flap, for a baby must be well buried, since it has had nothing else of life" (266). Naturalizing social insurance, Steinbeck traces the organic, spontaneous emergence of a down-home Social Security Administration.

But the ostensible instrumentalism of Steinbeck's insurance notwithstanding, this is self-interest of a necessarily impersonal kind. As the Hartford executive Wallace Stevens would have been quick to point out, or as James Cain so often insisted in his noir depictions of the industry, the actuarial engine at the heart of insurance calculates probability and sustains continuity for population groups, not for individuals. Whether offered by a state or a private company, insurance guarantees only macro-economic harmony: by definition, it would never be in the best self-interest of *everyone* in Steinbeck's camp to feed hungry strangers. This presents something of a problem as Steinbeck's families get larger and larger; as he moves from the local to the national, Steinbeck is confronted with the problem of how to justify the quasi-public care so prevalent in his migrant communities. A local community preserves its families, ostensibly, because it knows them, in which case charity is motivated either by friendship or by the fact that individuals within that community can imagine themselves in their neighbor's shoes. Adam Smith famously claims that sympathy for another — based on "conceiving what we ourselves should feel in the like situation" — is self-interested in just this way.[24] But sympathy does not work, Smith insists, with strangers. Railing against those who advocate "commiseration for those miseries which we never saw, which we never heard of, but which we may be assured are at all times infesting such numbers of our fellow-creatures," Smith writes in *The Theory of Moral Sentiment* (1759) that "whatever interest we take in the fortune of those . . . who are placed altogether out of the sphere of our activity, can produce only anxiety to ourselves, without any manner of advantage to them. To what purpose should we trouble ourselves about the world in the moon?"[25]

This question cuts to the heart of the welfare state and its revision of laissez-faire. It was one thing to stress the family as an object of concern, but quite another to convince Americans to care for families they would never know. Why exactly should a worker in Delaware care about the fate of a family in California? Michael Ignatieff observes that the welfare policy of the modern state is driven by what he calls "the needs of strangers." "This phrase," Linda Gordon argues, reminds "us that aid and mutual aid are harder to organize and justify among strangers than among intimates. This was a major lesson of the Great Depression."[26] A lesson relevant to policymaker and novelist alike: both *The Grapes of Wrath* and New Deal social policy turn primarily on the question of how to organize and justify care for strangers (albeit American ones) during an economic climate that had gone a long way in eroding traditional distinctions between the public and the private, between domestic and reproductive labor on the one hand and wage labor on the other.

Steinbeck's writing wrestled with this central problem throughout and then long after the thirties. Steinbeck's first commercially successful work, *Tortilla Flats* (1935), depicts men struggling heroically to perform altruistic deeds against their otherwise selfish natures. The mock epic centers on a band of unemployed, racially caricatured Mexican Americans who justify their invariably selfish actions with the rhetoric of charity. One character is described as "a pathway for the humanities. Suffering he tried to relieve; sorrow he tried to assuage; happiness he shared. . . . His heart was free for anyone who had a use for it."[27] "Urged on by altruism more pure than most men can conceive" (513), Steinbeck's men are so preoccupied with ethics that they are seized with a "philanthropic frenzy" (423) in the process of trying to steal gold from a close friend who has denied himself the fruits of his considerable fortune. "Would it not be a thing of merit," one of the men reasons, "to do those things for him which he cannot do for himself? To buy him warm clothes, to feed him food fit for a human?" (418). The group's joviality fails them, however, when they take in an army corporal who has absconded from his wife with their newborn child. While the men lament the bad treatment the corporal received from his wife (who took up with a higher-ranking officer), the baby dies in its crib.

Steinbeck's next novel, *In Dubious Battle* (1936), takes as its protagonists two Communist Party agitators who attempt to organize a strike of fruit pickers in the San Joaquin Valley. Here also, an unmistakably homoerotic altruism impacts on the fate of a young child. Willing to sacrifice their own lives as well as the lives of those about them for a revolutionary cause they hold to be greater than any individual, Mac and Jim — polar opposites of the inhabitants of Tortilla Flats — are almost inhuman in their ability to put their personal interests and well-being aside. Armed with an unwavering belief in the greater good, the two are terrifying in their stone-faced righteousness. Just after arriving in the workers' camp, Mac pretends to be experienced in delivering children so that he can assist in the birthing of the camp leader's grandchild. He brushes the midwife aside and takes control of the delivery in the hope of furthering the strike. "We've got to use whatever material comes to us," he later tells Jim. "That was a lucky break. We simply had to take it. 'Course it was nice to help the girl, but hell, even if it killed her — we've got to use anything. . . . With one night's work we've got the confidence of the men" (576). But ultimately, Mac gets more than he bargained for: he loses his cherished objectivity by developing a covetous obsession with his younger comrade Jim, soon after Jim begins a flirtation with the mother of the child Mac brought into the world. Jim is saved from his heterosexual desires when a local reactionary kills him at close range with a shotgun. Sanctified with buckshot, Jim survives as an ideal for Mac to revere and follow.

This ideal was New Deal through and through. Steinbeck's most apparently radical novel, *In Dubious Battle* seems sympathetic enough to the left for Michael Denning to term it a proletarian novel.[28] But, as even the title to his novel might suggest, Steinbeck vociferously denied precisely this reading of his work. He declared in a letter to George Albee in 1935, "I'm not interested in strike as a means of raising men's wages, and I'm not interested in ranting about justice and oppression" (*Letters,* 98). "I don't like communists," Steinbeck explained to a friend the year *In Dubious Battle* was published. "I mean I dislike them as people. I rather imagine the apostles had the same waspish qualities and the New Testament is proof that they had equally bad manners" (*Letters,* 120). On the other hand, there is reason to believe that Steinbeck meant to align *In Dubious Battle* with the New Deal. Steinbeck was every bit the government man, meeting twice with Roosevelt in the thirties, delivering lectures for the Federal Theater Project, and befriending influential New Deal cultural officials such as Pare Lorentz.[29] In the novel, the camp leader, who usually listens to his communist advisors with open mind, speaks for Steinbeck by establishing reasonable parameters to his revolutionary spirit: "Always when I hear them they're mad. 'God damn the cops,' they say, 'T'hell with the government.' They're goin' to burn down the government buildings. I don't like that, all them nice buildings" (748).

Steinbeck's next novel, *Of Mice and Men* (1937), takes up where *In Dubious Battle* leaves off. Here, the gruff but good-natured George looks out for the slow-witted Lenny and dreams with him of a day when the two can form their own nonreproductive family. This novel is plagued by the fear of female reproduction. Urging Lenny to stay away from women, George tells him of a future that will involve just the two of them and, of course, plenty of rabbits, which serve principally to displace women's reproductive capacities onto fetish objects that Lenny can safely hold (that is, that Lenny can safely kill). But though Lenny stays away from women, they do not stay away from him. Consequently, he accidentally kills Curley's new wife when she comes to talk to him (given no name of her own, Curley's wife is pertinent to the narrative only as an incitement to sexual jealousy). Thirteen years later, Steinbeck still refused to reclaim for his characters the reproductive dimension of male-female relationships. "A man can't scrap his blood line, can't snip the thread of his immortality," declares the sterile Joe Saul in Steinbeck's novella *Burning Bright* (1950), who starts the story, appropriately enough, as a professional clown. "There's more than just my memory," agonizes Saul, who is just beginning to sense that he is unable to have children. "More than my training and the remembered stories of glory and the forgotten shame of failure. There's a trust imposed to hand my line over to another, to place it tenderly like a thrush's egg in my child's hand."[30] Saul cries out to his wife that he wants a child who will be "a piece of me, and more, of all I came from — the blood stream, the pattern of me, of us, like a shining filament of spider silk hanging down from the incredible ages" (92).

Selflessly in love with her husband, Saul's wife, Mordeen, decides to become pregnant by another man and then to convince her husband that the child is his. As Mordeen grows larger, Steinbeck waxes eloquent depicting the "slow ecstasy" (86) of this nonetheless "frantic beingness": "The secrets of her body were in her eyes — the zygote new thing in the world, a new world but formed of remembered materials: the blastoderm, the wildly splitting cells, and folds and nodes, the semblance of a thing, projections to be arms and legs and vague rays of ganglia, gill slits on the forming head, projections to be fingers and two capacities from which to see one day, and then, a little man, whole formed, no bigger than the stub of a pencil and bathed in warm liquor, drawing food from the mother bank and growing" (85). As his wife basks in her biological ferment, Saul goes to a doctor and discovers that the baby could not be his. At first outraged at what he considers to be his wife's treachery, Saul later learns the moral lesson around which *Burning Bright* is constructed when he comes face to face with his wife's child. In an outpouring of emotion, Saul declares to his wife, "The eyes, the nose, the shape of the chin — I thought they were worth preserving because they were mine. It is not so. It is the race, the species that must go staggering on. Mordeen, our ugly little species, weak and ugly, torn with insanities, violent and quarrelsome, sensing evil — the only species that knows evil and practices it — the only one that senses cleanness and is dirty, that knows about cruelty and is unbearably cruel" (157). As the melodrama builds, Saul works his way to his final verity: "I had to walk into the black to know — to know that every man is father to all children and that every child must have all men as father." No need to be jealous, he reasons: "This is not a little piece of private property, registered and fenced and separated" (158).

As I have been suggesting, *The Grapes of Wrath* is premised on the notion that "every man is father to all children"; moreover, the novel suggests that men fulfill the requirements of this form of paternity not in local acts but as avatars of a persistently displaced vision of social justice. *Burning Bright* displaces this vision onto the good of the species. Saul's incipient sociobiology suggests that, ultimately, individuals understand their local commitments in terms of the propagation of a larger gene pool. Utterly devoid of any group other than White Americans, *The Grapes of Wrath* is uninterested in "humanity" per se. Rose does not nurse her dying man because she cares only for "the race, the species." But at the same time, neither does she help him because she sees her own well-being in his salvation. In fact, Steinbeck goes out of his way to describe Rose's aid to the dying stranger in decidedly impersonal terms that intentionally complicate the relevance of sympathetic identification to the novel's sentiment. Insisting on the disinterested nature of Rose's act, the author writes to his editor of the man she helps that the "Joads don't know him, don't care about him, have no ties to him" (*Letters,* 178). And indeed, Rose does not imagine herself in the stranger's position: there is no moment of sympathetic identification between the two; the stranger remains as unknown to Rose as he does to the reader. Granted, Rose acts out a gendered moral code forcefully promulgated by her mother, but even so, there is little to no motivation attached to the novel's concluding scene.

But if this is the case, if Rose does not care about the man, why does she nurse him at all? If Rose does not care for him emotionally, then why does she care for him physically? What, finally, is the social role Steinbeck imagines for sentiment and sympathy when the objects of an individual's emotion — whether a stranger or a public abstraction such as "the people," let alone the species — offer at best a problematic basis for personal identification?

As I have already pointed out, Steinbeck sees the women in his novel as embodying, literally, the crux of this issue. Initially icons of private, biological selfishness, Steinbeck's women are instructed to sacrifice their bodies for increasingly disembodied men who, as the novel progresses, become figures for impersonal national publics. *The Grapes of Wrath* thus detaches women's reproductive abilities and family loyalties from what Steinbeck takes to be the natural caregiving functions of their bodies. Initially, the otherwise gracious Ma Joad is filled with conflict when it comes to caring for strangers. "I dunno what to do," she cries out when confronted with begging children. "I can't rob the fambly. I got to feed the fambly" (351). When Ma Joad, tire iron in hand, wrests the family leadership from her husband, she does so in an attempt to halt this blurring of priorities. The Joads have been traveling with the Wilson family, whom they have just met, when the Wilson truck breaks down. Tom Joad suggests that the two families go ahead while he and Preacher Casey stay and fix the engine, because, as Pa Joad puts it, there is "almost a kin bond" between the two families. But Ma Joad inflexibly refuses to acknowledge the Wilsons as her kin. "All we got is the fambly unbroke" (231).

Yet the Joad family does eventually break, and *The Grapes of Wrath* teaches Ma Joad the necessity of this fissure. Most painfully to her, Tom ends up leaving the family like Connie before him, though not before teaching his mother that families "go on" with the resilience of "the people" precisely because family members are replaceable with strangers. One critic of the novel thus observes that its movement is "toward larger and more inclusive structures," and another that "for Steinbeck, any kind of boundary — whether it's drawn around forty acres or forty thousand, around a family or a class — is wrong."[31] Ma Joad herself concludes at the end of the novel, "Use' ta be the fambly was fust. It ain't so now. It's anybody" (606). If not exactly everyone, then at least all Americans: Steinbeck's novel is preoccupied with preserving the integrity of what his characters continually refer to as "the country" (207). Steinbeck's characters are bound together by a shared national identity and by their respective place under the aegis of the government meant to secure that identity. Land owners and workers thus contest government policy by debating whose tax dollars should go toward what particular form of federal aid. Steinbeck's vision of social justice, then, is in service of a resolutely national population group. If the good of the species provides the ultimate justification for Saul's actions, then the good of "the country" — or at least the good of those citizens whose tax dollars fund its government — serves finally to underwrite Steinbeck's social justice. Toward this end, women in *The Grapes of Wrath* are taught by the anxious men around them to not distinguish between strangers and blood relations, to extend even the most personal forms of maternal aid to those who are not kin but are nevertheless compatriots in a national enterprise. Rose's almost mechanical extension of herself to a stranger for whom she has no personal feelings is the apotheosis of this process. For Rose has been taught not so much to care for strangers as if they were a part of her family, but to care for strangers in the complete absence of producing even an imaginary personal relation to them.[32] Steinbeck's national welfarism is potent not because it extrapolates from codes of familial care, but because it supplants them entirely, eschewing the sentimental justifications and personal identifications once required for such care.

3.

"Folks gonna look," Ma Joad informs her bashful, pregnant daughter in *The Grapes of Wrath* just before the dance held at the Weedpatch campsite. She is quick to add that they will like what they see: "It makes folks happy to see a girl in a fambly way — makes folks sort of giggly an' happy" (460). But Ma Joad's wisdom aside, the novel's men respond with unadulterated terror when confronted with pregnant women. Certainly Ma Joad does not speak of her own husband. Long before he is displaced from his farm, Pa Joad is overcome by an irrational fit during the birth of his child Noah: "Pa, frightened at [his wife's] spreading thighs, alone in the house, and horrified at the screaming wretch his wife had become, went mad with apprehension. Using his hands, his strong fingers for forceps, he had pulled and twisted the baby" (106). Despite his frenzied midwifery, his child is born and grows up with a character trait that Steinbeck ascribes to the physical damage done him by his father, a trait that anticipates the moral and sexual progress of the Joads' voyage: Noah is resolutely, almost pathologically asocial. He has no interest in or sympathy for either strangers or family. Steinbeck writes that Noah "didn't seem to care; there was a listlessness in him toward things people wanted and needed" (107). Whereas Connie leaves the Joads to go into politics and Tom leaves to fight for the people, Noah flees into nature, absconding down a river when his family isn't looking.

It is tempting to see Noah's social apathy as a distinctly masculine characteristic, in which case, his indifference to others emerges as a critique of his father's pregnancy mania. "A woman knows," Ma Joad declares. "Man, he lives in jerks — baby born, an' a man dies, an' that's a jerk. Woman, it's all one flow, like a stream, little eddies, little waterfalls, but the river, it goes right on" (577). But Ma's account of what a woman knows is more striking for its almost causal account of "a baby [being] born, an a man [dying]" than it is indicative of an intrinsically feminine impulse to nurture. Women in *The Grapes of Wrath* are not in fact more caring than the men. Rather, they are marked with a maternal capacity for domestic sympathy that, the novel insists, needs to be translated into more public terms. As much as women seem to carry within them the capacity for a certain kind of maternal care, they are enjoined never to have children of their own. As Ma's ominous words might suggest, the last thing Steinbeck's men want is new children. For despite the fact that the novel imagines women's domestic labor reinvigorating men's wage labor, Steinbeck is far less sanguine about the regenerative possibilities promised men by reproductive labor itself. Steinbeck's men (none of whom, as agricultural workers, would have been eligible for Social Security benefits) have at best limited access to wage labor, and are terrified by the collapse of separate spheres ideology. Pregnancy does not, as one might suspect, preserve this ideology so much as it erodes it even further.

In fact, one has to look hard in Depression-era writing to find working-class men embracing the "fambly way." If there was one resounding conclusion to political fiction of this period, it was that men either could not or would not take care of their own. Erskine Caldwell's short story "Daughter" (1935) is emblematic; here a father shoots his daughter in the head with a shotgun because she cannot stop crying from hunger. In Tillie Olsen's *Yonnondio* (1932–1937), gothic renditions of reproduction and pregnancy suggest that male labor is literally eaten up by pathologically voracious female bodies. Try as they might, Olsen's men are no match for the gaping female maw — figured as a mine shaft — that swallows them whole. Similarly, in Pietro di Donato's *Christ in Concrete* (1937), a construction worker loses his leg and is forced into the domestic economy of piecework; trapped in his sister's home, the character is joined each day by the neighborhood women who teach him how to use a needle and thread. Proper order is restored when his male coworkers buy him a prosthetic limb and, even more significantly, when, that same day, he marries a woman unable to have children. Lest we miss the way salaried male companionship displaces reproductive labor throughout the novel, di Donato concludes with a mother who literally beats herself to death by punching her womb: "Quietly," di Donato writes, "her mother-strength sent shafts against the bag of life."[33] Betty Smith's *A Tree Grows in Brooklyn* powerfully extends this tradition. As in *The Grapes of Wrath,* men are overcome with curiously tortured responses when faced with pregnant women, responses whose agonized vehemence seem to belie the very principles of social justice they aim to reinforce. Smith's classic tearjerker is especially useful because it situates its heroine's explicitly sentimental writing with respect to both wage and reproductive labor. Francie Nolan learns to be a sentimental writer by cleaving to the men around her; internalizing a male antipathy to reproductive labor, she eschews her selfish mother for the civic-minded, liberal ethos of her departed father.

Picturing a fatherless family thrown precipitously beyond the confines of the traditional home, *A Tree Grows in Brooklyn* — Smith's bittersweet, quasi-autobiographical account of Francie's coming-of-age in working-class Brooklyn — is of a piece with Steinbeck's *The Grapes of Wrath,* even if, at first pass, Smith's introspective and episodic narrative seems to have little in common with Steinbeck's epic populism. Most of Smith's characters are aggressively dismissive of the leftist-humanist sentiment that absorbs Steinbeck's tale of migrant Oklahoma farmers. *A Tree Grows in Brooklyn* does share some striking similarities with the more radical writings of Federal One employees Tillie Olsen and Meridel Le Sueur. In particular, Le Sueur's *The Girl,* like Smith's novel, explores the simultaneous development of sexual and economic self-consciousness in a newly fatherless young woman.[34] But Smith's women echo the Jeffersonian anti-Federalism of Laura Ingalls Wilder's *Little House on the Prairie* series more than they do socially conscious fiction of any kind. Katie, Francie's mother, prides herself on the independence of her family and insists on her abhorrence of unearned aid. "When the time comes . . . that we have to take charity baskets," she vows, "I'll plug up the doors and windows and wait until the children are sound asleep and then turn on every gas jet in the house" (267). Choosing pre-Depression hardship over the more proximate variety, the novel covers the years between 1902 and 1919 despite the fact that it was published in 1943. Smith generates heady nostalgia for simpler times, and turns back to an era when, ostensibly, poverty was the result of bad luck (if not more dire moral shortcomings) and families took care of themselves regardless.

Smith's novel does take place in the heyday of Progressivism, when reformers such as Jane Addams, Mary McDowell, and Florence Kelley worked tirelessly to improve the working conditions of women and children, and when the Supreme Court, on its way to insisting on a minimum wage for this group in *Muller v. Oregon* (1908), said that the "physical structure [of the modern woman] and a proper discharge of her maternal functions — having in view not merely her own health, but the well-being of the race — justify legislation to protect her from the greed as well as the passion of man." The White House seemed not far behind when, one year later, it celebrated the home as "the highest and finest product of civilization" while backing a policy of federally supported cash grants to widows with children.[35] As historians of the welfare state are quick to point out, mothers and children, along with war veterans, were the first recipients of organized government solicitude.[36] It is perhaps not surprising, then, that even as Katie rails against private charity, Smith's tear-jerking Bildungsroman gradually weans Francie from her mother's antisentimental and draconian politics. "The Nolans were individualists," writes Smith. "They conformed to nothing except what was essential to their being able to live in their world. They followed their own standards of living. They were part of no set social group." Such strength of character takes its toll. The family's intense idiosyncrasy "was fine," Smith continues, "for the making of individualists, but sometimes bewildering for a small child" (143). Francie finds her family so bewildering and distasteful that she leaves her mother and Brooklyn behind at the end of the novel, never to see either again. Falling in step with a modernity her mother cannot fathom, Francie moves beyond Katie's suddenly archaic conceptions of sentiment and domestic economy. Not coincidentally, Francie's emancipating departure from her mother and Brooklyn takes place in 1919, the year decades of suffrage movements bore fruit in the congressional approval of the Nineteenth Amendment.[37]

But Betty Smith was more than simply a progressive-minded reformer, and she was more than simply a New Deal liberal; she was a "client" of the government throughout the thirties. Employed first by the Civil Works Administration in the early thirties, Smith was an ardent participant in the WPA's Federal Theater Project from 1935 to

1937.[38] If Smith was little like Katie Nolan, Smith's first husband shared even less with Johnny Nolan. Coauthor with liberal historian Charles A. Beard of, among others, *The Future Comes: A Study of the New Deal* (1933), *Current Problems of Public Policy* (1936), and *The Old Deal and the New* (1940), Smith's once-liberal ex-husband George H. E. Smith had undergone a political conversion by the time his estranged wife wrote her first novel. Betty Smith was living hand to mouth in garrets finishing *A Tree Grows in Brooklyn* in early 1943 as her husband set up the Republican Policy Committee in the U.S. Senate with Robert E. Taft.[39]

During her years on the Theater Project, Smith was widely recognized as an accomplished playwright and turned out dozens of plays. She was so highly esteemed on the New York Project that she was one of four New Deal playwrights sent to develop North Carolina's struggling theater program in 1936. Apparently, Smith's interest in the stage was inextricable from the government's patronage of it. She ended her career as a playwright soon after the FTP was terminated in 1937 to take up the writing of novels, basing her style, she claimed, on the radical social realism of James T. Farrell.[40] But Diana Trilling saw things differently. In a *Nation* review, Trilling lacerated *A Tree Grows in Brooklyn*: "In Miss Smith's picture of American poverty there is neither ugliness nor rebellion, only sentiment; the explosive family life of James Farrell's realistic novels is replaced, in the 'realism' of *A Tree Grows in Brooklyn,* by a sweet co-operativeness. National unity reflects itself in family unity, and fiction arms us with the illusion of domestic security against the insecurity of the world."[41]

It is hard to disagree with Trilling, for though Smith gave up the theater to write novels, she seems simply to have translated the essentially melodramatic form of her plays into a more novelistic sentimental structure. Smith's putative apprenticeship to the politically radical and hyperbolically masculine tales of Farrell seems to overlook not simply the affective extravagance of her own writing, but the extent to which that writing quite consciously situated itself within the traditions of American sentimentalism. One of Smith's early plays, *Little Immortal,* is actually taken from the early life of Harriet Beecher Stowe; years later, *A Tree Grows in Brooklyn* readily exemplifies many of the characteristics that critics have attributed to a nineteenth-century form most famously expressed by Stowe.[42] The centrality of Johnny Nolan's death to *A Tree Grows in Brooklyn* suggests Joanne Dobson's definition of sentimental literature: a form "premised on an emotional and philosophical ethos that celebrates human connection, both personal and communal, and acknowledges the shared devastation of affectional loss." Francie's subsequent venture into the Manhattan labor force, where she is preyed on by an unscrupulous G.I., likewise echoes Cathy Davidson's claim that an "unstated premise of sentimental fiction is that the woman must take greater control of her life and must make shrewd judgments of the men who come into her life."[43]

But most important, *A Tree Grows in Brooklyn* develops Francie's sentimentalism as a function of the breakdown of the divisions of labor in her family. "Dear God," prays Katie Nolan, "give me two months. . . . When I'm boss of my own mind and my own body, I don't need to ask You for anything. But now my body is boss over me and I've got to ask You for help" (267). At the time she makes this prayer, Katie has recently been forced by the death of Johnny to become the head of the Nolan household. "From now on, I am your mother and your father" (263), Katie tells Francie and her brother. In fact, the tyranny of Katie's body, as she will later reason, is partly responsible for Johnny's death. After Katie tells him that she expects a third child, Johnny realizes he must now bring more money into the Nolans' working-class home. As a result, he tries to wean himself from his addiction to alcohol, catches pneumonia, and then stays out on the street to die.

While Katie remains in the family's building as its washerwoman, Francie is now forced to support her mother and brother in an entirely new economy. Whereas Johnny was a unionized singer, paid to croon the folk tunes of preindustrialized Ireland to the beer-guzzling patrons of the local saloon, Francie confronts a new public sphere in all of its Taylorized grandeur. First, Francie is paid daily to read all of the nation's newspapers for a press-clipping agency, and later, by a "Communications Corporation" that teaches her to teletype. Smith sharply distinguishes Francie's new life in the modern workplace from her mother's traditional domestic arrangements. When she is proposed to by a local gentleman at the close of the novel, Katie makes clear just how domestic she will remain: "A man like you — in public life — needs a wife who knows social business — who can entertain his influential business friends. I'm not that kind of a woman," she declares. Her pleased suitor replies, "My office is where

I do my business entertaining. My home is where I live. Now I'm not meanin' you wouldn't be a credit to me — you'd be a credit to a better man: But I'm needin' no woman to help me out in my business. I can handle that myself, thank you" (412). All he wants, he tells Katie, is her infant child to be considered his own. Katie accepts this arrangement, she tells her suitor, for the simple reason that she has grown used to it.

But if, as Katie reasons, Francie is forced into the workplace because Katie's pregnancy drives Johnny to his death, it is also the case that Francie understands her newfound employment in terms of crucially ineffectual feelings of sympathy she has for a fatherless child. On her thirteenth birthday, just before her father dies, Francie sees neighborhood women taunt a young mother, Joanna, who dares to flaunt her illegitimate child in public. Tempers flare, and the neighborhood women begin throwing stones, one of which hits the baby. Unable to motivate herself to help Joanna, or even to show sympathy when the mother beseechingly looks her way, Francie passively watches as "a clear thin trickle of blood ran down the baby's face and spotted its clean bib" (205). This thin trickle of blood reasserts itself later that day, when Francie hides in the basement of her building: "She had heard papa sing so many songs about the heart; the heart that was breaking — was aching — was dancing — was heavy laden — that leaped for joy — that was heavy in sorrow — that turned over — that stood still. She really believed that the heart actually did those things. She was terrified thinking her heart had broken inside her over Joanna's baby and that the blood was now leaving her heart and flowing from her body" (208). Imagining she is being punished for withholding her sympathy, Francie believes her first period to be the bleeding of her broken heart.[44] Francie is not entirely wrong, for *A Tree Grows in Brooklyn* physically manifests women's emotional relationships with strangers, such that women are biologically transformed by their sympathetic identifications with them. In this instance, Smith understands the sexualization of Francie's body as inextricable not simply from her failed sympathy for Joanna but also from the waning of sentiment occasioned in the Nolan family by Johnny's death. Weeping for a fatherless child as well as for the failure of her own sympathetic facilities, Francie unwittingly mourns the imminent loss of her own hopelessly sentimental and sympathetic father.

In fact, Johnny's eventual death constitutes more than just a personal loss for Francie: it marks the passing from the novel of liberal political commitment. Elizabeth Ammons suggests that *Uncle Tom's Cabin* "proposes as the foundation of a new democratic era, in place of masculine authority, feminine nurture."[45] Both *The Grapes of Wrath* and *A Tree Grows in Brooklyn* also invoke the politically redemptive nature of feminine nurture: Ma Joad, for example, serves as the moral lightning rod for broadly socialist notions of collective responsibility in Steinbeck's novel. But it is also the case that, for Steinbeck and Smith, women need to be taught their feminine nature by the men around them. These authors suggest that, left to its own, feminine nurture remains relatively unconcerned with democratic governance or even social policy of any kind. Thus Smith contrasts the socially indifferent and humorless Katie Nolan to her populist, sentimental, and departed husband. Before he dies, Johnny is the romantic of the Nolan family; his liberalism is set apart from his wife's Republican rationality. Much to Katie's chagrin, the unionized Johnny is an avid supporter of the Tammany Hall Democrats because, he says, "the party does a lot of good for the people" (157).

At the same time, Johnny's political attachments, such as they are, stand in sharp relief from those he forms at home. He is no model of domestic virtue. Quite the opposite: the kind of public sympathy he demonstrates in liberal politics stands in direct contrast to the affection and caring he is unable to demonstrate at home. Johnny feels most powerfully for those he does not himself have to love or provide for. Francie grows up knowing not simply that her father is a failure as a breadwinner, but that, more hurtfully, he never wanted to provide for a family in the first place. "I drink because I don't stand a chance and I know it," Johnny tells young Francie. "I drink because I got responsibilities that I can't handle. . . . I am not a happy man. I got a wife and children and I don't happen to be a hard-working man. I never wanted a family" (34). Further, Johnny's shortcomings as a breadwinner appear the product of his wife's first pregnancy. Johnny loses it when his wife delivers the child. Overcome by panic, he goes out on an all-night drinking spree and fails to show up for both Katie's delivery and his job the next day. As a result, he is fired from the last steady job he will ever have. After skulking to the hospital the day after his child is born, "Johnny hardly looked at the baby." He "knelt by Katie's bed and sobbed" (72).

Johnny's antipathy to Katie's pregnancy, to his having children of his own, is a staple feature of the male characters in the novel, who are able to care for children only when they belong to others.[46] Francie's Aunt Sissy has had ten miscarriages — with ten interchangeable husbands, each of whom she calls her "John" — before she decides that it is time to adopt. First, Sissy discovers a pregnant adolescent possessed of an unwanted child. She then tells her latest John that she is pregnant and proceeds to act out her pregnancy over the course of nine months. When John protests that her body does not look any larger than it had before she was pregnant, Sissy dismisses him and retorts that she simply carries a small child. After initial skepticism, and after Sissy unveils her surprise, John accepts the child as his own, partly because it has his chin, and partly, we must intuit, because he appreciates the fact that his wife was never pregnant, that the infant is not in fact his.[47] Thus, whereas Steinbeck's women are taught to transform their familial attachment into impersonal detachment, Smith's women and men produce their families in the first place only through the mediation of an essentially impersonal mechanism, here the adoption of a stranger's child. In Steinbeck, women are transformed into socially responsible persons by their engagement with strangers; these encounters divorce them from their biological drives even as they preserve those drives as the necessary ground or catalyst of their sympathy. As we saw with Francie, on the other hand, Smith figures the onset of reproductive sexuality as a function of her inability to implement liberal policy, of her own distance from her father's bleeding heart.

In fact, Smith's families take on whatever intimacy they have only through impersonal mediations. McGarrity, owner of the local saloon, explains that he is unable truly to care for his children because they came from his wife's body. McGarrity dreams that his wife "would come to him and confess that the children were not his. He felt that he could love those children if he knew that they were another man's. Then he could see their meanness and their stupidity objectively; then he could pity them and help them. As long as he knew they were his, he hated them because he saw all of his own and [his wife's] worst traits in them" (270). As it turns out, McGarrity is sexually paralyzed by the suspicion that his wife sleeps with other men. As if in response to this imagined emasculation, McGarrity pretends that Johnny's children are his own. "In the eight years that

Johnny had been patronizing McGarrity's saloon," Smith writes, McGarrity "pretended that he was Johnny and that he, McGarrity, was talking so about [his own] wife and his [own] children" (270). Feeling "pity" for the children after Johnny's death, McGarrity offers them a job; in a pattern axial to *The Grapes of Wrath,* sentiment is translated into aid only when the giver of aid has no biological relation to the persons with whom he or she sympathizes.

Still more miraculously, McGarrity's employment of the Nolan children produces in him a biological transformation akin to Francie's menstruation. Confronted with Francie's mother, who has come to thank him for employing her children, McGarrity feels "his lost manhood stirring within him" (274). McGarrity's transformation echoes Francie's, whose menstruation is something of a punishment for her failure to help Joanna's child. McGarrity is given sexual potency only insofar as he learns to sublimate it in acts of kindness directed at children other than his own. The last thing McGarrity wants is new children of his own. Conversely, Francie is made fertile after failing to care for another's child. *A Tree Grows in Brooklyn* locates the onset of Francie's sexuality not in her sympathetic identification with the strange girl and her child but in its insufficiency and in her concomitant feelings of guilt for not having done anything to help the two: Francie imagines she is "getting her lesson" (206) when she menstruates. As much as she feels for Joanna's child, the outpouring of her broken and bleeding heart is primarily an expression of regret. Francie "remembered how Joanna had smiled at her and how she had turned her head away without smiling back. Why hadn't she smiled back? Now she would suffer — she would suffer all the rest of her life every time that she remembered that she had not smiled back" (206).

In this context, Francie's failure to help the beset child — her failure to translate sympathetic identification into action — feels like an inescapably gendered inadequacy. The men in Smith's novel might have prevented the stoning, not because they are brave or heroic, but, Smith suggests, because they are more prone than women to implement their identifications (provided, that is, those identifications take place outside the family). In fact, a passing man tries to help Joanna, who refuses his aid. Francie thus learns a rather stark lesson: "From that time on, remembering the stoning women, she hated women." Francie reasons, "Most women had the one thing in common: they had great pain when they gave birth to their children. This should make a bond that held them all together; it should make them love and protect each other against the man-world. But it was not so. It seemed like their great birth pains shrunk their hearts and their souls" (209). Francie thus opposes the exigencies of the reproductive female body to its capacity to feel sympathy for others. Women's hearts shrink because of their labor pains, and it is no coincidence that all of the women who stone Joanna and her child are themselves mothers.

Francie's sexual maturation and the virtually concurrent death of her father consequently become occasions for the same nostalgia. Francie's two losses — of her sexual innocence and of her father — inscribe the unavailability to her of masculine forms of public sympathetic identification. Francie is forced out of the home and into the workforce not simply because Johnny is unable to reconcile his congenial liberal political ideals with a desire to care for a new child, but also because Francie herself is unable to form a strong sentimental identification with Joanna's child. In turn, Francie's salaried employment militates against the authority of the dispassionate women to whom she is asked to submit. "As her capacity to feel things" grows, Francie experiences an increasing number of "disillusionments" (114). No wonder, then, that as she develops sexually without her father, she becomes more and more "like her mother," "afraid of being openly sentimental" (414).

The workplace awaiting Francie across the East River would seem to be in perfect sync with this deracinated sensibility. Walking down the teeming streets of Manhattan on her way back from work, Francie imagines that she hears "voices." *"Everything is machines,"* the voices tell her. But this mechanical dystopia could not be less like the traditional domestic sphere overseen by Katie Nolan. Francie hears one voice in particular say, *"I heard a joke the other day. Feller and his wife going around the other day getting food, clothes, everything out of machines. So they come to this baby machine, and the feller puts money in and out comes a baby. So the feller turns around and says, 'give me the good old days' "* (308). At this point in the novel, Francie herself is the last person who wants the good old days back. Holding Sissy's child in her arms just before she leaves Brooklyn for good, Francie suggests that she hopes to find this same form of mechanical reproduction beyond Brooklyn. As she cradles the child, she feels a rush of visceral excitement in the recognition that babies can be produced with the same detached, mechanized efficiency of other household commodities. Holding the child, Francie dreams a new consumerism: "A thrill started at her finger tips, went up her arm, and through her entire body. When I get big, she decided, I'll always have a new baby in the house" (279).

This erotic but nonetheless impersonal maternal dispensation makes Francie more like the men in the novel than her mother. Part and parcel of her becoming more like a man — more adept at caring for children to whom she is not related — is Francie's developing career as a writer. From the start, Katie's stringent and selfish use of sentiment is reinforced at Francie's school, where her creative-writing teacher offers her the same emotional repression as her mother. After composing a heart-wrenching account of her father's life and death, Francie is chastised by her genteel schoolmarm, who urges Francie to avoid unseemly material: "Poverty, starvation, and drunkenness are ugly subjects to choose. We all admit these things exist. But one doesn't write about them" (283). Most of all, Francie's teacher does not want her to produce writing that sympathizes with those who are less than ideal citizens. Censured for her elegiac recollections, Francie places her most personal stories, those about her father, into a box that she will open only after she leaves her mother and moves out of Brooklyn with her future husband.[48]

But as much as the women around her militate against sentimental writing, Francie knows better. At this point in the novel Francie has already discovered a core function of New Deal sentimental writing, namely, its ability to displace private, biologically defined relationships of sympathy into impersonal, public form. Making amends to Joanna for her indifference, for her failure to help when her baby is stoned, Francie gives the mother the only copy she has of her first published short story, "Winter Time." If, as David Marshall suggests, experiencing sympathy for another is in many respects akin to witnessing a theatrical tableau or, in fact, to reading a novel, then Francie's gift emerges with especially symbolic power. Francie makes available to Joanna precisely the experience she herself is not able to act out: reading a sentimental story is akin to watching a child abused in public, Francie seems to intuit, because both displace passive, heart-wrenching moments of sympathy. This displacement — of the biographical to the impersonal, of the private and biological to the abstract and public, indeed, of the literal to the realm of fiction — helps explain Smith's curious desire to locate her own literary genealogy not in the sentimental, but in the more obviously masculine novels of James Farrell. Whereas "great birth pains" shrank the "hearts and souls" of women, writing — offered in remembrance of departed, public-minded fathers — provided a safe vehicle for the spectacles of sympathy.

4.

The marriage of John and Carol Steinbeck began to come to an end, biographer Jay Parini reports, during a paternity suit brought against the author while he was writing *The Grapes of Wrath.* A young woman whom Steinbeck had known as a child declared that she was pregnant by him. Steinbeck vigorously denied the claim, and did so in a manner that sheds considerable light on the politics of his novel. Protesting his innocence to his literary agent, he makes an abrupt segue: "I must go over into the interior valleys. There are about five thousand families starving to death over there, not just hungry, but actually starving. The government is trying to feed them and get medical attention to them with the fascist group of utilities and banks sabotaging the thing all along the line and yelling for a balanced budget. In one tent there are twenty people quarantined for smallpox and two of the women are to have babies in that tent this week" (*Letters,* 158). Translating his vexed personal relation to reproduction and paternal responsibility into a more selfless concern with public aid, Steinbeck performs one of the many displacements that form the core of *The Grapes of Wrath.* One such displacement occurs when Uncle John of the Joad family explains that he inadvertently killed his first wife by ignoring her acute labor pains. She asked for a doctor, and he told her, "Hell, you jus' et too much." Uncle John's wife is dead the next morning. "Sence then," he declares, "I tried to make it up — mos'ly to kids" (306). Uncle John devotes himself to caring for children of unknown origin as a way of making appropriate amends for his tragic indifference to his wife's labor pains. In by now familiar fashion, he commits himself to public forms of sympathy because, we must assume, he was unwilling to accept a child of his own. But I have been suggesting that, according to the perverse logic of *The Grapes of Wrath,* it makes just as much sense to put this in exactly the opposite terms: Uncle John kills his wife and child precisely so he can care for other children. In either event, the brutal trade-off to which he bears testimony seems not only acceptable but urgently necessary to an author whose novels worry that individuals care for "the people" only to the extent that this group remains abstract and impersonal, detached from discernible origins.

Steinbeck responded like one of his characters to the discovery, soon after his opus was published, that Carol was pregnant. As it was, John had already refused Carol even the most minimal participation in public life to which his best-seller had given him access, this despite the fact that Carol had logged countless hours editing the manuscript of *The Grapes of Wrath* while she was working for the State Emergency Relief Administration. He would refuse her a child as well. Previously committed to "the people," Steinbeck was not prepared to be equally so to his own. Imagining himself already burdened down by overwhelming public responsibilities, and in what Parini calls a state of absolute "panic," Steinbeck forced Carol to get an abortion against her better judgment. As a result of the operation, "an infection developed in [her] uterine tubes that led, within months, to a complete hysterectomy."[49]

A loss for Carol but not, perhaps, for the national economy. In Betty Smith's *Tomorrow Will Be Better* (1948), Margy muses over her husband's unwillingness to have children by noting, "There was a class of comfortably fixed, educated, altruistic people who made a profession or a hobby out of uplifting the masses. They would claim that . . . there should be no children unless economic conditions were favorable" (269). Steinbeck, it seems fair to point out, was one such person. But Steinbeck's insistence that Carol abort her pregnancy had as much to do with his own conception of literary labor as it did with national economic conditions. Underwriting this insistence was his belief that he was, as a writer, already engaged in procreative labor. Locked within his home struggling to write, the author made numerous analogies between pregnancy and authorship in the journal he kept while working on *The Grapes of Wrath*. Nervously remarking on the fiscal authority his confinement at home accorded his wife, Steinbeck remarks, "Carol is paying the bills [while] I'm changeable and skittish." All the same, he reassures himself, "I don't have to produce until the pressure inside me does it."[50]

Steinbeck's anxiety that his trade made him something less than distinctly masculine is in no sense unique. Writing at home during the Depression, male writers from different class backgrounds persistently understood themselves to be domestic laborers. Before Gordon Graham finds employment on the Writers' Project in Norman Macleod's *You Get What You Ask For,* he works at home while his wife earns her money at an office job. "Gordon would put on his apron, roll up his sleeves, and dig again into the interminable business of cooking. . . . Housekeeper, chief cook and bottle washer, butler and servant, Gordon was and he knew it as he made the bed, swept the floor and washed the dishes with the radio turned on to Make Believe Ballroom."[51] Graham is unable to maintain this role, in part because his working-class politics seem to require that he leave his wife to take up with other working-class men. As Paula Rabinowitz points out in *Labor and Desire,* most male radical novelists of the thirties and forties figured the masses as male and the bourgeoisie as female. "The bourgeois woman," Rabinowitz notes, "represented the epitome of false consciousness."[52] The working-class Harry in Hemingway's "The Snows of Kilimanjaro" sees himself emasculated and his writing career sold down the river by the simple fact that he has been supported by his well-to-do wife. In Jack Conroy's *A World to Win,* Robert Hurley similarly attributes his literary idiom to his financial dependence on his wife. Kept unforgivably comfortable by her income, he decides that his effete and pretentious modernist style is a product of the fact that "He'd been a gigolo. . . . She had kept plenty for him to eat, and she had a warm and loving body."[53] It was only a small leap from here to associate the writer's domestic labor with reproductive labor itself. In Tess Slesinger's 1934 short story "A Life in the Day of a Writer," a writer loses his mind when confronted with the fact that his wife is out earning a salary while he sits at home suffering from writer's block. To drive home the implications of his feminization, namely, that writer's block is tantamount to abortion, the writer types out a grotesque and endless series of coat hangers on the blank pages that face him. When the wife of radical novelist Richard Gordon in Hemingway's *To Have and Have Not* rails against her husband for the abortion he forced her to have, she concludes by declaring, "If you were just a good writer, I could stand for all the rest of it maybe."[54] The suggestion here is not simply that Gordon's desire for the abortion had something to do with his literary vocation, but also that "quality" writing might otherwise have taken the place of an aborted fetus.

Steinbeck conjoins literary and reproductive labor most powerfully in his journal the day he notes that Carol had recently been reading *Tristram Shandy* (1759–67), Laurence Sterne's novel of a child deformed at birth by his father's indifference to the conditions of his delivery. Writing in his journal, he guesses that Carol's reading material accounts for his dream the previous night, "a confused mess made up of Dad and his failures and me and my failures" (*Working Days,* 28). Steinbeck's sense of "Dad's" failures emerged at least in displaced fashion later that afternoon: this was to be the day Steinbeck would write about Pa Joad's frenzied and damaging midwifery of his son Noah. Steinbeck's account of his own failures was more vexed: he writes that "This book has become a misery to me because of my inadequacy" (76). His inadequacy, he reasons, involves a failure to become the appropriate kind of father to his own text. Explaining his desire "to create something which is larger and richer than I am," he goes on to observe that a writer writes to transcend his paternal failings. The satisfaction of an author, he says, is "much like that of a father who has seen his son succeed where he has failed" (*Letters,* 119).

At the same time, everything about the way Steinbeck describes his process of composition suggests that he imagines himself something of a mother to his texts as well. And as we have seen, nothing makes Steinbeck more anxious than motherhood. Following this analogy through, we begin to see Steinbeck himself shadowing Rose's growing form. Amid the numerous and remarkable identifications Steinbeck effects between himself and the Joads in his working journal, he makes clear that, as much as he is like the men in the novel, he is perhaps most like Rose, whose child grows within just as surely as *The Grapes of Wrath* took form over its carefully planned and executed composition. Steinbeck decided to allow himself no more than seven months of home confinement. Accordingly, he sat down to write his novel at the start of May 1938 and, working at home every day for the next six months, finished at the end of October. And as his journal makes clear, Steinbeck had in mind the novel's remarkable final image from the moment he began this deliberate process. The one thing of which he was certain from the start was that his novel would conclude with Rose, suddenly deprived of her child, offering her breast to a dying stranger. Rose's stillborn delivery, like the rigidly scheduled completion of the novel itself, is the "huge and symbolic" action "toward which the whole story moves." So, even as Rose's delivery seems to fuse with Steinbeck's, even as the writing of the novel is almost exactly coterminus with Rose's pregnancy, Steinbeck plans from the start to abort his own delivery in richly symbolic fashion.

"The ruthlessness of my design to be a writer," Steinbeck wrote at this time, needs to win out over "mother and hell."[55] The ruthlessness of Steinbeck's male appropriation of female creative powers, in other words, entailed more than simply appropriating a sentimental genre that had seemed the exclusive domain of both female authors and a laissez-faire market for writing. It involved as well a distinctly process-oriented, agentless poetics: just as fathers were to teach mothers to forget about their own and to attach themselves, through moments of public sympathy, to objects external to themselves, Steinbeck imagined writing itself as a process that, ultimately, renounced its relation to whatever object it produced. Steinbeck insisted that "the whole future [of my] working life is tied up in [a] distinction between work and person" (*Letters,* 119). Winning out over mother and hell meant brutally enforcing this distinction. "Forget that baby," Ma Joad urges her daughter. "He'll take care of hisself." For Steinbeck, this advice extended readily to writing itself. "The way to write," Steinbeck would declare in his introduction to *Cannery Row* (1945), is "to open the page and to let the stories crawl in by themselves."[56]

Steinbeck's repression of his authorial agency in writing went hand and hand with his symbolic disavowal of ownership in the writing he did produce. Despite the fact that he and Carol were closing on an extremely large property as he was finishing the book, despite as well that the enormous proceeds anticipated from his novel were Pat Covici's only hope to stay independent of Viking Press, Steinbeck imagined himself something of a worker, a day laborer with no real recourse to capital. He imagined himself, like the Joads, en route to a market for his labor. Thus his working journal documents in painstaking detail the day-to-day travails of his writing, the grueling hardships he endured during its composition.

Promoting copyright reform in the July 1946 *Screen Writer,* James M. Cain made exactly the opposite claim; he urged writers to view themselves as capitalists and not as wage laborers. The problem with copyright law, he argued, was that it saw a writer's earnings as income from his labor, as opposed to income from a property that he owned. Not only should a writer be taxed on capital gain as opposed to regular income, Cain reasoned that copyright law should be changed to grant writers unambiguous ownership of their work. Meaning to drive home this point, Cain analogized babies to books: a writer creates "property," he argued, "and he knows that he has just so many of these ova in his belly, and indeed he is never sure that the latest one he produced will not be his last; it is a special, peculiar, heart-breaking business."[57] Cain compared novels to ova to insist that literary works were artifacts uniquely bonded to their creators. These artifacts could never, he insisted, be valued simply in terms of the labor that produced them: "One's work," he reasons in his 1946 essay, "done at great labor, time, and expense, may bring almost no return, while another done with comparative ease may be a gold mine and may, more importantly, be the only gold mine the writer ever sees."[58]

Never one to insist on the unbreakable bond between a mother and her child, Steinbeck used the same analogy toward an entirely different end: books needed to be separated from their authors precisely because they were like children, who also needed to be separated from their mothers. Steinbeck left his own book just as surely as the men in his novel leave their families; he dispossessed himself of his artifact just as surely as he dispossesses Rose of her child. "I want this book to be itself with no history and no writer" (*Letters,* 181), Steinbeck held forth. Just as he insists that Rose knows nothing about the origins of the man for whom she cares — that, in general, aid be rendered precisely in the absence of a personal relation between giver and recipient — he claimed to want his book to approach readers with a similar strangeness. A character in *Tortilla Flats* states, "The good story lay in half-told things which must be filled in out of the hearer's own experience" (407). In this context, Steinbeck's flight from his own literary object — manifest in his attempts to detach authorial intention from the public consumption of that object — is of a piece with Stevens's claim that "the basis of criticism is not the hidden intention of the author," and even more so with W. K. Wimsatt and Monroe C. Beardsley's claim that the poem belongs to "the public" because "it is detached from the author at birth and goes about the world beyond his power to intend about it or control it."[59] Orphaned, the literary text throws itself upon the kindness of an impersonal public.

If Steinbeck's disavowal of his completed novel makes him less like a reproductive laborer (or more like the kind of reproductive laborer Rose is taught to become), it simultaneously frees him to engage in commerce with exactly this public. For Steinbeck, books need to be separated from their authors — in the same way that children need to be separated from their mothers — precisely so authors can gain entrance to the civic ether inhabited by figures like Connie and Tom. Accordingly, Steinbeck could reassure himself that, as much as he seemed like Rose, freighted with commodity and en route to an uncertain market, he was in fact more like Connie and Tom, more like a salaried shaper of public policy than a reproductive laborer.

So, while Carol Steinbeck assisted in New Deal relief efforts, Steinbeck stayed at home writing his novel, as well as the occasional letter to Roosevelt, all the while figuring out how it made sense to engage readers instead of hungry bodies. The dying stranger — a figure for Steinbeck's readers, I want finally to suggest — emerges with such force at the close of *The Grapes of Wrath* not because he is more in need than the Joads themselves, but because he is resolutely anonymous. Steinbeck's stranger is no mere person; he is nothing less than a reading public that could imagine itself both giver and recipient of aid, a reading public that, in the narcissistic self-identifications explored in the next chapter, could sympathize mainly with itself. Rose's delivery must be stillborn, it now becomes possible to see, precisely so Rose can engage in the novel's most emblematically theatrical act, so that Steinbeck can give sustenance to his reading public through Rose. Thus Steinbeck offers the substance of a new kind of sentiment. As committed to the theatrical, spectatorial relations of sympathy as *The Grapes of Wrath* proves to be, one can see in its staged conclusion a by now familiar turn back toward the absorptive, back toward the New Deal project of collapsing aesthetic production and consumption so completely that no difference remains between a writer and his audience, between a writer's literary labors and the eventual enjoyment of his work. Male abstraction is as important as it is, Steinbeck concludes, in parenthood and in literary production both, not simply because it chastens the otherwise selfish, anticivic impulses of maternal care but because it substitutes for these values a paternal code that binds the hardships of wage labor to the very principle, if not the actual practice, of social justice.

Chapter Five

"The Death of the Gallant Liberal"

Robert Frost, Richard Wright, and Busby Berkeley

. . . I am a totalist
And hope that others soon may see the light.
Co-operation is the breath and blood
Of true democracy, while we have made
A god of rugged individualism
As if it meant a sacred right to pick
Your neighbor's pocket undisturbed by law.
And should that neighbor starve, the help he gets
Is charity, and not his rightful share
In harvests that were made by all for all.
We have been told democracy must mean
That every man is held responsible
For what we call the state. Is it not time
To turn around and start considering
The state's responsibility for all?
The man who has no food, or clothes, or home,
Can be of little use as citizen,
And it is foolish to expect his vote —
The only thing of value he has left —
To register much interest in a whole
Of which he cannot feel himself a part.
— Edwin Bjorkman, from "Old Barham on Democracy"[1]

At a memorial service held just after Robert Frost's death in 1963,
John F. Kennedy eulogized the poet, surprisingly enough, as a lone
figure standing against a monolithic state. Kennedy, the highest representative of that state, declared that Frost, who had figured so
prominently in the public ritual of Kennedy's own inauguration, em-

· · ·

bodied the artist's position as "the last champion of the individual mind and sensibility against an intrusive society and an officious state." "The great artist," the president proclaimed, is "a solitary figure. He has, as Frost said, 'a lover's quarrel with the world.' "[2] Although this might seem to have assigned the state too oppressive a role, it actually explained why the state needed artists. "I see little of more importance to the future of our country and our civilization," Kennedy said, "than full recognition of the place of the artist. If art is to nourish the roots of our culture, society must set the artist free to follow his vision wherever it takes him." That Frost's particular vision took him to pay an unauthorized visit to Nikita Khrushchev in 1962 did not, apparently, diminish his ability to nurture the roots of American culture. For Kennedy's language suggested that the artist was of public value precisely in his or her opposition to the government's absorptive mechanisms, including even those ideological formations that so strenuously enlisted Americans in the cause of the cold war.

But Kennedy reasoned that the artist was most free when bound to the state with federal support for his or her work, not when engaged in political acts. Unfortunately, in Kennedy's eyes, writers had not been supported as a group by the state since 1943, when the New Deal terminated its Federal Arts Projects. Twenty years later, the president wanted the writer back. Earlier that year, he had established the Advisory Council on the Arts, forerunner of the NEA, toward just this end. In his statement announcing the formation of the Council, Kennedy invoked an argument that had been at the core of the Federal Arts Projects: "The concept of the public welfare," he insisted, "should reflect cultural as well as physical values, aesthetic as well as economic considerations."[3] In this context, Frost embodies for Kennedy the necessary relation between "the public welfare" and a form of public art designed to facilitate the individual's amicable resistance to the state. But though the president makes Frost a guardian of the public welfare — by 1963, conceived in terms of national as opposed to social security — his eulogy captures equally well how the New Deal structured the poetry it praised.

Standing over Frost's grave, Kennedy declared that Frost had "a lover's quarrel with the world," borrowing from Frost's "The Lesson for Today" (1942). In this poem, a speaker discusses the relation of the individual to the state while standing by the side of his own grave;

the line Kennedy cites — "I had a lover's quarrel with the world" — is the epitaph this speaker imagines for himself. It is, he says, what "I would have written of me on my stone."[4] In what follows, I take up similar epitaphic doublings in New Deal modernist texts from the thirties, forties, and fifties, all of which use imaginative conjurings of future death to negotiate the politics of welfare. Busby Berkeley's gleeful *Gold Diggers of 1937,* for example, discussed below with "The Lesson," depicts a manager of an insurance company telling his salesmen that the best way to close a sale is to get the prospective buyer to "see himself in his own grave." Richard Wright makes a strikingly similar gesture in *The Outsider* (1953). Strolling in a cemetery, the existential antihero Cross Damon pictures his own epitaph on a tombstone and shortly thereafter starts "thinking about taking out some insurance."[5]

There are any number of accounts of the split personality in modernity that might accurately describe these imaginary flights of self-transcendence; Henry David Thoreau's "being beside ourselves in a sane way," Walt Whitman's "Both in and out of the game, and watching and wondering at it," and William James's examination of "The Divided Self" in *The Varieties of Religious Experience* (1902) offer a start. Also pertinent are W. E. B. Du Bois's *The Souls of Black Folks* (1903), Jean-Paul Sartre's *Being and Nothingness* (1943), Frantz Fanon's *Black Skin, White Masks* (1952), and Deleuze and Guattari's *Anti-Oedipus: Capitalism and Schizophrenia* (1972), all of which offer broadly psychological accounts of similar self-displacements.[6] In what follows, however, I explain the distinctly visual conjuring of one's death not in terms of the complexities of what Kennedy called "the individual mind," but in terms of structures of psychic identification mobilized both in acts of sympathy and in the pursuit of social security. One-time Communist Party activist, "client" of the New Deal's Federal Writers' Project, civil servant, and insurance agent, Richard Wright epitomizes this pursuit and all of its attendant doublings.

James Farrell's *Yet Other Waters* offers a ready example of the conjunction between insurance and sympathy that I wish to point out. In Farrell's novel, the author Bernard Carr (modeled on Farrell) reveals a tendency to confuse himself with his fictional character, Paddy Stanton (modeled on Studs Lonigan). Carr "had imagined himself being battered and beaten with police clubs, and then as going insane because he'd been hit on the head, the fate of his hero in *Paddy Stanton.* He had seen himself becoming a martyr, an object of sympathy and pity. He had even imagined himself killed, and he'd visualized his own funeral, with hundreds attending it. Last night in bed he'd actually composed his own obituary for the Left and liberal press."[7] But whereas Carr confesses his theatrical tendency to make himself as much an object of sympathy as Stanton, he also insists on a cruel distinction between himself and Stanton. Responding to the question, "But isn't he [Paddy Stanton] you?" Carr answers that for Stanton, "the world has to be one of certitude. . . . That's why I used the title of one of John Dewey's books on the quotation page — 'The Quest of Certainty.' That's Paddy Stanton's real quest — for certainty. I neither look for nor believe in certainty. Intellectually, Paddy is the exact opposite of me" (88). Carr is more than just skeptical when it comes to certainty; he wants none of it. When his father-in-law asks, "You don't have insurance, do you, Bernard?" he responds, "No, I don't need any" (245); the truth is he "knew nothing about insurance . . . he didn't want to take out insurance because of his views on the downfall of capitalism, and it excited him to be able to ignore taking out an insurance policy" (245). But in fact, Carr admits that he does have a policy of his own: "Reading," he thinks to himself, "was his intellectual insurance" (246).

Carr's suggestion that reading is a form of insurance might seem particularly difficult given Carr's tendency to confuse himself with Stanton; for Carr does more than read, he persistently imagines that he is an object read by himself and others. But as Adam Smith might have pointed out, this confusion is fundamental to Carr's becoming "an object of sympathy" (the condition that leads him to a discussion of insurance in the first place). For Smith, sympathetic identification depends on a series of such displacements through which individuals read themselves and others through borrowed lenses. "As Adam Smith contends," observes Elizabeth Barnes, "we not only sympathize with others according to what we imagine they feel, we judge our own actions according to whether or not we can imagine others sympathizing with them. 'We can never survey our own sentiments and motives,' nor 'form any judgement concerning them,' says Smith, 'unless we remove ourselves, as it were, from our own natural station' and 'view them with the eyes of other people.' "[8] This holds equally, Smith reasons, when, like Bernard Carr, we objectify our own abject condition and feel sympathy for ourselves. Barnes again: "Smith theorizes a primary alienation from oneself, the result of a kind of 'mirror of sympathy' in David Marshall's words, whereby initial sufferers become 'spectators to [their] spectators and thereby spectators to [themselves].' Putting himself in the position of the observer, the sufferer acts as observer to himself, becoming at once both spectator and spectacle. This sense of alienation is for Smith the greatest affliction, just as the strongest desire is not a relief *from* pain but *for* a 'more complete sympathy. [The sufferer] longs for that relief which nothing can afford him but the entire concord of the affections of the spectators with his own.' Of course this is exactly what the experience of sympathy has taught him he cannot have" (34). The self-scrutinizing sufferer cannot have this experience, Barnes reasons, because, at least "for Smith, sympathetic identification is a relational dynamic. Total identification with the other person might extinguish sympathy altogether since sympathy operates by a simultaneous awareness of separateness and inclination to overcome it." Barnes explains that "as Smith presents it, sympathy denotes both psychological attachment — or empathy, as we might term it — and psychological distance. That is, the self is constituted by acts of the imagination that simultaneously connect and distinguish it from projected images of other selves not unlike one's own" (21).

Reading about his own threatened body (in the form of Stanton's), Carr engages in exactly this contingent identification with a larger group, for he is alternately part of the reading public that consumes his fiction as well as the subject of that fiction itself. It makes sense to think of this kind of reading as a form of New Deal social insurance because insurance depends on this same double identification. As I have already pointed out, Michael Denning's *Cultural Front* insists that the New Deal was committed to preserving the legacy of individualism so central to nineteenth-century liberalism. For cultural critic C. L. R. James, on the other hand, the sudden emergence of social security as the dominant cultural paradigm during the New Deal effectively collapsed the difference between the state and the more overtly collectivizing strategies of the left. Writing between 1938 and 1953 in what would become *American Civilization,* he claimed that "the outstanding social fact of the United States is that the population has gone a long way on the road to recognizing that freedom has been lost." The "welfare state," he consequently argues, "actually proposes now no longer freedom but security."[9] But in fact, both Denning and James are correct, for social security involves a reconciliation of liberalism to very real losses of freedom made manifest during the Great Depression. François Ewald notes that the "abstract technology of insurance" offers "a form of association which combines a maximum of socialization with a maximum of individualization. It allows people to enjoy the advantages of association while still leaving them free to exist as individuals. It seems to reconcile those two antagonists, society-socialization and individual liberty."[10] In its effort to "reconcile" the classical-liberal "antagonists" of self and society, an "abstract technology of insurance" such as social security does more than simply make money available: it offers its recipients an imaginative mechanism for organizing their relations to the world, a phenomonology that produces the same acute schizophrenia found in Farrell and explained in Smith. Because social security understands individual action both as the result of an intention to act and as a predictable instance of structurally determined behavior patterns, it is continually offering its consumers a picture of the world in which they are both passive and active, isolate victims of circumstance and collectivized agents of their own salvation.

Comparing the phenomenological procedures attendant on the execution of sympathy and the consumption of insurance might seem to ignore what is most characteristic of sympathy, namely, its ability to generate affect. Insurance, it would seem, renders affect an altogether irrelevant category. Insurance is not charity; we don't collect from insurance companies because they feel sorry for us, but rather because we have paid for the benefits we receive. In this account, insurance affiliates individuals with financial collectives precisely to moot the role of sympathy in producing harmonious social outcomes (Social Security is preferable to straight welfare, we might reason, because its recipients earn their payments, because the state need not sympathize with them to provide them with funds). But from another perspective, insurance reworks the dynamics of sympathy in purely formal terms precisely because it is able radically to adumbrate the range of "fellow feeling" on which it need draw to perform its functions. Far from depending on the emotional experience of others, insurance requires an entirely narcissistic form of self-sympathy; it requires, in other words, that doubled condition in which individuals are spectators to their own suffering. "The mood of a man insuring his life is not unlike that of a man signing his will," observes Truman Capote in *In Cold Blood* (1965), "thoughts of [his own] mortality must occur."[11] Seen from this vantage, insurance does not get rid of sympathy so much as it squares the circle between its consumption and production; it asks the individual to anticipate, experience, and then come to the rescue of his or her own abject condition. In the case of private insurance, this rescue might involve nothing more than purchasing an insurance plan. In the case of the social insurance with which Wright is preoccupied, self-salvation comes by recognizing the extent to which one is always already contributing to and represented in the state collectives that rescue one from insecurity.

Though the sympathy of others is not literally required in the individual consumption of insurance, some vestigial interest in group affect remains integral. Having internally generated sympathy for his own future state, the consumer of insurance, the texts that follow all suggest, proceeds to displace his affective experience of himself onto the actuarial collective of which he is a part. Carr does not rush out to purchase insurance after witnessing his own death, as do characters in Berkeley and Wright; finding insurance only in the equivocal identifications of reading, Carr needs to imagine he becomes "an object of sympathy" not simply to himself but to the hundreds he envisions attending his funeral. Frost, Berkeley, and Wright, on the other hand, don't need Carr's funeral scene because the collective sympathy it stages has already been internalized in the forms of insurance toward which they turn. Insurance is as compelling as it is in their texts because it suggests that the only sympathy necessary to secure the individual from harm is the kind of anticipatory self-sympathy that leads one to purchase insurance in the first place. Consequently, Frost, Berkeley, and Wright equate the dynamics of sympathy and social security not by asking what it means to be loved by a collective but rather by asking how it is that one loves such a group oneself. What we find in these texts are not absolute equations between individual and group feeling, but partial, ambivalent gestures at union: Frost's "lover's quarrel with the world," or the musical number "All's Fair in Love and War" in *The Gold Diggers of 1937*. These curiously incomplete couplings of personal and impersonal affect continue Steinbeck's project of questioning exactly how individuals establish meaningful relations with abstract publics; so too they serve more broadly to interrogate how and to what extent a liberalism organized around social security is able to reconcile not simply individual and group interest, but individual and group feeling as well.

Wright might seem a counterintuitive choice here, if only because of his insistence that in writing *Native Son* he wished to avoid garnering undue sympathy for Bigger Thomas. In "How 'Bigger' Was Born" he states that prior to starting the novel he realized, "I had written a book of short stories which was published under the title of *Uncle Tom's Children*. When the reviews of that book began to appear, I realized that I had made an awfully naïve mistake. I found that I had written a book which even bankers' daughters could read and weep over and feel good about. I swore to myself that if I ever wrote another book, no one would weep over it; that it would be so hard and deep that they would have to face it without the consolation of tears."[12] James Baldwin was quick to point out some nine years later that *Native Son* hardly constituted a victory over its author's naïveté. *Native Son* is hopelessly sentimental, Baldwin maintains in "Everybody's Protest Novel," regardless of whether or not it brings bankers' daughters to tears. Speaking out in defense of the "unpredictable" human being, condemning at the same time James M. Cain's *The Postman Always Rings Twice* (a novel terrified by the unpredictable), Baldwin accuses Wright's opus of buying into the theologically laden, black-and-white presuppositions of *Uncle Tom's Cabin*; "shouting curses" at the self-evident horrors of racism, looking for clarity where there can be none, Wright's novel, Baldwin concludes, wallows in self-indulgent and ultimately specious moral indignation.[13]

Baldwin's astute but often needlessly vindictive observations depend on an unambiguously severe definition of sentimental literature: "Sentimentality," he declares, "the ostentatious parading of excessive and spurious emotion, is the mark of dishonesty, the inability to feel; the wet eyes of the sentimentalist betray his aversion to experience, his fear of life, his arid heart; and it is always, therefore, the signal of secret and violent inhumanity, the mask of cruelty" (14). These accusations, I think, do not ring true with *Native Son*. But at the same time, the novel does work within the orbit of sentimental fiction, specifically within the spectral politics of sympathy mentioned above. Wright's sentimental fantasy of weeping bankers' daughters is simply displaced into his novel: Mary Dalton is exactly the kind of reader Wright says he wishes not to bring to tears. Her subsequent death at Thomas's hands seems explainable in part by the fact that she shows Thomas forms of sympathy to which he is unaccustomed. Far from constituting a refusal of the sentimental form, this dynamic in which women are punished for inappropriate uses of sympathy is, we have seen, absolutely constitutive of the New Deal sentimental novel. So, despite Wright's stoic commentary — indeed, despite Max's anguished response when on the last page of the novel Thomas turns his back, refuses any final gestures of sympathy, and declares, "What I killed for, I *am*!" (501) — it is not surprising that *Native Son* was trumpeted in *The Herald Tribune* as "*The Grapes of Wrath* of 1940."[14] In many respects, this comparison was dead-on: following Bigger Thomas's passage out of his own home and into the home of a WPA sponsor, out of that home and into jail, and then, finally, out of jail and into the disembodied ether of the New Deal public sphere, *Native Son* essentially duplicates Tom Joad's ascension into the realm of "spirit." That Bigger Thomas effects these transitions by accidentally and then intentionally killing women is less a corruption of Steinbeck's sentimental form than its logical completion.

The Outsider follows *The Grapes of Wrath* even more closely, as it chronicles Cross Damon's flight from his family and children and even his body into the existential world of political philosophy. "The Negro," Wright proclaimed in 1945, had been "a more or less free agent for more than 75 years."[15] *The Outsider,* however, would show just how insubstantial this juridical claim truly was. Damon is decidedly not a free agent because, he reasons, his body blocks the realization of his thoughts and desires; he begins the novel "despairingly aware of his body as an alien and despised object over which he had no power, a burden that was always cheating him of the fruits of his thought, mocking him with its stubborn and supine solidity" (16). Damon's recalcitrant body finds a natural home in the novel's world of contingency. "Time alone," he declares, "made this teeming world gush and roar like a Niagara with its richness of unforeseeable events; it was only by plunging rashly onward that one could see at all" (443).[16] Thus the murderous Damon, characterized as "an accident going somewhere to happen" (89), plunges forward into the "richness of unforeseeable events" by inscribing what he calls "the death of the gallant liberal" (481) on the bodies of his victims. The gallant liberal, however, dies only a symbolic death; he dies to be reinvented. Damon, we will see, manages to rid himself of his body and join Tom Joad in his quest for social justice.

But Damon does not stay disembodied for long, and his eventual reembodiment — a rebirth of the gallant liberal — has everything to do with the New Deal revision of liberalism. "A change came over the spirit and meaning of liberalism," observes John Dewey in *Liberalism and Social Action,* his philosophical defense of the New Deal. "It came surely, if gradually, to be disassociated from the laissez-faire creed and to be associated with the use of government action for aid to those at economic disadvantage and for alleviation from their conditions."[17] Likewise, Wright's liberalism is premised on the substantial revision of a laissez-faire philosophy that posited abstract persons dispossessed of precisely those material conditions that put Black Americans, from the start, "at economic disadvantage."[18] Imperative to this revision is Damon's need to reestablish himself in relation to what he calls "the claims of others" (196). He becomes a killer at the start of the novel in part because he makes a rational choice to disavow all manner of social responsibility but also because he experiences a complete failure to feel himself in any kind of meaningful relation to those around him. If, as Barnes notes, the sympathetic self is "constituted by acts of the imagination that simultaneously connect and distinguish it from projected images of other selves not unlike one's own," then Damon begins the novel utterly unwilling to establish sympathetic connections with those around him; he starts out, he says, wanting "to sever all ties . . . of sentimentality" (114). *The Outsider* follows Damon in his efforts to return to the community-building functions of sentiment, an ultimately fruitless quest that concludes when he tearfully confesses just before he dies his inability to feel "a direct bridge between the subjective worlds of people" (446).

In both *Native Son* and *The Outsider,* Wright's characters find their way to this bridge to the degree that they reconcile an account of their agency in which intention is paramount, to an opposed account in which decisions are structurally determined, whether by racism or less malevolent environmental determinants. As determined as Bigger Thomas seems to be by the racism around him, Wright is quick to qualify that he "was not black all the time," and insists that *Native Son* itself, like a "swinging pendulum" moving between "concrete picture[s]" and "abstract linkages," understands Thomas in both representative and idiosyncratic terms.[19] Critics have used similar terms to describe Wright's other work as well. Situating him in the context of modern urban sociology, Carla Cappetti notes that Wright's autobiographies are torn between "the tendency toward a more subjective sociology, a sociology that rediscovered the subjectivity of the individual as a social and cultural being," and "the tendency toward a more objective literature, a literature that rediscovered the individual's unbreakable ties with the larger cultural and social spheres." Cappetti sees Wright as preoccupied with the desire to reconcile the "contradictions between individual and group," between the antithetical categories of "personality" and "environment."[20] In turn, criticisms of Wright often focus on his perceived inability to reconcile these antinomies: Kwame Anthony Appiah says of *Black Power* (1954), for example, that Wright's interest in emotional depth is "oddly in conflict with the high purpose announced in Wright's preface and the 'scientific' language of the informational discourse that he promised."[21]

But Wright's liberalism absolutely depends on the fact that the emotions are never in conflict with the impersonal mechanisms of scientific discourse. His most objectifying representations of the social come on the heels of his most subjective, affective identifications. This is the function of the epitaphic moments mentioned above: characters move toward the spatializing, objectifying mechanisms of insurance only after they become spectators of their own suffering. Hence Frost's speaker, who declares himself "liberal," is able to find solace from "this uncertain world in which we dwell" in the doubling that characterizes his epitaphic encounter. He decides, we will see, that he is, at one and the same time, both autonomous and subsumed within what he calls a "total race." Whereas Frost's speaker claims membership in a "total race" after he serenely contemplates the universal experience of death, Wright's characters, less abstractly conceived, feel part of a total race only when faced with the traumatic immediacy of their own impending deaths. But they do in fact get to leave their race behind just before they die: in *Native Son,* with moments left to live, Bigger imagines himself absorbed into a "vast crowd of . . . white men and black men and all men" (420). Thus Wright suggests that "general social and employment insurance without discrimination" might take on the role of social institutions that, at least according to Henry James, had been conspicuously absent in the American novel. Wright imagines state insurance replacing race as a paradigm that mediates between the individual and those uncontrollable forces so central to the history of American naturalism; for Wright, I suggest, the actuarial engine of insurance helps give shape to "the items, political, social, and personal [that determine] character-destiny" in his fiction.[22]

In *The Outsider,* Damon's brash individualism leads him to declare that he has no race, that "being a Negro is the least important thing in his life" (385). "The slaves of today," Damon reasons as he transposes the racial to the existential, are those who "fall on their knees and break into a sweat when confronted with the horrible truth of the uncertain and enigmatic nature of life" (484). But *The Outsider* also insists that being Black brings with it a phenomenology particularly adequate, we will see, to the requirements of sympathy and social security. "Negroes," declares a character in the novel, "are going to be gifted with a double vision, for, being Negroes, they are going to be both inside and outside our culture at the same time" (163). This is clearly a legacy of Du Bois's "double consciousness," which describes the alienating process whereby the Black subject anticipates and internalizes the responses White culture has to him. And Wright's use of the word "gifted" suggests that, like Du Bois, he is acutely aware of the extent to which a "double vision" can be, in the words of Paul Gilroy, "neither simply a disability, nor a consistent privilege."[23] But this is Du Bois with a significant difference, for if Du Bois characterized double consciousness as the Black subject's tendency to see himself through the eyes of an externalized White world, Wright's double consciousness — absolutely constitutive of his social security — involves exactly the reverse dynamic, one in which the Black subject looks back at the world spatially, from the outside. The doubleness constitutive of Frost, Berkeley, and Wright, in other words, requires both the capacity to imagine oneself in the future — either damaged and receiving the benefits one has paid for, or dead and dispensing those benefits to others — and the capacity to transcend embodiment and look on oneself and one's encompassing group from without. These authors replace the temporal project of imagining future contingency with a spatial mechanism for addressing it: looking on themselves from without, the characters in Frost, Berkeley, and Wright recognize the extent to which they are engaged both by the double logic of liberalism and its protocols of congenial dissent.

1.

And it comes to this: That always I feel another hand, not mine,
   has drawn and turned the card to find some incredible
   ace,
And another word I did not write appears in the spirit parch-
   ment prepared by me,
Always another face I do not know shows in the dream, the
   crystal globe, or the flame.
— Kenneth Fearing, "Readings, Forecasts, Personal Guidance,"
in *The Agency, 1938–1940*

"This man is with Uncle Sam, win, lose, or draw," declares the civil
servant Jake Jackson in Wright's posthumously published *Lawd Today* (1963). Moments later, Jackson stares transfixed at a sign that
boldly reads "GUARANTEED INSURANCE." Jackson will subse-
quently say of New Dealers, in suspicious respect — for their ide-
alism — but mainly in cynical derision — for their failure to adjust
these ideals to reality — that they "don't know white from black."[24]
   During the Depression, Uncle Sam's "Guaranteed Insurance" was
the preserve of a distinctly White population. Social Security was
essentially insurance for White males who were in the position to
receive steady wages. The Social Security Administration, which did
not begin collecting taxes until 1937 and dispensing benefits until
1942, did almost nothing to help the Black community, which was
crippled by an unemployment rate between 40 and 50 percent. Helping only those who were already steadily employed, the administration offered limited assistance at best to the out-of-work or to nontraditional laborers: out of the 5.5 million Blacks working in 1935,
roughly 2 million were in agriculture and another 1.5 were in domestic service; neither group was eligible for benefits.[25] This is why, one
suspects, Wallace Stevens is able to include the poem "Like Decorations in a Nigger Cemetery" in *Ideas of Order,* a book of poems that,
he claims, "reflects" "changes occurring today . . . that raise questions of political and social order."[26] For despite these changes, the
political and social order initiated by the New Deal remained in many
ways fundamentally racist and hostile to Blacks. The NRA, to take
another example, was derisively referred to as the Negro Removal
Act, and the WPA for which Wright worked persistently doled out

undesirable jobs to its Black participants.[27] Thus, just as the speaker of "The Idea of Order at Key West" turns toward "order" as a function of turning away from a woman, so it appears that *Ideas of Order* uses "Nigger Cemetery" in similar fashion. In the poem, a speaker muses on the death and burial of a Black population at Key West, symbolically excluding "niggers" from the "perfect insurance" that (as I argue in chapter 3) the book of poems is meant to embody.[28] In fact, the death of non-White populations is built into the very name of Key West, which the WPA *Key West Guide* informs us is so named "because early explorers of the Caucasian race found bones scattered about the island, and . . . called the little reef 'Cayo Hueso,' or 'Bone Key.' Key West is the English corruption of the Spanish 'Cayo Hueso.' "[29]

Still, the Black press was divided over how to view the New Deal. The Democratic Black Congressman from Chicago, Arthur W. Mitchell, was predictably sanguine about its racial orientation: "Mr. Roosevelt," he declared to Congress on 13 August 1935, "promised not only a 'new deal' but a square deal to the Negro during his campaign. He knew then as he knows now that the Negro is the most forgotten of all forgotten men in this country. He has kept his promise. Every instance of race discrimination that has been properly brought to the attention of the President has not only received immediate attention but has been amicably adjusted as far as the authority of the Executive Office could go."[30] Those not directly involved in New Deal politics were less wide-eyed. George Edmund Haynes castigated "lily-white social security" in *The Crisis*;[31] in the same journal, John P. Davis observed that Roosevelt's programs were neither "new" nor "square," but rather part of a "raw deal" that perpetuated all the worst pre–New Deal forms of American racial discrimination.[32] Writing in *Opportunity,* Robert Weaver was slightly more circumspect. "It is impossible," he reasons, "to discuss intelligently the New Deal and the Negro without considering the status of the Negro prior to the advent of the recovery program. The present economic position of the colored citizen was not created by the recent legislation alone." Pointing out the persistent discrimination in agriculture and housing, Weaver nonetheless concludes, "Given the economic situation of 1932, the New Deal has been more helpful than harmful to Negroes. We had unemployment in 1932. Jobs were being lost by Negroes and they were in need. Many would have starved had there been no Federal relief program."[33] In *Black Metropolis,* a sociological study of Chicago for which Wright wrote an introduction, Horace Cayton and St. Clair Drake confirm this view: "Data concerning pre-Depression incomes assembled for this study indicate that in a significant number of cases even the bare subsistence level permitted by relief allowances and WPA wages constituted a definitely higher material standard of living for the lowest income group than did the wages earned in private industry."[34]

No surprise, then, that despite the racism rampant in its programs, Black communities began in 1932 to turn to the New Deal in unprecedented numbers. Lizabeth Cohen observes that by 1937, Black workers were declaring, "Our survival depends on a strong federal government, and the Democrats, both in Chicago and Washington, are the only ones who can give it to us." The WPA in particular, notes Cohen, was "one of the New Deal programs most responsible for orienting blacks toward the federal government."[35] Wright was part of this new orientation, particularly from 1935 to 1939, when he wrote parts of *Native Son* while receiving a government wage from the WPA's Writers' Projects in Illinois and New York. By all accounts, this experience was profoundly formative for Wright. Wright biographer Michel Fabre suggests that the Writers' Project more adequately spoke to Wright than the Communist Party ever did. "It seems that Wright's motives for joining," Fabre reasons, "were more literary than political. Since he had never had the chance to escape his total intellectual isolation by going to college or associating with his white contemporaries, the [John Reed] club was the only bridge between his cultural ghetto and the American intellectual world."[36] Margaret Walker, who served with Wright on the Illinois Project, notes that "the explosion of [Wright's] genius coincided with the [cultural] explosion of the WPA."[37] According to Nelson Algren, who served with Wright on the Creative Writers Project, Wright was "more alert" to the advantages of the project than any other so employed.[38]

Wright was alert as well to the fact that most Black Americans suffered without any such advantages. Speaking for Southern Blacks migrating to Chicago during the thirties in *Twelve Million Black Voices* (1941), Wright says: "We hear talk vaguely of a government in far away Washington, a government that stands above the people and desires the welfare of all. . . . More to keep faith alive in our hearts than from any conviction that our lot will be better, we cling to the hope that the government would help us if it could."[39] Although *Twelve Million Black Voices* is itself a product of the government it describes — Wright's prose is accompanied by photographs from the Farm Securities Administration — these lines insist on the chilling remoteness of New Deal social policies. This same remoteness is evident six years later when Wright declares that "perhaps never in 2000 years has the reality of the state been so dim in men's mind."[40] This just one year after he documented his persecution at the hands of the American intelligence community in his "FB Eye Blues" (1947):

> Woke up this morning
> FB eye under my bed
> Said I woke up this morning
> FB eye under my bed
> Told me all I dreamed last night,
>   every word I said.[41]

If the social security state was dim, the national security state loomed uncomfortably. But as much as his intimate brushes with the FBI made the state unavoidably palpable, the "reality" of the state did not register for Wright in its authoritarian transgressions, but in its commitment, however sporadic, to the "welfare of all."

Perhaps more than any other of his novels, *The Outsider,* written some thirteen years after he left the WPA, embodies Wright's commitment to this ideal. At the novel's start, Damon is a debased personification of the New Deal. Comparing him to Roosevelt's Triple-A Farm Program, a friend jokes, "Cross is trying to imitate the United States' government. They said the trouble with Cross is his four As. *Alcohol. Abortions. Automobiles.* And *alimony.* They called C-cross the Q-quadruple-A Program. Said that the best thing for Cross w-was to plow h-himself under" (4). Like the fields that Roosevelt's Triple-A paid to be left fallow, Damon is plowed under in an accidental train wreck just pages later at "Roosevelt Street Station." The authorities mistakenly identify a body mangled in the wreck as Damon's, bury it, and presume him dead. Emerging as a politically marked specter from this premature death, Damon spends the remainder of the novel trying to revive what he calls "a third set of ideas" between communism and fascism (376).[42] The ideal of social security, it seems, played no small part in this "third way." As early as 1935, Wright had formulated what he called a "Personalist Aesthetic" bent on striving "to heighten the consciousness of the [petty bourgeoisie] to all those progressive forces making for security in American life."[43] Eighteen years later, the year he published *The Outsider,* his views had not changed: he observed that "Europe has a dilemma. . . . It stands before the choice of defending itself against [its own] military powers, or deciding to provide complete social security for its population."[44] Wright was convinced that the United States had already made the incorrect choice, that the New Deal had been, like Damon, ploughed under; he mourned the passing of "the glorious Rooseveltian experiment — the liberalism of the Roosevelt era"[45] and complained while he wrote *The Outsider* that "Southern Democrats and Northern conservatives — most of them Republicans — [were] chopping away at whatever was good in the New Deal."[46] Published just after the electoral victory of the first Republican president since Herbert Hoover, the novel suggests that Damon — like Tom Joad before him, a ghost without a family — "had to be born again, come anew into the world" (167).

Whereas Damon struggles to replace his family with a third set of ideas that might reinvigorate the New Deal welfare state, *Native Son*'s Bigger Thomas is "born again" into the state in a more immediate sense. Thomas goes to work for the Daltons as part of his WPA relief; they become his first substitute, state-sponsored family. As biographer Fabre notes, the WPA was just such a family to Wright: the organization offered Wright "an ideal brotherhood of intellectuals"; his friends on the project, Willard Maas, Marie Mencken, Helen Neville, Ralph Ellison, Claude McKay, and Roi Ottley, "were Wright's new spiritual family, the stimulating and varied company he enjoyed when tired from writing *Native Son.*"[47] Part of this group, Chester Himes expresses a similar sentiment in his recollections of the Writers' Project: "We were all, black and white alike, bound together into the human family by our desperate struggle for bread."[48] The Daltons seem to offer Thomas just such a family. Mrs. Dalton, for example, is blind and cannot see Thomas's Blackness. But even as the Daltons treat him as if he were not Black at all, Thomas is betrayed by embodiment at every turn, first when his own body seems to act of its own accord and kill Mary, and second, when the ashen remains of Mary's bones are discovered in the basement furnace. If the New Deal family could not tell White from Black, the rest of the world could: reporters immediately release to the public the discovery of Mary's bones, and the manhunt is on.

New Deal relief is thus quickly collapsed into the Illinois penal code.[49] So, while Thomas is on trial before the state of Illinois, this same state — eager first to ignore the difference between Black and White and eager later to collapse manslaughter into murder when that difference reasserts itself — is on trial for not understanding how its own willful naïveté renders it complicitous with Thomas's accidental crime. Both Thomas and the New Deal itself await judgment as the court decides whether or not to "uphold those two fundamental concepts of our civilization, those two basic concepts upon which we have built the mightiest nation in history — personality and security — the conviction that the person is inviolate and that which sustains him is equally so" (*Native Son,* 472).

Wright's own liberalism — and his concomitant distance from 1930s hard-line communism — might be gauged by his obsession with "personality." Cappetti points out that Wright uses the term "with stubborn insistence." "Personality," she explains, is seen as a "bulwark against the rising tide of conformity," particularly the conformity espoused by an axis joining "the family, the church, the school, the south, and the Communist Party."[50] The party in particular seemed to Wright unforgivably shortsighted in its refusal to come to terms with the idiosyncrasies of individual personality. One year after the publication of *Native Son* and three years before he would formally break with the Party, Wright queries Michael Gold in a letter: "Are we Communist writers to be confined merely to the political and economic spheres of reality and leave the dark hidden places of the human personality to the Hitlers and the Goebbels? I refuse to believe such."[51] In *The Outsider,* Damon reviles communist models of collectivism because they have no interest in "personality." "Do you think the party exists to provide an outlet for your personal feelings?" Damon is asked. "Hell, no! . . . Being a communist is not easy. It means negating yourself, blotting out your personal life" (248). Such acts of self-extinction could not be farther from the sensibility of *Native Son,* or, specifically, from Max's sense that the state has failed to offer Thomas the right admixture of personality and security. Thomas needs both personality and security for the same reason that Adam Smith imagines sympathy involving, in Barnes's words, "both psychological attachment . . . and psychological distance." For Smith, "the self is constituted by acts of the imagination that simultaneously connect and distinguish it from projected images of other selves not unlike one's own"; for Max, security comes when the self is connected to a group, personality when the self is distinguished from it.

Max imagines that Thomas comes closest to experiencing this double bond after he kills Mary Dalton. He says that Thomas's "accidental murder placed [Thomas] into a position where he had sensed a possible order and meaning in his relations with the people about him" (316). Thomas gets this "order and meaning," the attorney reasons, to the extent that he and the "people about him" feel themselves equally victimized by the accidental. The order and meaning to which Max gestures is constructed not in terms of the agency people share, but in terms of the agency they do not. Max would have Thomas embrace exactly the kind of powerlessness so much a part of male identity in *The Grapes of Wrath*; only then, the attorney reasons, might Thomas become an object of the court's sympathy, only then might the jury "connect and distinguish [Thomas] from projected images of other selves not unlike [their] own." That Thomas refuses this identification — he felt "there was one angle that bothered him . . . he should have *planned* it. He had acted too hastily and accidentally" (147) — is to Max the truest sign of his degradation. "He murdered Mary Dalton accidentally," Max pleads to the judge, "without thinking, without plan, without conscious motive. But after he murdered he accepted the crime. And that's the important thing. It was the first full act of his life . . . it made him free, gave him the possibility of choice" (461).

But of course, this is exactly what the court wants to hear. For if nothing else, Thomas is convicted and sentenced because he makes claim to forms of agency he should not possess. Thomas would seem at first to be set apart from White America precisely in his limited agency. The enclosed ghetto of the South Side, for example, restrains Thomas's social movement as surely as his later imprisonment: living there, he complains, "is just like living in jail" (20). But far from being willing to see him as powerless, the State of Illinois instead attributes to him actions he never performed. District Attorney Buckley is above all interested in convicting him for raping Dalton, the one crime he unambiguously did not commit. This point is crucial, for though it makes clear that Thomas would have been put to death regardless of how he responded to Dalton's suffocation, it demonstrates as well the court's categorical refusal to imagine Thomas victimized by the accidental. The frenzied racism confronting Thomas drives home more than the sexual threat White men perceive in Blacks. For in the context of the novel's concern with the difference between planned and accidental events, the hysterical response to Thomas exposes the absolute inability of the public at large to imagine Thomas as anything other than a dangerously unfettered "free agent." This is the work of the primitivism attributed to Thomas: he is derided as a "black ape" by Whites who imagine that he is capable only of acting directly and without restraint on animal instincts. As James Baldwin points out in "Everybody's Protest Novel," *Native Son* is as tragic as it is because Thomas internalizes this accusation completely, because he imagines that only violent and unimpeded action can rescue him from the social oblivion to which White America has consigned him. Baldwin points out that "it is the particular triumph of society — and its loss — that it is able to convince those people to whom it has given inferior status of the reality of this decree; it has the force and the weapons to translate its dictum into fact, so that the allegedly inferior are actually made so, insofar as the societal realities are concerned" (20). Convinced in this manner of his own inferiority, Thomas fails to see that the capacity to commit an accident is one of the most valuable of the resources persistently denied him: "Though he had killed by accident, not once did he feel the need to tell himself that it had been an accident. He was black, and he had been alone in a room where a white girl had been killed; therefore he had killed her. That was what everybody would say anyhow, no matter what he said" (*Native Son,* 119).

Thomas's intentions, such as they are, thus remain at best a secondary concern in *Native Son*. Indeed, the novel's sophistication lies in its incessant displacement of these intentions to sites both internal and external to Thomas. For example, Thomas experiences his own intentions as if they were performed by another, "doubled" version of himself. He imagines himself caged within a body that acts of its own accord. Thomas describes his own decisions as if they "were being handed down to him by some logic not his own, over which he had no control, but which he had to obey" (264). This alienation in turn leads Thomas to imagine a second agent responsible for doing what he does. He says of Dalton's death, "It was like another man stepped inside of my skin and started acting for me" (407).

Such doublings are the hallmark of numerous New Deal texts concerned to account for determining "logics" not the product of individual agents. In Wright's *Savage Holiday* (1954), for example, the protagonist Erskine Fowler is locked out of his apartment without any clothes. Fowler, a retired insurance executive, suddenly appears naked before a child on a balcony and causes the child to fall to his death. Fowler is confounded by the nature of the event, for though he caused the child's death, he fervently believes he did not intend it. As the novel progresses, he becomes less and less sure of his innocence: his Christian middle-class conscience and his fascination with Freudian psychology lead him to believe that he did in fact intend the crime. Yet Wright, who tried to start his own insurance program in 1932,[52] is not interested in ferreting out Fowler's unconscious intention, but rather in demonstrating how insurance presides over the elimination of intention altogether, how insurance effects a transition from the criminal to the civil, from the penal code to tort law. As in *Native Son*, Wright represents a world in which intentions, though inferable from outcomes, are never themselves treated as the primary determinants of actions. Fowler continually observes himself, watches himself execute actions that seem to take place in advance of his intention to perform them: "Once again he broke the elevator's descent by pressing the red button . . . and the elevator went into action too quickly, so quickly that he was not certain if he, or someone else had pressed the button, if he or someone else had put the elevator into action. In suspense he watched the floors pass. He couldn't stand it; he had to know who had put the elevator into motion."[53] In one of many similar instances, Fowler experiences his actions as if they are performed by someone else. Positing a second agent, he invents a conspiracy. But there is no one at the other end of the elevator. Watching himself perform out of character, Fowler instead watches the eclipse of intention: he experiences his own agency as utterly alienated, as a reified social force performing actions beyond his control.

Fowler's sense that his actions have been performed by an alienated double pervades most insurance narratives. Cora Papadakis and Frank Chambers, the lovers in James Cain's 1934 runaway best-seller *The Postman Always Rings Twice,* murder Cora's husband and collect $10,000 from his life insurance policy. When Cora is later killed in a car accident in exactly the manner that she and Chambers had used to kill her husband, Chambers is convicted of both killings. Haunted by the thought that Cora might have believed, the instant before she died, that he planned her death, Chambers reassures himself, "You know what you're doing, and you do it."[54] But everything about *The Postman* denies this simple assertion. Chambers goes to his death mystified by his own intentions, paralyzed by the idea that he has "two selves," and that one of them did indeed plan Cora's death.[55] These "two selves" in turn take center stage in Cain's next work, *Double Indemnity,* the locus classicus of the insurance-scam narrative. *Double Indemnity* makes Chambers's bifurcation of identity seem like an effect of insurance coverage itself; the doubleness in the title signifies the way insurance produces agents who passively observe themselves perform unintended actions. Here the insurance-salesman protagonist describes watching himself perform unintended actions, caused, he says, by "that thing . . . in me."[56]

Insurance salesman for General Fidelity of California, Walter Huff describes accident insurance by insisting that there are always two such consumers of insurance: the one who thinks he is buying insurance and the one to whom insurance is sold. It is the salesman's job to make his customers think that they are choosing to buy insurance. But Huff insists that, in point of fact, "accident insurance is sold, not bought" (6). Accident insurance happens to consumers, as a kind of accident.[57] Huff's plan to kill the innocent Mr. Nirdlinger and collect on his policy simply extends this logic. Huff plans to commit the "perfect murder" (20) by buying accident insurance in Nirdlinger's name without his knowledge, killing him, and then collecting from Huff's company. Huff explains to his accomplice Mrs. Nirdlinger by doubling Nirdlinger, by describing a knowing, active agent, and a passive, duped victim: "I didn't spend all this time in this business for nothing, did I? Listen, he knows all about this policy, and yet he don't know a thing about it. He applies for it, in writing, and yet he don't apply for it. He pays me for it with his own check, and yet he don't pay me. He has an accident happen to him and yet he don't have an accident happen to him" (22). The murdered husband gets accident insurance the only way one ever can get accident insurance—it happens to him, as Huff puts it, "accidentally on purpose" (16).

The "double indemnity" clause referred to in the title deceptively mitigates against the kind of powerlessness that Nirdlinger's murder symbolizes. Huff notes that the clause is used as a come-on meant to confuse buying insurance with the agency required to prevent the contingencies it covers. The clause provides extra money for particular contingencies and leads the customer to believe that the decision to construct a personalized policy constitutes some form of control over the events for which that policy provides. Even though the clause covers only things that almost never happen, it leads to the belief that insurance somehow safeguards one's control over the future when, in point of fact, insurance simply compensates for the individual's complete lack of such control. Huff is not himself immune to this form of false consciousness, for he falls victim to and purchases the very come-on that he foists on unwitting consumers. Huff's plan to murder Nirdlinger is nothing if not an attempt to orchestrate and direct, to perfectly plan the course of future events. Convinced that he can "crook the wheel" (24), Huff decides to cash in on Nirdlinger's double indemnity clause. Still, he is haunted by the possibility that this scheme has been sold to him, that it is not in fact his own. "That thing was in me," he reports, "pushing me still closer to the edge" (15). "I knew where I was at, of course," Huff states. "I was standing right on the deep end, looking over the edge, and never coming back. But that was what I kept telling myself. What I was doing was peeping over the edge, and all the time I was trying to pull away from it, there was something in me that kept edging a little closer, trying to get a better look" (14).[58] Huff's eventual realization that he has been a puppet of Phyllis, his partner in crime, that all along she "had plans of her own," hardly constitutes a significant moment of epiphany. Phyllis is no more a fully realized agent than Huff is; instead, she is a projection, a double invested with the agency Huff would like to have but doesn't.

Huff's ultimate downfall confirms less the insufficiency of his will than his mistake in believing in it at all. Huff falls victim to the false allure of the product he sells; his downfall is attributable not to the fact that he lacks the means sufficient to execute his will, but rather to the fact that he decides to execute his will at all. Seduced by the double indemnity clause, he opts to plan the accidental. In so doing, he forgets his own words. From the start, he observes that insurance is "the biggest gambling wheel in the world. It don't look like it, but it is, from the way they figure the percentage on the 00 to the look on their face when they cash your chips. You bet that your house will burn down, and they bet that it won't, that's all. What fools you is that you didn't want your house to burn down when you made the bet, and so you forget it's a bet. That don't fool them. To them a bet is a bet, and a hedge bet don't look any different than any other bet" (23). The insurance agency is able to win the preponderance of its bets by searching for statistical patterns as they emerge independently of any organizing will. Large numbers of events follow recognizable patterns in the actuarial table only when they are *not* intended.

Barton Keyes, the head of the Claims Department who intuits that Nirdlinger's death was not an accident, explains to the president of his company why he ruled out suicide as a cause of death. Study the actuarial tables, he tells his boss, "you might find out something about the insurance business." He continues:

> You were raised in private schools, in Groton and Harvard. While you were learning to pull bow oars there, I was studying these tables. Take a look at them. Here's suicide by race, by color, by occupation, by sex, by locality, by seasons of the year, by time of day when committed. Here's suicide by method of accomplishment. Here's method of accomplishment subdivided by poisons, by firearms, by gas, by drowning, by leaps. Here's suicide by poisons subdivided by sex, by race, by age, by time of day. Here's suicide by poisons subdivided by cyanide, by mercury, by strychnine, by thirty-eight other poisons, sixteen of them no longer procurable at prescription pharmacies. And here — here, Mr. Norton — are leaps subdivided by leaps from high places, under wheels of moving trains, under wheels of trucks, under the feet of horses, from steamboats. *But there's not one case here out of all these million cases of a leap from the rear end of a moving train.* That's just one way they don't do it. (60)

For Keyes, conspiracy is evident as events *deviate* from this table; he deduces nefarious intent only insofar as Nirdlinger's death disrupts the otherwise consistent patterning of human behavior.

To Cain, this backward glance, this insistence on the primacy of the already manifest, served as the basis not simply for an insurance practice, but for a conception of government as well. Four years before inventing the insurance scam, Cain dabbled with a more strictly political form of criminality when he wrote *Our Government* (1930), a withering satire of the executive, legislative, and judiciary branches of his contemporary American government. The scam here lies not in any kind of criminal conspiracy but in the apparent irrelevance of deductive thought to the operation of government. Cain opens the preface to the volume with the following:

We live in an age that has abandoned theory, except when theory can be made to serve as working hypothesis, in favor of fact. No longer do we start with *cogito, ergo sum* as a basis for deducing the principle of the universe; no longer do we believe that the principle of the universe can be deduced, or even stated. We incline to table such profundities as this in favor of things more objective: instead of concluding, by syllogistic processes, that since the patient is insane he must have a devil inside of him, we study his symptoms, trying to find out something about them; instead of indulging in great debates about the fairness of the income tax, we study the minutiae of economic phenomena, accumulating great columns of tables; instead of saying *cogito,* and letting it go at that, we study ourselves, seeking to find out how we cogitate, if at all.[59]

Cain "tables" thinking, first metaphorically, and then literally, as he gestures to a new dispensation that registers events not as the product of particular thoughts — cognitions — but after the fact. Cain's bureaucratic state, run by statisticians and social scientists, deflates pretensions to collective agency even as it oversees the emergence of self-consciousness in its place, as "we study ourselves." Thus thought is inferred, if at all, from great columns: not stone columns enshrining great leaders, self-possessed agents of history, but those on the page, columns of actuarial data.

In *Double Indemnity,* Walter Huff invents internal phantoms meant to register the elusive origin of his own otherwise inscrutable intentions. At the same time, Barton Keyes registers intentions only as they deviate from the actuarial. In *Our Government,* the actuarial emerges as an objectifying bent that renders "theory" moot altogether; government dismisses the "devil" that appears to drive Huff, it closes its eye to causes and concerns itself instead simply with the manifest. Richard Wright does not dismiss the devil in Bigger Thomas as much as he displaces it onto a larger collective. Thus, Max ultimately claims in *Native Son* that Thomas's crime is no accident — not, he reasons, because Thomas planned it, but because society did: "We planned the murder of Mary Dalton" (459), he cries. This claim requires no recourse to a conspiratorial account of Dalton's death. Rather, Max simply relocates the site of significant social agency from Thomas to the systemic. Invoking an "environmental" account of behavior, Max qualifies the accidental nature of Thomas's crime by understanding it less in terms of what Thomas intended than in terms of how he was socially conditioned to do exactly what he did. In this case, Thomas's environment, broadly conceived, emerges as the agent responsible for Dalton's death. Dismissing the category of intentional agency by superseding it with forces seen to script individual action, Max attempts to convince the judge that Thomas is a product of debased living conditions, which range from Jim Crow housing to an oppressive climate of racial hate.

Wright makes similar arguments in *Black Boy* (1945), where he describes individuals "claimed wholly by their environment," and in his introduction to *Black Metropolis,* where he takes up the question of "the system that provides" for "our individual experiences."[60] Wright notes in the latter that "the huge mountains of fact piled up by the Department of Sociology at the University of Chicago gave me my first concrete vision of the forces that molded the urban Negro body and soul" (xxvii). His interest in systemic and environmental accounts of agency reached its pinnacle when he worked for the U.S. Postal Service. There, he recalls, he would eagerly study tables of figures "relating population density to insanity, relating housing to disease, relating school and recreational opportunities to crime, relating various forms of neurotic behavior to environment, relating racial insecurities to the conflicts between whites and blacks."[61] Within such a framework, Thomas's crime does not appear accidental at all. Cross-referencing columns "relating school and recreational opportunities to crime," and columns "relating racial insecurities to the conflicts between whites and blacks," Wright might have seen, for example, just how often and at what interval black males subject to Thomas's educational and recreational conditions killed as Thomas did. The table would not have listed why each individual killed, or whether he intended to kill, for it would have been designed precisely to demonstrate patterns of behavior that emerged regardless of the intentions of the individual actors in question.

In his essay "How Bigger Was Born," Wright suggests that he understood even the form of *Native Son* along these strikingly statistical lines. The essay describes Thomas as if he were the focus group in an actuarial study, as if, in other words, *Native Son* were that study. Thomas, we are told, is a walking population group; he is a composite character, one who represents a distinct "behavior pattern" derived from no fewer than five figures Wright encountered while growing up. Having recalled the manifold sources for this personified tendency, Wright asks: "Why should I not try to work out on paper the problem of what will happen to Thomas? Why should I not, like a scientist in a laboratory, use my imagination and invent test-tube situations, place Thomas in them, and, following the guidance of my own hopes and fears, what I had learned and remembered, work out in fictional form an emotional statement and resolution of this problem?" (*Native Son,* 523). Gesturing to his novel's ability to mediate between the objective and the subjective, Wright claims that the situations Thomas confronts are the product of his imagination, but that Thomas's responses to them are not, but are instead the projection in fictional form of "what I had learned and remembered." He thus describes his writing as a mediation of the individual's creative expression and more objective, statistically measurable events: "An imaginative novel represents the merging of two extremes; it is an intensely intimate expression on the part of a consciousness couched in terms of the most objective and commonly known events. It is something at once private and public by its very nature and texture" (505). Of course, *Native Son* is private and public in an obvious sense: the fictional novel based loosely on Wright's experiences was written in part while Wright was, to recall Kennedy, "set free" by funds from the WPA Writers' Project. In fact, Wright was one of the few writers on the Project actually paid to work on his own material.[62] I will argue in the following sections, however, that *Native Son* — like Frost's "The Lesson," Warner Brothers' *Gold Diggers of 1933,* and Toni Morrison's *Song of Solomon* — reconciles the private to the public in its very form, principally by rewriting narrative linearity as spatial totality.

2.

At first glance, Frost's "The Lesson for Today" seems to accommodate Kennedy's account of the benign antagonism between the solitary artist and the officious state. The poem is addressed to a "Master of the Palace School" (351), a medieval court poet of King Charles with whom Frost's speaker feels a kinship. Skeptical that times are as bad as his contemporaries say, Frost's speaker turns back to "the world's undebateably dark ages" (350) to engage a series of comparisons between then and now. The New Deal first enters the poem as an object of satire, a modern counterpart to King Charles that takes too seriously its task of ameliorating the problems of what the poem calls "this uncertain age in which we dwell" (350). "Could it be brought under state control," the poem says of the human soul, "Its separateness from Heaven could be waived" (353). But the state begins to appear more ominous than farcical in its efforts at salvation, because those efforts seem to endanger the solitary individual.

This threat emerges in the context of the speaker's concern with statistics, the technology devoted to figuring out practically how to eliminate uncertainty:

> You and I
> Would be afraid if we should comprehend
> And get outside of too much bad statistics,
> Our muscles never could again contract:
> We never could recover human shape,
> But must live lives out mentally agape
> Or die of philosophical distention. (351)

This is the first of a series of moments in the poem where the speaker decides against transcendence, that is, the effort to "get outside" the environment in which he is situated and see it as a whole. Later, we are told:

> Space ails us moderns: we are sick with space.
> Its contemplation makes us small
> As a brief epidemic of microbes
> That in a good glass may be seen to crawl
> The patina of this the least of globes. (352)

In the first stanza, the hypothetical attempt of an individual to transcend the social totality results in the monstrous distortion of the body (muscles cannot "contract," leaving one unable "to recover human shape"). In the second stanza, the very existence of such a point of view distorts scale in the opposite way, shrinking bodies until they become an undifferentiated swarm. In both cases, the individual becomes something other than a distinct person in trying to take in the whole of which he or she is a part.

Examining events as they occur at the level of entire populations, actuarial science generates certainty (probabilities worth betting on) from uncertainty by occupying precisely the totalizing perspective from which persons look, to Frost's speaker, like microbes. That such an objectifying strategy came to seem a tool of writers as well is, in the context of the New Deal modernism I have been pointing out, hardly surprising. As Joan Didion later writes in *Democracy* (1984), "When novelists speak of the unpredictability of human behavior they usually mean not unpredictability at all but a higher predictability, a more complex pattern discernible only after the fact. Examine the picture. Find the beast in the jungle, the figure in the carpet."[63] In a similar vein, Malcolm Cowley urged writers at the First American Writers Congress to affiliate with the left because, he said, such an affiliation offered certain "practical benefits." One of those benefits was the fact that "the revolutionary movement gives the artist a perspective on himself — an idea that his own experiences are not something accidental and unique, but part of a vast pattern." The writer was in this way able to derive from the movement a "sense of human life, not as a medley of accidents, but as a connecting and continuing process."[64]

But, although getting a "perspective on oneself" might expose "the beast in the jungle," such potentially vertiginous self-reflection also brought with it a distinctly liberal set of anxieties. In *Double Indemnity*, for example, characters find it so difficult to provide accounts of their own intentions in part because they repeatedly discover that what at first seem to be accidents are not accidents at all, but parts of designs whose scope always extends beyond their immediate sphere of perception. Thus Cain lights on the phrase "accidentally on purpose" (Frost will later borrow it to title one of his poems), meant to describe the dizzying renegotiation of agency that occurs when analytic and perceptual frames shuttle between the personal and the impersonal (91). In "The Fetish of Being Outside" published in *New Masses*, Meridel Le Sueur responds to politically middle-of-the-road critics who, she reasons, have embraced exactly this equivocation between the personal and the impersonal, "liberal" critics who let concerns over their own autonomy keep them from embracing the kind of panopticism Cowley mentions.[65]

She begins by observing, "In times like these, points of view are important; they represent what you will be called upon to act from tomorrow" (299). In part, Le Sueur uses "point of view" only in a loose metaphorical sense, as a general orientation toward the world. Objecting to the assumption that "the creative worker is not an economist and cannot understand deviations, and political theory," she reasons that "the artist can no longer take refuge in infantilism, or the supposition that he has not the kind of mentality to understand economic thought because this is the dynamic stuff of the composition of our time and he cannot take a double course and be part of it and still apart from it" (300). As the essay progresses, however, Le Sueur's sense of what it means to be "part of it" begins to take on a more literal topography. She insists that the writer must be unambiguously a part of it, completely and totally embedded both in the reality of the times and in political responses to it. "Why want to be an outsider when you see and admit sight of the promised land?" she asks. "Why choose to walk around the wall of Jericho merely? . . . it seems very dangerous to me to want at the same time to be in and to be out. . . . You must accept the discipline of the party and yet you must be objective and individual and outside. You must act and yet *you* must not act, you must be individual and again objective" (301). For Le Sueur, disgusted, she says, with her own recidivist middle-class commitment to individual identity, any sense of self is dangerous to the degree that it leads to a paralyzing self-consciousness. Wanting "at the same time to be in and to be out," she concludes, is "like saying I will fall in love and I will not fall in love" (301).

Or perhaps, Le Sueur might have added, wanting "at the same time to be in and to be out" is like trying to fall in love with the world only half way. But Frost's speaker, who declares at the conclusion of "The Lesson" his "lover's quarrel with the world," manages just this. He does so first by discovering the extent to which he is already "part of it." "Like a good Christian disciplined to bend / His mind to thinking always to the end" (353), the speaker wends his way to a cemetery, where he is overcome by the advice of an imagined interlocutor. *Memento mori,* he is told: remember that you will die. The terms of the poem now switch, as the speaker soberly realizes that he is in fact already part of a community, comprising those who, like himself, are fated to die: "We are all doomed," he intones, "to broken off careers / And so's the nation, so's the total race." Suddenly, community is something of a comfort: "I take my incompleteness with the rest" (355). The epitaph the speaker will invent for himself — "I had a lover's quarrel with the world" — expresses just this sentiment. "Loving the world," the speaker accepts his place in a community defined by the inevitability of death. The specific nature of the epitaph, however, speaking at once of a love and a quarrel, further suggests that the speaker has now accepted precisely the statistics-oriented community of the living that he seemed earlier to reject. For the image of the speaker standing outside of and perceiving his entombed body, like the word "quarrel" itself, echoes a moment earlier in the poem, when the speaker explains the paradoxes of liberalism. He claims, not without biting irony, that the liberal — the truest supporter of the New Deal — is the true spectator of himself. He is that person who chooses to argue, not only against his own best interest, but literally with himself: "Don't let the things I say against myself / Betray you into taking sides against me," Tityrus warns Meliboeus in "Build Soil."[66] The speaker in "The Lesson for Today" is similarly self-divided: "I never," the speaker professes, "take my own side in a quarrel" (354).

As in much of Frost's political poetry, irony — the trope of self-difference — prevails. In fact, as F. R. Ankersmit reminds us, liberal politics have long been figured in terms of irony and schizophrenia: "Friedrich Schlegel wrote: 'He is liberal who is free from all sides and in all directions, and who realizes his entire humanity.' One is 'liberal,' that is to say, one is a democrat, if one is aware of the multipolarity of each political position, if one succeeds in mobilizing that multipolarity for 'the entire humanity.' "[67] Indeed, "democracy" itself, Ankersmit adds, "puts us in relation to ourselves" (347). But this kind of liberalism emerges in particularly anguished form under the reign of the welfare state, during what Ankersmit calls "the Age of Unintended Consequences," when "the ironic discrepancy between our intentions and the results of our actions so often and so disagreeably surprises us." In such an age we are "forced to subsume, as much as possible, the consequences of our actions in these actions themselves." "The picture emerging from all of this," he concludes, is "self-ironization" (237). "Standing in relation to oneself" (349), the modern citizen "is confronted with the inconsistency of his or her own seemingly legitimate desires. The citizen him- or herself now becomes a microcosm of traditional ideological politics. . . . We could describe this remarkable internalization of political conflict in Freudian terms: the citizen now learns to see himself or herself as the place where the conflict is fought out between the 'libido' of one's ideological desires and the 'superego' of one's new insight into the need to counter the unintended consequences effected by the realization of one's ideological desires" (362).

But if Frost's speaker seems to internalize political division in his willingness to engage himself in debate, the poem as whole also works insistently to externalize this self-ironization and to map the speaker's divided ego onto an almost geopolitical set of relations. Declaring that he never takes his own side in a quarrel, Frost's speaker would seem initially to define liberalism in terms of its morality, such that liberalism involves loving others more than loving oneself. But the transposition — to the objectified space of the epitaph — of the internalized "quarrel" in which the liberal opposes himself suggests that, through the contemplation of death, the speaker is now able to do what before he could not, namely, see himself and the world he inhabits from the outside. The contemplation of death, in other words, provokes a distinctly compensatory experience in which the looming and threatening future is displaced with a vision of a nurturing collectivity. Having invoked his end, the speaker sees himself as part of a whole in the present. Here, social security depends on a compensatory substitution of the diachronic, narrative project of seeing the future with the synchronic, spatial project of apprehending the present in its entirety. The liberal emerges, then, not simply as the product of a certain kind of affect — as the person who finds love for the world in the fact that he will die — but as the product of an optic technology as well, as the person who loves the world as a function of being able to picture himself within it. What Frost makes clear, in other words, is that his liberalism — constituted in this moment of loving the world — isn't simply a question of altruism or selflessness. On the contrary, Frost's speaker loves the world because he sees himself within it. For Frost, loving the world involves picturing the self embedded in the world such that this act of vision compensates for the ways in which one might appear indistinguishable from the others with whom it is shared. The speaker thus establishes a personal relationship with impersonality itself.

At the very least, this complicates Kennedy's vision of the "solitary artist" set against the world. It complicates also Richard Poirier's assertion that "the placement of the self in relation to the apparent organization of things is one of the major concerns of Frost's later poetry, but it is a political concern only while it also reveals his more general contempt for a tendency in modern liberalism to discredit the capacity of ordinary, struggling people to survive in freedom and hope without the assistance of state or any other kind of planning."[68] Frost's ambivalent fascination with the placement of the self, in this account, is compelling only until those systems of organization in which the self is placed become political, at which time they become repugnant. But the speaker of "The Lesson" is not discredited in his love of the world, nor is he completely lost in that love. This, I take it, is the force of the ambivalent phrase "lover's quarrel," which asserts a qualified identification, the possibility of an autonomy — here, a discreteness of identity — not compromised by complete identity with a subsuming system. The unresolved double bind, or oscillation, between an ostensibly homogenizing social totality on the one hand, and individuality or personality on the other, is not, as Poirier would have it, a movement between politics and something other than politics. Rather, this double bind *is* Frost's liberalism, imagined through a tropological substitution that replaces a narrative of the apprehension of death with a spatial representation of the moribund individual embedded in networks of connection that secure him from contingency.

3.

Concerted action is completely repellent to our nature. A gang of plumbers can easily sew up a city with extortionist regulations and hang together like wolves, but anybody who has tried to get three writers to act as a unit on the simplest matter knows what the difficulties are.

—James M. Cain, in *Screen Writers* (1946)[69]

During the thirties, film was without doubt the medium to manipulate most powerfully the visual dynamics of what it meant to establish a personal, affective relationship with structures grounded in impersonality. The particular kind of film I have in mind, however, is not Classical Hollywood Cinema — which provided omniscient perspectives on sealed-off worlds — but rather Busby Berkeley's *Gold Diggers* musicals, which self-consciously shuttled its spectators in and out of cinematic reality.[70] Whereas Frost achieves liberal transcendence with the meditative, memorializing, and ultimately compensatory function of epideictic poetry, Berkeley does so with codes of visual reflexivity that enable individuals to watch themselves perform within functioning populations.

Nothing might seem less integral to the dynamics of social insurance and the welfare state than the Hollywood musical, a form often derided during the Depression for its escapist frivolity. As the socially conscious director Sullivan asks his producer in Preston Sturges's comedy *Sullivan's Travels* (1941), "How can you think about musicals at a time like this, with the world committing suicide, with corpses piling up on the streets, with grim death gargling at you from every corner, with people being slaughtered like sheep?" Yet, Warners would claim that the entertainment offered in its Berkeley musicals was nothing less than a social necessity, a form of social insurance not unlike the work relief for which people lined up in the streets throughout the Depression. Launching its Busby Berkeley musical series in 1933, Warners thus pledged to provide American audiences with a "New Deal in entertainment."[71] The Warners steeped themselves in New Deal liberalism. Harry Warner wrote tirelessly about film's "implied duties to ethics, patriotism, and the fundamental rights of individuals" and firmly believed that "as Americans we try to make pictures which . . . will advance the public interest and welfare." Jack Warner campaigned for Roosevelt during the 1932 primaries — at one point using Warners' radio station KFWB to organize a rally attended by 175,000 supporters in the Los Angeles Coliseum — and remained a close friend of Roosevelt until the president's death in 1945.[72] Soon after he was elected, Roosevelt convinced Jack Warner to serve on and later chair the NRA board in California. More than any of the five major studios, then, Warners made good on the motto "Doing our part" that was printed under the NRA blue eagle with which pictures were then stamped.[73]

Malcolm Cowley declared that for the screenwriter during the Depression, the New Deal studio "was a Writers' Project retailored in mink." *Gold Diggers of 1933* insisted on this analogy, suggesting that the salaried employment Warners offered writers perfectly mirrored the kind available on the WPA Writers' Project. At the start of the film, the Broadway producer Barney Hopkins (who looks strikingly like Harry Hopkins) is forced to close his new stage production due to lack of funds, an action that results in the unemployment of the many dancers, actors, and musicians who depend on the show to see them through the hard times of the Depression. Like most events in the Warner Brothers' "back-stage musicals" of the thirties, the scene had a pointed parallel in the life of the studio: it echoes a decree issued by the major studios early in 1933 that all studio employees would need to take substantial pay cuts because of the Depression. As Larry Ceplair and Steven Englund report: "Ironically, President Roosevelt's bank holiday in March 1933 — which launched the New Deal — persuaded studio management that the moment had arrived to resurrect the *old* deal of paternalistic labor/management relations which the Academy had been created to camouflage. Throughout Hollywood, the artistic personnel (directors, actors, writers) were herded into studio commissaries or sound stages [and] . . . were informed of a 50 per cent salary slash for everyone making over $50 a week."[74] The fact that those within the film lose their jobs entirely and would willingly take a pay cut rather than face unemployment feels, in this light, like a celebration of "paternalistic" Hollywood producers willing to go out on a limb to help their employees. Imagining a Broadway scenario worse than the one it was offering its own employees, Warners goes the benevolent but financially limited Barney Hopkins one better.

But the screen writer was the one studio employee who refused to be placated by the studio's invocation of Depression hardship. For the well-paid writer's beef with studio management was not primarily financial, but rather centered around the issue of authorship, particularly over the dual questions of how much control writers would have over their work, and how much screen credit they would receive for it: "A writer without a credit on a script he has written is professionally emasculated," explained Carl Foreman.[75] The relation between the screenwriter and the studio came to a head in 1933, when writers banded together to form the Screen Writers Guild (SWG), an organization designed to become the principal union of writers in Hollywood. The first priority of the union was to secure for screenwriters more production control over and recognition for their efforts. The studio reaction to the SWG was swift and hostile, particularly at Warners, a studio famous for its desire to recognize its writers' labors with a salary alone. Notorious for its impersonal if not Taylorized production system, Warners had already built a fence around its writers' building and hired a security guard to keep track of its inhabitants.[76] It was no surprise, then, that Warners, with the

3. Allegories of screen writing in Berkeley's *Ready, Willing and Able,*
1937. *(Courtesy Photofest)*

other studios, refused to recognize or deal with the SWG. But despite
studio opposition, the SWG was launched in April 1933 with the
assertion of its president John Howard Lawson that "The writer is the
creator of motion pictures."[77] The SWG soon found, however, that
the New Deal stood in the way of this claim as much as the studios
did. The National Labor Relations Board (NLRB) would emerge in
the late thirties as an ally of the SWG, but in 1933 the NRA set into law
wage levels and production codes that were favorable to the studio.
Producers sat on NRA boards, writers did not. In the eyes of the New
Deal, the studio was the real creator of motion pictures.

Given Warners' obsession with keeping its writers in line, it is
tempting to see *The Gold Diggers of 1933* as a response to the
formation of the guild and what would soon become the first significant labor dispute in Hollywood. *The Gold Diggers of 1933* keeps its
authors in line, literally. Dick Powell, for instance, the urbane and
wealthy songwriter in the film, is only too happy to invest his money
in Hopkins's play and take his place in its chorus line. He is the star of
the production Hopkins stages, but a star of a humble sort, one who
gives way in almost every number to the visual spectacles that supplant him. Powell is not in the final number of the film, raising the
question of whether or not he is himself the departed "forgotten

man" the concluding number urges the viewer to recall. Replacing the author, Warners enjoins the audience to respect him in his anonymity, offering in his place a union more total, and yet more benign, than any achieved by the SWG. The Busby Berkeley musical "system" that supplants Powell, that renders the author invisible but not forgotten, is a perfectly unified, organic collective, starkly beautiful in its impersonal efficiency (see fig. 4).

But even though *The Gold Diggers of 1933* seems primarily directed at the studio's own, Warners insisted that its *Gold Diggers* films offered security for all who watched them as well. The *Gold Diggers* musical was, in the words of Warners' producer Hal Wallis, "the most important product we make."[78] This product was threatened in 1934 when Darryl Zanuck, Warners' chief producer and patron saint of the Berkeley musical, left the studio to found 20th-Century Pictures. Two years later, 20th-Century Pictures purchased the floundering Fox and became 20th-Century Fox.[79] Allegorizing the birth of his new dynasty, Zanuck immediately produced *Lloyd's of London* (1936), a story of the founding of the insurance house of that name. As if in answer to Zanuck's desertion, and in response to Dick Powell's suggestion in *Dames* (1934) that a Broadway show is tantamount to life insurance for those who watch it, Warner Brothers made *Gold Diggers of 1937* centrally concerned with the relation between insurance and the production of entertainment.

In the film, two scheming vice presidents of New York's premier theatrical agency plan to rescue the company from impending financial ruin by insuring and then killing its owner, J. J. Hobart.[80] The two persuade the reluctant Hobart to purchase life insurance because he has an obligation to the 50 million who watch his productions to provide for his possible death. His audience, they insist, is his extended family, the real beneficiary of his policy. The vice presidents make the mistake, however, of turning to an insurance company currently employing the ex-crooner Dick Powell and the ex–chorus girl Joan Blondell. Powell sells Hobart a $1 million policy and then, with Blondell, proceeds to protect Hobart against the machinations of his vice presidents. When Hobart's firm goes broke, Powell and Blondell protect their friend and client by organizing the insurance company into a musical production group that stages a benefit show to rescue Hobart from financial ruin (see fig. 5). By the end of the film, the insurance-turned–production company is indistinguishable

4.

(Opposite page, top image)

The collective nuptial in

Dames, 1934;

(Opposite page, bottom image)

Organic geometry in *Dames,* 1934;

(Above)

The language of abstraction in

Whoopee!, 1930.

(All images courtesy Photofest)

5. J. J. Hobart being screened for his life insurance in *Gold Diggers of 1937 (Courtesy Photofest)*

from the production-turned–insurance company: the insurance company saves the possibility of entertainment (Hobart's firm) by becoming a production company that saves lives and promotes financial liquidity more successfully than any insurance firm.

Made before the New Deal, but centrally concerned with the ideology of corporate paternalism, King Vidor's *The Crowd* (1927) offers a bleak version of this same claim. Vidor collapses insurance and entertainment into one industry by collapsing the difference between the corporate paternalism of the Atlas Insurance Co., which employs the film's protagonist, John Sims, and the show Sims goes to see with his family in the last scene of the film. Sims spends his life at Atlas waiting for his "ship to come in." But when his company boards a cruise-liner for a picnic, Sims has already quit the firm — missing, as it were, the boat. Out of work, he moves from one humiliation to the next, paying a heavy price for having asserted his individuality. His final reconciliation with his wife, along with the solidarity he achieves with his family and with strangers at a vaudeville show, teach Sims to embrace that humiliation — teach him, in other words,

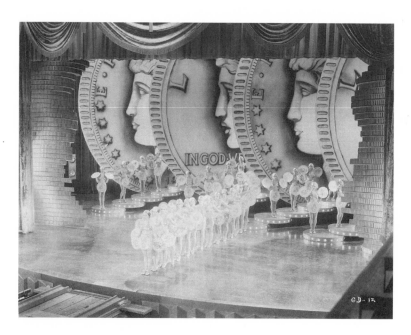

6. "In the money": The financial sublime in *Gold Diggers of 1933*
(*Courtesy Photofest*)

that his hopes for personal advancement must be subordinated to selfless participation in a self-identical group. When Sims joins the Atlas Insurance Co., he comments, "You guys all talk the same," and *The Crowd*'s final scene of entertainment offers little more than this aggregated equivalence. To the extent that entertainment offers a kind of insurance, Vidor argues, it seems to do so for populations, never for particular persons.

But from the start of the *Gold Digger* series (*Gold Diggers of 1937* is the fourth installment of five), Berkeley had reconciled personality to security — to recall Max's language in *Native Son* — by depicting populations bent on accommodating the autonomous person. *Gold Diggers of 1933* begins with persons as interchangeable as coins — insisting "We're in the Money" — but ends by recalling the dignity of the empirical individual with the number "Forgotten Man," precisely the man of which any representation of totality threatens to lose sight (see fig. 6). More strikingly, the relation between the narrative and musical segments of the *Gold Diggers* films conforms perfectly to François Ewald's sense that insurance "allows people to enjoy the advantages of association while still leaving them free to exist as individuals."[81] The narrative sections of the film are committed to the possibility of intentional agency. Here, individuals regulate events based on the idea that cause precedes effect. The musical sections, however, represent the external management of wholly organic populations, and develop a visual language as abstract as Wallace Stevens's impersonal poetic language.[82] The musical sections are "arranged"; they are closed, restricted economies that follow nonlinear patterns not the product of intentional agents operating within them. The absolute interchangeability of persons within these groups is taken to an extreme in "All's Fair in Love and War," the final number of *Gold Diggers of 1937*. During this number, Joan Blondell's character becomes at times indistinguishable from Glenda Farrell's, recalling actions Farrell's character performed earlier as her own. This kind of interchange, the number suggests, comes from the disruption of the linear temporality of narrative: at moments, Berkeley runs the film in reverse, manipulating his actors and dancers technologically, so they pointedly cease to appear as self-authoring agents. Stepping from narrative to musical and back again, the protagonists of Warner Brothers' musicals thus avail themselves of both autonomy and security, as they slide in and out of different mechanisms for representing social relationships.

Berkeley's musical numbers themselves internalize this oscillation, this strategic reconciliation of socialization and individualization, suggesting that there is never any moment when one needs to choose between the person and the population. This, I take it, is the significance of the mind-bending reflexivity of the numbers, the impossible ways they provide frame-breaking perspectives that continually renegotiate the individual's point of view with respect to that of the collectivity's. Always beginning on a stage located within the film's diegesis, these numbers soon transcend that literal space, reconciling individual to group in a manner unavailable to Classical Hollywood Cinema. Berkeley continually collapses frames of reference such that a person in a chorus line can (paradoxically) look upon herself as she performs in that line. As we saw with James Farrell's Bernard Carr, reflexivity aspires to an essentially absorbed narcissism, as theatrical individuals become their own best audiences. In "I Only Have Eyes for You" in *Dames* (1934), for example, Ruby Keeler watches herself in a mirror that she holds in her hand. The camera pulls away, and reveals that this entire scenario is reflected in a second mirror, held by a second Keeler. The sequence repeats itself

7. "All's fair in love and war" in *Gold Diggers of 1937 (Courtesy Photofest)*

ad infinitum. Here, then, is a state of perfect sympathy, a double-ness — indeed, an endlessly repeating process of reproduction — deeply implicated in the promises of liberal government and the welfare state. Easing characters in and out of both hypotactic narrative linearity and paratactic musical economy, Warners promises that individuals can, at one and the same time, be individuated and affiliated with populations.

Affiliated, that is, in explicitly erotic terms. In the show-stopping and film-ending musical number "All's Fair in Love and War," gendered armies line up against each other. Kisses fly across the lines as if they were bullets. Perfume wafts into hostile trenches as if it were tear gas. And all the while, parodically smiling chorus girls and boys watch themselves perform, watch themselves get swept into a conflagration that transposes interpersonal sexual dynamics onto a vast scale (see fig. 7). Coupling large-scale mechanized group behavior with the affect constitutive of one-on-one relationships, Berkeley produces displaced, doubled individuals who have, quite literally, a lover's quarrel with the world. This lover's quarrel, coupled as it is with a recursive escape from cause and effect, saves Hobart's life, and makes good on the film's initial claim that entertainment is a form of life insurance.[83] So, even as the manager of Powell's insurance firm tells his agents that he wants every prospective buyer of life insurance to be able to "see himself in his own grave," the film insists that such imaginings in turn produce a compensatory moment in which insurance consumers visually contextualize themselves in the present. Hobart seems to understand this logic perfectly well, for he believes he will die if he does not get to watch the insurance company perform "All's Fair in Love and War" at the close of the film, a musical number that, in typical Berkeley fashion, starts out as a stage play and turns into a film. Hobart is saved from the grave by imagining himself on the screen, by becoming absorbed into the frame-breaking space of Berkeley's concluding extravaganza. He escapes death, impossibly, by witnessing and transcending his own embodiment. He is protected by a beneficent technology of insurance that depends on his imagining himself in two places at the same time.

With this miraculous form of life insurance, characters need never die to cash in. Hobart gets to live and cash out his 50 million beneficiaries. In fact, any filmgoer who takes seriously the inaugural insistence of the *Gold Diggers* series — "We're *in* the money" — gets to benefit from this insurance. Berkeley's frame-breaking is, after all, designed to do nothing so much as transport the moviegoer into the cinematic apparatus itself. Here, avant-garde reflexivity does not produce alienation so much as the possibility conditions of franchise. "Picturing" themselves, not in the grave but on the screen, these moviegoers get to watch themselves perform, realizing, in the circulation of their money, the fantasy of New Deal liberalism.

4.

Yes; insurance was a shifty-eyed, timid, sensual, sluttish woman trying, with all of her revolting and nauseating sexiness, to make you believe that she'd been maimed in an automobile accident, and you wouldn't, couldn't believe her or take her word for it, and you'd smiled at her and led her to believe that you believed her and you easily beat her at her crooked game by just looking into her eyes and letting her fool herself into thinking that maybe you were falling for her. — Richard Wright, *Savage Holiday*[84]

The start of Toni Morrison's *Song of Solomon* (1977) finds Robert Smith, agent for the North Carolina Mutual Life Insurance Company, leaving a suicide note: "At 3:00 P.M. on Wednesday the 18th of February, 1931, I will take off from Mercy and fly away on my own wings. Please forgive me. I loved you all." Robert Smith signs his suicide note "Ins. agent," and then, true to his word, jumps from the top of Mercy Hospital.[85] Less true to his word, he plummets to the earth and dies.

Later in the novel we discover that Smith's leap has little to do with the official capacities of the Mutual Life. The company, one of the first all-Black insurance firms to operate on a national scale, is the headquarters of a conspiracy, the Seven Days, of which Robert Smith was a member. The Seven Days is a Black separatist group committed to countering racial violence perpetrated on Blacks with equal responses perpetrated on Whites. But nonetheless, the group is understood as a kind of insurance practice. Despite the violent nature of the Seven Days, Guitar Bains, a practicing member who witnesses Smith's leap as a child and joins in the fifties as a young man, describes the group in actuarial terms. Racial violence has to be answered in kind because "the numbers have to remain static" (158); the group, Guitar explains, is an effort "to keep the ratio the same" (155) between Whites and Blacks. Guitar argues further that the Seven Days is not an instrument of revenge, but a purely statistical practice. The Seven Days is not, for example, understood in penal or paralegal dimensions: its members do not kill out of revenge, for they never kill the perpetrators of the crimes to which they respond, but instead kill random persons. In fact, the group operates with an emblematically New Deal commitment to statistical impersonality; its members "don't choose" their work and are "indifferent as rain" (154) to the actions they perform. Each member is assigned a particular day, and executes the group's office whenever an act of violence against a Black individual is committed on that day.

The fact that the Seven Days is concerned above all with "Numbers. Balance. Ratio" (158) and that it is housed within an all-Black insurance company look in one respect like a commentary on the role of private insurance practice in constructing and consolidating racial identity. What makes both the Seven Days and the Mutual Life private, Morrison suggests, is the insistence on race, the insistence that insurance is a technology for policing racial distinction. Since the turn of the century, private insurance practice has often done just this. Lizabeth Cohen points out that in the twenty years leading up to the Depression, racially identified communities would regularly provide insurance for their own in the form of Mutual Benefit Societies. "Mutualism," Cohen notes, "helped to sustain a . . . sense of ethnicity." Nowhere was the role of insurance more prominent in sustaining group identity than in the Black community, which, according to a 1918 study, carried more life insurance than any other population group. (Wright parodies this tendency in *Lawd Today!,* where Jackson prioritizes paying "the insurance bill and the milk bill" [23] over the removal of his wife's tumor.) As the twenties wore on, large-scale insurance corporations tended to replace the benefit societies, though even these corporations sold their product mainly within racial lines. By the end of the twenties, Cohen notes, "more and more blacks were choosing to insure the life of the black community along with their own."[86]

Until the advent of federal laws forbidding red-lining by insurance firms, insurance was sold primarily along racial lines. In Philip Roth's *Portnoy's Complaint* (1967), for example, Portnoy's father works for Boston and Northeastern Life, an insurance conglomerate Portnoy refers to as the "Holy Protestant Empire."[87] Portnoy Senior refers to the firm as "The Most Benevolent Financial Institution in America" (6); " 'The Home Office,' " Portnoy complains; "my father made it sound to me like Roosevelt in the White House in Washington" (8). Portnoy's father sells insurance only to all-Black communities. "What hope is there for these niggers' ever improving their lot?" he asks his son. "How will they ever lift themselves if they ain't even able to grasp the importance of life insurance? Don't they give a single crap for the loved ones they leave behind? Because 'they's all' going to die too, you know — 'oh,' he says angrily, 'they sho' is' " (10). Racked with guilt over his father's racism, Portnoy grows up an avid participant in the Great Society, inflecting the sins of his father through the welfare state once again. At twenty-five, Portnoy is "special counsel to a House Subcommittee — of the United States Congress." Later he becomes the "Assistant Commissioner of Human Opportunity for the City of New York"; he shouts to his mother, "I am conducting an investigation of unlawful discriminatory practices in the building trades in New York — *racial discrimination!*" (110).

But of course, insurance does not produce racial discrimination simply by choosing to sell to one group as opposed to another. More fundamentally, insurance constructs race in its statistical procedures. When the claims adjuster Keyes lists the headings under which suicide is broken down in his actuarial tables in *Double Indemnity*, he reads off "suicide by race, by color," and only then follows with "by occupation, by seasons of the year, by time of day" (59). Needless to say, a group organized around race is about as meaningful as a group organized around occupation; each group has coherence only as an object of statistical analysis (individuals are not biologically Black or White any more than they are workers or capitalists). This is why Morrison's private insurance industry turns out to be just as murderous as Cain's, why both the Seven Days and *Double Indemnity*'s Walter Huff seem to express in their murderous actions the logic of the insurance itself. *Song of Solomon* starts from the premise not simply that a commitment to private insurance is a commitment to racial identity, but that a commitment to either is potentially murderous even where it intends to be beneficial.

Members of the Seven Days, on the other hand, explain their actions as expressions of love. "What I'm doing," says Guitar, "ain't about hating white people. It's about loving us. Loving you. My whole life is love" (159). The object of Guitar's affection — his "us" — is an imagined racial population: the Seven Days "don't off Negroes" (161), he explains. This claim refers us back to Robert Smith's suicide declaration, "I loved you all": we are left to wonder whether Smith, private "Ins. Agent," member of the Seven Days, loved his race or the world, and concomitantly, whether his leap from on high is meant to exemplify or reject what Guitar will later call the Seven Days' embrace of "race-consciousness." For Guitar, Smith's longing for flight is indistinguishable from the desire to transcend racial difference. "They want us, you know, 'universal,' 'human,' no 'race consciousness' " (222), Guitar tells Milkman. He goes on to insist, however, that no visual perspective, however high, will provide for such fantasies: "Even if you make it, even if you stubborn and mean and you get to the top of Mt. Everest — that still ain't enough" (222–23). Thus, Smith's tormented declaration "I loved you all" is later understood as resistance to what the novel calls "graveyard love," the misguided but nonetheless lethal process whereby individuals imagine themselves in love with a statistical entity such as race. By his own admission, Guitar is unable to love individual women, principally because they seem to threaten his personality. "Black women," he says, "they want your whole self. Love, they call it" (222). "It was hard for me to latch on to a woman," he explains. "Because I thought if I loved anything it would die" (307). If Busby Berkeley fetishizes women by absorbing them into abstract population groups, Guitar does the same. His alternative to "latching on" to one woman is a latching on, a cathexis, to race. Loving race, Guitar imagines himself negotiating the equally threatening alternatives of a universal human identity and the love of one woman.

Like "that red-headed Negro named X" (160), Guitar is violently opposed to status quo American politics. He asks Milkman, "Where's the money, the state, the country to finance our justice?" (160). As it happens, there is no such money for the Black separatism that Guitar espouses. There is, on the other hand, no shortage in the novel of what Morrison calls "mild liberalism" (190). The civic-minded poet Michael-Mary Graham, who employs Milkman's sister Corinthians as a maid, is the personification of this decidedly New Deal ethos. Graham's poetry had been published "first in 1938, in a volume called *Seasons of My Soul*; there was a second collection in 1941 called *Farther Shores*. What is more, her poems had appeared in at least twenty small literary magazines, two 'slicks,' six college journals, and the Sunday supplements of countless newspapers. She was also the winner, between 1938 and 1958, of nine Poet of the Year awards, culminating finally in the much coveted State Poet Laureateship" (191). Robert Frost, whose New Deal poems were collected in *A Further Range* (1936), is probably not Morrison's object of derision. But the "mild liberalism" Graham personifies is traced unambiguously to the New Deal. Born on the day Smith leaps from the top of Mercy Hospital, Milkman is himself an emblem of the New Deal for which Smith does not wait. "By the time Milkman was fourteen he had noticed that one of his legs was shorter than the other" (62). Instead of mourning his handicap, he embraces it as a source of identification with President Franklin D. Roosevelt: "He favored it, believed it was polio, and felt secretly connected to the late President Roosevelt for that reason. Even when everybody was raving about Truman because he had set up the commission on Civil Rights, Milkman secretly preferred FDR and felt very very close to him. Closer, in fact, to him than to his own father" (62–63). In this light, Milkman is something of a bookend for Wright's Cross Damon, whose official death at "Roosevelt Street Station" marks the close of the New Deal.

Like Damon, Milkman exists in the shadow of his imagined death. His real name, Macon Dead Jr., causes friends to joke that he is free from danger because he is already dead. What is more, Milkman imagines his own death just as surely as Damon pictures his own tombstone: "He lay in Guitar's bed face-up in the sunlight, trying to imagine how it would be when the ice pick entered his neck" (113). As if in response to these visions, Milkman, like Damon, later masquerades as insurance agent.

The nickname "Milkman" itself transforms the unavoidable contingency in Macon's last name into a condition of dependency, for it designates his extremely late weaning and his more general dependency on women. "Everybody he was close to seemed to prefer him out of this life. And the two exceptions were both women, both black, and both old" (331). *The Song of Solomon*'s resonance with *The Grapes of Wrath* is thus unmistakable, whether or not it is intended. We might well imagine that Morrison's novel chronicles the life of any one of the many children in Steinbeck's epic who are left to their mothers after their fathers flee the scene. A more likely reference for *The Song of Solomon,* of course, is the notorious "Moynihan Report," which, forgetting *The Grapes of Wrath,* pathologized the Black male's supposed tendency to flee his domestic responsibilities. But in Morrison's novel, which brings the reader up to the moment just before the report is issued in 1965, men don't simply flee — they fly away: *The Song of Solomon* follows Milkman's quest to trace his lineage to "Solomon," a legendary slave who literally flies back to Africa, leaving his family behind.

Despite his identification with FDR (or perhaps because of his identification with the hobbled man), Milkman too feels the pull of taking to the air. Born in the shadow of the flightless Robert Smith, Milkman longs to leave the ground, longs for the colorless universalism Guitar derides. When he does, he feels himself possessed by utter security: "The airplane ride exhilarated him, encouraged illusion and a feeling of invulnerability. High above the clouds . . . it was not possible to believe he had ever made a mistake, or could. . . . In the air, away from real life, he felt free, but on the ground, when he talked to Guitar just before he left, the wings of all those other people's nightmares flapped in his face and constrained him" (220). Echoing Wright, Morrison contrasts this feeling of unfettered individuality with Milkman's experience of life on the ground. "Under the moon, on the ground," we are told, "his self — the cocoon that was his 'personality' — gave way" (277). But, needless to say, fleeing from "other people's nightmares" takes its toll. The epigraph of *The Song of Solomon* is thus double-edged: "The fathers may soar / And the children may know their name." If the lines suggest that knowing your father's name brings with it a talismanic power (Milkman is in fact reinvigorated by discovering his relation to Solomon), the second equivocal "may" suggests that the possibility of knowing your father's name is small recompense indeed for actually knowing him. Without any particularly strong attachment to his own father — who does not leave, but who remains emotionally distant — Milkman learns instead to love his aunt Pilate, not simply because she saves his life, but "because without ever leaving the ground, she could fly" (336). Pilate sticks around; her love remains local and individual, as she refuses the abstracting flights toward totality so characteristic of the men around her.

5.

Like *Song of Solomon, The Outsider* depicts individuals struggling unsuccessfully to love individual persons, as opposed to races. Damon is desirable to his White lover, the painter Eva Blount, primarily because he is Black. Like Damon, Blount has had her fill with the communism of her lover Gil, so much so that the colors she uses in her nonobjective art reflect her disillusionment with both the left and the skin color of those pursuing its agenda. She writes in her diary, "My loathing of Gil has gone so far that I cannot any longer abide the color pink. I no longer want to paint in reds and blues and greens. . . . They now remind me of Gil's deception. That's why I am beginning to adore colored people; I could live my life with sunburnt people; I wish a warm, rich, brown color" (284). Conflating pink as a literal color — for paint as well as for skin — and as a designation for middle-class leftism, Blount collapses the formal and the political. Blount's place in the novel, along with the white District Attorney who claims that Blacks are both inside and outside their culture, is in this respect crucial. For her abstract art, like the DA's topography, epitomizes the racial dynamics of the existential phenomenology of *The Outsider,* what Margaret Walker calls the novel's "move away from both naturalism and chronological organization into more symbolism and spatial organization."[88]

Wright had begun to associate Black identity with a spatial apprehension of the world at the end of the thirties, as his narrative style gradually gave up the oral and vernacular voice that characterizes *Uncle Tom's Children* (1938) in favor of a free-indirect style that depends on the topographical doubleness I have been associating with both social security and sympathy. Wright makes clear his interest in the spatial as early as 1937, in his essay "Blueprint for Negro Writing," where he claims that "the plight of the Negro in America is above all a question of perspective."[89] In a section titled "The Problem of Perspective," he asks, "What vision must Negro writers have before their eyes in order to feel the impelling necessity for an about face?" (341). The answer, it seems, is nothing less than a picture of the entire world. "A Spanish writer recently spoke of living at the height of one's time," Wright jokes. "Surely perspective means just *that*" (342). Conflating financial success with literal elevation, Wright binds together economic and visual security. But the function of Wright's essay is to argue that "Negro writers must . . . create a meaningful picture of the world today" (340) because they are in some sense emblematic of a crisis in the middle class. He reasons that "somewhere in his writings Lenin makes the observation that oppressed minorities often reflect the techniques of the bourgeoisie more brilliantly than some sections of the bourgeoisie themselves. . . . Lacking the handicaps of false ambitions and property, they have access to a wide social vision and a deep social consciousness. They display a greater freedom and initiative in pushing their claims upon civilization than even do the petty bourgeoisie" (335). *The Outsider* invokes this same claim when it informs us that "Negroes are going to be gifted with a double vision, for, being Negroes, they are going to be both inside and outside our culture at the same time" (163). According to this logic, Black subjects are most able to push their claims on civilization despite the fact that they are the very persons whose claims are most often denied; put only slightly differently, for Wright, Black subjects embody "complete social security" despite the fact that theirs is the one group most comprehensively denied its benefits.

This said, Damon in *The Outsider* finds it almost impossible to maintain this mediated double vision. "Some people are pushed deeper into their environment," he says, "and some are pushed completely out of it" (275). Damon suffers from too much perspective; he was "a man who had killed and fled, a man who had broken all of his ties and was free" (173). The problem, notes Damon two pages later, is that "he was *too* free" (175). Ties broken, Damon floats farther and farther from the world, unable any longer to picture himself within it: "In a strict sense he was not really in the world; he was haunting it for his place, he was pleading for entrance" (167). *Native Son*'s Thomas, on the other hand, is about as deep in his environment as you can get; he suffers from a stifling claustrophobia and the inability to find ground high enough from which he might survey his individual relation to the system that shapes him. Thomas's one dream, he reluctantly tells Max, is to be an aviator (409).[90] This ambition is absolutely constitutive of the *Native Son*'s welfare politics, for like Frost and Berkeley before him, Wright works out the question of whether Thomas's actions are his own or representative of more systemic tendencies in terms of Thomas's vision and point of view.

As we have already seen, Max argues that Thomas is "thrown by an accidental murder into a position where he had sensed a possible order and meaning with the people about him." And in fact, as the plan to pretend he has kidnapped Mary Dalton crystallizes in his head, "The world of sound fell abruptly away from [Thomas] and a vast picture appeared before his eyes" (155). But Thomas experiences "order and meaning" of the right kind, Max insists, only to the degree that he understands his actions as truly accidental. It seems appropriate, then, that Max see Thomas's life turning on the question of how and what he sees: "The central fact to be understood here," he argues at the trial, "is not who wronged this boy, but what kind of vision of the world did he have before his eyes" (461). When we are first introduced to Thomas, he sees the world beyond his ghetto as if from a vast distance; he feels he is on "the outside of the world peeping in through a knot-hole in the fence" (20). No doubt this describes as well Thomas's point of view when he and his cohorts masturbate in a movie theater. If Max wants to know what kind of vision Thomas had before his eyes, the answer seems to be simple: as numerous critics have pointed out, Thomas grows up on the dross of a glamorized popular culture he can see but never have, look at but never touch. But Max's question finds a more specific answer than just "the movies." The cinematic vision before Thomas's eyes (in this instance, the film *Trader Horn*) is above all nonreflexive. This is the case because *Trader Horn* is devoid of people like Thomas: while the newsreels introducing the film recount the "real-life" stories of wealthy scions of privilege like Mary Dalton, the film itself is populated only by leering African "savages."

As the novel progresses, Thomas speaks of vision as if it were a form of political critique. The blind Mrs. Dalton thus literalizes an accusation Thomas metes out to all around him: "Jan was blind. Mary had been blind. Mr. Dalton was blind. . . . Thomas felt that a lot of people were like Mrs. Dalton, blind" (120–21). But Thomas remains equally blinded; he does not come close to an appropriately mediated visual relationship to the world until the last moments of the novel. Before then, he experiences nothing but debased self-consciousness. Looking at the report of Dalton's death in the dailies, for example, Thomas sees himself in print for the first time in his life: "Yes; here was a large picture of him" (296). Murder abstracts Thomas into the eroticized public sphere in which he is first introduced to Mary Dalton, the blindingly White media arena of newspapers, radios, films, and billboards. Under normal circumstances, "Negroes have access to none of [the] highly crystallized modes of expression," explains Max (464).[91] Murder, on the other hand, gives Thomas access to the media, to modes of expression from which he is otherwise excluded. Yet this is hardly access of a useful kind; Thomas pays with his life for his presence in the media. Exceptions like Joe Louis aside, making it into the papers means death if you are a Black man such as Thomas. This is made clear when Thomas locates himself on the map accompanying the reports of his flight: "This time the shaded area [of the map] had deepened from both the north and the south, leaving a small square of white in the middle of the oblong Black Belt. He stood looking at that tiny square of white as though gazing down into the barrel of a gun. He was there on that map, in that white spot, standing in a room waiting for them to come" (296). Thomas is killed by what he sees: the image of himself "on the map" becomes a gun pointed in his face.

Thomas does finally achieve a nonlethal self-transcendence. He does so, in a by now familiar pattern, while contemplating his own impending death. Sitting in his prison cell, transfixed by the fact that "he had to die" (420), Thomas seems on the verge of the eroticized relation to totality captured in Frost's "lover's quarrel with the world." All at once, Thomas feels himself in sympathetic accord with totality. Perched atop a "pinnacle of feeling," in the grips of a "high hope," Thomas suddenly "is seized with a nervous eagerness. He stood up in the middle of the cell floor and tried to see himself in relation to other men, a thing he had always feared to try to do" (418). Gripped by his vision, Thomas sees "an image of a strong blinding sun sending hot rays down and he was standing in the midst of a vast crowd of men, white men and black men and all men, and the sun's rays melted away the many differences, the colors, the clothes, and drew what was common and good upward toward the sun" (420). Literally and figuratively, this is the high point of *Native Son,* the moment that anchors what little hope there is in the novel. Thomas wants, and seems to get, an experience of "union, identity," a "supporting oneness [and] wholeness which had been denied him all his life" (421).

Thomas's momentary vision of unity is, of course, an illusion, as laden with false consciousness as the visions offered up in a Busby Berkeley musical. The United States was not a colorless family and Thomas, sent to his death, is in the end unable to see himself as part of it or the state designed to secure it. Nothing "inside" or "outside" of Wright's novel actually offers Thomas social security. What Thomas gets instead is a resolutely aesthetic experience, one that negotiates the twin demands of personality and security, and in so doing allows him an affective experience of sympathy with a colorless whole the likes of which he has never known. After his vision, Thomas momentarily feels that he "would not mind dying" (420). "If he had to die," he concludes, he wanted "to die within" his experience of transcendence (421).

The novel's reader, however, whether a banker's daughter or not, gets this experience throughout, for the narrative voice of *Native Son* depends on the same topographical doubleness Thomas's vision does. Though the novel powerfully conveys the immediacy of Thomas's lived experience, its strikingly exaggerated free-indirect discourse insists on the permeability of those experiences by an omniscient narrator who moves in and out of Thomas's consciousness. Thus, when Thomas is described looking down at the map of Chicago, Wright's sentence reads: "He was there on that map, in that white spot, standing in a room waiting for them to come." As the frames of reference collapse (Thomas is simultaneously on the map and in the room with the map), it becomes impossible to tell how mediated Thomas's experience finally is. For the "he" in the sentence represents Thomas objectifying his own image on the map as well as Wright objectifying Thomas in the room looking at himself on the map.[92]

Thomas's final, ostensibly redemptive vision is equally confused, and Wright presents it with agonizing ambivalence. The sun that draws the "good upward" and into the light, we are told, is "blinding." But it is not at all clear who is blinded by this heart of light, this sanctifying Kilimanjaro. For though the image of Thomas in the crowd is figuratively blinded, Thomas's imagination is not. And Wright, it would appear, seems unwilling to be as blinded as his character. So, as Thomas's moribund imagination pictures a second version of itself looking blindly upward, trying unsuccessfully to discern the contours of "complete social security," we see perhaps a double of Wright himself, both inside and out, trying hard to believe in the experience he gives Thomas but at the same time somehow unable to convince himself. For Wright, this elusive vision, freighted with both promise and deception, is as utopian as it is ideological. Rejecting the ideal of "personality and security," State's Attorney Buckley describes Max's efforts to construct a "legendary No Man's Land of human thought and feeling" (434). In so doing, however, Buckley simply confirms the distance between his offices and "the glorious Rooseveltian experiment" that Wright would later extol. For Wright invokes the phrase "No Man's Land" in both *The Outsider* — where it describes Damon's ability to exist both inside and outside his culture — and "Personalism," where it describes the origin of "all those progressive forces making for security in American life." Trapped within the bounds of this "No Man's Land," this "no place" — the very definition of utopia — Wright conjures "the reality of the state."

Conclusion

New Deal Postmodernism

From the modernism you want, you get the postmodernism
you deserve. — David Antin, "Modernism and Postmodernism:
Approaching the Present in American Poetry"

In *The Origins of Postmodernity* (1998), a genealogy of postmodernism that serves also as a paean to the writings of Fredric Jameson,
Perry Anderson informs us that Charles Olson is responsible for "the
origination of the term [postmodern] in North America":

> Writing to his fellow-poet Robert Creely on return from the Yucatan
> in the summer of 1951, [Olson] started to speak of a "post-modern
> world" that lay beyond the imperial age of Discoveries and the Indus-
> trial Revolution. "The first half of the twentieth-century," he wrote
> soon afterwards, was "the marshalling yard on which the modern was
> turned to what we have, the post-modern, or post-West." On 4 No-
> vember 1952, the day Eisenhower was elected President, Olson —
> ostensibly supplying information for a biographical dictionary of
> *Twentieth Century Authors* — set down a lapidary manifesto, begin-
> ning with the words, "My shift is that I take it that the present is
> prologue, not the past," and ending with a description of that "going
> live present" as "post-modern, post-humanist, post-historic."

"The sense of these terms," Anderson adds, "came from a distinctive poetic project. Olson's background lay in the New Deal."[1]

Anderson does not himself evaluate Olson's relation to literary
postmodernism; before taking up this matter myself — and commenting on its implications for the New Deal modernism described
above — I should pause to point out just how firmly Olson was in fact
rooted in the New Deal. After the outbreak of the Second World War,
Olson went to work for Elmer Davis and the Office of War Information (OWI), where he assisted in the war effort by producing propaganda alongside such cultural notables as Archibald MacLeish, John
Houseman, Bernard DeVoto, Malcolm Cowley, and Arthur Schles-

· · ·

inger. In response to the Bataan campaign in the Pacific, Olson wrote *Spanish Speaking Americans in the War,* which, according to Olson's biographer, was a "sophisticated manipulation of patriotic feeling that managed to convert sadness over great loss of life into a rousing call to arms, reminding the 'fighters, workers, farmers' of the Southwest that — in the words of pamphleteer Olson — 'ACTION was America's answer to Bataan.' "[2] As the war drew on, the OWI came under increasing attack from Republicans for being a "New Deal publicity center" bent on churning out "window-dressing" for a fourth term for Franklin Roosevelt. Southern Democrats joined with their colleagues across the aisle by lamenting the office's outreach to minorities — in which Olson was heavily involved — as "a philosophy that is alien to us."[3] Frustrated by the restrictions the office began to place on its writers in response to these attacks, Olson quit the agency and was soon thereafter named director of the Foreign Nationalities Division of the Democratic National Committee. In this capacity, Olson was crucial in turning out the immigrant vote for FDR's fourth and closest victory.

Olson believed himself in line for a high-level appointment because of his electioneering — perhaps, he thought, as assistant secretary of the Treasury or State Department, or even as postmaster general.[4] But Roosevelt would not live long into his fourth term, and Olson had made the mistake of vociferously backing Henry Wallace over the more conservative Harry Truman as Roosevelt's running mate. Truman, Roosevelt's eventual choice, would learn of Olson's lobbying. Olson received news of Roosevelt's death while vacationing in Key West with the rest of the Democratic Party, and saw right away that his hopes for advancement within the Party were severely restricted with Truman in office. House-sitting for Pauline Hemingway, struggling with his still unrefined literary gifts at what was once Ernest Hemingway's desk, Olson decided to give up politics and devote himself full time to poetry. Pausing to point out that "the affairs of men remain a chief concern," Olson's early poem, "The K" (1945), announces the poet's self-imposed exile from the corridors of political power: "Full circle: an end to romans, hippocrats and christians."[5] According to his biographer, Olson felt that "American political life was not suited to a creative person, and accordingly he had 'left both politics and government again and gone back to writing.' The political realities of this country, he had discovered, denied artists any vital influence on government policy, instead forcing them into severely compartmentalized roles that guaranteed futility. The modern democratic artist could never be more than just another cog in the bureaucratic machine. His own vision of big government in action had left him with a nostalgia for simpler forms."[6]

But Olson's movement from "the bureaucratic machine" into "simpler forms" was not a pastoral retreat meant to consolidate a realm secure in its autonomy and unchallenged cultural "influence." Moving from big government to poetry, from political to literary form, Olson's career instead marks out a quintessentially New Deal modernist trajectory. His poetry constitutes a relocation of the same energies he brought to bear in Washington: essentially liberal energies that, I will show, use a performance-oriented poetics to consolidate the kind of contingency-free community that was one of the principal goals of the New Deal. After leaving political service, Olson became one of America's most relentlessly avant-garde poets, the pioneering and vastly influential rector of Black Mountain College, the first, Anderson reminds us, to formulate as postmodern a challenge to the increasingly imperial and authoritarian postwar American Century. But whether poet or party hack, Olson devoted himself to the ideals of big government. Robert von Hallberg maintains that as late as 1968, Olson remained an avid New Dealer, cleaving still to Roosevelt's liberal vision in the midst of considerably more radical alternatives.[7] Susan Vanderborg concurs when she notes that Olson's poetry is interested primarily in the civic procedures of "political reform."[8] Even critical accounts that grant Olson a more antihegemonic impulse end up insisting on his moderate, liberal politics. Andrew Ross characterizes Olson in terms of his fraught and ultimately self-defeating "modernist attempt to match formalism with humanism." Ross reasons that Olson's "literary drive feeds directly into politically positivist aims — to successfully produce a new cultural humanism out of novel and radical mutations in language, idiom, form, and subjectivity."[9] As radical, novel, or new as he wanted to be, Olson remained a humanist. This is most evident for Ross in the manner that Olson reaffirms precisely the political epistemology he seeks to undermine; the poet's project of deriving "a more authentic subjectivity" through "*process,*" Ross suggests, ends in an ambivalent and necessarily flawed attempt to "escape the rationalist discourses of authority." Engaged in what he took to be a quintessentially antiliberal project, Olson's attack on subjectivity comes full circle to reaffirm the most basic premises of liberalism. Thus Ross concludes that Olson's claim to the postmodern "may be premature."[10]

Leaving aside for a moment the question of how Olson's ostensibly failed attack on liberal subjectivity might bear on his postmodernism, I want to start by suggesting that Olson's poetry is identifiably New Deal modernist principally in its relentless performativity, in its commitment to what Ross, following Olson, calls *process*. Fascinated with what he called "the *process* of the thing," Olson insisted that "Art does not seek to describe, but to enact." In "A Bibliography on America for Ed Dorn" (1955), he insists on "*process* as the most interesting fact of fact (the overwhelming one, how it works, not what, in that what is always different if the thing or person or event under review is a live one, and is different because adverbially is changing)."[11] Commenting on this essay, Ross finds occasion to point out that, for Olson, poetic labor invariably "takes precedence over the object."[12] In fact, virtually all of Olson's most characteristic formal innovations worked to accentuate the performative dimension of poetry. His "open form" technique, for example, also called "composition by field," used nontraditional typography to accentuate the spoken, communal nature of poetic expression. Eschewing ordinary lineation, straight left-hand margins, and regular meter and verse forms, Olson used the often chaotic arrangement of his words on the page to indicate how to read his poems. He believed that the performance of a given poem should be determined not by metrical feet but by the natural rhythms of thought, breath, and gesture required to scan the poem. According to the *Norton Anthology of American Literature,* Olson used these techniques to bring "mental activity . . . in touch with its physical origins." An Olson poem is in this way "a graph of the process through which it was produced."[13]

These assertions do not themselves establish any particularly compelling compatibility between Olson and the New Deal modernism I have been describing. The American avant-garde turned to the codes of performance art en masse in the decades following World War II, often drawing on aesthetic traditions that had no immediate connection to the New Deal. Influenced by French existentialism, Blake, and Whitman — and apparently uninfluenced by Olson — Allen Ginsberg strove as well to enhance the performed poetic experience by replacing meter and traditional form with the natural syncopations of human breathing. Black Mountain College sported an equally eclectic lineage; "The performance — how it is done — that is the content of art," declared Joseph Alpers, the rector Olson succeeded, a Bauhaus artist who during the thirties introduced the nascent college to the European avant-garde.[14] Later additions to Black Mountain assimilated this avant-garde to more exclusively native traditions; John Cage, for example, came to the college after simultaneously studying with Arnold Schoenberg and laboring on the WPA Arts Projects. Despite its varied history, however, "performance art" broke onto the New York art scene in the early fifties as if it were an entirely new phenomenon. Apparently taking his cue from Black Mountain College's influential "untitled event" in 1952 — performed by Olson, Cage, Mary Caroline Richards, and Robert Rauschenberg — Allan Kaprow staged his *18 Happenings in 6 Parts* in 1959; two years later, the Fluxus group in New York began to bring this fascination with performance to still larger audiences.

Not surprisingly, traditional performing arts such as symphonic music, repertory theater, and modern dance became hotbeds of innovation in performance art: Cage's *4'33"*, in which a pianist sits before his audience opening and closing his piano to mark the progress of silent movements, is perhaps the most notorious case in point. But American artists and critics just as readily understood non-performance-based media in terms of an antagonism between objects and performances. A former consultant for the WPA Arts Projects, Harold Rosenberg described abstract expressionism as "action painting" in *The Anxious Object* (1964). Whereas Clement Greenberg celebrated painters like Pollock, Rothko, and de Kooning because of their tendency to stress the opacity of the painterly medium, Rosenberg maintained that such painters "focused on the inception of the work in opposition to, as Klee put it, the 'end product.' [Their] vocabulary tends to describe its creations in terms of their coming into being: expressions that conceive of a painting as beginning to 'happen' or as 'working itself out' are typical."[15] Rosenberg held that it was only a "logical step" from action painting to "happenings, which carry painting and sculpture over into theatre" (76).

Rosenberg's perception of the painterly investment in theater would find a counterstatement in Michael Fried's landmark essay "Art and Objecthood" (1967). Responding to the performance-oriented desire of minimalists like Robert Morris and Donald Judd to understand installation art not simply as an object, but as an object that needed to be engaged in time by an audience, Fried updated the modernist fascination with process and product. While observing that "modernist painting has come to find it imperative to defeat or suspend its own objecthood," he nonetheless finds fault with "literalist" attempts in minimalism to transform modernism's commitment to objecthood into a commitment to performance. Fried argues that "it is by virtue of their presentness and instantaneousness that modernist painting and sculpture defeat theatre. . . . faced with the need to defeat theatre, it is above all to the condition of painting and sculpture—the condition, that is, of existing in, indeed of secreting or constituting, a continuous and perpetual present—that the other contemporary modernist arts, most notably poetry and music, aspire."[16] Rosenberg had maintained that "the chief attribute of a work of art in our century is not stillness but circulation."[17] Against this claim, Fried insisted that painting defeated theater because it refused to circulate, because it qualified as best it could what Fried would later call "the primordial convention that paintings are made to be beheld."[18]

In his essay "How Modernism Works" (1982), Fried would go on to explain the distinction between presentness and theater laid out in "Art and Objecthood" as one obtaining between modernism and postmodernism proper: "In the years since 'Art and Objecthood' was written," he reasons, "the theatrical has assumed a host of new guises and has acquired a new name: postmodernism."[19] Statements like these suggested to some, principally those affiliated with the journal *October,* a way to map the distinction between artistic product and process onto a binary between a modernist, politically apathetic formalism on the one hand, and a proto-postmodern, proactive commitment to "the performative" on the other.[20] Castigating the ostensibly phallogocentric Clement Greenberg for his celebration of "three dimensional volume," Rosalind Krauss champions surrealists like Marcel Duchamp and Alberto Giacometti in *The Optical Unconscious* (1994), in part because both are committed to what Krauss terms "the temporal dimension" of art, but also because these commitments are seen to enable liberating modes of sexuality and identity unavailable to "pure phallus" modernists such as Fried.[21] Leapfrogging the American midcentury, Krauss uses performative aesthetics to link the European avant-garde with what Hal Foster considers a "postmodernism of resistance" that "seeks to deconstruct modernism and resist the status quo." [22]

This tendency to trace postmodernism — invariably identified as, at least initially, an American phenomenon — back to the performative practices of the European avant-garde is still more endemic in literary studies. We need not agree with Richard Poirier that Robert Frost, Gertrude Stein, and Wallace Stevens "shared [a] distaste for social or economic theory" to take seriously his observation that, despite their abiding interests in human labor and performative aesthetics, these figures are invariably ignored in accounts of the emergence of postmodernism: "Those who write most confidently about some dubious sequence from a putative modernism to a putative postmodernism," Poirier declares, "leave the American contingent from Emerson to William James on to Frost, Stein, and Stevens off the calendar altogether . . . choosing to locate the lines of force and development only among Continental figures." [23] No one has written more confidently on postmodernism — or more eloquently, for that matter — than Fredric Jameson; all the same, Jameson's accounts of postmodernism pass quickly and fitfully over American modernism, moving most forcefully from the political cells and coffee houses of continental Europe at the start of the century to the corporate venues of New York and Los Angeles in the 1970s. Relatively uninterested in distinguishing between the avant-garde and modernism proper, Jameson is most compelling when comparing a largely American postmodernism to its essentially European antecedents.

In a series of essays on the relation between modernism and postmodernism collected in *The Cultural Turn* (1998), we find Jameson reasoning, "Those formerly subversive and embattled styles — Abstract Expressionism; the great modernist poetry of Pound, Eliot, or Wallace Stevens; the International Style (Le Corbusier, Gropius, Mies van der Rohe); Stravinsky; Joyce, Proust and Mann — felt to be scandalous or shocking by our grandparents are, for the generation which arrives at the gate in the 1960s, felt to be the establishment and the enemy — dead, stifling, canonical, the reified monuments one has to destroy to do anything new." [24] Here, Jameson uses modernism proper as the *October* critics use the avant-garde, as the launching pad for all that might be salvaged within the postmodern; this is why, one suspects, Jameson elsewhere reads one of the most "familiar aesthetics of high-modernism" — Pound's "make it new" — as an early instance of the eventually lapsed postmodern performative.[25] The point here is that whereas modernism opposed itself to the institutions and practices of bourgeois society, postmodernism embraces both with glee. "There is some agreement," Jameson writes in *The Cultural Turn,* "that the older modernism functioned against its society in ways which are variously described as critical, negative, contestatory, subversive, oppositional, and the like. Can anything of the sort be affirmed about postmodernism and its social moment?"[26]

One is drawn up by statements such as these not so much by the too casual reference to an undisclosed critical consensus — there is, Jameson avers, "some agreement" on these matters — but by the series of equivalencies that works to install abstract expressionism, Pound, Eliot, and Stevens as, impossibly, "contestatory, subversive, [and] oppositional." If the reactionary poetics of Eliot and Pound represent the negative energy so lacking in postmodernism, we can only wonder why Jameson mourns their passing. If, on the other hand, this same energy can be represented by largely liberal figures like Pollock and Stevens — both deeply implicated in the mechanisms of the American state — then we must stop to wonder exactly what account of American modernism is most operative for Jameson.[27] Perry Anderson's *The Origins of Postmodernity* makes most sense, I think, as an attempt to forestall this signal problem in Jameson. While pausing to grant that his "initial formulations [of postmodernism] were focused principally on North America," Anderson goes so far as to read Jameson himself as the fulfillment of the oppositional energies of modernism, as the principal ligature between the European and the American: "Here," Anderson declares while speaking of Jameson, "is where the critical ambition and revolutionary *élan* of the classical avant-garde have passed. In this register, Jameson's work can be read as a single continuous equivalent of all the passionate meteorologies of the past."[28]

There is a sense in which this is indubitably correct; more than any of his contemporaries, Jameson has uncovered with often impressive nuance how various modernists integrated form and broadly "Western Marxist" systems of thought. But if these readings have seemed less than compelling in the American context, we can begin to understand why Charles Olson is so important to Anderson. Meticulously tracing the origins of the term "postmodernism," Anderson circumnavigates the periphery of the Western world in an effort to connect Jameson's later accounts of postmodernism and his earlier writings on modernism. The virtue of Olson to this project is his status as an American writer nonetheless committed to "a time when the dominance of the West would cease." It is crucial to Anderson that "Olson's visionary confidence," based on his conflation of postwar American imperialism with the Western tradition per se, "was not misplaced; *The Kingfishers* could virtually be read as a brevet for Jameson's achievement."[29] At the heart of that achievement, we are meant to understand, is the conviction that the artistic traditions of Europe transfer to the United States after 1945 as seamlessly as did the seat of global dominance. Thus, the postwar American order becomes symptomatic of an increasingly fluid multinational capitalism at the very moment that American cultural forms no longer seem meaningfully or exclusively American.

But of course, American cultural imperialism has come to seem as noxious as it has precisely because the dross it often foists on the rest of the planet is in fact distinctly American in any number of important ways. As we rush to theorize the multinational nature of contemporary capital, we risk missing entirely the historical contours of the American cultural forms that, Jameson is correct to point out, pave the way for that capital. We must pause and wonder, then, why a thinker as concerned with culture and finance as Jameson passes so completely over the New Deal, moves so indifferently past the immediate political and economic background of postmodernity. Certainly neither the New Deal nor Charles Olson make much of an appearance in his extensive corpus; when they do, both are mentioned in passing, to exemplify the concept of "late modernism." "We should probably make some place," Jameson grants in *Postmodernism, or, The Cultural Logic of Late Capitalism* (1991), "for what Charles Jencks has come to call 'late modernism' — the last survivals of a properly modernist view of art and the world after the great political and economic break of the Depression, where, under Stalinism or the Popular Front, Hitler or the New Deal, some new conception of social realism achieves the status of momentary cultural dominance by way of collective anxiety and world war."[30] With dizzying speed, the Third Reich collapses into the New Deal, ostensibly because both advocated "some new conception of social realism," a concept that takes its place under the aegis of "a properly modernist view of art and the world." This view of the world, we have already seen, is "contestatory, subversive, [and] oppositional"; just before nodding toward "late modernism," Jameson cites Perry Anderson, declaring that the "deepest and most fundamental feature shared by all the modernisms is . . . their hostility to the market itself" (304–5).

Nothing could be farther from the case with New Deal modernism, which was committed more to the liberal protocols of reform than to the eschatological ruptures important to any critic still invested in the idea of revolution. New Deal modernism might seem in this light caught between Jameson's account of the modern and the postmodern, between the fiercely autonomous, antimarket forces of an oppositional modernism and the complicit, corporation-friendly complacencies of postmodernism. In fact, how one feels about the welfare state — about whether, at bottom, it marks a significant revision of laissez-faire — may be all that separates New Deal modernism from New Deal postmodernism. Looking back on the thirties from the end of the nineties, there seems ample evidence for either hope or despair. The simple fact, however, is that the writers described above were "hostile" to the market only insofar as they wanted to reform it, to mediate its more egregious uncertainties. The New Deal modernist ethos of reform — articulated, I have argued, in consistently performative aesthetics — offered nothing like an avant-garde attack on the institutions of civil society, but instead set out to transform those institutions into organs of social security by the welfare state. Whether or not such an assertion changes when we mark the end of modernism and the emergence of postmodernism is, finally, of little consequence. For that matter, there is still less at stake in deciding whether a figure like Charles Olson was, strictly speaking, a late modernist or a postmodernist. There is, on the other hand, quite a bit at stake in how broadly we characterize aesthetic paradigms based on their supposed hostility to a concept as unrelentingly abstract as "the market." As I will show in a moment, Olson used the notion of projective verse to redress the atomizing contingency of laissez-faire culture. In doing so, he no more exposed a "deep" and "fundamental" hostility toward the market than he did in working tirelessly for Franklin Delano Roosevelt. Quite the contrary: his efforts to supplement the political and economic with the aesthetic expressed a profound commitment to the civic procedures — and attendant compromises — of the interventionist state.

New Deal modernists pointed out persistently that not all markets are laissez-faire; conversely, these writers tended to be hostile to markets only to the extent that they advocated not writing altogether. Almost invariably, however, even the most radical writers embraced the mechanisms of governmental reform, particularly as these reforms were brought to bear on the institution of bourgeois literary patronage itself. More than any other during the Depression, this particular institution seemed to encapsulate if not amplify a crisis of underconsumption crippling the national economy. As I have already pointed out, the Federal Writers' Project responded to this perceived crisis by embracing performative aesthetics, not, ultimately, as a means of bringing writers into sync with either working- or middle-class audiences, but as a means of escaping the idea of audience altogether. The Writers' Project understood writing as labor primarily to make coherent a salary form that released the writer from ever having to sell his or her work. A cornerstone of New Deal efforts to produce community through regulated, non-laissez-faire mechanisms, the Writers' Project described writing not as a commodity to be consumed but as a form of collective labor in which American citizens could participate and so become transformed into newly empowered producers. As John Dewey suggested in *Art and Experience,* the ideal experience of art should approximate as closely as possible the physical conditions of its creation; taking this observation seriously, the Writers' Project circumvented the vagaries of literary consumption by theorizing a form of writing that need never be bought.

The organic autonomy so important to Gertrude Stein and Ernest Hemingway seems at first to represent an alternative to this view: both authors commit to objects even as the New Deal they reviled committed to the trope of literature as labor. Conceived of as a non-relational "entity," writing defeated what Stein called "theater" by shutting itself off from ignorant audiences, by becoming a self-sufficient, inviolate identity, both oblivious and impervious to the conditions of its consumption. But Stein and Hemingway embraced literary objecthood for exactly the same reasons the Writers' Project rejected it: both camps released the writer from dependence on invariably equivocal markets. What the Writers' Project did as an institution, Stein and Hemingway accomplished through analogy; perfectly organic literary artifacts were absolved from contingency, they held, by achieving the unity so cherished by modern government. In this,

Stein and Hemingway were akin to Wallace Stevens, who completed the literary revision of market contingency by comparing poetry to New Deal mechanisms of social insurance. He reasoned that poetry could produce the effects of a risk-free human collectivity more effectively than even the New Deal that inspired him, principally because poetry embodied the market more than it served as a commodity within it. In this way, Stevens conceived of poetry as an interpersonal principle of circulation not unlike money itself, a formal ligature that closed the breach between consumers and producers.

Sentimental writers preoccupied with public sympathy and its relation to New Deal social programs, John Steinbeck and Betty Smith achieved this fusion of consumption and production in different terms. Both authors sought to articulate relations of sympathy that seemed emblematic of relations between writers and their readers, relations of sympathy that obviated the need for there ever being sympathetic spectators (or literary consumers) beyond the author himself or herself. Insofar as sympathy required imagining how others would respond to you in a given situation — or conversely, of how you would respond were it another in that situation — both authors found in the experience of sympathy a problem emblematic of laissez-faire consumption. Both found as well a schizophrenic doubling emblematic of the writer's relation to these markets, a doubling redressed through primarily narcissistic means. For Steinbeck and Smith, sentimental writing became a kind of performance art not unlike the act of writing itself, for despite its resolutely progressive overtones, the mechanisms of self-projection at the heart of sympathy suggested a form of solipsism in which authors became their only readers. Warner Brothers' *Gold Diggers* musicals work toward a related effect; as the audience is invited to imagine itself participating in the film, as spectators are transported into Busby Berkeley's extravagantly reflexive and frame-breaking organic arrangements, the circle closes between passive consumption and active production. This absolute identification between performer and audience is at the very heart of the New Deal modern fantasy, which consistently uses the aesthetic experience, initially as emblem and finally as solution to the looming specter of forms of consumption that cannot be rationalized.

Charles Olson's fascination with "process" belongs squarely within this characteristically New Deal set of concerns. In his most influential essay, "Projective Verse" (1950), Olson declares, "Verse now, 1950, if it is to go ahead, if it is to be of essential use, must, I take it, catch up and put into itself certain laws and possibilities of the breath, of the breathing of the man who writes as well as of his listenings."[31] Similar statements throughout the essay suggest an abiding concern with the exchange that takes place between literary producers and consumers. Olson maintains that "a poem is energy transferred from where the poet got it (he will have some several causations), by way of the poem itself to, all the way over to, the reader" (240). The poem, he declared, is "a passage of force from subject to object" (244). Poetry needed to replace traditional meter and form with the rhythms of human breath to render this passage of force as instantaneous as possible. "What we have suffered from," he declares, "is manuscript, press, the removal of verse from its producer and its reproducer, the voice, a removal by one, by two removes from its place of origin *and* its destination" (245). But live, interactive poetry — in which a poet could come face to face with his or her listeners — did not alone change the fact that the producer and reproducer of a poem (the poet and his or her voice) were still themselves removed from the destination of poetic verse, the ear of the listener. Poetry was projective, Olson reasoned, not simply because it achieved an almost instantaneous passage from subject to object but because, more radically, it collapsed the space separating subject and object altogether. Wanting "to emphasize the already projective verse as the sons of Pound and Williams are practicing it," he says, "already they are composing as though verse was to have the reading its writing involved, as though not the eye but the ear was to be its measurer, as though the intervals of its composition could be so carefully put down as to be precisely the intervals of its registration" (246). Here, finally, was to be the solution to the literary schizophrenia noted so persistently by writers such as Jack London, James Cain, James Farrell, and Richard Wright, doublings that split the author into both writer and reader, into both producer and consumer. Rendering identical "the intervals" of poetic "composition" and "registration," Olson collapses the difference between the poem's composition and its performance at the same moment that he renders the poet identical to his or her audience. Von Hallberg explains that for Olson, poetry "is less like painting, music, or sculpture than it is like guerrilla theatre, in which the conventional separation between audience and actor disappears. . . . The poem as artifact, the good poem, was not Olson's concern," von Hallberg reasons; rather, Olson found in poetry a way for engaged "experience [to] supplant [passive] spectacle."[32] Collapsing completely the separation between subject and object, between literary producer and literary consumer, Olson's performative could in this way complete his aborted New Deal career; financial markets may have been beyond his control, but poetic markets were not. Still absorbed by "the affairs of men," Olson claimed that poetry was "the only answer to the spectatorism which both capitalism and communism breed—breed as surely as absentee ownership (whether of a leisure class or of a dictatorship, in the 'proletarian' sense) doth breed it, separating men from action."[33]

Poetry was an alternative to capitalist passivity, from one perspective, because it allowed the reader (ideally a listener) to equate an act of consumerism with one of production. Like so much performance art, the poem is interactive precisely so the audience can confuse reception with composition. Thus, Susan Vanderborg sees Olson's *Maximus Poems* organized around a "need to make author and audience respond to each other"; in general, she declares that Olson was preoccupied with the question of how one can "make participation attractive to an audience." For Vanderborg, this account of audience participation leads very naturally into an account of politics: "Not only did Olson see the choice of poetic form as a political strategy of interpretation, but he believed that poetry could influence politics directly. He strove to make his own poems . . . a model for a new participatory polis that might spur his audience to political reform. Specifically, he tried to create a communal text that redefined its own borders to incorporate marginal voices and narratives, an alternative to the repressive public policies he described during the Second World War and its aftermath."[34] But putting matters this way confuses the desire to influence politics with the effort to embody its procedures in a manner unavailable to actual institutions. Olson did not see poetic form as a town hall for political debate so much as he used poetry to transform town halls into the kinds of fantasy markets at the heart of New Deal modernism. Collapsing the difference between consumers and producers, Olson produces an interactive community in which all can imagine themselves at work, laboring at the business of poetry.

This does not, I should stress, implicate Olson in a cynical vision of economic co-optation, in which otherwise emancipatory formal commitments are neutralized by their association — direct or otherwise — with the state apparatus. At the same time, the fact that some of the most performative New Deal writing that I take up above was paid for by the state and the modern corporation is not simply incidental, not simply an ironic page torn from the history of those compromises writers have had reluctantly to endure over the centuries to support their work. Rather, in turning to performance as an aesthetic touchstone, the New Deal picked up on the fundamentally corporate desire of the avant-garde, in Peter Bürger's terms, "to eliminate the antithesis between producer and recipient," a desire, I have been suggesting, that has cut at least two different ways since the New Deal. For if, from one point of view, the desire for unity between producer and consumer seeks to effect a radical redistribution in cultural wealth — in which individual citizens are endowed with the means for producing culture — from another it articulates a dream of uninhibited, purely rationalized consumption, in which the contingency embodied in the idea of an audience vanishes and leaves in its wake a demand for art as ineluctable as the demand for food.

The New Deal performative spanned these alternatives. From one perspective, it served as a mechanism for writers and the state to imagine the production and consumption of art as one and the same event, an event that seemed to eliminate the contingency of markets and endow artist and consumers alike with newfound agency. The performance artist was all at once able to rationalize the relation between his or her labor and the way he or she was paid for it. But from another perspective, the New Deal performative would end up meaning more to the consumers of culture than to its producers; in the grips of this aesthetic, consumer-participants were able to imagine themselves producing art in their experience of it. If the public was indeed a disembodied phantom, it seemed most corporeal, most like a human agent, when consuming art.

Just as beleaguered New Deal writers shored up their professional agency with what turned out to be an atavistic commitment to labor, so too they ushered in a postmodern sensibility that, crushingly, would enshrine consumption as a legitimate form of political action. To recall Roland Barthes, the goal of the readerly text — that touchstone of postmodern literary ideals — "is to make the reader no longer a consumer, but a producer of the text. Our literature is characterized by the pitiless divorce which the literary institution maintains between the producer of the text and its user, between its owner and its customer, between its author and its reader."[35] But what cold comfort must the readerly text ultimately be. Increasingly denied agency in Keynesian economies geared toward increasingly concentrated corporate hierarchies, American consumers — let alone academics — would find in performative art the kinds of participatory agency they could not in political or economic spheres. It is appealing to describe this difference in redemptive or emancipatory terms. But it makes far more sense to describe performative art as what it has been: a technology that, for better or for worse, has facilitated the organization of the American citizen into increasingly secure cultural and economic forms.

Notes

Introduction: The Literature of the Welfare State

1 Franklin Delano Roosevelt, "Annual Message to the Congress," in *The Court Disapproves,* vol. 4 of *The Public Papers and Addresses of Franklin D. Roosevelt* (New York: Russell and Russell, 1938–1950), 17.
2 Franklin Delano Roosevelt, "Presidential Statement upon Signing the Social Security Act," in ibid., 324.
3 Ibid.
4 Wallace Stevens, "Insurance and Social Change," in *Opus Posthumous,* rev. ed. (New York: Knopf, 1989), 233.
5 Milton Bates, *Wallace Stevens: A Mythology of Self* (Berkeley: University of California Press, 1985), 158.
6 Richard Wright, *Native Son and "How 'Bigger' Was Born"* (New York: Harper Perennial, 1993), 472.
7 Irving Howe, introduction to *Beyond the Welfare State,* ed. Irving Howe (New York: Schocken, 1982), 12, 5.
8 As Daniel T. Rodgers explains, the New Deal did not seem to offer anything like a consistent ideology even to its contemporaries: " 'Aimless experiment, sporadic patchwork, a total indifference to guiding principles or definite goals,' Lewis Mumford scolded Franklin Roosevelt's policies in the fall of 1934; there was no logic to the New Deal, he objected, only drift through a sea of 'confused and contradictory nostrums.' Mumford was in a particularly radical mood that season as the Roosevelt administration moved into its second Depression winter. But his exasperation at the incoherence of the New Deal was a commonplace of the 1930s. Even administration insiders like Rexford Tugwell and Frances Perkins admitted that finding the central tendency in Roosevelt's moves took a kind of lucky divination." Rodgers continues by observing that "the conundrum the New Deal poses" involves the question of "how to square its energy, in a decade that dealt so cruelly with progressive governments elsewhere, with its monumental confusions. Without intellectual and ideological passion, the New Deal is all but inexplicable, yet virtually every quest for the New Deal's logic seems only to unravel in contradictions. The riddle of the New Deal is how to understand the marriage of such striking success with such massive apparent incoherence." See Rodgers, *Atlantic Crossings: Social Politics in a Progressive Era* (Cambridge, MA: Harvard University Press, 1998), 409, 412. Need-

• • •

less to say, the point here is not that it is futile to characterize the New Deal; Rodgers does, and notes in particular that if the New Deal did not seem coherent to Americans, it remained powerfully so abroad: "Keynes saw in the New Deal the 'middle way' American progressives so often looked for in Europe: a 'half-way house' between Marxism and laissez-faire. In France, Léon Blum led a socialist-radical government to power in 1936 with a rhetoric of progressive experimentation explicitly derivative of the American New Deal. In Britain, David Lloyd George staged the Liberal Party's quest for renewed power as a 'new deal' for Britain." As Rodgers sees it, the New Deal was the first and most definitive crystallization of an early twentieth-century transatlantic progressivism whose legacy is still very much with us today: "In no other nation of the North Atlantic economy was the progressive response to the world Depression of the 1930s as vigorous as in New Deal America" (411).

9 It has taken a book like Astradur Eysteinsson's *The Concept of Modernism* (Ithaca, NY: Cornell University Press, 1990) to show just how contradictory and incoherent many of these formulations are. See chapter 1, "The Making of Modernist Paradigms."

10 Alan Filreis, *Modernism from Right to Left: Wallace Stevens, the Thirties, and Literary Radicalism* (New York: Cambridge University Press, 1994), 10, 5.

11 Eysteinsson, *The Concept of Modernism,* 15.

12 John Crowe Ransom, *The World's Body* (New York: Scribners, 1938), 41.

13 T. S. Eliot, *The Complete Poems and Plays, 1909–1950* (New York: Harcourt Brace, 1958), 291.

14 John Gabriel Hunt, ed., *The Essential Franklin Delano Roosevelt* (New York: Random House, 1995), 82, 83. Seven years after Roosevelt introduced the administration, the National Resources Planning Board's Committee on Long-Range Work and Relief Policies expressed the same sentiment in their *After the War — Toward Security,* a treatise on the centrality of social security to the modern welfare state. "Social insurance agencies are not and cannot be regarded as something wholly independent of other governmental activity or other economic activity," the report reads. But even more strongly, the report transforms social security into the guiding principle not simply of the New Deal but of modern democracy itself. "For many centuries and in many lands, the problem of social security has challenged the best efforts of man. In our occidental world the profound changes of the industrial revolution loosed technological and social forces which made it impossible for either the family or the churches to do the necessary job of caring for the needy, even when aided by other voluntary associations." The report continues: "It is not by accident that public aid policies are adopted by our governments, for without social and economic security there can be no true guarantee of freedom. Our efforts to establish life, liberty, and the pursuit of happiness are not effective unless and until they rest on a firm foundation of social and economic security" (1). See National Resources

Planning Board's Committee on Long-Range Work and Relief Policies, *After the War — Toward Security: Freedom from Want* (Washington, DC: U.S. GPO, 1942), 6.

15 Alan Brinkley, *The End of Reform, New Deal Liberalism in Recession and War* (New York: Vintage, 1995), 73; Linda Gordon, *Pitied but Not Entitled: Single Mothers and the History of Welfare 1890–1935* (New York: The Free Press, 1994), 3; Alan Dawley, *Struggles for Justice: Social Responsibility and the Liberal State* (Cambridge, MA: Harvard University Press, 1991), 4, 77.

16 I. M. Rubinow, *Quest for Security* (New York: H. Holt, 1934). In 1936 Roosevelt returned a copy of the book to Rubinow, inscribed "From the reader to the author." See Philip Elkin, "The Father of American Social Insurance: I. M. Rubinow," in *Modern Insurance Theory and Education: A Social History of Insurance Evolution in the United States during the Twentieth Century,* vol. 1, ed. Kailin Tuan (Orange, NJ: Varsity Press, 1972), 361, 354.

17 Rufus M. Potts, "The Altruistic Utilitarianism of Insurance" (1916), in Tuan, *Modern Insurance Theory,* 320.

18 Edwin Witte, in "What to Expect of Social Security" (1944), in Tuan, *Modern Insurance Theory,* 476.

19 Thurman Arnold, *Symbols of Government* (New Haven: Yale University Press, 1935), 241. For Arnold's use of the term "welfare state," see Fred Shapiro, "Thurman Arnold, Willmott Lewis, and the Origin of the term 'Welfare State,' " *Notes and Queries* 35, no. 233 (September 1988): 3.

20 See Francis MacDonnell, " 'The Emerald City Was the New Deal': E. Y. Harburgh and *The Wonderful Wizard of Oz,*" *Journal of American Culture* 13, no. 4 (1990).

21 Alfred Manes, "Progress of the Insurance Idea," in Tuan, *Modern Insurance Theory,* 304, 305.

22 Oliver Wendell Holmes, *The Common Law,* ed. Mark DeWolf Howe (Cambridge, MA: Belknap Press of Harvard University Press, 1963), 77. In 1936, Jean-Pierre Maxence, mourning France's commitment to the welfare state and its concomitant distance from the Axis powers, claimed, "While most countries of Europe are being led towards greatness and adventure, our leaders are inviting us to transform France into an insurance company" (quoted in Tony Judt, *Past Imperfect: French Intellectuals, 1944–1956* [Berkeley: University of California Press, 1992], 17).

23 Josephine Herbst, *The Rope of Gold* (New York: Harcourt Brace, 1939), 158, 33; emphasis in original. More recently, Daniel Defert has insisted that insurance is "a *generalizable technology* for rationalizing societies . . . a figure of social organization which far transcends the choice which some thinkers are currently putting to use between the alternatives of privatization and nationalization of security systems" (215). See Defert, " 'Popular Life' and Insurance Technology," in *The Foucault Effect: Studies in Governmentality,* ed. Graham Burchell, Colin Gordon, and Peter Miller (Chicago: University of Chicago Press, 1991).

24 F. R. Ankersmit, *Aesthetic Politics: Political Philosophy beyond Fact and Value* (Stanford: Stanford University Press, 1996), 276, 193, 152, 188.

25 Alain Desrosières, *The Politics of Large Numbers: A History of Statistical Reasoning,* trans. Camille Naish (Cambridge, MA: Harvard University Press, 1998), 194, 199. Desrosières points out that "as the etymology of the word shows, statistics is connected with the construction of the state, with its unification and administration. All this involves the establishment of general forms, of categories of equivalence, and terminologies that transcend the singularities of individual situations" (8).

26 Robert McElvaine, *The Great Depression: America, 1929–1941* (New York: Times Books, 1993), 75.

27 Kenneth Burke, *The Philosophy of Literary Form* (1941; Berkeley: University of California Press, 1972), 18.

28 Holly Stevens, ed., *The Letters of Wallace Stevens* (New York: Knopf, 1966), 286.

29 Wallace Stevens, *The Necessary Angel: Essays on Reality and the Imagination* (New York: Vintage, 1951), 21.

30 Max Horkheimer and Theodor Adorno, *The Dialectic of Enlightenment* (New York: Continuum, 1990), 145.

31 Michael Denning, *The Cultural Front: The Laboring of American Culture in the Twentieth Century* (London: Verso, 1996), 5. For other work concerned with the relation between class politics and literature during the 1930s, see Daniel Aaron, *Writers on the Left* (New York: Avon, 1952); Marcus Klein, *Foreigners: The Making of American Literature, 1900–1940* (Chicago: University of Chicago Press, 1981); Eric Homberger, *American Writers and Radical Politics, 1900–1939* (New York: St. Martin's, 1986).

32 Michael North, *The Political Aesthetics of Yeats, Eliot, and Pound* (New York: Cambridge University Press, 1991), 3.

33 Edward Berkowitz, *America's Welfare State, From Roosevelt to Reagan* (Baltimore: Johns Hopkins University Press, 1991), xiii.

34 Nelson Algren, *Nonconformity* (1950–1953; New York: Seven Stories, 1996), 38.

35 Norman Mailer, "The White Negro: Some Superficial Reflections on the Hipster" (1957), in *The Portable Beat Reader,* ed. Ann Charters (New York: Penguin, 1992), 584, 583, 600, 601.

36 James Baldwin, "The Black Boy Looks at the White Boy," in *Nobody Knows My Name* (New York: Michael Joseph, 1964), 188, 189.

1. "The Whole Question of What Writing Is": *Jack London, the Literary Left, and the Federal Writers' Project*

1 James Agee and Walker Evans, *Let Us Now Praise Famous Men: Three Tenant Families* (Boston: Houghton Mifflin, 1988), 41, 42.

2   Peter Cosgrove offers one version of this sentiment when he argues that *Let Us Now Praise Famous Men* "is a product of the Great Depression, which," he insists, "still occupies a mythic place as the moment when irrepressible private suffering publicly marked a faltering of capitalism." Cosgrove goes on to describe how Agee's "modernist aesthetic" works to "replicate the antinomies of private and public as a tension between artistic independence and corporate patronage." Cosgrove sees even Walker Evans's photographs operating "as a hinge between the internal relations of private life and its domination by public structures." In this account, artistic independence seems to mean privacy, and we are meant to understand that the history of the "modernist aesthetic" Agee shared with his contemporaries has been the history of art's betrayal at the hands of government and corporate modes of patronage antithetical to that privacy. Read this way, however, Agee's putative nostalgia for "artistic independence" misses entirely the significance of those formal and stylistic developments brought about by the rise of both state and corporate patronage — misses, in other words, the transformations undergone by American modernism as it impacted with the New Deal. See Cosgrove, "Snapshots of the Absolute: Mediamachia in *Let Us Now Praise Famous Men*," *American Literature* 67 (June 1995): 329, 352. Another critic uses this same antinomy when he describes Wallace Stevens responding to Social Security by "redoubl[ing] his rhetorical efforts to establish a private poetic that can reduce the anxiety occasioned by current history" (Joseph Harrington, "Wallace Stevens and the Poetics of National Insurance," *American Literature* 67 [1995]: 110). This reading is crucially incorrect for Stevens, as I show in chapter 3.

3   In its ambivalent and ultimately counterfactual commitment to "the actual," Agee's text is a curious amalgam of American pragmatism and European avant-gardism; his painstaking accounting of his host's finances, indeed his sustained fascination with what it means for his art to retreat so completely from the pretenses of civilization into a purifying natural setting of vigorous work, gesture to Thoreau's *Walden* at the same time that his aesthetics of quotidian inclusion gesture to the ready-made or the objet trouvé. In either context, it is easy to see *Let Us Now Praise Famous Men* as a performance: the eclectic work is essentially an ongoing diary; a record of its own construction, the text is a palimpsest of material written over a span of four years, material Agee does not bother to unify or reconcile under a single publication date.

4   Cited in Malcolm Cowley, *The Literary Situation* (New York: Viking Press, 1954), 172.

5   My use of the term "performative" here and in each of these chapters makes unavoidable reference both to J. L. Austin's *How to Do Things with Words* (1962) and subsequent responses to Austin, from Jacques Derrida's *Limited Inc.* (1983) to Judith Butler's *Gender Trouble* (1990) and *Excitable Speech* (1997). As one critic has recently noted, "The concept of the performative is now a complex accretion, continually

evolving over the last thirty-odd years from its introduction into philosophy by J. L. Austin, through its qualification by speech act theorists such as John Searle and Paul Grice and linguists such as Emile Benveniste, through post-structuralist critiques by Jacques Derrida and Shoshana Felman and its adoption in rhetorical criticism by Barbara Johnson and J. Hillis Miller, to recent use in poetry studies and a burgeoning appropriation by anthropology, queer theory, and performance studies" (E. Warwick Slinn, "Poetry and Culture: Performativity and Critique," *New Literary History* 30, no. 1 [1999]: 60). I am not, however, concerned with language theory per se; rather, I use the term to describe New Deal discourses that understand art generally and literature specifically as an activity not necessarily or primarily productive of an artifact. These discourses have as much in common with what Richard Poirier has called Emersonian pragmatism as they do with poststructuralism. "We can learn a great deal about art by telling the dancer from the dance," writes Poirier, nodding to Paul de Man. "Dancers themselves do; and writers are always more anxious than are their critics to distinguish between writing as an act and the book or poem" (Richard Poirier, *The Performing Self: Compositions and Decompositions in the Languages of Contemporary Life* [New York: Oxford University Press, 1971], 87). " 'Art' itself," Poirier declares, is constituted in "the performative acts out of which texts are produced" (Richard Poirier, *Poetry and Pragmatism* [Cambridge, MA: Harvard University Press, 1992], 65). I will have more to say at different points in *New Deal Modernism* about the relation between the New Deal performative and both poststructuralism and American pragmatism. Here, I want simply to note that although I take up exactly those authors Poirier describes as modernist inheritors of Emersonian pragmatism (Frost, Stein, and Stevens in particular), I do not construct a strictly American genealogy for the modernist commitment to performance. An avant-garde formation such as Dada, we will see, figured every bit as powerfully in the construction of New Deal writing as did, say, Emerson and Thoreau. Conversely, the discourses I point out do more than simply reiterate a fascination, as old as aesthetic theory itself, with distinctions between artistic processes and products (not even Poirier would claim this distinction originates with Emerson).

6 Edward Bruce, "Implications of the Public Works of Art Project," *American Magazine of Art* (March 1934): 114.

7 Alfred Kazin, *On Native Grounds* (New York: Reynal and Hitchcock, 1942), 501.

8 Cowley, *Literary Situation,* 176. Cowley argues that, by 1954, one could be a professional writer without ever producing literary artifacts; the university instructor, for instance, teaches creative writing "without any interlude for writing creatively, or even commercially" (166). Cowley notes that in the 1920s writing "had consisted — according to commonly quoted figures — of seventy per cent of fiction and thirty per cent of

nonfiction; in the 1950s the proportions had been reversed" (176). This leads Cowley to conclude that "authors as a class [had become] replaceable persons" (170).

9 In Marcus Klein, *Foreigners: The Making of American Literature, 1900–1940* (Chicago: University of Chicago Press, 1981), 64.

10 Jim Thompson, *Now and on Earth* (1942; New York: Vintage, 1994), 236.

11 Jack London, *Martin Eden* (1909; London: Penguin, 1985).

12 William Dean Howells, *Literature and Life: Studies* (New York: Harpers, 1902), 20.

13 Poirier, *Performing Self*, 88.

14 When Marx distinguishes between "abstract" alienated labor and the "concrete" unalienated labor inimical to labor power, concrete labor is characterized by its ability to coalesce in a singular artifact that, not incidentally, resembles a work of art. Marx notes in the *Grundrisse*: "The economic relation—the character assumed by capitalist and worker as the two extremes of a relationship of production—develops, consequently, in a manner all the more pure and adequate in proportion to the extent that labor loses its character of art; that is to the extent that its particular skill is converted into something that is increasingly abstract and undifferentiated, into an attitude that is more and more purely abstract, merely mechanical and, consequently, indifferent to its specific form; into a purely formal activity or, what is the same thing, a purely material activity which is indifferent as to its form" (quoted in Adolfo Sanchez Vazquez, *Art and Society: Essays in Marxist Aesthetics,* trans. Maro Riofrancos [New York: Monthly Review Press, 1973], 205). When the producer of a singular artifact (a "specific form") receives a wage, he becomes engaged in a "purely formal activity" (one "indifferent" to that form). This has led Adolfo Sanchez Vazquez to assume that "the threat which constantly hangs over art in capitalist society is precisely this: that it will be treated in the only way that interests a world ruled by the law of surplus production, that is, according to economic criteria, as wage labor" (200). Vazquez notes that "the attempt to subject artistic activity to the laws of wage labor entails both the alienation of the laborer, with all the negative consequences that implies, and the introduction of coercion to the sphere of art, which by its very essence is the sphere of creativity and freedom" (224).

15 Louis Menand, *Discovering Modernism: T. S. Eliot and His Context* (New York: Oxford University Press, 1987), 61.

16 Jack London, *The Letters of Jack London* (Palo Alto: Stanford University Press, 1988), 759.

17 Henry James, *The Portrait of a Lady* (New York: Norton, 1975), 12.

18 William Dean Howells, *A Hazard of New Fortunes* (1890; New York: E. P. Dutton, 1952), 3.

19 Christopher Wilson generalizes the problem of literary professionalism

in the Progressive era in terms of the demands of mass markets and a conflicted naturalist aesthetic that wants to be both romantically transcendent and socially critical. Wilson uses Howells's "The Man of Letters as a Man of Business" to emblematize the Progressive fear that "professionalism might be bound, almost inevitably, to the principle of exchange; that their credentials would be established only in practice, and not before it; and that their status as expert or professional would rely rather heavily on the often elusive plebiscite of mass-popularity." For Wilson, London is transfixed and ultimately incapacitated by his inability to get beyond the insoluble dilemma posed by his desire for " 'mastery' and the status of the artisan" on the one hand, and by his dependence on the recognition of a mass public on the other. See Wilson, *The Labor of Words: Literary Professionalism in the Progressive Era* (Athens: University of Georgia Press, 1985), 16, 123. See also Burton Bledstein, *The Culture of Professionalism* (New York: Norton, 1976), 34, 36, 38.

20 Cited in Thomas Riha, ed., *Readings in Russian Civilization* (Chicago: University of Chicago Press, 1969), 694.

21 *The First American Writers Congress* (New York: Equinox, 1935), 10.

22 Statistics from Arthur Domenic Casciato, *Citizen Writers: A History of the League of American Writers, 1935–1942* (Ph.D. diss., University of Virginia, 1986), 48–50.

23 Cited in ibid., 46.

24 The John Reed Clubs were dissolved in September 1934 to make way for the League of American Writers, which was affiliated with the International Union of Revolutionary Writers, the literary wing of the Comintern. Despite the fact that writers in attendance such as Kenneth Burke were eager to unite radicals and liberals in their opposition to war, fascism, and just simply the economic dislocation of the Depression itself, the League's elision of class and professional concerns was not, strictly speaking, the product of the Popular Front, which was announced later in the summer of 1935 by the Seventh World Congress of the Comintern.

25 Joseph Freeman, introduction to *Proletarian Literature in the United States: An Anthology* (New York: International Publishers, 1935), 16.

26 Quoted in Douglas Wixson, *Worker-Writer in America: Jack Conroy and the Tradition of Midwestern Literary Radicalism, 1898–1990* (Chicago: University of Illinois Press, 1994), 296.

27 James T. Farrell, *Yet Other Waters* (New York: Vanguard, 1952), 23.

28 Granville Hicks, "The Crisis in American Criticism," *New Masses* 5 (1933): 8.

29 Rideout observes, "During the decade seventy examples of the form were published, fifty of them, a significantly large majority, appearing between 1930 and 1935" (*The Radical Novel in the United States, 1900–1954: Some Interrelations of Literature and Society* [New York: Columbia University Press, 1992], 171).

30 *The Writer in a Changing World: The Proceedings of the Second American Writers' Congress* (New York: Equinox, 1937). For a recent recollection of the League of American Writers, see Franklin Folsom, *Days of Anger, Days of Hope: A Memoir of the League of American Writers, 1937–1942* (Boulder: University of Colorado Press, 1994).

31 Cited in Harvey Klehr, *The Heyday of American Communism* (New York: Basic Books, 1984), 353.

32 Alan Filreis, "Stevens, 'J. Ronald Latimer,' and the Alcestis Press," *Wallace Stevens Journal* 17, no. 2 (fall 1993): 181.

33 Monty Noam Penkower, *The Federal Writers' Project: A Study in Government Patronage of the Arts* (Urbana: University of Illinois Press, 1977), 5.

34 Williams replied, "There is a place in our economic system for literature as a profession but all the elevators are broken down. Nobody can get up there. It's too high. One life is not long enough for a man to make the ascent in." See "The Situation in American Writing," *Partisan Review* 6, no. 4 (1939): 43. Early in his own literary career, Wallace Stevens mused, "Is literature really a profession?" T. S. Eliot would later emphatically answer yes; in 1918 he railed against the British "dislike of the specialist" and noted, "The opposite of the professional is not the dilettante, the elegant amateur, the dabbler who in fact only attests to the existence of the specialist. The opposite of the professional, the enemy, is the man of mixed motives" (quoted in James Longenbach, *Wallace Stevens: The Plain Sense of Things* [Oxford: Oxford University Press, 1991], 18, 19). Explaining why "the great corrupting force in literary activity in this country is that its object is to make money," Stevens notes that the writer "must apparently choose between starvation and that form of publishing (or being published) in which it is possible to make money. His problem is how to support himself while engaged in the most honorable capacity. There is only one answer. He must support himself in some other way" (quoted in Milton Bates, *Wallace Stevens: A Mythology of Self* [Berkeley: University of California Press, 1985], 161).

35 Quoted in Richard Fine, *James M. Cain and the American Authors' Authority* (Austin: University of Texas Press, 1992), 64.

36 See Wilson, *Labor of Words,* 113–40, for a discussion of this conviction in Upton Sinclair.

37 Quoted in Fine, *James M. Cain,* 66. The long-fought battles between the AFL and the CIO might be said to emblematize a distinction in the disputes of American labor made between white-collar trade specialties and the desire to unite all trades under the "working-class" category of the laborer. The lot of the writer had changed so significantly by 1935, however, that the once high-brow ALA, along with the Unemployed Writers Association, headed the list of guild organizations lobbying Washington for a federal writing project. See Penkhower, *Federal Writers' Project,* 12–15.

38 Quoted in Klein, *Foreigners,* 79.

39 Lewis Corey, *The Crisis of the Middle Class* (New York: Covici Friede, 1935), 179.

40 Richard H. Pells, *Radical Visions and American Dreams: Culture and Thought in the Depression Years* (Middletown, CT: Wesleyan University Press, 1973), 92. Pells explains: "Corey insisted that the growth of monopoly capitalism, the centralization of wealth and power, the emergence of collectivist institutions like the corporation and the labor union had all destroyed the old middle class of small property owners and independent entrepreneurs. In its place there arose a new group of salaried employees, government bureaucrats, industrial managers, clerks, salesmen, technicians, and professionals, who were now dependent on the organization for which they worked, who desired steady employment and economic security more than personal advancement, whose jobs were essentially 'social' in nature, and who found themselves 'wavering between the proletariat and the bourgeoisie" (91).

41 James Livingston, *Pragmatism and the Political Economy of Revolution* (Chapel Hill: University of North Carolina Press, 1994), 173.

42 Walter Benjamin, "The Author as Producer," in *The Essential Frankfurt School Reader,* ed. Andrew Arato and Eike Gebhardt (New York: Continuum, 1990), 257.

43 William Carlos Williams, *The Autobiography of William Carlos Williams* (New York: Random House, 1951), 264.

44 Quoted in Michael Davidson, "Dismantling 'Mantis': Reification and Objectivist Poetics," *American Literary History* (fall 1991): 522.

45 Diego Rivera, "The Revolutionary Spirit in Modern Art," excerpted in *Art and Theory: An Anthology of Changing Ideas,* ed. Charles Harrison and Paul Wood (Cambridge, MA: Blackwell, 1992), 405.

46 Rosalind E. Krauss, *The Optical Unconscious* (Cambridge, MA: MIT Press, 1994), 13.

47 Peter Bürger, *Theory of the Avant-Garde,* trans. Michael Snow, foreword by Jochen Schulte-Sasse (Minneapolis: University of Minnesota Press, 1984), 22.

48 Malcolm Cowley, *Exile's Return* (New York: Norton, 1934), 188.

49 Responding to Bürger's book, Raymond Williams's *The Politics of Modernism* (1989) suggests an approach to the avant-garde, whose politics, he suggests, were never unqualifiedly committed to the "overthrow and remaking of existing society" (67). Without challenging Bürger's sense of which artists and movements comprised "the avant-garde as a complex of movements from around 1910 to the late 1930s" (67), Williams urges us "to recall that the politics of the avant-garde, from the beginning, could go either way" (62). He argues that " 'bourgeois,' in all its rich range of meanings, turns out to be the key to the many movements which claimed to be its opposite" (53). "Thus what we have observed synchronically in the range of positions covered by the anti-bourgeois

revolt we observe also, diachronically, within that evolution of the bourgeoisie which in the end produced its own successions of distinctively bourgeois dissidents" (56–57). See Williams, *The Politics of the Avant-Garde: Against the New Conformists,* ed. Tony Pinkey (New York: Verso, 1989).

50 Bürger, *Theory of the Avant-Garde,* 66.

51 Cited in Rose Lee Goldberg, *Performance Art: From Futurism to the Present* (New York: Henry Adams, 1988), 70.

52 Agee, *Let Us . . . Famous Men,* 203.

53 Carl Sandburg, *The People, Yes* (1936; New York: Harcourt, 1948), 36.

54 Kenneth Fearing, *The Collected Poems of Kenneth Fearing* (New York: Random House, 1940), 60.

55 Josephine Herbst, *The Executioner Waits* (New York: Harcourt Brace, 1934), 281. Chance's father is situated firmly in the camp of economic and political reaction; he is a rentier capitalist of the worst sort. One of "the worst enemies of progress" (129), his speculative trade urges him "to accept accidents as the hand of god" (229).

56 Josephine Herbst, *The Rope of Gold* (1939; New York: Harcourt, 1984), 33.

57 Jack Conroy, *A World to Win* (New York: Covici and Friede, 1935), 198.

58 Jack Conroy, *Disinherited* (New York: Covici and Friede, 1933), 195.

59 Sherwood Anderson, "A Writer's Notes," *New Masses* 8 (1932): 14.

60 Richard Wright, "How 'Bigger' Was Born" (1940), in *Richard Wright: Early Works* (New York: Library of America, 1991), 877.

61 Nicos Poulantzas makes just this assumption in his explanation of why artists do not engage in what Marx calls "productive labor." Poulantzas notes that "labor can take the commodity form without producing surplus-value for capital. This is particularly the case with the work of painters, artists, and writers, which is concretized in a work of art or a book, i.e. a commodity form, even though what is involved are services exchanged against revenue." But to imagine that a writer exchanges services against revenue is to imagine that the publisher pays writers, in whatever form they pay them (with a flat sum or on a percentage system), for the labor of writing and not for the commodity they produce. Writers from the Progressive era to the Depression, however, wanted to believe, but couldn't, that they were exchanging their services for revenue. See Poulantzas, *Classes in Contemporary Capitalism,* trans. David Fernbach (London: NLB, 1975), 219. For a historical analysis of the relationship between the middle class and the evolution of the regulation of time, see E. P. Thompson, "Work, Time, Discipline," in *Customs in Common* (London: Merlin Press, 1991).

62 Poulantzas states of his term "structural class determination": "In so far as capital is concerned, I stress the forms assumed by the articulation of the two relationships (economic ownership, possession) that delimit in a definitive manner its place" (175). He notes later, "The criterion of

class membership is not one of behavioral motivation . . . but an objective category referring to one form in which surplus-value is realized" (*Classes,* 179).

63 In *Proceedings of the First American Artists' Congress* (New York: Equinox, 1936), 56.

64 Franklin Delano Roosevelt, *The Public Papers and Addresses of Franklin Roosevelt,* 13 vols. (New York: Russell and Russell, 1938–1950), 1:659.

65 Stuart Chase, *A New Deal* (New York: Macmillan, 1933), 3.

66 See also Elaine Scarry's writings on the relationship among work, the accidental, and human identity. Speaking of Thomas Hardy, she notes that "his essential subject is the reciprocal alterations between man and world, and though these reciprocal alterations occur inevitably in almost any activity (walking, watching, reading, playing cards), they occur there (however inevitably) accidentally and incidentally, almost as by-product: in work, in contrast, they do not simply happen to occur but are consciously sought; they are not simply the outcome of the activity but seem instead to constitute the very activity itself" (*Resisting Representation* [Oxford: Oxford University Press, 1994], 54–55). Scarry's work is a response to Derrida's claims concerning the invariably differential and alienated nature of properties and rights. For Derrida, work produces something necessarily not the self; for Scarry, work, regulated in a way that play is not, remakes and reconstitutes the self. See Jacques Derrida, "The Law of Genre," *Critical Inquiry* 7 (autumn 1980): 55–81.

67 A substantial amount of attention has been given to the role of speculative money in Naturalist and Progressive era fiction. See in particular Walter Benn Michaels, *The Gold Standard and the Logic of Naturalism* (Berkeley: University of California Press, 1987), chaps. 2 and 7. See also Howard Horwitz, *By the Law of Nature: Form and Value in Nineteenth-Century America* (New York: Oxford University Press, 1991), 218–239, for a consideration of how different legal conceptions of ownership played out in the debate over earned money.

68 Quoted in Robert McElvaine, *The Great Depression, America, 1929–1941* (New York: Times Books, 1984), 211.

69 Jack Balch, *Lamps at High Noon* (New York: Modern Age, 1941), 297.

70 Ira Wolfort, *Tucker's People,* introduction by Alan Filreis (1943; Urbana: University of Illinois Press, 1997), 24.

71 Franklin Delano Roosevelt, "Facsimile of Typed Draft of Roosevelt's First Inaugural Address," National Archives and Records Administration, 1988, 4.

72 Harold Rosenberg, *Art on the Edge: Creators and Situations* (New York: Macmillan, 1975), 197.

73 Forbes Watson, "A Steady Job," *American Magazine of Art* (April 1934): 168.

74 Forbes Watson, "The Chance in a Thousand," *American Magazine of Art* (March 1936): 473, 474.

75 Head of the FSA program that paid Walker Evans his salary, Rexford Tugwell remarked of Hoover's early and inadequate attempts to regulate markets that "the difference between guessing and planning is the difference between laissez-faire and social control" (quoted in Stuart Kidd, "Collectivist Intellectuals and the Idea of National Economic Planning, 1929–1933," in *Nothing Else to Fear: New Perspectives on America in the Thirties,* ed. Stephen Baskerville and Ralph Willet [Manchester, England: Manchester University Press, 1985], 27).

76 Forbes Watson, "The Artist Becomes a Citizen," *Forum* (May 1934): 278. The New Deal was wary of modernism for more overtly political reasons. Senator George Dondero (R, Michigan) was to provide the definitive example of this bias when he presented his treatise "Modern Art Shackled to Communism" to the U.S. Congress in 1949. From Dada to the Russian Suprematists, the history of modern art — principally abstract art — seemed to the senator to be the history of political movements that, at least by the late forties, could be united in their subversive proclivities. This perception was not entirely spurious, as American champions of abstraction, such as Stuart Davis, had stressed the form's left-wing heritage throughout the thirties. Herbert Read put this best in 1935 when, disagreeing with Diego Rivera, he argued that the abstract artist was "the true revolutionary artist, whom every Communist should learn to respect and encourage" (in Harrison and Word, *Art and Theory,* 503). See Gary Larson, *The Reluctant Patron: The United States Government and the Arts, 1943–1965* (Philadelphia: University of Pennsylvania Press, 1983), 34.

77 Quoted in McElvaine, *Great Depression,* 153.

78 Quoted in William R. Brock, *Welfare, Democracy, and the New Deal* (New York: Cambridge University Press, 1988), 270.

79 The WPA work-relief philosophy was derived from what has been called the "Elberfeld system," an early nineteenth-century German system that "required that each recipient of relief, after having been judged worthy through investigation, be obliged to do work suited to his capacity in return for the given help" (William F. McDonald, *Federal Relief Administration and the Arts* [Columbus: Ohio State University Press, 1969], 5). On a different note, the wage the workers received in place of Roosevelt's "market baskets" was originally determined in such a way as to avoid those unpredictable and unregulated free market forces that led to the nation's massive unemployment. The predecessor of the WPA, the Civil Works Administration, calculated its wages at the going local rate, deriving wages backward from the demand for any given service or product on the market. The WPA's "security wages," however, were fixed, set between relief rates and going market rates. The security wage was consequently insulated from the marketability of whatever it was that the wage produced.

80 Quoted in ibid., 681.

81 See Jonathan Harris for an exposition of how FAP art "interpolated" the

newly formed state-citizen subject position through a dynamic of positioning: "State Power and Cultural Discourse," *Block* 13 (1987–1988): 28–42.

82 *Life* 16 (17 April 1944): 85–86. For a brief discussion of this, see Richard McKinzie, *The New Deal for Artists* (Princeton, NJ: Princeton University Press), 1973.

83 George Biddle, "Art under Five Years of Federal Patronage," *American Scholar* (July 1940): 333.

84 Terry Smith, *Making the Modern: Industry, Art, and Design in America* (Chicago: University of Chicago Press, 1995), 296.

85 Michael Sandel explains the uniqueness of such an endeavor when he points out that in "the democratic tradition in America, the [New Deal's] embrace of the nation was a decisive departure. From Jefferson to the populists, the party of democracy in American political debate had been, roughly speaking, the party of the provinces, of decentralized power, of small-town and small-scale America. And against them had stood the party of the nation — first Federalists, then Whigs, then the Republicans of Lincoln — a party that spoke for the consolidation of the union. It was thus the historic achievement of the New Deal to unite, in a single party and political program, what Samuel Beer has called 'liberalism and the national idea.' What matters . . . is that, in the twentieth century, liberalism made its peace with concentrated power." See Sandel, "The Procedural Republic and the Unencumbered Self," in *Twentieth-Century Political Theory,* ed. Stephen Eric Bonner (New York: Routledge, 1997), 81.

86 Key West Administration, *Key West Guide* (fall–winter, 1935–1936), 9.

87 Robert Cantwell, "America and the Writers Projects," *New Republic* (26 April 1939).

88 John Kenneth Galbraith takes this one step farther in his claim that the welfare state is itself a product of an agentless history. Notes one reviewer in the *New York Times Book Review* (19 May 1996): "The fundamental error made by Republicans out to roll back the welfare state, Mr. Galbraith contends, is that they think politicians and their actions drive history. In fact, he argues persuasively, it's the reverse: Liberals didn't create big government, history did." See Galbraith, *The Good Society: The Humane Agenda* (Boston: Houghton Mifflin, 1996).

89 Alexander Williams, *Murder on the WPA* (New York: Robert M. McBride, 1937), 49. No coincidence, then, that the innocent fall guy for the murder of the head of the Arts Project rejected "the theory that he was a charge on the public purse, an object of charity being given a chance to work to maintain his self-respect. He was all for government subsidization of art on a permanent basis" (72). As it turns out, the real killer wants to do away with the Arts Project entirely.

90 Norman Macleod, *You Get What You Ask For* (New York: Harrison-Hilton, 1939), 14.

91 George Biddle, "Art under Five Years of Federal Patronage," *The American Scholar* (July 1940): 331.

92 Archibald MacLeish in *The New Republic* (15 April 1946), quoted in Jerre Mangione, *The Dream and the Deal: The Federal Writers' Project, 1935–1943* (New York: Little Brown, 1972), 349.

93 Holger Cahill, quoted in *Fortune* (May 1937): 114–15. As Jerrold Hirsch points out, "Various publications by Holger Cahill, FAP director, were used by Federal Writers as authoritative sources. . . . A former student of John Dewey's, he shared his mentor's belief in art as experience." See Hirsch, *Portrait of America: The Federal Writers' Project in an Intellectual and Cultural Context* (Ann Arbor: UMI Dissertation Services, 1984), 130.

94 John Dewey, *Art as Experience* (New York: Minton, Balch and Co., 1934), 345. The Cleveland Center for Contemporary Art's *Outside the Frame: Performance and the Object: A Survey History of Performance Art in the USA Since 1950,* Catalogue Coordination, Gary Sangster (Cleveland: Cleveland Center for Contemporary Art, 1994), cites John Dewey's *Art as Experience* on its "Performance Art Time Line" as "a major influence on the Works Progress Administration" (149).

95 Thomas M. Alexander, in *John Dewey's Theory of Art, Experience, and Nature: The Horizons of Feeling* (Albany: State University of New York Press, 1987), has the following to say on this matter: "Dewey is forced to search for the aesthetic initially by conscientiously ignoring works of fine art. The origin of art is not to be found in the desire to become housed in a museum. Instead, art originates when life becomes fulfilled in moments of intelligently heightened vitality. . . . The artistic-aesthetic event, *an* experience, is a primary instance of expression for Dewey. . . . Form becomes the temporal process through which the 'substance' of the work, what the work is ultimately about, shows itself. Not only is form the enactment of the work in individual experience, it is also the *historical* enactment of the work within a culture. The work of art is a social event, and it lives within a culture." Alexander continues: "Art is social not because it occurs within culture, but because in a very real sense art is culture. It becomes one with the community's ability to realize itself in a significant manner (xix–xx).

96 Bürger, *Theory of the Avant-Garde,* 53. Roland Barthes expresses a similar ideal on his way to distinguishing between the "writerly" and the "readerly" text in *S/Z.* "The writerly text is not a thing," Barthes declares; "we would have a hard time finding it in a bookstore" (5). Barthes lionizes the writerly over the readerly nonetheless. In readerly texts, he reasons, "everything holds together"; "controlled by the principle of non-contradiction," readerly texts present their readers with the artifactual, fixed embodiment of their author's intentions (156). Conversely, "the writerly is the novelistic without the novel, poetry without the poem, the essay without the dissertation . . . production without product" (5). What meaning, what product there is, ends up being produced not by the author in question, but by those who read his or her work. Writerly texts, Barthes reasons, need their readers, need the audiences

that an organic work of art denies. Consequently, the meaning of a writerly text is not derived from "the book" in question, but from a necessarily infinite performance staged in the minds of its readers. Barthes presents this hermeneutic mise-en-abyme in decidedly populist registers: "The goal of literary work (of literature as work)," he states, "is to make the reader no longer a consumer, but a producer of the text. Our literature is characterized by the pitiless divorce which the literary institution maintains between the producer of the text and its user, between its owner and its customer, between its author and its reader" (4). Readerly texts are emancipatory, it would appear, because they promise something like a Marxist restructuring of the means of literary production. But all at once, this suggests that the opposition between the readerly and the writerly simply marks out two different degrees of absorption. For writerly texts do not simply render their consumers literary producers by fiat, they do so by internalizing within themselves the potentially infinite equivocations of their readers. This is what separates a writerly from a readerly text: the former anticipates the potentially infinite terms of its empirical consumption, and the latter does not. See Barthes, *S/Z*, trans. Richard Miller, preface by Richard Howard (New York: Hill and Wang, 1974). Further still down the critical pipeline, Jerrome McGann takes such claims to their natural (if not entirely convincing) conclusion. Speaking of his own presentation in *The Textual Condition* (Princeton, NJ: Princeton University Press, 1991), McGann notes, "Properly understood, *this text,* every text, is unique and original to itself when we consider it not as an object but as an action. That is to say, this text is always a new (and changed) originality each time it is textually engaged" (183).

97 Paul Sporn, *Against Itself: The Federal Theater and Writers' Projects in the Midwest* (Detroit: Wayne State University Press, 1995), 45.

98 Quoted in Mangione, *Dream,* 99. Roger Cahill quoted in *Fortune* (May 1937): 114–15.

99 Hirsch, *Portrait,* 131, 137.

100 Folsom, *Days of Anger,* 240.

101 Jerre Mangione recalls not simply that there were enormous numbers of leftists on the Writers' Project, but that the John Reed Clubs in particular had been crucial in "agitating for a government-sponsored agency that would give jobs to needy artists and writers" (*Dream,* 33).

102 Richard Wright, "Blueprint for Negro Writing," in *The Black Aesthetic,* ed. Addison Gayle (New York: Doubleday, 1971), 343, 344.

103 Recent critical opinion varies considerably over the extent to which writers affiliated with the Communist Party and other politically radical organizations embraced more than the money offered it by the Writers' Project. In *The Cultural Front: The Laboring of American Culture in the Twentieth Century* (New York: Verso, 1996), Michael Denning notes the large numbers of radical writers employed by the WPA only to con-

firm the right-wing assumption that these figures "infiltrated" the government and other such organs of the cultural apparatus (83). Douglas Wixson suggests just the opposite of the Writers' Project, namely, that "the United States government filled a vacuum created when the left largely abandoned its sponsorship of worker-writing" (*Worker-Writer in America*, 421). Helen Harrison contends that "In the early 1930s, a significant number of American artists who were aligned, either practically or theoretically, with the Communist Party became supporters of the New Deal. Artist members of the John Reed Club, a party-directed cultural organization, were enjoined to develop 'revolutionary art' as a vehicle for the type of social change that had transformed tsarist Russia into the Soviet Union. Yet many of them found Roosevelt's 'peaceful revolution' worthy of the highest accolade they could bestow on a subject: its inclusion as an affirmative theme in their work" ("The John Reed Club Artists and the New Deal: Radical Responses to Roosevelt's 'Peaceful Revolution,' " *Prospectus* 5 [1980]: 241). Robert McElvaine concurs when he notes that "leftist intellectuals were basically in tune with the values of the public aspirations of the New Deal. Franklin Roosevelt often employed the same class-oriented rhetoric and symbols that the leftists used. The leftists were calling for a liberal socialism, while FDR was offering a social liberalism" (*Great Depression*, 206). At the other extreme, critics such as David Lawrence blame the Writers' Project in particular for diluting the radicalism of the literary left of the period: "The anarchist critic David Lawrence answered his own query, 'Who Slew Proletcult?' by blaming the appointment of writers sympathetic to the CPUSA to positions of power in the Federal Writers' Project of the Works Progress Administration (WPA), an action that tempered their radicalism" (Paula Rabinowitz, *Labor and Desire: Women's Revolutionary Fiction in Depression America* [Chapel Hill: University of North Carolina Press, 1990], 30).

104 Robert Warshow, "The Legacy of the 30s" (1947), in *The Immediate Experience: Movies, Comics, Theater and Other Aspects of Popular Culture* (New York: Doubleday, 1962), 35.

105 Malcolm Cowley, *The Dream of the Golden Mountains: Remembering the 1930s* (1964; New York: Penguin, 1980), 283.

106 Quoted in Daniel Aaron, *Writers on the Left: Episodes in American Literary Communism* (New York: Harcourt, 1961), 282.

107 Ibid., 294.

108 Cited in Cowley, *Dream*, 287.

109 Cited in Frank Warren, *Liberals and Communism: The Red Decade Revisited* (1966; New York: Columbia University Press, 1993), 39.

110 For an analysis of the relation between formal concerns and forms of regularized social control during a slightly earlier period, see Martha Banta, *Taylored Lives: Narrative Productions in the Age of Taylor, Veblen and Ford* (Chicago: University of Chicago Press, 1993).

111 Quoted in Wilson, *Labor of Words,* 192.

112 Quoted in McElvaine, *Great Depression,* 270.

113 Ralph Ellison, *Shadow and Act* (1953; New York: Quality Paperback Book Club, 1994), xii.

114 Penkower notes that many FWP writers "could never completely adjust to the collective authorship of the state guides. Without their individual literary outlets, they felt, even their sincerest efforts would be lost in the anonymity of the guidebooks and forgotten in numerous manuscripts which would forever rest in file drawers" (*Federal Writers' Project,* 170).

115 Quoted in Hirsch, *Portrait,* 432.

116 Meridel Le Sueur, *The Girl* (1935–1945; New York: West End, 1995), 133; emphasis added.

117 Bledstein, *Culture of Professionalism,* 87, 92.

118 George Biddle, "The Writer and the State," *New Republic* (1940): 40.

119 From an unpublished and undated office memo, Works Projects Administration Records, Record Group 69/8. National Archives.

2. The Politics of Textual Integrity: *Ayn Rand, Gertrude Stein, and Ernest Hemingway*

1 Malcolm Cowley, *Exile's Return* (New York: Norton, 1934), 207.

2 Cleanth Brooks and Robert Penn Warren, *Understanding Poetry: An Anthology for College Students* (New York: Holt, 1938), 32.

3 Clement Greenberg, "Abstract, Representational, and So Forth," in *Art and Culture* (Boston: Beacon, 1965), 136. All further references to Greenberg are from *Perceptions and Judgments* (1939–1944), ed. John O'Brien (Chicago: University of Chicago Press, 1992), 139.

4 Astradur Eysteinsson, *The Concept of Modernism* (Ithaca, NY: Cornell University Press, 1990), 10.

5 Samuel Taylor Coleridge, *The Complete Works of Samuel Taylor Coleridge.* Vol. 3: *Biographia Literaria* (New York: Harper Brothers, 1884), 46.

6 Ayn Rand, *The Fountainhead* (1943; New York: Signet, 1993), 579.

7 Theodor Adorno, *Aesthetic Theory,* ed. Gretel Adorno and Rolf Tiedemann, trans. and introduced by Robert Hullot-Kentor (1970; Minneapolis: University of Minnesota Press, 1997), 1.

8 Insofar as this "progress" had been systemic to numerous modernisms, Adorno concedes that "the technically integral, completely made artwork converges with the absolutely accidental work" (ibid., 26). Moreover, he insists that "Art is not to be reduced to a polarity between the mimetic and the constructive, as if this were an invariant formula, for otherwise works of high quality would be forced to strike a balance between the two principles" (44). Taken as a whole, Adorno character-

izes modern art in terms of its oscillation between organic, autonomous, or mimetic art, and constructivist works concerned with "the process of their own production." But at the same time, he makes plain that the best of modern art did not attempt this synthesis themselves, an effort that led to a bland "middle ground" (44). "What was fruitful in modern art," he declares, "was what gravitated toward one of the extremes, not what sought to mediate between them; those works that strove after both, in search of synthesis, were rewarded with a dubious consensus" (44).

9 Max Horkheimer and Theodor Adorno, *The Dialectic of Enlightenment* (1944; New York: Continuum, 1990), 146.

10 Fredric Jameson, *Marxism* (Princeton: Princeton University Press, 1972), 7, 36.

11 Ibid., 8.

12 According to Leland Monk, "Mallarmé understood that, though a throw of the dice will never do away with chance, narrative will." Monk goes on to declare that "chance is that which cannot be represented in narrative" (*Standard Deviations: Chance and the Modern British Novel* [Stanford: Stanford University Press, 1993], 9).

13 *Outside the Frame: Performance and the Object: A Survey History of Performance Art in the USA Since 1950,* Catalogue Coordination, Gary Sangster (Cleveland: Cleveland Center for Contemporary Art, 1994), 35.

14 Jackson Pollock, "My Painting," in *American Artists on Art, from 1940 to 1980,* ed. Ellen H. Johnson (New York: Harper and Row, 1982), 8.

15 Alan Kaprow, " 'Happenings' in the New York Art Scene," excerpts, in Johnson, *American Artists,* 64.

16 Michael North, *The Political Aesthetic of Yeats, Eliot, and Pound* (New York: Cambridge University Press, 1991), 15.

17 John Gabriel Hunt, ed., *The Essential Franklin Delano Roosevelt* (New York: Random House, 1995), 61.

18 Ernest Hemingway, "The Gambler, The Nun, and The Radio," in *The Complete Short Stories of Ernest Hemingway* (New York: Charles Scribner's Sons, 1987), 367.

19 Quoted in Frank Folsom, *Days of Anger, Days of Hope: A Memoir of the League of American Writers, 1937–1942* (Boulder: University of Colorado Press), 82.

20 Rand is most likely writing in response to reformist works such as Catherine Bauer's *Modern Housing* (1934) and Lewis Mumford's *Technics of Civilization* (1934) and *The Culture of Cities* (1938), all three of which are pro–New Deal and lobby for more equitable and affordable social housing programs. That the New Deal itself embraced a formal vision of architecture almost identical to Rand's must have seemed to her beside the point. Like Roark, Roderick Seidenberg and Lewis Mumford — the two largest influences on the architectural essays of the *Guides* — championed Louis Sullivan's dictum, "The very essence of every problem is that it

contains and suggests its own solution." The architectural manual accompanying the *American Guide Series* embraced a modern, functionalist account of architecture and urged federal writers "to avoid the pitfall of relying solely upon the externals of style — the ornamental earmarks of a period." Instead, writers were instructed to attend to "the main elements of a structure and [their] relation to each other and the building as a whole." Elements were thus to be clarified "in terms of . . . purpose and function." See Jerrold Hirsch, *Portrait of America* (Ann Arbor: UMI Dissertation Services, 1984), 142–43.

21   See Alaina Lemon, "Maiakovskii and the 'Language of Lenin,' " *Chicago Anthropology Exchange* 19 (winter 1990–1991): 11.

22   Ayn Rand, *Letters of Ayn Rand,* ed. Michael Berliner (New York: Dutton, 1995), 50–51.

23   Quoted in James D. Bloom, *Left Letters: The Culture Wars of Mike Gold and Joseph Freeman* (New York: Columbia University Press, 1992), 114.

24   Gertrude Stein, "Money," as well as "More about Money," "Still More about Money," "All about Money," "My Last about Money," and "The Capital and Capitals of the United States of America" are all collected in *How Writing Is Written,* ed. Robert Bartlett Haas (Los Angeles: Black Sparrow Press, 1974); the quotation is from p. 112.

25   Cited in James Mellow, *Charmed Circle: Gertrude Stein and Company* (New York: Praeger, 1974), 371, 420.

26   Gertrude Stein, *The Geographical History of America, or, The Relation of Human Nature to the Human Mind* in *Gertrude Stein, Writings, 1932– 1946* (New York: Library of America, 1998), 370. All references to *Lectures in America* and "What Are Master-pieces and Why Are There So Few of Them" are also from this edition.

27   Stein bases this analogy between *domus* and *polis,* between domestic and national economy, on more than the ostensible titillation the father "feels . . . when he says no." Heads of families, Stein insists, understood money in ways that heads of government could not. "Public money" is abstract and impersonal, and operates by its own set of rules: "When you earn money and spend money every day anybody can know the difference between a million and three. But when you vote money away there really is not any difference between a million and three" (*How Writing,* 106). Money "ought to be the same whether it is what a father of a family earns and spends or a government" (107). But whereas "everybody who earns it and spends it every day in order to live knows that money is money, anybody who votes it to be gathered in as taxes knows money is not money. That is what makes everybody go crazy" (106).

28   Gertrude Stein, *Four in America* (New Haven: Yale University Press, 1947), 1.

29   Writing on the essay "What Are Master-pieces," Karin Cope observes that for Stein, a work of art "is an entity, a thing, owned, exchanged, and speculated upon. For Stein, a work, even if of or about a person, re-

mains a persistent object, without subjectivity, and thus at some level impervious or indifferent to the vicissitudes of identity that surround it" ("Painting after Gertrude Stein," *diacritics* 24, nos. 2–3 [summer–fall 1994]: 196–97). Needless to say, Cope's analysis complicates Marjorie Perloff's claim in *The Poetics of Indeterminacy: Rimbaud to Cage* (Princeton, NJ: Princeton University Press, 1981) that Stein is a deeply "performative" writer. Perloff makes no effort to differentiate among Stein's myriad writings, which leads her to the entirely mistaken generalization that for Stein, "the symbolic evocations generated by words on a page are no longer grounded in a coherent discourse, so that it becomes impossible to decide which of these associations are relevant and which are not. This is the 'undecidability' of the text I spoke of earlier" (18).

30 Gertrude Stein, "What Is English Literature" in *Lectures in America,* 198. This essay refines what Jennifer Ashton terms Stein's "career-long project of representing the whole in and as literature." This project, Ashton explains, tirelessly explores similarities in "questions of identity — not only of persons, but of nations and literatures." Ashton explains that Stein analogized the failure of nineteenth-century English literature to the failure of British imperialism: Stein understood both projects to involve "indirection, incompletion, and partiality," and reasoned that both are replaced by the more successful ventures of American nationalism and the American paragraph. "How Stein imagines the paragraph is how she imagines America itself. It is, above all, a bounded or boundaried whole" ("Gertrude Stein for Anyone," *ELH* 64 [1997]: 289, 292).

31 Franklin Delano Roosevelt, *The Public Papers and Addresses of Franklin D. Roosevelt* (New York: Russell and Russell, 1938–1950), 1:658.

32 Stein was nonetheless popular on the Writers' Project, as one Project writer's spoof on the *Guide Series* suggests: "A tour is a tour is a tour is a tour. To go on a tour is to be on a tour is to stay on a tour is not so bad as to write a tour is not to get a headache on a tour. A tour is a main tour, a side tour, a well-paved tour, a graveled tour" (quoted in Monty Noam Penkower, *The Federal Writers' Project* [Urbana: University of Illinois Press, 1977], 87).

33 Ernest Hemingway manuscript 252, John F. Kennedy Library, Boston.

34 Both letters cited in Stephen Cooper, *The Politics of Ernest Hemingway* (Ann Arbor: UMI Research Press, 1985), 78.

35 Ernest Hemingway, *By-Line: Ernest Hemingway* (New York: Charles Scribner's Sons, 1967), 216. Hemingway would continue to associate Stein with solidity in *For Whom the Bell Tolls:* " 'An onion is an onion is an onion,' Robert Jordan said cheerily and, he thought, a stone is a stein is a rock is a boulder is a pebble" (*For Whom the Bell Tolls* [New York: Charles Scribner's Sons, 1940], 289).

36 Ernest Hemingway, *Selected Letters, 1917–1961* (New York: Charles Scribner's Sons, 1981), 837.

37 Ernest Hemingway, "An Interview with George Plimpton," in *Heming-way,* ed. Harold Bloom (New York: Chelsea, 1987), 136.

38 Both cited in Kenneth Lynn, *Hemingway* (New York: Simon and Schuster, 1987), 106.

39 Mark Spilka's *Hemingway's Quarrel with Androgyny* (Lincoln: University of Nebraska Press, 1990) shifts the wounding in Italy to "the wound of androgyny" and premises Hemingway's ambivalence toward androgyny on what are ultimately fears of the wounding inflicted by castration (106). Lynn likewise shares with Spilka the "working through" hypothesis, reading Hemingway's writing as the proleptic expression of those neuroses that eventually lead to his suicide. This essay is not intended to attack these more than plausible accounts of Hemingway's personal disorders but instead attempts to more precisely consider and specify what Hemingway himself understood to be the relation between the wound and his writing.

40 Ernest Hemingway, *To Have and Have Not* (1937; New York: Collier, 1987), 97.

41 This excerpt from William Carlos Williams's "The Term" (1937) mocks the conviction that inorganic objects can seem most like "living things" due to their literal size and shape:

> A rumpled sheet
> of brown paper
> about the length
>
> and apparent bulk
> of a man was
> rolling with the
>
> wind . . .
>
> a car drove down
> upon it . . .
>
> . . . Unlike
> a man it rose
> again . . .

For Williams, paper takes on the attributes of personhood to the degree that it takes on human form. But putting matters this way, Williams points out a possible misinterpretation of the organicist project itself. The paper survives to the degree that the similarity between its form and the human body is incidental at best. "The length / and apparent bulk" of the paper is a red herring; the paper is less vulnerable than a man not because it resembles one, but because its resemblance to the human turns out not to speak to the paper at all. Free from the synthetic instrumentalism lethally embodied in the car, the paper possesses its invulnerability because it is "inspired" by the wind, and not a poet. "Paper bleeds little," concurs Robert Jordan in Hemingway's *For Whom the Bell Tolls* (152).

42 Such a relational conception of identity qualifies the relevance of "the material" to modernism so insistently declared by such critics as Tom Cohen, T. J. Clark, and Jerome McGann. Eager to insist on what he terms modernism's "extreme performativity," for example, McGann holds that the physical nature of the literary artifact undermines its claims to unity. Confidently asserting that "everyone agrees, of course, that meaning is a wild variable" (184), he insists that "no stability in the material object can be assumed with respect to texts" (185). He explains by debunking exactly the kind of relational identity insisted on by Hemingway: "If we define a text as words in a certain order, then we have to say that the order of the words in every text is, *in fact,* at the factive level, unstable. No text, either conceptually or empirically, can have the 'ordering of its words' defined or specified as invariant. Variation, in other words, is the invariant rule of the textual condition" (185). See McGann, *The Textual Condition* (Princeton, NJ: Princeton University Press, 1991).

Responding to Clement Greenberg, T. J. Clark argues that modernism's attention to the material attributes of its medium causes that art to "present itself as a work of interminable and absolute decomposition." For Clark, modernist materiality signals the "ending" of the medium in question, in which the medium "turns back into mere unworked material." Clark's materiality, unspecified and totalized, is loosely defined as the "negation" of whatever artistic identity is at hand. The moment a medium becomes pure material, it forsakes its identity as that medium, falling into an empty and opaque abyss of "mere" material set against that medium's capacity to mean and to be what it once was. This particular conception of materiality is endemic enough to warrant a much more sustained address, which is not the subject of this essay. Suffice it to say that there is something problematic about a "mere material" that can negate specific mediums and specific identities. It is reasonable to expect that any principle of negation be as specific as the thing that it negates; "mere" material per se is not necessarily anything and as such has no necessary relationship to either meaning or identity. See Clark, "Clement Greenberg's Theory of Art," *Critical Inquiry* 9 (1982): 139–56.

Tom Cohen pursues linguistic materiality in the context of the body. He notes that "legs may be understood as a corporeal analogue for the material base of language itself, that entails the brute dependence of semantic relations on what precedes mimesis and figuration; on what, in the course of marking itself, gets woven into and alters meaning production" (7). Cohen's account of modernism in this way produces a whiggish history of linguistic poststructuralism and uses the breakup of the human body in modernist texts to register the collapse of meaning in those texts; for Cohen, the amputated body enacts the invariably arbitrary and disconnected relation between signified and signifier. See Cohen, *Anti-Mimesis from Plato to Hitchcock* (Cambridge: Cambridge University Press, 1994).

For an account of the relational with respect to signification and materiality, one to which this essay is indebted, see Frances Ferguson, "Historicism, Deconstruction, Wordsworth," in *Solitude and the Sublime: Romanticism and the Aesthetics of Individuation* (New York: Routledge, 1992). Ferguson's account echoes Benjamin Whorf's desire to study "pattern over reference." The linguist claimed in 1942 that "sentences and not words are the essence of speech, just as equations and functions, and not bare numbers, are the real meat of mathematics" (261). See Whorf, *Language, Thought, and Reality* (Cambridge, MA: Technology Press of MIT, 1956).

43 Richard Godden, *Fictions of Capital: The American Novel from James to Mailer* (New York: Cambridge University Press, 1990), 60; see also 55.

44 Quoted in Cooper, *The Politics,* 78.

45 Ernest Hemingway, "Who Murdered the Vets: A First-Hand Report on the Florida Hurricane," *New Masses* (17 September 1935): 9.

46 Stanley Burnshaw, *Robert Frost Himself* (New York: George Braziller, 1986), 33.

47 Needless to say, this pleased no one on the left. Philip Rahv noted that "a proletarian critic's evaluation of Hemingway's subject matter and detailed content cannot but show its uselessness to the proletarian writer" (Review of "Winner Take Nothing," *Partisan Review* 1 [February–March 1934]: 59).

48 James Agee and Walker Evans, *Let Us Now Praise Famous Men: Three Tenant Families* (Boston: Houghton Mifflin, 1988), 56.

49 Writing in *Partisan Review* in 1935, Wallace Phelps argued that what he called "*patterns* of writing" needed to be distinguished from the mistaken conviction that "form" is a "shape," "structure," or "mold" into which "something else is poured." Phelps states that the sundering of form from content "is not very surprising when we consider that the fundamental premise of idealist philosophy is a detachment from the material conditions of life, and a severance of the necessary social derivation of ideas and forms ("Form and Content," *Partisan Review* 2 [January–February 1935]: 31). Echoing Phelps, and also writing in the *Partisan Review,* Clement Greenberg provides a similar definition for abstract art in his essay "Avant-Garde and Kitsch" (1939): "Content is to be dissolved so completely into form that the work of art or literature cannot be reduced in whole or in part to anything not itself" (in *Perceptions and Judgments,* 8). For Greenberg, a modernist painting belonged "to the same order and space as our bodies" only when it acted "solely in terms of [its] separate and irreducible sel[f]" (in *Art and Culture,* 136, 139). Because of a "confusion" in the arts epitomized for Greenberg by Dada and surrealism, the modernist avant-garde found it "important to

determine the essential elements of each of the arts" (in *Perceptions and Judgments,* 23, 29). Greenberg felt, for example, that painting needed to rediscover the identic singularity of its medium by exploring the two-dimensional flatness of the canvas and its relationship to the three-dimensional nature of paint inscribed on it. Greenberg's much-referred-to emphasis on "materiality," similar to Bois's reading of Matisse, is significant not because it exposes as exhausted the raw physical matter used in making paintings but because it signifies the requirements of a generic identity that cannot be translated between different systems of expression. "To *restore* the identity of an art," Greenberg claimed that "the opacity of its medium must be emphasized" (32). This is not to imagine that any given painting's "opacity" somehow interferes with the process of representation; it does not, for example, recur to Gombrich's phenomenological claim that one can see pigment as well as picture, but never both at the same time. Instead, "opacity" suggests that what will count as painting needs at every moment to engage the conditions of the medium as it has previously been defined by artists confining themselves to the genre of easel painting. Generic parameters, Greenberg insisted, could not be seen through and instead at every moment determined the criteria by which any art would be judged. Salvaging Greenberg from assaults that have taken his formalist account of abstraction as a willful and didactic effacing of specific contents, Yves-Alain Bois has demonstrated with respect to Matisse's "Modernism and Tradition" (1935) that those categories usually referred to as form and content are never separable for abstract modernists. Bois argues that color for Matisse, like all linear forms of shading, does not merely fill spaces on a canvas but instead takes on identity through its relation to those spaces; it is inextricable from its specific relational and positional encoding in that painting. Blue between two thick black lines one inch apart is categorically different from that same pigment between two thin black lines two inches apart. In this account, claims concerning the inseparability of form and content do not, as I. A. Richards points out, indicate an interest in reference but instead an investment in the self-defining autonomy of identity. See Bois, *Painting as Model* (Cambridge, MA: MIT Press, 1990).

50 Cited in Kenneth Johnston, "The Silly Wasters: Tzara and the Poet in 'The Snows of Kilimanjaro,'" *Hemingway Review* 8 (1988): 52.

51 George Ribemont-Dessaignes, "History of Dada" (1931), in *The Dada Painters and Poets,* 2d ed., ed. Robert Motherwell (Boston: G. K. Hall, 1981), 110.

52 Peter Bürger, *Theory of the Avant-Garde,* trans. Michael Snow, foreword by Jochen Schulte-Sasse (Minneapolis: University of Minnesota Press, 1984), 56.

53 Tristan Tzara, "An Introduction to Dada," in *The Dada Painters and Poets,* 404.

54 Dada's violence targeted the most literal form of art: the actual physical

artistic body. The assertion that "the poem is not the aim of poetry," for example, expresses a discontinuity between the generic essence of Poetry and the physical form of any one poem. Dada imagines that the very presence of the Dada artifact is unrelated to what is being performed through it. But unlike Hemingway, Dada's performative violence undermines the coherence and singularity of identity as such. Dada does not simply play out a resistance to the physical; instead, it subverts the possibility that any identity exists as a single and coherent unit. The artistic body, when it does exist in Dada, becomes the performance of its own contingency and irrelevance, not just because the "printed" poem is superfluous to the identity of any one poem but because any one poem is superfluous to the identity of "Poetry." The destruction of Poetry with its own weapons thus precludes the possibility that any artistic identity could be expressed in one poem or one artifact and advances the claim that art is never immanent in form but is instead perpetually, safely, "elsewhere." Dadaist art can never be altered, mutilated, or changed, because any violence performed on an artifact (such as a Tzara poem) or on a performance never touches a generalized and curiously transcendent conception of art that, resisting finite identity, bears no necessary relation to either that artifact or performance. This goes against the tradition that understands Dada and surrealism in terms of an insistent nominalism. Yet, the most sophisticated version of this tradition, Thierry de Duve's *Pictorial Nominalism,* is premised on an ambivalence central to Duchamp that provides for both the nominalist and idealist positions. Duve argues that Duchamp was caught between the desire to be a significant and serious artist and the recognition that being such an artist at that historical moment necessitated the destruction of art as it was then constituted. The same ambivalence exists in Dada in general, a movement that declared its intentions to destroy the bourgeois category of art, but one that did so through artistic means, always preserving the abstract category of art while it destroyed its historical and institutional articulations. See Duve, *Pictorial Nominalism: On Marcel Duchamp's Passage from Painting to the Ready-made* (Minneapolis: University of Minnesota Press, 1991). For a compelling theoretical exposition of this structural ambivalence in modernist neo-Kantian aesthetics, see Stephen W. Melville, "Notes on the Reemergence of Allegory," *October* 19 (1981): 55–93; and "On Modernism," in *Philosophy beside Itself: On Deconstruction and Modernism* (Minneapolis: University of Minnesota Press, 1986).

55 Ernest Hemingway, *Green Hills of Africa* (New York: Charles Scribner's Sons, 1935), 29.

56 Theodor Adorno, "On the Fetish Character of Music and the Regression of Listening" (1938), in *The Essential Frankfurt School Reader,* ed. Andrew Arato and Eike Gebhardt (New York: Continuum, 1990), 289.

57 Karl Marx argues in *Capital* that the marketplace is a public site of

abstraction in which value and identity are not only extracted from specific physical forms but are produced by being extractable from them. Where value, for Marx, should reflect the historically specific quantity of labor required for any one object's construction (labor that is not commodified as labor power), it instead becomes a category that establishes relative systems of relations and equivalencies among always changing forms. Value in this model becomes increasingly ethereal, first as use value, then as exchange value — first as money, then as capital — and moves among different physical objects at the moment that it intends to substitute itself for them. Marx insists that a commodified identity under capitalism is neither singular nor possessed of only one form. Central to Marx's thesis is that all identity loses its specificity in the same moment that it loses its irreducible material form. "Killing itself in advance," Dada preempts and parodies this system of abstraction in its ability to assert identity as *totally* alienated — something neither coherent nor intrinsic to an object's physical form. Dada's identity, like Marx's conception of value, is always "elsewhere"; for both Marx and Dada, "everything solid melts into air" as identities are abstracted from the bodily form that once defined their singularity.

58 Gertrude Stein, *Everybody's Autobiography* (1937; New York: Vintage, 1973), 39.
59 Gertrude Stein, "Plays," in *Lectures in America.*

3. Wallace Stevens and the Invention of Social Security

1 Robert Frost, "Build Soil," in *The Poetry of Robert Frost* (New York: Holt, 1975), 316.
2 Richard Poirier, *The Performing Self* (New York: Oxford University Press, 1971), 89.
3 Richard Poirier, *Poetry and Pragmatism* (Cambridge, MA: Harvard University Press, 1992), 89.
4 "Provide, Provide," in *The Poetry of Robert Frost,* ed. Edward Latham (New York: Holt, Rinehart, and Winston, 1969), 307.
5 For a discussion of the pronoun in pastoral, see the introduction to Annabel Patterson, *Pastoral and Ideology, from Virgil to Valéry* (Berkeley: University of California Press, 1987).
6 Quoted in Richard H. Pells, *Radical Visions and American Dreams: Culture and Thought in the Depression Years* (Middletown, CT: Wesleyan University Press, 1973), 165.
7 Wallace Stevens, "The Irrational Element in Poetry," in *Opus Posthumous* rev. ed. (New York: Knopf, 1989), 229.
8 John Gabriel Hunt, ed., *The Essential Franklin Delano Roosevelt* (New York: Random House, 1995), 96. Stevens parodies Marxist attempts to plan the future when he has a Burnshaw-styled ideologue declare, "Ev-

erything is dead / Except the future" in the first stanza of "Mr. Burnshaw and the Statue" (in *Opus Posthumous,* 78).

9 John Steinbeck, *In Dubious Battle* (1936), in *John Steinbeck, Novels and Short Stories, 1932–1937* (New York: the Library of America, 1994), 641.

10 Franklin Delano Roosevelt, *The Public Papers and Addresses of Franklin D. Roosevelt* (New York: Russell and Russell, 1938–1950), 4: 448.

11 Wallace Stevens, "Notes Toward a Supreme Fiction," in *The Collected Poems of Wallace Stevens* (New York: Knopf, 1955), 388.

12 Harold Bloom, *Wallace Stevens, The Poems of Our Climate* (Ithaca, NY: Cornell University Press, 1977), 189.

13 Holly Stevens, ed., *The Letters of Wallace Stevens* (New York: Knopf, 1966), 434.

14 Wallace Stevens, "The Idea of Order at Key West," in *The Collected Poems* (New York: Vintage, 1982), 128.

15 Fredric Jameson, *Marxism and Form* (Princeton: Princeton University Press, 1972), 36.

16 Cited in Milton Bates, *A Mythology of Self* (Berkeley: University of California Press, 1985), 157.

17 François Ewald, "Insurance and Risk," in *The Foucault Effect: Studies in Governmentality,* ed. Graham Burchell, Colin Gordon, and Peter Miller (Chicago: University of Chicago Press, 1991), 203. Also see Gordon's introduction, where he notes that risk is "an omnivorous, encyclopaedizing principle of the objectification of possible experience — not only of the hazards of personal life and private venture, but also of the common venture of society" (38).

18 James Farrell, *A Note on Literary Criticism* (1936; New York: Columbia University Press, 1992), 109.

19 James Farrell, *Yet Other Waters* (New York: Vanguard, 1952), 48.

20 T. S. Eliot, *Selected Prose of T. S. Eliot,* ed. Frank Kermode (New York: Harcourt, 1975), 40.

21 Wallace Stevens, "Adagia," in *Opus Posthumous,* rev. ed. (New York: Knopf, 1989), 189.

22 Insurance cannot guarantee that individuals do not experience accidents; further, the indemnification it offers is never an exact substitute for the loss incurred in any given experience. Bent on immunizing populations from the vicissitudes of individual experience, insurance instead guarantees that one person's experiences will not be transferred to others as a loss (when, for example, an insured individual is able to continue to meet his financial obligations after a work-stopping injury).

23 Oliver Wendell Holmes, *The Common Law,* ed. Mark DeWolf Howe (Cambridge, MA: Belknap Press of Harvard University Press, 1963), 76.

24 Stanley Burnshaw, "Turmoil in the Middle Ground," *New Masses* (October 1935): 41, 42.

25 Nicholas Barr, *The Economics of the Welfare State* (London: Weidenfeld and Nicolson, 1987), 111.

26 Quoted in Stanley Burnshaw, *Robert Frost Himself* (New York: George Braziller, 1986), 10.

27 George Bernard Shaw, *Everybody's Political What's What* (New York: Dodd, Mead and Company, 1945), 109.

28 For Foucault's work on insurance and Social Security, see "Social Security" and "The Dangerous Individual," in Michel Foucault, *Politics, Philosophy, and Culture: Interviews and Other Writings, 1977–1984* (New York: Routledge, 1988).

29 Michel Foucault, "Governmentality," in Burchell et al., *The Foucault Effect,* 102. In "Governmental Rationality: An Introduction," Colin Gordon distinguishes Foucault's interest in social security from more Marxist accounts of the modern state. "In a nutshell, [Foucault] suggests that recent neo-liberalism, understood (as he proposes) as a novel set of notions about the art of government, is a considerably more original and challenging phenomenon than the left's critical culture has had the courage to acknowledge, and that its political challenge is one which the left is singularly ill equipped to respond to, the more so since, as Foucault contends, socialism itself does not possess and has never possessed its own distinctive art of governing" (6). Gordon thus explains at least one source of Foucault's suspicion of social security: "If the state is the only institution within society possessed of that degree of solidity requisite in a provider of certain kinds of insurance, it then follows that the continued survival of the state will itself become a peculiarly social imperative. The existence of insurance is . . . an insurance against revolution" (41).

30 Frank Warren, *Liberals and Communism: The Red Decade Revisited* (1966; New York: Columbia University Press, 1993), 106.

31 For the benchmark account of the NRA, see Ellis Hawley, *The New Deal and the Problem of Monopoly: A Study in Economic Ambivalence* (Princeton, NJ: Princeton University Press, 1966). See also Arthur Schlesinger Jr., *The Age of Roosevelt: The Politics of Upheaval* (Boston: Houghton Mifflin, 1960).

32 Rexford G. Tugwell, *Industrial Discipline and the Governmental Arts* (New York: Arno, 1977), 189.

33 Walter Lippmann, *The Phantom Public* (1927; New Brunswick, NJ: Transaction Publishers, 1993), 67, 67, 93, and 93. Bruce Robbins has recently noted the "urgency" of confronting Lippmann's claims because he is speaking *"from the right"* (emphasis in original). See Robbins, introduction to *The Phantom Public Sphere,* ed. Bruce Robbins (Minneapolis: University of Minnesota Press, 1993), x. Lippmann's currency during the early New Deal was made clear by Carrol D. Clark, "The Concept of the Public," *The Southwestern Social Science Quarterly* 13 (March 1933): 311–20. Not incidentally, Clark specifies Habermas's news-center coffee house as an insurance company, citing the maritime

insurance center of Lloyd's Coffee House as one of the forerunners in the founding of the public sphere (316 n. 8). See Jürgen Habermas, *Structural Transformations in the Public Sphere* (Cambridge, MA: MIT Press, 1989).

34 Ayn Rand, *Atlas Shrugged* (New York: Signet, 1957), 953.

35 Ayn Rand, "What Is Capitalism," in *What Is Capitalism* (New York: Signet, 1966), 7.

36 Ayn Rand, *The Fountainhead* (1943; New York: Signet, 1993), 679.

37 Quoted in Howard Brick, "The Reformist Dimension of Talcott Parsons's Early Social Theory," in *The Culture of the Market: Historical Essays,* ed. Thomas L. Haskell and Richard F. Teichgraeber III (New York: Cambridge University Press, 1993), 375.

38 Thurman Arnold, *Symbols of Government* (New Haven: Yale University Press, 1935), 269.

39 Thurman Arnold, *The Folklore of Capitalism* (1937; New Haven: Yale University Press, 1966), 5.

40 John Dewey, *Liberalism and Social Action* (New York: G. P. Putnam's Sons, 1935), 90, 67.

41 John Dewey, *The Public and Its Problems* (1927; Athens: Ohio University Press, 1954), 34.

42 Dewey's desire to objectify relations between "modes of associated behavior" and "consequences beyond those directly engaged in" might have led him to the actuarial, as it did for more than one of his pragmatist predecessors. As Ian Hacking has argued, C. S. Peirce, 30-year federal employee, based his conception of human community not on a Cartesian "introspective individual ego," but on the objective quantification of group experience; Peirce's was a life, Hacking observes, "permeated by statistics and probabilities." In 1914, the more idealist and Hegelian Josiah Royce argued in *War and Insurance* that a harmonious global community could best be maintained by an international organization modeled along the lines of an insurance company. See Hacking, *The Taming of Chance* (New York: Cambridge University Press, 1990), 212, 201.

43 John Dewey, *Art as Experience* (1934; New York: Perigee Books, 1980), 347, 343.

44 Walter Lippmann immediately saw in Keynes an ally, and wrote to the economist urging him to step up his communications with Roosevelt: "I have been on the point of writing you for some time," Lippmann starts, "to urge you to write another article, following up your letter to the President of December last. I don't know whether you realize how great an effect that letter had, but I am told it was chiefly responsible for the policy which the Treasury is now quietly but effectively pursuing. . . . Our greatest difficulty now lies in the President's emotional and moral commitments to the N.R.A. and to the various other measures which he regards as the framework for a better economic order. . . . Nobody could

make so great an impression upon the President as you could if you undertook to show him the meaning of that part of his policy" (in John Maynard Keynes, *The Collected Writings of John Maynard Keynes* (Cambridge, England: Macmillan, 1973), 11:305.

45 John Maynard Keynes, *The General Theory of Employment, Interest, and Money* (1936) in *The Collected Writings,* 7:13.

46 John Maynard Keynes, "Art and the State," part 1, *The Listener* (26 August 1936): 372.

47 For Keynes's role on the British Arts Council, see Eric White, *The Arts Council of Great Britain* (London: Davis and Poynter, 1975).

48 Alan Brinkley, "The New Deal and the Idea of the State," in *The Rise and Fall of the New Deal Order, 1930–1980,* ed. Stephen Fraser and Gary Castle (Princeton, NJ: Princeton University Press), 93.

49 Robert E. Goddin, "Reasons for Welfare: Economic, Sociological, and Political — but Ultimately Moral," in *Responsibility, Rights, and Welfare: The Theory of the Welfare State,* ed. J. Donald Moon (Boulder, CO: Westview Press, 1988), 21.

50 For a detailed discussion of the *General Theory*'s relation to uncertainty, see chapter 5 in Athol Fitzgibbons, *Keynes's Vision: A New Political Economy* (Oxford: Clarendon, 1988).

51 Goddin, "Reasons for Welfare," 27.

52 In his *Pragmatism and the Political Economy of Cultural Revolution, 1850–1940* (Chapel Hill: University of North Carolina Press, 1994), James Livingston suggests that the modern and postmodern fascination with money — understood as a performative medium utterly devoid of content — marks a particularly liberal stage in the evolution of the modern state: "The monetary forms specific to a modern 'credit economy' (e.g., deposits, checks, bills of exchange, securities) approached the status of pure symbols precisely because they represented potential claims on future outcomes — they were in fact 'floating signifiers' — to adduce these meanings was to posit a certain relation between material circumstances and inscription, between object and subject, and to situate this hypothetical subject within a corresponding symbolic or rhetorical universe. Thus the money question was the idiom in which seemingly abstract philosophical or epistemological issues became the predicates of political arguments as well as popular fiction — and vice versa" (184). Money functioned as a "floating signifier," Livingston suggests, not because it undermined an ossified hegemonic order but, quite the contrary, because it epitomized the infinitely labile, adaptable fungibility of modern capital.

Like Livingston, F. R. Ankersmit's *Aesthetic Politics: Political Philosophy beyond Fact and Value* (Stanford: Stanford University Press, 1996) reasons that "Money provides the political theorist with the language that enables free movement through all the areas of political reality, and is the language that can render commensurable all the objects encountered there" (90). Ankersmit treats this pure fungibility as nothing less than the performative condition of postmodernity itself; he imagines that the kind of performativity embodied in money proves resistant to the modes of analysis once offered by traditional notions of political economy. But for Ankersmit, the modern fascination with money — most purely articulated, he suggests, in the Rawlsian concern with distributive justice — leaves the modern political theorist strikingly unable to understand and provide accounts of contemporary political formations, particularly of the welfare state. Commenting on the massive infiltration of the modern state into the lives of its citizens, as well as the concomitant dissemination of "politics" far beyond considerations of state and government, Ankersmit reasons, "We may witness today the evanescence or the evaporation of the political object, precisely because of its omnipresence" (65). Consequently, the kind of pure fungibility promised in a politics centered on the control and distribution of money might on the one hand "look ideal to us, as now everything has been made commensurable with everything else, but for that same reason we have now become blind to all the differentiations and frictions that constitute the political realm" (95). So blinded, the contemporary political theorist remains particularly unable to answer the question " 'Who acts?' or, rather, 'To whom or to what must we ascribe the kind of political action "that makes a difference" in politics?' " (95). If Rawles's investment in ethics proves, for Ankersmit, particularly inadequate to these questions, then so does traditional Marxism, principally because of its conviction that "explaining what goes on in political reality in terms of the intentions and actions of human individuals will provide us with a far less satisfactory explanation of politics than explanations adopting the phraseology of the class struggle" (96). For Ankersmit, the contemporary turn away from questions of intention allows us to "observe with regard to the notion of political action an evolution that is an exact parallel of . . . the absorption of the political object by the tertia against which it used to articulate and define itself" (96). The elision of the category of intention, in other words, leaves us strikingly unable to understand a modern state presiding over "an age where the ironic discrepancy between our intentions and the results of our actions so often and so disagreeably surprises us" (237). Ankersmit concludes that our inability to understand and theorize the political consequences of this discrepancy has enabled the modern state to succeed "in removing the results of our collective actions from their original intentions at a scale hitherto unparalleled in the whole history of mankind. . . . Surely, if future historians would decide to refer to our time as 'the Age of Unintended Consequences,' what more appropriate label could they find for characterizing (and condemning) the political world that we have shaped?" (13).

53 See Alan Filreis, *Modernism from Right to Left: Wallace Stevens, the Thirties, and Literary Radicalism* (New York: Cambridge University

Press, 1994), 68–70, for a discussion of money and banking in Stevens's "Lions in Sweden."

54 Quoted in James D. Bloom, *Left Letters: The Culture Wars of Mike Gold and Joseph Freeman* (New York: Columbia University Press, 1992), 128.

55 Carl Sandburg, *The People, Yes* (1936; New York: Harcourt, 1948), 102.

56 Ezra Pound, "In the Wounds" (1935), in *Ezra Pound, Selected Prose: 1909–1965,* ed. William Cookson (London: Faber and Faber, 1973), 418.

57 William Carlos Williams, *Paterson,* ed. Christopher MacGowan (New York: New Directions, 1992), 7.

58 Christopher MacGowan, in ibid., explains that these sections are extracts from a mimeographed sheet — addressed to "Dear Citizen" and most probably written by Pound — put out by Alfredo and Clara Studer and dated January 1947: Clara Studer one year earlier had written to Williams and asked if he wanted to see Social Credit materials.

59 Sentences taken and rearranged from a pamphlet, "Tom Edison on the Money Subject," accompanying the Studer sheet, in Williams, *Paterson.*

60 Jean-François Lyotard, *The Postmodern Condition: A Report on Knowledge* (1979), trans. Goeff Bennington and Brian Mussumi, introduction by Fredric Jameson (Minneapolis: University of Minnesota Press, 1984), 11.

61 The nexus I have been attempting to trace among Dewey's pragmatism, Keynes's economics, and broadly performative aesthetics depend on the same basically functionalist suppositions as insurance itself. As the pragmatist legal theorist Felix Cohen writes in the *Columbia Law Review* in 1935, "A definition of law is *useful* or *useless.* It is not *true* or *false,* any more than a New Year's resolution or an insurance policy. A definition is in fact a type of insurance against certain risks of confusion. It cannot, any more than can a commercial insurance policy, eliminate all risks. Absolute certainty is as foreign to language as to life." As messy as this conjunction is among the legal, the commercial, and the linguistic, it importantly demonstrates the ease with which insurance made itself available during the thirties in pragmatist inquiries into the nature of linguistic meaning and intention. See Cohen, "Transcendental Nonsense and the Functional Approach," *Columbia Law Review* 35 (1935): 835–36.

62 Jacques Derrida, "Signature, Event, Context" in *Limited Inc.,* ed. Gerald Graff (Evanston, IL: Northwestern University Press, 1983), 14. Also see Barbara Johnson, "Poetry and Performative Language: Mallarmé and Austin," in *The Critical Difference: Essays in the Contemporary Rhetoric of Reading* (Baltimore: Johns Hopkins University Press, 1980), and Stanley Fish, "With the Compliments of the Author: Reflections on Austin and Derrida," in *Critical Inquiry* 8 (1982): 693–721. For a response to the deconstructive notion that intention exists in a "prior or exterior state of things" in the first place, see Steven Knapp and Walter Michaels, "Against Theory," *Critical Inquiry* 8 (1982): 723–42. For an

account of how Austin's linguistic performative might be compared to David Antin's performance art, see Rei Terada, "Austin and Antin about "About," *SubStance* 78 (1995): 49–69.

63 Alan Filreis finds in these lines Stevens's unqualified dismissal of the rationalism of the New Deal. He glosses the above: "No explanation of market forces, whether offered by far or moderate left, was plausible; no 'secret' was to be discovered, no new deal to be struck, no trick played or comprehensive solution wrought, no fully confident reading tendered — of stock prices or of poetry. The forces at work on contemporary verse were largely beyond individual, let alone social, control" (*Modernism,* 14). Although Filreis is dead-on to suggest that Stevens rejects the New Deal penchant for social planning, he overlooks the extent to which Stevens, like the second New Deal itself, understands the compensatory mechanisms of insurance as necessary at the private and public level precisely because of the impossibility of planning. As a result, Filreis concludes — incorrectly, I think — that Stevens here rejects New Deal "rationalism" altogether.

64 Cleanth Brooks and Robert Penn Warren, *Understanding Poetry: An Anthology for College Students* (New York: Holt, 1938), 5.

65 The two offer a slightly more comprehensive account of how poems are intended in the third edition of their textbook: "An architect intends a certain kind of house and he can predict it down to the last nail. The carpenter simply follows the blueprint. But at best, the poet cannot en-visage the poem as the architect can envisage the house. . . . As he begins to work with the poem, he is never simply following a plan; he is also exploring the possibilities of imagination and language. Until the poem is actually written down to the last word, the poet cannot be sure exactly what it will mean — for we know that the meaning of the poem is fuller than the paraphrasable idea" (*Understanding Poetry,* 526).

66 Wallace Stevens, *Owl's Clover,* in *Opus Posthumous,* 82. James Longen-bach also notes that *Owl's Clover* values the activity of making over the made ("Elizabeth Bishop's Social Conscience," *ELH* 62 [summer 1995]: 485 n. 20). For an astute analysis of the relation between Stevens and statuary, see Michael North, "The Nobel Rider," in *The Final Statue: Public Monuments and Modern Poets* (Ithaca, NY: Cornell University Press, 1985).

67 Douglas Mao, *The Solid Object: Modernism and the Test of Production* (Princeton, NJ: Princeton University Press, 1998), 211.

68 Anzia Yezierska, *Red Ribbon on a White Horse* (New York: Scribners, 1950), 198.

69 Richard Wright, *Native Son and "How Bigger Was Born"* (New York: Harper Perennial, 1993), 540.

70 Ramon Fernandez, "I Came Near Being a Fascist," *Partisan Review* 1, no. 4 (1934): 20, 25.

71 Quoted in Walter Benjamin, "The Author as Producer," in *The Essential*

Frankfurt School Reader, ed. Andrew Arato and Eike Gebhardt (New York: Continuum, 1990), 255.

72 Quoted in Jennifer Wick, "Mrs. Dalloway Goes to Market: Woolf and Keynes and Modern Markets," *Novel* 28 (fall 1994): 21.

73 Wallace Stevens, "Jacket Statement from *Ideas of Order,*" in *Opus Posthumous,* 222.

74 Mao, *Solid Object,* 220.

75 Michael Denning, *The Cultural Front: The Laboring of American Culture in the Twentieth Century* (New York: Verso, 1996), 265.

76 The first two quotations are from the *New York Times,* 30 March 1935; the third is from the *Philadelphia Inquirer,* 30 March 1935. They are taken from clippings in an untitled notebook held at the Key West Public Library, Key West, Florida.

77 Bernard A. Weisberger, ed., *The WPA Guide to America: The Best of 1930s America As Seen by the Federal Writers' Project* (New York: Pantheon, 1985), 208.

78 Elmer Davis, "New World Symphony, with a Few Sour Notes," *Harpers Magazine* 170 (May 1935): 642.

79 Wallace Stevens, "Surety and Fidelity Claims" (1938), in *Opus Posthumous,* 239.

80 Wallace Stevens, "Insurance and Social Change," in *Opus Posthumous,* 234.

81 Wallace Stevens, "A Duck for Dinner" (1936), in *Opus Posthumous,* 66.

82 Alan Filreis and Harvey Teres, "Interview with Stanley Burnshaw," in *The Wallace Stevens Journal* 13, no. 2 (fall 1989): 124. Harold Bloom sees the song as evidence of Stevens's interest in a transcendental order that is "not our own," but can be located "nowhere else" but in ourselves (*Poems of Our Climate,* 101). Despite his avowed interest in the topographical, J. Hillis Miller, like Bloom, locates the poem's order in the romantic imagination and voice of the singer, and not in the town toward which the speaker turns (*Topographies* [Palo Alto: Stanford University Press, 1995], 288). For an in-depth analysis of Stevens's often hostile interest in romanticism during the 1930s, see Filreis, *Modernism,* 39–180.

83 William Wordsworth, *Selected Poetry and Prose,* ed. Philip Hobsbaum (London: Routledge, 1989), 129.

84 Kenneth Burke, *The Philosophy of Literary Form* (1941; Berkeley: University of California Press, 1972), 21.

85 Frank Lentricchia makes this point in *The Gaiety of Language: An Essay on the Radical Poetics of William Butler Yeats and Wallace Stevens* (Berkeley: University of California Press, 1968); see also Frank Dogget, *Wallace Stevens: The Making of a Poem* (Baltimore: Johns Hopkins University Press, 1980). Michael North and Walton Litz also make versions of this claim; see North, *The Final Statue,* 222; and Walton Litz, "Wallace Stevens's Defense of Poetry," in *The Romantic and Modern:*

Revaluations of Literary Tradition, ed. George Bornstein (Pittsburgh: University of Pittsburgh Press, 1977).

86 Benjamin Whorf, "The Relation of Habitual Thought and Behavior to Language" (1939), in *Language, Thought, and Reality,* ed. John Carroll (Cambridge, MA: MIT Press, 1991), 155.

87 Wallace Stevens, "Esthétique du Mal" (1944), in *The Collected Poems,* 322.

88 Wallace Stevens, "The Man with the Blue Guitar" (1937), in *The Collected Poems,* 168.

89 Wallace Stevens, "The Creation of Sounds" (1944), in *The Collected Poems,* 311.

90 Like a natural object, but not identical to one: Stevens writes to Richard Latimer at the start of 1935 that "while poems may very well occur, they had very much better be caused" (*Letters,* 274).

91 W. K. Wimsatt Jr. and Monroe C. Beardsley, "The Intentional Fallacy," in *The Verbal Icon: Studies in the Meaning of Poetry,* ed. W. K. Wimsatt Jr. (Lexington: University of Kentucky Press, 1954), 5.

92 It is therefore Stevens's proto–New Critical dogma, and not simply his job at Hartford, that leads Gerald Graff to claim that Stevens's poetry protects itself from "referential liabilities," the "risks of assertion." See Graff, *Poetic Statement and Critical Dogma* (Chicago: Northwestern University Press, 1970), 25.

93 Wimsatt and Beardsley, "The Intentional Fallacy," 5.

4. The Vanishing American Father: *Sentiment and Labor in* The Grapes of Wrath *and* A Tree Grows in Brooklyn

1 John Steinbeck, *The Grapes of Wrath: Text and Criticism,* ed. Peter Lisca (New York: Viking, 1972), 129–30.

2 Betty Smith, *A Tree Grows in Brooklyn* (New York: Harper, 1992), 78.

3 James Cain, *Double Indemnity* (New York: Vintage, 1992), 7. Phyllis is strikingly uninterested in using her husband's insurance policy to care for his daughter. Far from it: her accomplice, Walter Huff, discovers that she once killed six of a previous husband's children to collect from his policy.

4 Kenneth Fearing, *The Collected Poems of Kenneth Fearing* (New York: Random House, 1940), 56.

5 Philip Fisher, *Hard Facts: Setting and Form in the American Novel* (New York: Oxford University Press, 1985), 122. Bakhtin attributes to sentimental literature "a pathos occasioned by helplessness and weakness rather than by heroic strength" (quoted in Joanne Dobson, "Reclaiming Sentimental Literature," *American Literature* 69, no. 2 [June 1997]: 272). Daniel Born observes a similar phenomenon in Dickens: " 'The system! I am told on all hands,' cries Mr. Gridley in *Bleak House,* 'I

musn't look to individuals, it's the system' " (*The Birth of Liberal Guilt in the English Novel* [Chapel Hill: University of North Carolina Press, 1995], 5).

6 Jane Tompkins, *Sensational Designs: The Cultural Work of American Fiction, 1790–1870* (New York: Oxford University Press, 1985), 124.

7 Fisher, *Hard Facts,* 99.

8 Elizabeth Barnes, *States of Sympathy: Seduction and Democracy in the American Novel* (New York: Columbia University Press, 1997), 2.

9 Steinbeck's politics reinvigorate a patriarchal state precisely by manifesting male powerlessness, and in this respect, Steinbeck's novel partakes in what Laura Wexler terms the "imperial project of sentimentalism." Wexler maintains that "sentimentalization was an *externalized* aggression that was sadistic, not masochistic, in flavor. The energies it developed were intended as a tool of control of others, not merely as aid in the conquest of self. This element of the enterprise was . . . aimed at the subjection of different classes and even races who were compelled to play not the leading roles but the human scenery before which the melodrama of middle-class redemption could be enacted, for the enlightenment of an audience that was not even themselves." See Laura Wexler, "Tender Violence: Literary Eavesdropping, Domestic Fiction, and Educational Reform," in *The Culture of Sentiment: Race, Gender, and Sentimentality in Nineteenth-Century America,* ed. Shirley Samuels (New York: Oxford University Press, 1992), 15.

10 David Marshall, *The Surprising Effects of Sympathy: Marivaux, Diderot, Rousseau, and Mary Shelley* (Chicago: University of Chicago Press, 1988), 12.

11 John Steinbeck, *Working Days: The Journals of* The Grapes of Wrath, *1938–41,* ed. Robert DeMott (New York: Viking, 1989), 36.

12 John Steinbeck, *A Life in Letters,* ed. Elaine Steinbeck and Robert Wallsten (New York: Penguin, 1976), 178; hereafter cited as *Letters.*

13 Carl Sandburg has these two senses of "domestic economy" in mind when he conflates the national impetus to care for an abstraction like "the people" with the individual's desire to care for children. In *The People, Yes,* he intones,

> The people, yes, the people,
> Until the people are taken care of one way or another,
> Until the people are solved somehow for the day and hour,
> Until then one hears, "Yes, but the people what about the people?"
> Sometimes as though the people is a child to be pleased or fed . . .
> (221)

Sandburg's often maudlin, sentimentalized lamentations on behalf of the downtrodden prove as appropriate a vehicle as any for exploring the parameters of the New Deal's domestic economy. Carl Sandburg, *The People, Yes* (1936; New York: Harcourt, 1948).

14 See Gillian Brown's *Domestic Individualism: Imagining Self in Nineteenth-Century America* (Berkeley: University of California Press, 1990) for a refutation of the critical opposition of the domestic and the market.

15 Ralph E. Flanders, *The American Century* (Cambridge, MA: Harvard University Press, 1950), 12, 19.

16 Ann Douglas, *The Feminization of American Culture* (New York: Avon Books, 1977), 12.

17 John Gabriel Hunt, ed., *The Essential Franklin Delano Roosevelt* (New York: Random House, 1995), 80.

18 Kalin Tuan, ed., *Modern Insurance Theory and Education: A Social History of Insurance Evolution in the United States during the Twentieth Century* (Orange, NJ: Varsity Press, 1972), 1:478.

19 Linda Gordon, "New Feminist Scholarship on the Welfare State," in *Women, the State, and Welfare,* ed. Linda Gordon (Madison: University of Wisconsin Press, 1990), 23. In *Engendering Culture: Manhood and Womanhood in New Deal Public Art and Theater* (Washington, DC: Smithsonian Institution Press, 1991), Barbara Melosh notes that "The New Deal stands as the single example of a liberal American reform movement not accompanied by a resurgence of feminism. Instead, the strains of economic depression reinforced the containment of feminism that had begun after the winning of suffrage (1).

20 Nancy Fraser, *Justice Interruptus: Reflections on the Postsocialist Condition* (New York: Routledge, 1997), 41.

21 As Gwendolyn Mink points out, the Social Security Administration was crucial in institutionalizing the assumptions behind Roosevelt's "him and his": "To the extent that the 'welfare state breakthrough' of the New Deal hangs on the development of national social insurance, we can say that the modern U.S. welfare state was crafted (mostly) by men — for men, capitalism, and democracy. But to the extent that the welfare crisis springs from contradictions among work, race, and motherhood, we must credit maternalist New Dealers for helping implant these distinctions in the women's and children's provisions of the Social Security Act. The Social Security Act rewarded (men's) work, succored (women's) dependency, and treated working women collectively as an anomaly and individually as in transition to mature, domestic, maternal citizenship" (127). And as it turned out, "maternal citizenship" entailed little more than producing the right kind of children. In its *Report to the President,* the Economic Security Bill had this to say about the provisions for "Aid to Dependent Children" within the Social Security Act: "These are not primarily aids to mothers but defense measures for children. They are designed to release from the wage-earning role the person whose natural function is to give her children the physical and affectionate guardianship necessary not alone to keep them from falling into social misfortune, but more affirmatively to rear them into citizens capable of contributing to society" (132). See Gwendolyn Mink, *The Wages of Motherhood:*

Inequality in the Welfare State, 1917–1942 (Ithaca, NY: Cornell University Press, 1995), 127, 132.

22 The camp provides services that are still more personal. Rose rejoices when she discovers not simply that the camp has a nurse to oversee childbirth and child care, but that the migrants in the camp collectively name the children who are born there.

23 In her study of interwar American popular fiction, Suzanne Ellery Greene observes that "the novels published from 1928 to 1937 mark a partial retrogression [from the feminism of the twenties] in that men are again more central to the stories and more dominant over women." But Greene observes that in "1938–1945, the strong role of women is restored. The rebellions of the twenties are now restored" (159). Greene's account is no doubt overly schematized, but it is the case that after 1937, women began to win back some of the rights that had been denied them by the New Deal. Section 213 of the 1932 National Economy Act, for example, made legal the firing of a woman from the Civil Service if her husband was also so employed. The act was repealed in 1937. See Greene, *Books for Pleasure: Popular Fiction, 1914–1945* (Columbus, OH: Bowling Green Popular Press, 1974).

24 Cited in Barnes, *States of Sympathy,* 21.

25 Cited in Julie Ellison, "A Short History of Liberal Guilt," *Critical Inquiry* 22 (winter 1996): 360. Some two hundred years later, the heroine of Betty Smith's second novel, *Tomorrow Will Be Better,* takes up a similar question. The young Margy asks herself, "If you'd press a button and a Chinaman died in China, leaving you a million dollars, would you press that button? Sometimes Margy had decided that she'd press it very firmly; other times, she had decided that a million dollars would never compensate for causing a death — not even a Chinaman's on the other side of the world." In one respect, Margy's effort to identify with a quasi-colonial population perfectly demonstrates Ellison's claim that "from the very beginning [liberal guilt] is bound up with self-conscious racial difference" as well as "the feeling of being implicated in systems of domination." Axiomatic of liberal guilt — as critics like Ellison and Daniel Born describe it, in the eighteenth and nineteenth centuries, respectively — is its always ambivalent attempt to situate the individual in relation to faceless and exploited populations, from which the individual in question knows himself or herself to have benefited. But the population Margy imagines is most obviously salient to her because it exists on exactly the other side of the globe. Margy knows little about China, and probably less about colonialism. She does, however, know that strangers persistently provide her with the love, sympathy, and financial support that her emotionally abusive mother does not. Just moments after musing on her relation to the fate of the Chinese, Margy is separated from her indifferent mother on a city street. She is immediately rescued by an unfamiliar woman, fed ice cream, and returned to her furious

parent. Margy is castigated by her mother for being too much like her father — who is hounded by his wife for not earning enough money to feed their family — and her quandary about the relation between personal hunger and the existence of strangers less fortunate than she invokes a cognizance of the gendered labor relations of her family more than a consciousness of her complicity in late colonialism. See Betty Smith, *Tomorrow Will Be Better* (New York: Harper and Brothers, 1948), 3. Ellison, "Short History," 352, 350.

26 Gordon, "New Feminist Scholarship," 23.

27 John Steinbeck, *Novels and Stories, 1932–1937* (New York: Library of America, 1994), 456; further references to *Tortilla Flats* and *In Dubious Battle* are from this volume.

28 Michael Denning, *Cultural Front: The Laboring of American Culture in the Twentieth Century* (New York: Verso, 1996), 260.

29 Lorentz, head of the U.S. Film Service from 1935 to 1940, was a principal New Deal influence on *The Grapes of Wrath.* The documentary filmmaker reportedly convinced Steinbeck to give up writing about left politics and to write *The Grapes of Wrath* in its present form instead.

30 John Steinbeck, *Burning Bright* (New York: Macmillan, 1950), 29.

31 David Wyatt, introduction, and Stephen Railton, "Pilgrims' Politics: Steinbeck's Art of Conversion," both in *New Essays on the Grapes of Wrath,* ed. David Wyatt (New York: Cambridge University Press, 1990), 19, 31.

32 The incipient universalism governing these and many similar moments in Steinbeck's corpus might seem to suggest sympathies with a quasi-Christian, humanist left. Most obviously, it's hard not to think of Rose of Sharon and her stranger as a Mary cradling Christ; her name alone is a reference to The Song of Solomon. But though Christian in its allegorical structure, Steinbeck's novel insistently secularizes Christian ethics. Hence the presence of the Preacher Casey, who turns away from his calling and enlists himself as a strike organizer. He has lost God, he reiterates, and consequently apprentices himself to "the people." Moreover, as much as Rose seems a religious icon, she is also what Barbara Melosh describes as the idealized "moral mother" of the peace movement during the late thirties. Melosh points out that in New Deal stage productions, the "moral mother" is invoked to regenerate a degraded democratic society, because, as a mother, she is presumed to have an inside track on modes of nurturing then thought necessary to civic life. See Melosh, *Engendering Culture,* 146, 138, 141. William Howarth also notes the prevalence of the "nurturing Madonna" in FSA photography in his essay "The Mother of Literature: Journalism in *The Grapes of Wrath,*" in Wyatt, *New Essays,* 80.

33 Pietro di Donato, *Christ in Concrete* (New York: Bobbs-Merrill, 1939), 297.

34 In *The Girl,* a domineering father roars to his wife, "I worked all my

life . . . ain't any lady reliefers gonna snoop around here I tell you" (30). But as much as relief palpably threatens men in Le Sueur's working-class novel, it threatens women even more. "The Girl," Le Sueur's pregnant heroine, is turned over by her case worker to an Orwellian relief agency that locks her up and plans to sterilize her after she delivers her child. The Girl escapes, and triumphantly delivers her child before a crowd of women picketing the agency's office for more milk for their children. See Meridel Le Sueur, *The Girl* (1935–1945; New York: West End Press, 1995).

35 See Alan Dawley, *Struggles for Justice: Social Responsibility and the Liberal State* (Cambridge, MA: Harvard University Press, 1991), 101, 103.

36 See Theda Skocpol, *Protecting Soldiers and Mothers: The Political Origins of Social Policy in the United States* (Cambridge, MA: Belknap Press of Harvard University Press, 1992).

37 For treatments of the relation between gender and state politics during the Progressive era, see Paula Baker, "The Domestication of Politics: Women and American Political Society, 1780–1920," in *Unequal Sisters,* ed. Ellen Carol DuBois and Vicki L. Ruiz (New York: Routledge, 1994).

38 Smith's only biographer argues that Smith "believed in the ideology of the New Deal — that art and education were the keys to solving all manners of social ills." See Carol Siri Johnson's dissertation, *The Life and Work of Betty Smith, Author of* A Tree Grows in Brooklyn (Ann Arbor: UMI, 1995), 87. For Johnson's account of Smith's tenure with the Federal Writers Project, see 87–104.

39 Ibid., 79.

40 Ibid., 107.

41 Trilling condemned Smith's novel on charges of sentimentalism twice, both times in *The Nation,* on 3 September 1943, and, cited above, May 1944. Cited in Johnson, *The Life,* 162–64.

42 See Johnson, *The Life,* 109.

43 Dobson, "Reclaiming," 266. Cathy Davidson, *The Revolution and the Word: The Rise of the Novel in America* (New York: Oxford University Press, 1986), 113.

44 What this means in part is that Francie loses her brother even as she loses her father: Katie feels that it is suddenly inappropriate for Francie to sleep in the same room as her brother. Forced out of a once comforting household, Francie learns that fathers can't live either with their own children or with daughters who can make children.

45 Elizabeth Ammons, "Heroines in Uncle Tom's Cabin," in *Critical Essays on Harriet Beecher Stowe,* ed. Elizabeth Ammons (Boston: G. K. Hall, 1980), 154.

46 Katie's father "never forgave any of his daughters for marrying. His philosophy about children was simple and profitable: a man enjoyed

himself begetting them, put in as little money and effort into their up-bringing as was possible, and then put them to work earning money for the father as soon as they got to their teens" (55).

47 Suddenly, Sissy is able to do what previously she could not. After the adoption, Sissy becomes pregnant and gives birth to a healthy child of her own for the first time. "I've never seen it to fail," exclaims Katie. "Let a childless woman adopt a baby and bang! A year or two later she is sure to have one of her own. It's as if God recognized her good intentions at last" (387). It is not at all clear what Katie means by "good intentions." On the one hand, Katie seems to imply that her sister deserves a child of her own because she is committed to having children, as opposed to just having sex. On the other hand, it seems that Sissy gets to have children because she first demonstrates her commitment to motherhood on another's child, in which case biological reproduction is further displaced from her body. In either event, Katie later decides that Sissy's successful pregnancy has nothing to do with "intentions" of any kind. "Life's funny," she muses to her sister. " 'A couple of accidental things come together and a person could make a lot out of them. It was just an accident that you got to know about that girl. That same fellow must have told a dozen men in the shop. Steve just mentioned it to you accidentally. It was just by accident that you got in with that family, and just accidental that the baby has a round as opposed to a square chin. It's even less than accidental. It's . . . ' Katie stopped to search for a word. . . . 'You mean coincidental, Mama?' she called out. A shocked silence came from the bedroom. Then the conversation was resumed. This time in whispers" (368). This moment of almost religious reverence for an otherwise nebulous distinction between the accidental and the coincidental is striking. Just as Steinbeck's characters are unable to do anything other than have feelings about the actions they perform like automatons, Katie needs to believe that there is some subsuming pattern — providential or otherwise — that organizes what seem to be accidental events, that make child bearing and rearing less a matter of male sentiment than one of an almost providential formalism.

48 See Dobson, "Reclaiming," on the relation between sentimentalism and the keepsake.

49 Jay Parini, *John Steinbeck: A Biography* (New York: Henry Holt, 1995), 227.

50 John Steinbeck, *Working Days: The Journals of* The Grapes of Wrath, *1938–41,* ed. Robert DeMott (New York: Viking, 1989), 108. Steinbeck was so skittish about this reversal of traditional gender roles that he insisted on keeping Carol out of the fragile domestic world he occupied while writing. Steinbeck thus lived out the anxieties captured in *Of Mice and Men,* where a lethal bourgeois female sexuality is imagined to intrude on and destroy an idyllic but threatened sphere of working-class male labor. As Parini notes, Steinbeck embraced a "traditionally sexist view of the world, seeing the male environment of the bunkhouse as a

kind of idyll that is interrupted by the evil woman who can't help herself" (*John Steinbeck,* 184). See also *Working Days,* 13.

51 Norman Macleod, *You Get What You Ask For* (New York: Harrison-Hilton, 1939), 18.

52 Paula Rabinowitz, *Labor and Desire: Women's Revolutionary Fiction in Depression America* (Chapel Hill: University of North Carolina Press, 1991), 54.

53 Jack Conroy, *A World to Win* (New York: Covici and Friede, 1935), 344.

54 Ernest Hemingway, *To Have and Have Not* (1937; New York: Collier, 1987), 186.

55 Cited in Howarth, "Mother of Literature." Steinbeck anxiously frets over what looked to be the impending financial ruin of Covici and Friede, his publishing house, in his working diary of *The Grapes of Wrath.* In fact, he worries over the fact that he will never get the large sums owed him exactly on the very days that he writes chapter 18, which analogizes the migrant's collective family to government insurance.

56 John Steinbeck, *Cannery Row* (1945; New York: Bantam, 1982), 2.

57 Quoted in Roy Hoopes, *Cain: The Biography of James M. Cain* (Carbondale: Southern Illinois University Press, 1982), 394.

58 Ibid.

59 W. K. Wimsatt Jr. and Monroe C. Beardsley, "The Intentional Fallacy," in *The Verbal Icon: Studies in the Meaning of Poetry,* ed. W. K. Wimsatt Jr. (Lexington: University of Kentucky Press, 1954), 5.

5. "The Death of the Gallant Liberal":
Robert Frost, Richard Wright, and Busby Berkeley

1 Printed in The Guild's Committee for Federal Writers' Publications, Inc. *American Stuff: An Anthology of Prose and Verse by Members of the Federal Writers' Project, with Sixteen Prints by the Federal Art Project* (New York: Macmillan, 1937), 125.

2 Quoted in Lawrence Thompson and R. H. Winnick, *Robert Frost: A Biography,* ed. Edward Latham (New York: Holt, Rinehart, and Winston, 1981), 515.

3 John F. Kennedy, "Statement by the President upon Establishing the Advisory Council on the Arts," 12 June 1963.

4 Robert Frost, "The Lesson for Today" (1942), in *The Poetry of Robert Frost,* ed. Edward Latham (New York: Holt, Rinehart, and Winston, 1969).

5 Richard Wright, *The Outsider* (1953; New York: Harper Perennial, 1993), 199, 204.

6 Thoreau and Whitman cited in Richard Poirier, *Poetry and Pragmatism* (Cambridge, MA: Harvard University Press, 1992), 67.

7 James T. Farrell, *Yet Other Waters* (New York: Vanguard, 1952), 21.

8 Elizabeth Barnes, *States of Sympathy: Seduction and Democracy in the American Novel* (New York: Columbia University Press, 1997), 18.

9 See Michael Denning, *The Cultural Front: The Laboring of American Culture in the Twentieth Century* (New York: Verso, 1996), xvii, 5, 8, 10, 61, 96, 128, 436, 447. C. L. R. James, *American Civilization,* ed. Anna Grimshaw and Keith Hart (Cambridge, MA: Blackwell, 1993), 107, 106.

10 François Ewald, "Insurance and Risk," in *The Foucault Effect,* ed. Graham Burchell, Colin Gordon, and Peter Miller (Chicago: University of Chicago Press, 1991), 204. Michel Foucault also reasons that, since the invention of the modern welfare state, "one ought to be able to expect from social security" that it "gives each individual autonomy in relation to the dangers and situations likely to lower his status or subject him." In its ideal form, he claims, social insurance would enhance a person's experience of distinctiveness by affiliating him with populations greater than himself; it would provide "optimal social security combined with maximum independence." See Foucault, *Politics, Philosophy, Culture: Interviews and Other Writings, 1977–1984* (New York: Routledge, 1988), 160, 165.

11 Truman Capote, *In Cold Blood* (New York: Random House, 1965), 47.

12 Richard Wright, *Native Son and "How 'Bigger' Was Born"* (New York: Harper Perennial, 1993), 531.

13 James Baldwin, "Everybody's Protest Novel" in *Notes of a Native Son* (Boston: Beacon Press, 1984), 16, 22.

14 See Michel Fabre, *The Unfinished Quest of Richard Wright* (New York: William Morrow, 1993), 178.

15 Richard Wright, introduction to *Black Metropolis: A Study of Negro Life in a Northern City,* ed. St. Clair Drake and Horace R. Cayton, foreword by William Wilson (1945; Chicago: University of Chicago Press, 1993), xxvi.

16 Claims such as these would lay the groundwork for a distinctly existentialist political philosophy. For an in-depth account of Wright's break with the Communist Party, see Fabre, *Unfinished Quest,* 228–31. For an account of Wright's relation to French existentialism, see 320–22, 374–76, 528–29. See also Yoshinobu Hakutani's *Richard Wright and Racial Discourse* (Columbia: University of Missouri Press, 1996).

17 John Dewey, *Liberalism and Social Action* (New York: G. P. Putnam's Sons, 1935), 21. For accounts of American corporate liberalism that stress the role of a centrist state, see Martin J. Sklar, *The Corporate Reconstruction of American Capitalism, 1890–1916: The Market, the Law, and Politics* (New York: Cambridge University Press, 1988), and Thomas Streeter, *Selling the Air: A Critique of the Policy of Commercial Broadcasting in the United States* (Chicago: University of Chicago Press, 1996).

18 Abdul R. JanMohamed makes a similar argument in terms of race, in "Negating the Negation as a Form of Affirmation in Minority Dis-

course," where he notes that, for Wright, "racist negation becomes the opposite of what it is initially — it becomes a site of freedom" (in *Richard Wright: A Collection of Critical Essays,* ed. Arnold Rampersad [Englewood Cliffs, NJ: Prentice Hall, 1995], 122).

19 Wright, *Native Son,* 514, 516.

20 Carla Cappetti, *Writing Chicago: Modernism, Ethnography, and the Novel* (New York: Columbia University Press, 1993), 199, 206, 202.

21 Kwame Anthony Appiah, "A Long Way from Home: Wright in the Gold Coast," in Rampersad, *Wright,* 192.

22 Richard Wright, *Conversations with Richard Wright,* ed. Keneth Kinnamon and Michel Fabre (Jackson: University of Mississippi Press, 1993), 159.

23 Paul Gilroy, *The Black Atlantic, Modernity and Double Consciousness* (Cambridge, MA: Harvard University Press, 1993), 161.

24 Richard Wright, *Lawd Today* (New York: Walker, 1963), 32.

25 Gwendolyn Mink, *The Wages of Motherhood: Inequality in the Welfare State, 1917–1942* (Ithaca, NY: Cornell University Press, 1995), 137.

26 Wallace Stevens, "Like Decorations in a Nigger Cemetery," in *Opus Posthumous,* rev. ed. (New York: Knopf, 1989), 222.

27 Lizabeth Cohen, *Making a New Deal: Industrial Workers in Chicago, 1919–1939* (Cambridge, England: Cambridge University Press, 1990).

28 As Edward D. Berkowitz points out in *America's Welfare State from Roosevelt to Reagan* (Baltimore: Johns Hopkins University Press, 1991), "The distinction between social insurance and welfare [is] important." People who receive benefits from social insurance "pay for at least some of those benefits themselves, or, alternatively, employers make contributions on behalf of their employees. People claim social insurance benefits as a matter of right, an entitlement. Welfare differs from social insurance on both counts. Its benefits come from general revenues and require no prepayment. Accepting welfare as a gratuity, people must prove to the state's satisfaction that they meet the entry conditions, such as having a dependent child in their care. Social Security constitutes our major form of social insurance, Aid to Families with Dependent Children (AFDC) our major form of welfare" (xviii). Few have imagined the welfare state as an institution designed exclusively for wage-earning Whites. In fact, just the opposite has been the case. Presuming to speak for an exclusively White readership, Berkowitz concurs: "On some gut level," he claims, the term welfare itself "evokes an instant shock of recognition and produces an almost visceral reaction. When we think of welfare, we envision a black woman, who lives in a sinister section of the city, taking care of her illegitimate children and cashing government checks" (xiii). For a recent and especially offensive linking of Blacks and welfare, see Dinesh D'Souza's *The End of Racism: Principles for a Multiracial Society* (New York: Free Press, 1995).

29 Key West Administration, *Key West Guide* (fall–winter 1935–1936): 1.

30 Quoted in Herbert Aptheker, ed., *A Documentary History of the Negro People in the United States, from the New Deal to the End of World War II,* 4 vols. (1974; New York: Citadel Press, 1992), 4:180.

31 George Edmund Haynes, "Lily-White Social Security," in Aptheker, *Documentary History,* 4:164.

32 John P. Davis, "A Black Inventory of the New Deal," in Aptheker, *Documentary History,* 4:172.

33 Quoted in Aptheker, *Documentary History,* 4: 174, 179.

34 "The New Deal," notes Lizabeth Cohen, "provided workers with federally funded relief programs, and eventually a permanent Social Security system, to take the place of the welfare previously dispersed by private organizations, often sponsored by their ethnic and religious communities" (*Making a New Deal,* 261). The New Deal would thus initiate a major shift of Blacks to the Democratic Party.

35 Cohen, *Making a New Deal,* 268.

36 Fabre, *Unfinished Quest,* 103.

37 Margaret Walker, *Richard Wright: Daemonic Genius* (New York, Warner Books, 1988), 81, 69, 70.

38 Quoted in Addison Gayle, ed., *The Black Aesthetic* (New York: Doubleday, 1971), 82.

39 Richard Wright, *Twelve Million Black Voices* (1941), preface by Eric Bently (New York: Thunders Mouth Press, 1988), 49. Considerations of the racial politics of the New Deal struggle to reconcile the often racist practices of specific federal agencies with the fact that on the whole the New Deal was beneficial to Blacks. In his preface to *Twelve Million Black Voices,* for example, Eric Bently reasons, "Theoretically, the relief was granted equally. In fact, it was created in the racist image of American Society. . . . Under the Social Security Board, unemployment benefits were provided to workers, but domestic and agricultural workers were exempted. . . . The Works Progress Administration (wpa), although it never employed as many as it was supposed to, nevertheless constructed black hospitals, college buildings, and playgrounds" (x–xi).

40 Richard Wright, "Two Letters to Dorothy Norman," in *Art and Action,* ed. Dorothy Norman (New York: Twice a Year Press, 1948). Wright has not, needless to say, ever been taken as a defender of the welfare state. Indeed, the politics of Wright's novels have been notoriously difficult to identify, particularly in terms of a cold war spectrum — bounded by the extreme left and right, ostensibly balanced by a vital center — that has rarely granted the welfare state a coherent valence of its own.

41 The unpublished poem is kept in the rare books section of the Schomburg Center for Research in Black Culture, New York Public Library, New York City. For an assessment of the accusation that Wright was in fact working for the fbi, see Addison Gayle, introduction to *Ordeal of a Native Son* (Gloucester, MA: P. Smith, 1983). For the files the fbi kept

on Wright, see Natalie Robbins, *Alien Ink: The FBI's War on Freedom of Expression* (New York: William Morrow, 1992).

42 Damon's quest also plugs into a cold war fascination with "the third man," that shadowy individual seen to throw off the ideological ruins of the Second World War in favor of pure economic self-interest. The same is true of *The Outsider*'s fascination with politically motivated murder, forged documents, and concealed identity: "What a system of life!," declares Damon. "Spies spying on spies who are being spied upon!" (453).

43 Richard Wright, "Personalism," microfiche, Schomburg Center for Research in Black Culture, New York Public Library, New York City.

44 Wright, *Conversations*, 159.

45 Constance Webb, *Richard Wright: A Biography* (New York: Putnam, 1968), 262.

46 Wright, *Conversations*, 89.

47 Fabre, *Unfinished Quest*, 168.

48 Chester Himes, *The Quality of the Hurt* (New York: Paragon, 1990), 72.

49 Nelson Algren claims that "In *Native Son*, [Wright] asserted specifically that, when a crime is committed by a man who has been excluded from civilization, civilization is accomplice to that crime. In defense of Bigger Thomas he demanded of the prosecution: 'Let's see your hands' " ("Remembering Richard Wright," *The Nation* 192 [28 January 1961]: 85).

50 Cappetti, *Writing Chicago*, 209, 189.

51 Quoted in Joseph T. Skerrett Jr., "Composing Bigger: Wright and the Making of Native Son," in Rampersad, *Wright*, 37.

52 See Fabre, *Unfinished Quest*, 91.

53 Richard Wright, *Savage Holiday* (1954; Jackson: University Press of Mississippi, 1994), 49.

54 James M. Cain, *The Postman Always Rings Twice* (1934; New York: Vintage, 1978), 119.

55 Albert Camus claimed *The Postman* as the inspiration for *The Stranger* (1946). In *The Stranger*, the apparent automatism of Chambers's actions finds expression in the trigger of a gun that "gives," a gun that fires five shots into the body of an Arab without the intention of the person pointing it. Camus's character, like Chambers before him, claims not to understand why he has done what he has done. It is also worth noting the explicitly welfare context in which *The Stranger* takes place. The main character is condemned by the court, not simply for killing an Arab, but for committing his mother to a state facility.

56 James M. Cain, *Double Indemnity* (1936; New York: Vintage, 1992), 15. In Kenneth Fearing's *The Big Clock* (1946), in *Crime Novels: American Noir of the Thirties and Forties*, ed. Robert Polito (New York: Library of America, 1997), the CEO of a publishing corporation developing a private industry alternative to the Social Security Administration — "Funded Individuals" — explains a murder he just committed by imagin-

ing another being within: "It wasn't me any more. It was some giant a hundred feet tall, moving me around, manipulating my hands and arms and even my voice. He straightened my legs, and I found myself standing" (431). Jim Thompson's *A Swell Looking Babe* (1954) — in which, as in *The Postman Always Rings Twice,* police solve a case by discovering that a killer is the unwitting recipient of his victim's life insurance money — concludes in a similar manner.

57 As Albert H. Mowbray, Professor of Insurance at Berkeley, puts it in "Insurance in Social Evolution" (1930), "Insurance must be sold, or its purchase compelled. . . . The transfer must be forced upon us, or we must be persuaded to it." Cited in Kalin Tuan, ed., *Modern Insurance Theory and Education: A Social History of Insurance Evolution in the United States during the Twentieth Century* (Orange, NJ: Varsity Press, 1972), 339.

58 Framing *Double Indemnity* in a flashback (a technique that would prove axial to the noir canon), Billy Wilder's film version of Cain's novella provides this "better look." Narrating his past actions to claims adjuster Barton Keyes — and yet unable to explain why he performed them — Huff (renamed "Neff" in Wilder's film) entreats Keyes and the audience to join him in watching his second self perform amidst Wilder's ominous shadows, predatory phantoms that accentuate the split between the individual and the spectral agency he does not himself possess. When Neff explains that Keyes missed his performance the first time around because "he was too close," Keyes replies, "Closer than that, Walter." "I love you too," replies Neff, just before he dies. But of course, the two are not quite close enough, in the same way that Huff can never manage to close the gap between his intentions and his actions. For valuable accounts of Billy Wilder's film of the novel, see *Double Indemnity,* ed. Richard Schickel, BFI Classics (London: BFI Publishing, 1992), 65. For an interesting account of Raymond Chandler's work on the film, see William Luhr, *Raymond Chandler and Film* (New York: Unger, 1982).

59 James M. Cain, *Our Government* (New York: Knopf, 1930), 1.

60 Richard Wright, *Black Boy* (1945; New York: Signet, 1963), 116; *Black Metropolis,* xix, xx.

61 Richard Wright, *American Hunger* (New York: Harper Perennial, 1977), 20.

62 Wright was one of only five writers selected to participate on the FWP's Creative Writers' Unit, which paid him a wage while he worked on material that would become *Native Son.* For an account of Wright's relation to the Creative Writers' Unit, see Jerre Mangione, *The Dream and the Deal: The Federal Writers' Project, 1935–1943* (New York: Little Brown, 1972).

63 Joan Didion, *Democracy* (1984; New York: Vintage, 1995), 215.

64 Quoted in *The First American Writers Congress* (New York: Equinox, 1935), 63–64.

65 Meridel Le Sueur, "The Fetish of Being Outside," in *Writing Red: An Anthology of American Women Writers, 1930–1940*, ed. Charlotte Nekola and Paula Rabinowitz (New York: The Feminist Press, 1987).

66 Robert Frost, "Build Soil," *The Poetry of Robert Frost* (New York: Henry Holt, 1979), 316.

67 F. R. Ankersmit, *Aesthetic Politics: Political Philosophy beyond Fact and Value* (Stanford: Stanford University Press, 1996), 96.

68 Richard Poirier, *Robert Frost and the Work of Knowing* (Palo Alto, CA: Stanford University Press, 1977), 264.

69 Quoted in Roy Hoopes, *Cain: The Biography of James M. Cain* (Carbondale: Southern Illinois University Press, 1982), 394.

70 Rudy Behlmer, ed., *Inside Warner Brothers, 1935–1951* (New York: Viking Press, 1985), 15. For the classic account of the relation between film and social escapism during the Depression, see Andrew Bergman *We're in the Money: Depression America and Its Films* (New York: New York University Press, 1971).

71 Richard Barrios, *A Song in the Dark; The Birth of the Musical Film* (New York: Oxford University Press, 1995), 377.

72 Stephen Vaugh, *Ronald Reagan in Hollywood: Movies and Politics* (New York: Cambridge University Press, 1944), 33, 35, 40. On the eve of the presidential election between Nixon and Kennedy, Harry and Jack Warner, now conservative Republicans, urged Nixon to take an even harder line on the welfare state by making it James Stewart's first task in *FBI Story* (1959) to rid the country of murderous sociopaths who "have become overly sentimental about insurance." It was clear by 1959 that, in Jack Warner's eyes, these sentimentalists threatening the nation were, at least in part, Hollywood screenwriters. Testifying before the House UnAmerican Activities Committee in 1947, Jack Warner set the FBI loose on all those screenwriters he so much as suspected of left leanings, a group principally composed of those who had formed the SWG. But during the thirties, Warner Brothers would show that it was perfectly consistent to be sentimental about both the FBI and insurance. This assertion came most powerfully in the form of a young actor under exclusive contract to Warners by the name of Ronald Reagan. During the thirties, Reagan was a "child of the Depression," by his own account "a near hopeless hemophilic liberal" who "bled for causes" (Stephen Vaugh, *Ronald Reagan in Hollywood: Movies and Politics* [New York: Cambridge University Press, 1944], 41). In his first years with Warners, Reagan starred in four FBI films, including *Secret Service of the Air* (1938) and *Smashing the Money Ring* (1939). Reagan's "insurance" films include *Girls on Probation, Angels Wash Their Faces,* and *Accidents Will Happen,* all centrally concerned with the overcoming of insurance fraud, all made in 1938, when Warners had turned to insurance companies for financial backing. In *Accidents Will Happen,* Reagan plays Eric Gregg, a

claims adjuster working to smash "an organized accidents racket." Like Neff, this racket, run by corrupt insurance men, attempts to plan accidents, to orchestrate events, and then to vanish as their cause. Gregg, like the welfare state, is committed to eliminating the planned. But Gregg's wife, "fed up with great gobs of ideals being fed to me morning, evening and night," deserts Gregg for the racket. Reagan, not yet so tired, takes on the conspiracy in the name of his company and of the system of government it allegorizes: "You don't know what a big company I work for," Gregg trumpets.

During the 1950s, a more conservative Reagan would himself work for both big business and the FBI: making public appearances and broadcasts against the welfare state for companies like GE and MCA and working with the FBI as president of the Screen Actors Guild to rid Hollywood of those hard-to-spot communist screenwriters. The important point here is that Reagan associated his fifteen years in front of the camera at Warners (1937–1952) not simply with insurance but with the welfare state itself; he facilitated his move from behind the camera into the political arena (first as president of the Screen Actors Guild, later as president of the United States) by consolidating the doubleness explored above. Reagan reports that his biggest problem with acting was getting "used to seeing myself." And as Michael Rogin argues, the president took from his acting years the unmistakable tendency "to present political events of his own making as if he somehow were not responsible for them." "There are not two Ronald Reagans," Nancy Reagan would later insist, disavowing the notion that Reagan performed roles more than he directed events (Michael Rogin, *Ronald Reagan, The Movie, and Other Episodes in Political Demonology* [Berkeley: University of California Press, 1987], 33, 6, 7). Rogin explains that Reagan himself believed he was integrating his "two selves" when he gave up acting for conservative politics. Specifically, Reagan wanted more control over what kind of roles he would play, and Warners, perhaps more than any of the five majors, was committed to refusing creative input from actors. Reagan's departure from the structured paternalism practiced at Warners would seem in turn to have direct political overtones: Reagan's autobiography *Where's the Rest of Me* (titled from Reagan's favorite Warners film, in which he plays a man whose legs are cut off) perfectly sets up Rogin's claim that "cutting" patients off welfare later would become for Reagan a symbolic gesture tied up with his emergence (out of film and welfare, into conservative politics) as a unified and self-authoring agent (see Rogin, 8, 21, 35).

73 Warner Brothers' retooling of its gangster genre into the FBI genre mentioned in the first chapter, for example, was done in large part to support an administration recently challenged by the Supreme Court's overturning of the NRA. Roosevelt's programs had been taking a beating from the Supreme Court, and Warners' FBI films were designed to curry public

support for legislation that allowed the agents to carry handguns. The FBI as we know it today is in fact a welfare-state invention. Though the agency existed before the New Deal, it was Roosevelt who provided the FBI with most of its modern-day powers, such as the ability to carry handguns. For an in-depth account of Warners' move to the FBI picture, see Nick Roddick, *A New Deal in Entertainment: Warner Brothers in the 1930s* (London: BFI, 1983).

74 Larry Ceplair and Steven Englund, *The Inquisition in Hollywood: Politics in the Film Community, 1930–1960* (Berkeley: University of California Press, 1979), 19.

75 Quoted in ibid., 23.

76 Ibid., 10.

77 Quoted in ibid., 27.

78 Quoted in ibid., 29.

79 Ibid., 25.

80 *Double Indemnity* lurks somewhere behind *The Gold Diggers of 1937.* In *Double Indemnity,* for instance, we find out that Phyllis has killed four people previous to her husband by inducing pneumonia in them. In the screenplay for *Gold Diggers of 1937,* the two vice presidents likewise attempt to kill Hobart by inducing pneumonia.

81 Ewald, "Insurance and Risk," 204.

82 In his account of Berkeley's influence on the Hollywood musical, Martin Rubin observes, "This rigid alignment of performance space and performance discourse is crucial to the development of the Berkeleyesque in the classic Warners musicals of the early 1930s. The clear and absolute separation of performance space/discourse (the partitioning off of the films' 'musicalness') imparts to the musical numbers a revue-like autonomy, freed from the demands of even the most tenuous narrative-to-numbers consistency. This allows full, unrestrained indulgence and extension of the impulse toward spectacle, of the Berkeleyesque." See Rubin, *Showstoppers: Busby Berkeley and the Tradition of Spectacle* (New York: Columbia University Press, 1993), 39.

83 Don DeLillo's *Libra* (London: Penguin, 1988) pushes this association between narrative form and death further still, to the claim that narrative plots lead to burial plots: "Plots carry their own logic. There is a tendency of plots to move toward death. . . . A narrative plot no less than a conspiracy of armed men. The tighter the plot of a story, the more likely it will come to death" (221).

84 Wright seems to have worked from exactly these associations when he was employed with an insurance company in the early thirties. Wright's company, he explains in *American Hunger,* would sell only to Black families, but would target the women in those families. This was done so that the company could have its way with those perceived to be unwilling to question authority. Beyond the fact that he would sexually exploit his female customers by sleeping with them in place of collecting their pol-

icy payments, Wright partook of a scam designed to prey on his customers' lack of familiarity with insurance. One insurance agent would distract the customer, while the second would switch policies, exchanging one form of coverage for another, less comprehensive in nature. Thus, either in its actuarial analysis, which might demonstrate that Black housewives were less likely to suffer accidental physical harm than working Black males, or in the kind of flagrant abuse described by Wright—premised, no doubt, on the belief that working-class Black housewives would know less about their policies than, say, educated middle-class White housewives—the insurance company divides and conquers by continually refining the criteria through which it identifies salient social groups. Claims adjuster Keyes urges Huff to resist the sex appeal of insurance in *Double Indemnity,* when he tells him to give up chasing women and take a job at his side as an assistant claims man. Keyes makes his case by suggesting that the claims man doesn't need women because he is already his own autoerotic corporate plurality: "The claims man, Walter, is a doctor, and a blood hound, and a cop, and a judge, and a jury, and a father confessor, all in one." Keyes's collectivization is unmistakably autoerotic: Keyes's "all in one" is given a home when Keyes refers to the "little man" living in his stomach who helps him with his cases. If Huff's heterosexual desire leads to a "something inside me" that he cannot control, Keyes's little man is professionally enabled, sanctioned by the insurance workplace.

85 Toni Morrison, *Song of Solomon* (1977; New York: Plume, 1987), 3.

86 Cohen, *Making a New Deal,* 75, 151.

87 Philip Roth, *Portnoy's Complaint* (1967; New York: Random House, 1969), 6, 39.

88 Walker, *Richard Wright,* 236. For a comprehensive account of the relation between race and the Communist Party during the thirties, see Barbara Foley, *Radical Representations: Politics and Form in U.S. Proletarian Fictions, 1929–1941* (Durham, NC: Duke University Press, 1993), 170–213. See also Jonathan Harris's "State Power and Cultural Discourse," *Block* 13 (1987–1988), where he argues that during the Depression, "abstraction was conceived not as a philosophical or aesthetic problem, but as one pertaining to the relation of the individual—and also, crucially, that of the artist—to both the State and social order" (40).

89 Richard Wright, "Introduction: Blueprint for Negro Writing," in *The Black Aesthetic,* ed. Addison Gayle (New York: Doubleday, 1971), 341. For an excellent discussion of this text, see Houston Baker Jr., "On Knowing Our Place," in *Richard Wright, Critical Perspectives Past and Present,* ed. Henry Louis Gates Jr. and K. A. Appiah (New York: Amistad, 1993). We find Wright's topographical imagination working at full force in his introduction to Drake and Cayton's *Black Metropolis,* where he declares, "There is yet another vista now open for us, a vista of which only artists have so far availed themselves: what new values of action or

experience can be revealed by looking at Negro life through alien eyes, or under the lens of new concepts?" (xxxi).

90   Wright's next novel, *Savage Holiday,* further connects the failure of perspective with the failure of social security. Fowler unintentionally causes a young child to fall from a highrise just moments after he is let go without warning by his insurance firm. Insurance, Wright seems to suggest, keeps the child suspended safely overhead. In "Discovering America: Generational Shifts, Afro-American Literary Criticism, and the Study of Expressive Culture," in *Blues, Ideology, and Afro-American Literature: A Vernacular Theory* (Chicago: University of Chicago Press, 1984), Houston A. Baker Jr. characterizes Wright in his adherence to what Baker describes as an "Integrationist Poetics." "The black spokesman who champions 'Integrationist Poetics,' " Baker explains, "is constantly in search of social indicators (such as the *Brown* decision) that signal democratic-pluralism in American life. The implicit goal of the paradigm's democratic-pluralistic philosophical orientation is a future raceless, classless society of men and women in America. The Integrationist critic, therefore, as Wright demonstrates, founds his prediction of such a future, homogeneous body of Americans on such social *evidence* as the Emancipation Proclamation, constitutional amendments, Supreme Court decisions, or any one of the many other documented claims that suggest America is moving toward AMERICA" (69). The "Integrationist spokesman" is thus defined in legal terms: he finds hope for a raceless and classless America in court enactments. Baker is of course correct to point out that Wright was, with characteristic ambivalence, committed to a raceless and classless vision of America. He is wrong, however, to suggest that this social vision is inaugurated by *Brown v. Topeka Board of Education* in 1954. For though the Brown decision offered some cause for celebration, *Savage Holiday* speaks more to the erosion of the New Deal, with which Wright was more concerned.

91   In this light, Wright might seem to draw attention to the need for multicultural media, principally because Thomas's experiences of alienation seem to be the product of his inability to see himself or his race actively participating in a public sphere. This would correspond to what Charles Taylor has termed "the politics of recognition" inherent in multiculturalism. The refusal to recognize cultural groups, Taylor reasons, "can inflict damage on those who are denied it. . . . Not only contemporary feminism but also race relations are subtended by the premise that the withholding of recognition can be a form of oppression" (55). Taylor goes on to reason that "espousing collective goals on behalf of a national group can be thought to be inherently discriminatory" because "the pursuit of the collective end will probably involve treating insiders and outsiders differently" (36). The problem we confront here, however, is that Wright's characters aspire to being enfranchised in a national group that subsumes and, ideally, dissolves *Native Son*'s "nation within a nation."

The last thing Thomas would seem to want is the public affirmation of the cultural and racial distinctions on which multiculturalism is premised. See Charles Taylor, *Multiculturalism and "The Politics of Recognition,"* ed. Charles Taylor and Amy Gutmann (Princeton, NJ: Princeton University Press, 1992).

92 For a discussion of Wright's free-indirect discourse, see John Reilly's "Giving Bigger a Voice: The Politics of Narrative in *Native Son,*" in *New Essays,* ed. Keneth Kinnamon (New York: Cambridge University Press, 1990), 45–47.

Conclusion: *New Deal Postmodernism*

1 Perry Anderson, *The Origins of Postmodernity* (New York: Verso, 1998), 7. In the inaugural issue of *boundary 2* in 1972, David Antin's keynote essay, "Modernism and Postmodernism: Approaching the Present in American Poetry," confirmed Olson's right to the term he helped invent. Antin lauded Olson and his Black Mountain followers for having cleared the ground in American poetry; Olson did so, Antin argued, by reviving an earlier, international modernism — marked by Apollinaire, Marinetti, Khlebnikov, Lorca, Jozsef, and Neruda — temporarily occluded by the provincial and meretricious writings of Eliot and Pound, Tate and Lowell. See Anderson, 15.

2 Tom Clark, *Charles Olson: The Allegory of a Poet's Life* (New York: Norton, 1991), 79.

3 Ibid., 82.

4 Ibid., 93.

5 Charles Olson, *The Collected Poems of Charles Olson,* ed. George Butterick (Berkeley: University of California Press, 1997), 14.

6 Clark, *Charles Olson,* 94.

7 Robert von Hallberg, *Charles Olson: The Scholar's Art* (Cambridge, MA: Harvard University Press, 1978), 11–12.

8 Susan Vanderborg, " 'Who Can Say Who Are Citizens?' Causal Mythology in Charles Olson's Polis," *Modern Language Quarterly* 59, no. 3 (September 1998): 364.

9 Andrew Ross, *The Failure of Modernism: Symptoms of American Poetry* (New York: Columbia University Press, 1986), 95.

10 Ibid., xvii, 118, 95.

11 Charles Olson, *Collected Prose,* ed. Donald Allen and Benjamin Friedlander (Berkeley: University of California Press, 1997), 240, 162, 297–98.

12 Ross, *The Failure of Modernism,* 96.

13 "Charles Olson, 1910–1970," in *The Norton Anthology of American Literature,* 3d ed., ed. Nina Baym, Ronald Gottesman, Laurence Holland, David Kalstone, Francis Murphy, Hershel Parker, William Pritchard, and Patricia B. Wallace (New York: Norton, 1989), 2:2422.

14 Cited in Rose Lee Goldberg, *Performance Art: From Futurism to the Present* (New York: Harry Abrams, 1988), 121.

15 Harold Rosenberg, *The Anxious Object: Art Today and Its Audience* (New York: New American Library, 1964), 76.

16 Michael Fried, "Art and Objecthood" (1967), in *Art and Objecthood: Essays and Reviews* (Chicago: University of Chicago Press, 1998).

17 Rosenberg, *Anxious Object*, 77.

18 Michael Fried, *Absorption and Theatricality: Painting and Beholder in the Age of Diderot* (Chicago: University of Chicago Press, 1980), 93.

19 Michael Fried, "How Modernism Works," *Critical Inquiry* 9 (September 1982): 229 n.17. It would be a mistake to take from this the suggestion that postmodernism has a particular affinity to the performative. For Fried, the condition of "theater" designated an artwork's consciousness of its audience as much as it did a process-oriented aesthetic. Likewise, he celebrated the absorbed ideal of presentness as a means for painting to respond to a perceived problem in its relation to its audience. If Fried's modernism seemed in this way to deny the existence of the audience so integral to the requirements of painting, it did so precisely by seeing the eventual consumption of a given work as internalized within itself. Or at least this is the story Fried would tell of eighteenth-century French painting in *Absorption and Theatricality*. If the paintings Fried takes up in this work aimed to deny or seal themselves off from the existence of a community of spectators, they did so by insistently staging dramatic scenes within the worlds they represented. Fried reasons that French painters working within the anti-Rococo tradition championed by Denis Diderot embraced the dramatic grandeur of history painting, for example, precisely to anticipate and internalize within their paintings the essentially theatrical moment when spectators would stand before them. Paintings would seem "absorbed," oblivious to the actual spectators gathered around them, by representing scenes of dramatic tension that depicted individuals gripped by the kind of involvement that, ideally, overcame those standing before great works of art. In this context, Fried's criticism of minimalism was not that it embraced either a temporal or an artifactual account of art; in fact, it embraced both, and this indicated to Fried a broader problem, which was the self-conscious relation of minimalist works to their spectators. The point for Fried was not that all investments in objecthood were literalist, or that all investments in temporality were theatrical, but rather that minimalism had given in to a dead-end modernist fascination with literal objects.

20 The perception that performativity constitutes a subversive practice is by no means exclusive or even endemic to those affiliated with *October*. See, for example Judith Butler's influential claim in *Gender Trouble: Feminism and the Subversion of Identity* (New York: Routledge, 1990) that a performative conception of gender — understood not as an essence but as "a regulated process of signification" — subverts the hegemonic order of "compulsory heterosexuality" (145). I hasten to note that my

aim in identifying modernist-period writing as performative has not been
to join the chorus of critical voices that have found poststructuralist
truths confirmed, avant la lettre, in modernist poetics. Quite the contrary:
I mean to insist on the ultimately hollow nature of distinctions between
the historical avant-garde and modernism (as well as between postmodernism and modernism) that turn on associations between performative
aesthetics and antibourgeois politics. In Michael Benamou and Charles
Caramello, eds. *Performance and Postmodern Culture* (Madison WI:
Coda Press, 1977), for example, Benamou declares "performance the
unifying mode of the postmodern." Benamou opposes the postmodern
interest in performance to what he deems to be the modernist commitment to the book: "What is a book is the question. Modernism . . .
compensates for a lost presence; hence an art oriented towards texts and
pictures rather than events and performance. But the postmodern acknowledges what is at stake: the play of the will that takes place where
presence once was" (6). This play of the will, Benamou reasons in turn,
is the key to performance's emancipatory politics. Paraphrasing anthro-
pologist Victor Turner (also a contributor to the volume), he proclaims
that "Play decenters the authoritarian rule." He continues: "Thus, making the letters dance again and the voice sing independently of any
script — small achievements in the glaring light of social injustices —
may not be such insignificant performances after all, as they attack the
very system of signification on which the state was historically founded"
(7). Even in 1977, such a claim was not without considerable precedent.
In "Force and Signification" (1963), for example, Jacques Derrida declared that there is "no insurance against the risk of writing" (25). Writing is "dangerous and anguishing," he reasons, because of its "infinite
equivocality," because, like meaning itself, it is an activity that knows
"no rest" (11). Derrida thus celebrates Mallarmé — who "unrealized the
unity of the Book" — in terms that seem at once potentially political and
formal (in *Writing and Difference,* trans. Alan Bass [Chicago: University
of Chicago Press, 1978]. In *Of Grammatology* [1967], Derrida derides
the "security with which . . . [critics consider] the self-identity of the
text." See "The Exorbitant: Question of Method," from *Of Grammatology,* in *Art in Theory: An Anthology of Changing Ideas,* ed. Charles
Harrison and Paul Wood [Cambridge, MA: Blackwell, 1992], 920). A
decade later little had changed. Rose Lee Goldberg writes in *Performance Art: From Futurism to the Present* that performance art "has
always been anarchic" (9). Similarly, Elin Diamond begins her introduction to *Performance and Cultural Politics* (New York: Routledge, 1997)
with the extraordinarily broad declaration that "postmodern notions of
performance embrace . . . different ways of knowing and doing that are
constitutively heterogeneous, contingent, and risky" (1, 2). With equal
confidence, Peggy Phelan declares in *Unmarked: The Politics of Performance* (New York: Routledge, 1993) that, as such, "Performance clogs

the smooth machinery of reproductive representation necessary to the circulation of capital" (148). Phelan imagines this clogging by conjoining Austin's linguistic performative with performance art itself; her book begins with the epigraph, "Against Being Right." The rather fantastical notion here is that, mooting the intentional, we simultaneously eschew conservative, reactionary politics; believing in the possibility of performance art and an au courant hermeneutics, we pledge our allegiance to the subversive. If what follows points to the fatuity of such easy conjunctions of the formal and the political, I am more specifically concerned to show how entirely reconciled the performative was with American capital in the thirties and forties. Far from clogging "the smooth machinery . . . necessary to the circulation of capital," the New Deal performative instead underwrites the state's decidedly liberal adaptations of laissez-faire to an increasingly postindustrial, state-regulated credit economy. The New Deal performative does not entail a "constitutively heterogeneous, contingent, and risky" politics. Rather than being opposed to bourgeois society, it is understood — in and through the advent of the salaried artist — as a stratagem crucial to its insulation from chance and risk by the welfare state.

21 Rosalind E. Krauss, *The Optical Unconscious* (Cambridge, MA: MIT Press, 1994), 103, 98, 139.

22 See Hal Foster, "Postmodernism: A Preface," in *The Anti-Aesthetic: Essays on Postmodern Culture,* ed. Hal Foster (Port Townsend, WA: Bay Press, 1983), xii.

23 Richard Poirier, *Poetry and Pragmatism* (Cambridge, MA: Harvard University Press, 1992), 119, 155.

24 Fredric Jameson, *The Cultural Turn* (New York: Verso, 1998), 2.

25 Fredric Jameson, introduction to *The Postmodern Condition: A Report on Knowledge,* by Jean-François Lyotard, trans. Geoff Bennington and Brian Massumi (Minneapolis: University of Minnesota Press, 1988), ix.

26 Jameson, *The Cultural Turn,* 20.

27 For an account of the relation between Pollock and the State Department, see Serge Guilbaut, *How New York Stole the Idea of Modern Art: Abstract Expressionism, Freedom, and the Cold War* (Chicago: University of Chicago Press, 1983).

28 Anderson, *Origins,* 74, 117–18.

29 Ibid., 75.

30 Fredric Jameson, *Postmodernism, or, The Cultural Logic of Late Capitalism* (Durham, NC: Duke University Press, 1991), 305.

31 Olson, *Collected Prose,* 239.

32 Von Hallberg, *Charles Olson,* 32.

33 Quoted in ibid., 35.

34 Vanderborg, " 'Who Can Say Who Are Citizens?,' " 373, 380, 364.

35 Roland Barthes, *S/Z,* trans. Richard Miller (New York: Hill and Wang, 1974), 4.

Index

• • •

and laissez-faire, 267; Rexford Tugwell and laissez-faire, 285 n.75; uncertainty and, 9, 49–52, 60; "up to date capitalism," 142, 145; value and, 32–33, 299 n.57; welfare state and laissez-faire, 59, 64, 132, 176, 265
Capote, Truman: *In Cold Blood*, 207
Cappetti, Carla, 211, 218
Capra, Frank: *It's A Wonderful Life*, 164
Cayton, Horace, and St. Clair Drake: *Black Metropolis*, 215, 226, 324 n.89
Ceplair, Larry, 235
Chance, 24, 31, 49, 51, 71, 82, 130–31, 291 n.12, 329 n.20; aesthetics of, 48; utopian eradication of, 81. *See also* Risk
Chase, Stuart: *A New Deal*, 56
Cheever, John, 62
Civil Works Administration, 185, 285 n.79
Cohen, Lizbeth, 215, 246
Cohn, David, 26–27
Coiner, Constance: *Better Red*, 17
Colby, Merle, 40–41, 43
Coleridge, Samuel Taylor: *Biographia Literaria*, 78
Collectivism, 44, 85; rejection of, 122
Collins, Tom, 174
Committee on Government Statistics and Information Services (COGSIS), 13. *See also* Actuarial
Communism: abstract art and, 285 n.76; James Agee and, 25; James T. Farrell and, 39; form and, 86–87; Ernest Hemingway and, 106; intellectuals and, 70; liberalism and, 17; loyalty and, 4; Norman Macleod and, 71; Charles Olson and, 269; Seventh Congress of the Communist International, 71; John Steinbeck and, 177–78; Richard Wright and, 203, 215–16, 218, 250
Communist Party of the United States of America (CPUSA), 37, 71, 86, 289 n.103

Congress, 9, 61, 88, 121, 143, 246
Conroy, Jack, 37, 50, 52, 55; *Disinherited*, 50; *A World To Win*, 50–51, 196
Copyright law, 198–99
Corey, Lewis: *The Crisis of the Middle Class*, 43–44, 46, 282 n.40
Corsair (film), 57
Cosgrove, Peter, 277 n.2
Covici, Pat, 198
Cowley, Malcolm, 28–29, 37, 39, 54, 70, 76–78, 112, 229, 234, 256, 278–79 n.8; *Exile's Return*, 48, 75, 111; "What the Revolutionary Movement Can Do for a Writer," 39
Crane, Hart, 98
Creeley, Robert, 256
Crowd, The (film), 240–41
Cubism, 47

Dada, 47–48, 75–76, 79–82, 111–16, 278 n.5, 285 n.76, 297 n.49, 298 n.54, 299 n.57; Berlin Dadaists, 48; performance and, 112
Dahlberg, Edward, 62
Dames (film), 237, 239, 242–43
Davidson, Cathy, 187
Davidson, Michael, 47
Davis, Elmer, 256; "New World Symphony, with a Few Sour Notes," 149–50; "Some Aspects of the Economics of Authorship," 26
Davis, John P, 214
Defert, Daniel, 275 n.23
Deleuze, Gilles, and Felix Guattari: *Anti-Oedipus: Capitalism and Schizophrenia*, 203
Dell, Floyd, 43, 62
Democratic National Convention, 55, 124
Denning, Michael, 20–21, 148, 178, 288 n.103; *Cultural Front*, 17, 19, 205–6
Depression. *See* Great Depression
Derrida, Jacques, 144, 278 n.5, 284 n.66, 328 n.20
Desrosières, Alain, 14; *The Politics of Large Numbers*, 13–14, 276 n.25

Freeman, Joseph, 29, 43, 45–46, 52–53; *American Testament*, 123; *Proletarian Literature*, 37, 40. See also *New Masses*

Freud, Sigmund: *Civilization and Its Discontents*, 98

Fried, Michael, 114, 327 n.19; "Art and Objecthood," 260–61; "How Modernism Works," 261

Frost, Robert, 2, 76, 121–24, 129–30, 155, 201–2, 207, 211–12, 227, 248, 252–53, 262, 278 n. 5; "Build Soil," 120, 122, 231; "Desert Places," 104; *A Further Range*, 122, 248; irony in, 231; "The Lesson For Today," 202–3, 227–33; "Provide, Provide," 122

Gambling, 31, 49, 56, 60

Garland, Hamlin, 43

George, David Lloyd, 274 n.8

Giacometti, Alberto, 261

Gilroy, Paul, 212

Ginsberg, Allen, 259

G-Men (film), 57

Godden, Richard, 105

Goddin, Robert, 139–41

Godin, Alexander, 53

Gold Diggers musicals (films), 233, 244, 267; *of 1933*, 227, 234–37, 241, 321 n.71; *of 1937*, 11, 203, 207, 237, 240–43, 323 n.80. See also Berkeley, Busby

Gold, Michael, 29, 37, 43, 88 , 142, 218; *Change the World*, 88

Gordon, Linda, 9, 173, 176

Gottlieb, Adolpho, 63

Government/State: allegories of, 10–11; central planning and, 131–32; comparisons with art and, 2, 8, 80–81, 83–84, 86, 92–93, 109–10; consumption of art and, 6, 266–71; displacement of, 12–13; as employer, 24–25, 28–29, 36, 55, 59, 121, 201–2, 227, 257–58; the family and, 173–76, 181, 185; humanizing of, 124; insurance companies and, 12, 224–25; John Maynard Keynes and, 138–41; legitimation crisis

of, 3; liberalism and, 21–23, 210, 217–18, 286 n.88; literary criticism and, 4, 19–22; loyalty to, 3–4, 70–71; money and, 143–44, 146; racism and, 215–16; social insurance and, 131–32, 165, 205–6, 255; statistics and, 9, 276 n.25

Grant, Ulysses S., 90

Great Depression: James Agee and, 277 n.2; Jack Balch and, 69; bourgeois stability and, 22; collectivities and, 123, 132; federal aid and, 176, 206, 213; Federal Arts Projects and, 63–64; Ernest Hemingway and, 107; Josephine Herbst and, 50; industry and, 5, 42; Meridel Le Sueur and, 73; Norman Macleod and, 71; Marxist responses to, 19; musicals and, 234; progressivism and, 274 n.8; Ayn Rand and, 85; social realism and, 264; statistics of, 14; Wallace Stevens and, 148–49; unemployment and, 172, 234; wages and, 56; writing and, 3, 13, 28–29, 39, 47, 49, 59, 70, 183, 196, 283 n.61

Greenberg, Clement, 77, 86, 96, 260–61; "Avant-Garde and Kitsch," 55, 296 n.49

Hallberg, Robert von, 258, 268–69

Happenings, 67, 82, 260

Harburg, E. Y., 11

Hartford Fire and Indemnity Company, 1, 157, 159. See also Wallace Stevens

Hart, Henry, 37, 41–42, 52–53, 60, 72

Haynes, George Edmund, 214

Hellman, Lillian, 37

Hemingway, Ernest, 2, 75, 77, 79, 82–86, 94–102, 106, 112–13, 126, 148, 266–67, 294 n.39, 295 n.42, 296 n.47; "In Another Country," 98–99; "The Battler," 98; "Big Two-Hearted River," 95; *A Farewell to Arms*, 99; *The Fifth Column and Four Stories of the Spanish Civil War*, 96; *For Whom*

108–9, 112, 115, 126, 291 n.8, 294 n.41; autonomy of, 115; form and, 91, 109, 119; Ernest Hemingway and, 98, 111; in nineteenth-century literature, 119; the musical and, 242; rhetoric of, 123; Romantic conceptions of, 77; unity and, 79–81, 93, 129, 145. *See also* Form

Ottley, Roi, 217

Parini, Jay, 195, 314 n.50
Parker, Dorothy, 85
Parsons, Talcott, 134, 144, 174
Partisan Review, 25, 42, 86, 147
Pastoral, 121–23, 258. *See also* Frost, Robert
Patronage: bourgeois, 27, 266; governmental, 68, 121, 186, 277 n.2, 286 n.89, 288 n.103; laissez-faire, 42; of modern art, 54; of radical writers, 28
Pearson, Ralph: "The Economic Status of the Artist Today," 54
Pells, Richard, 44, 282 n.40
Performance: audience and, 113, 119, 261, 270; gender and, 327 n.20; opposed to artifacts, 25–27, 261, 288 n.96; performative, 277 n.5, 278 n.5, 295 n.42, 304 n.52, 305 n.61, 329 n.20, and the "performing self," 32, 67; as process of composition, 67, 120, 270; as staged event, 139, 169, 277 n.3
Perkins, Frances, 273 n.8
Perkins, Maxwell, 96, 101
Plato: "Gorgias," 82
Plimpton, George, 96
Poirier, Richard, 32, 120–23, 232–33, 262, 278 n.5; *The Performing Self*, 67; *Poetry and Pragmatism*, 67
Pollock, Jackson, 63, 82, 260, 263
Popular Front, 17, 19, 41, 65, 71, 264, 280 n.24
Postmodernism, 144, 256, 258, 261–65, 270, 320 n.20; "New Deal postmodernism," 256; performativity and, 263, 304 n.52, 327 n.19

Potts, Rufus M.: "The Altruistic Utilitarianism of Insurance," 10
Poulantzas, Nicos, 53, 283 n.61, 283–84 n.62
Pound, Ezra, 32, 83–84, 142–44, 262–63, 268; formalism of, 47; "In a Station of the Metro," 32; "The Individual and His Milieu," 143; objectivism of, 32, 47; "What Is Money For?," 143
Pragmatism: American, 67, 277 n.3, 278 n.5; Emersonian, 66–68, 278 n.5
Pregnancy, 169–74, 179, 195, 198, 311 n.22, 313 n.34, 314 n.47; relation of to authorship, 195; relation of to sympathy, 170
Professionalism, 17, 25, 30, 32, 35, 41–42, 53, 72–73, 278–80 n.19, 281 n.34; culture of, 53, 74; identity and, 34, 55, 57; professional/managerial class, 28, 34–35, 44; the writer and, 14, 41–43, 53–54, 62, 76
Proletariat, 40, 43–46, 51–54, 87, 282 n.40; writers and, 29, 32, 34, 39–40, 44, 50, 55, 106, 296 n.47
Proust, Marcel, 262
Public Works of Art Project, 59, 63
Publishing, 26–27, 31, 41–42, 49, 52–53, 315 n.55; destruction of, 112; government and, 29; Houghton Mifflin, 26; Macmillan, 33; G. P. Putnam's Sons, 37; strikes against industry, 39; Viking, 170, 198

Rabinowitz, Paula: *Labor and Desire*, 16, 196
Race: discrimination and, 13–14, 208–10, 214–15, 246, 309 n.9, 311 n.25; identity and, 245, 316 n.18; insurance and, 212; New Deal and, 213–16, 318 n.39; violence and, 245; Richard Wright and, 213
Radicalism, 17, 19, 75; artists and, 25, 28–29, 39–40, 45, 47, 54, 196, 289 n.103; intellectualism and, 45; the left and, 87; mod-

Smith, George A. E., and Charles A. Beard: *Current Problems of Public Policy*, 186; *The Future Comes: A Study of the New Deal*, 186; *The Old Deal and the New*, 186

Smith, Terry, 63

Socialism, 4, 29, 189, 289 n.103, 301 n.29

Social security, 232, 251, 254–55, 274 n.14; Michel Foucault and, 301 n.29, 316 n.10

Social Security Administration, 1, 2, 4–5, 9–11, 13–14, 18, 21, 36, 45, 109, 121–22, 126, 128, 131–32, 140, 165, 173, 175, 183, 202–8, 212–17, 277 n.2, 310 n.21, 317 n.38, 318 n.34, 319 n.56; French, 131; Social Security Act, 1, 173, 310 n.21; Social Security Bill, 12; Social Security Board, 10, 318 n.39; Wallace Stevens and, 1–3, 11, 17–18. *See also* Insurance

Southern Agrarians, 7, 76

Speculation, 56, 59–61

Stalinism, 19, 71

Statistics, 14–15, 18. *See also* Actuarial

Stein, Gertrude, 2, 42, 49–50, 75, 77, 79, 82–91, 94–95, 117, 121, 126, 142–43, 262, 266–67, 278 n.5, 292 n.27, 293 n.29; "The Capital and the Capitals of the United States of America," 92–93; *Everybody's Autobiography*, 117–18; *Four in America*, 90; *The Geographical History of the United States*, 87–88, 90; *How Writing Is Written*, 88; *Lectures in America*, 90; *The Making of Americans*, 118; "Plays," 119; "What Are Master-pieces and Why Are There So Few Of Them," 90–93, 117–18; "What is English Literature," 93, 119, 293 n.30

Steinbeck, Carol, 194, 200; work for State Emergency Relief Administration, 195

Steinbeck, John, 2, 163, 190, 194–200, 207, 209, 267, 312 n.32,

315 n.55; *Burning Bright*, 178–79; *Cannery Row*, 198; gender politics and, 166–67, 314 n.50; *The Grapes of Wrath*, 10, 114, 162–71, 174–76, 179–84, 189, 191, 194–95, 198, 200, 249, 312 n.29, 314 nn.47, 50; *In Dubious Battle*, 123–24, 177–78; national welfarism and, 182; *Of Mice and Men*, 178, 314 n.50; populism and, 184; sentimentalism and, 162, 309 n.9; *Tortilla Flat*, 176–77, 199; wage labor and, 175

Stevens, Wallace, 1–3, 5, 7, 11, 16–18, 42, 120–21, 123, 130, 142–46, 149, 152, 156–58, 160, 163, 175, 199, 242, 262–63, 267, 277 n.2, 278 n.5, 281 n.34, 308 nn.90, 92; "Adagia," 129, 142, 152, 156, 159–60; "The Creation of Sounds," 159; "A Duck for Dinner," 152, 159; "Esthétique du Mal," 158; "The Idea of Order at Key West," 125, 130, 147–48, 150–62, 166, 214; *Ideas of Order*, 148, 213–14; "Insurance and Social Change," 1, 2, 5, 127, 129, 151, 157, 159; interest of in transcendental order, 307 n.82; "Like Decorations in a Nigger Cemetery," 213–14; "major man" and, 124–27; "The Man with the Blue Guitar," 158; "Mr. Burnshaw and the Statue," 145, 147; "The Noble Rider and the Sound of Words," 17; performative aesthetics of, 82; "Notes Toward a Supreme Fiction," 124–26, 145, 152, 158, 160; "The Old Woman and the Statue," 147; *Owl's Clover*, 145–47; "The Pleasures of Merely Circulating," 145; "Surety and Fidelity Claims," 151

Stock market, 48, 144–45; analogy with poetry and, 76–77, 145, 148

Stone, Julius, 149

Stowe, Harriet Beecher, 186; *Uncle Tom's Cabin*, 167, 189, 208

Stravinsky, Igor, 262

Sturges, Preston: *Sullivan's Travels* (film), 234
Surrealism, 48, 79, 116, 261, 297 n.49
Sympathy: James T. Farrell and, 204, 206; insurance and, 207; in New Deal literature, 171; pregnancy and, 170; Adam Smith and, 176, 204–6, 218; Betty Smith and, 188–89; John Steinbeck and, 168–70, 174, 177, 180, 182–83, 200; theater and, 170; Richard Wright and, 208–9, 212, 218, 251, 254. *See also* Sentimentalism

Taft, Robert, 186
Theater, 114, 169, 174, 200, 261; sympathy and, 170; theatricality, 169
Third American Writers Congress. *See* American Writers Congress: Third
Thompson, Jim: *Nothing More Than Murder*, 11; *Now and on Earth*, 29, 35–36; *A Swell Looking Babe*, 11
Thoreau, Henry David, 203; *Journal*, 67; *Walden*, 277 n.3
Tompkins, Jane, 167
Trilling, Diana, 186
Trilling, Lionel, 42
Truman, Harry, 248, 257
Tugwell, Rexford, 63, 133, 273 n.8, 285 n.75
Tzara, Tristan, 111–15, 119; "Dada Manifesto," 113; "An Introduction to Dada," 112

Underconsumption, 2, 5–6, 267
Unemployment, 4–5, 9, 13–14, 37, 48, 93, 140, 163, 166–69, 172, 176, 213–14, 234–35, 285 n.79, 318 n.39; compensation and, 13, 36, 140; federal programs and, 93; insurance and, 4, 140
Unions, 39, 41–42, 44, 282 n.40. *See also* Labor

Vanderborg, Susan, 258, 269
Vidor, King, 240–41

Wald, Alan: *The Revolutionary Imagination*, 16
Walker, Margaret, 62, 215, 250
Wallace, Henry, 257
Wallis, Hal, 237
Warner Bros., 11, 57, 234–37, 243, 267, 321 n.72; *Bullets or Ballots*, 57; *Corsair*, 57; *Dames*, 237, 239, 242–43; *G-Men*, 57; *Gold Diggers of 1933*, 227, 234–37, 241, 321 n.71; *Gold Diggers of 1937*, 11, 203, 207, 237, 240–43, 323 n.80; musicals of, 242; *Ready, Willing and Able*, 236; Harry Warner, 234; Harry and Jack Warner, 321 n.72
Warren, Frank, 132
Warren, Robert Penn, 42, 77–79, 145; *All The King's Men*, 10–11; *Understanding Poetry*, 76, 145
Warshaw, Robert, 70
Washington, George, 90
Watson, Forbes, 59–61, 65; "The Artist Becomes a Citizen," 60; "A Steady Job," 60; "The Chance in a Thousand," 59
Weaver, Robert, 215; *Opportunity*, 214
Welfare, 6, 21–22, 164, 206, 317 n.28, 318 n.34; collective welfare, 149; policies of, 176; politics of, 11
Welfare state: abandonment of, 4; F. R. Ankersmit and, 304 n.52; Edward Berkowitz and, 22; families and, 172–73, 185; Michel Foucault and, 316 n.10; French, 275 n.22; insurance and, 12, 164, 234, 275 n.22, 310 n.21, 316 n.10, 321 n.72; C. L. R. James and, 205–6; John Maynard Keynes and, 138–39; laissez-faire and, 132, 134, 176; liberalism and, 231; literature and, 2–3, 16; loyalty and, 4; Jean-François Lyotard and, 144; musicals and, 234; New Deal performative and, 329 n.20; political compromise and, 20; as product of agentless history, 286 n.88; Ayn Rand and, 86, 134; Philip Roth and, 246;

social security and, 10, 45, 205–
6, 265, 274 n.14; Wallace Stevens
and, 18; utopia and, 5; Richard
Wright and, 217

Whitman, Walt, 124, 203, 259

Whoopee! (film), 239

Whorf, Benjamin, 11, 156–59,
296 n.42; "The Relation of Habitual Thought and Language to
Behavior," 156–57; and Whorfian hypothesis, 157

Wilder, Laura Ingalls: *Little House
on the Prairie*, 184

Williams, Alexander: *Murder on the
WPA*, 65

Williams, Raymond, 20, 282 n.49

Williams, William Carlos, 32, 42,
46–47, 143, 268; Objectivism
and, 47; and *Paterson*, 143; "The
Term," 294 n.41

Wilson, Christopher, 43, 279–
80 n.19

Wilson, Edmund, 148

Wimsatt, W. K., and Monroe C.
Beardsley, 160–61, 199; "heresy
of paraphrase," 77, 145; "The
Intentional Fallacy," 160

Witte, Edwin, 10

Wolfort, Ira: *Tucker's People*, 57–58

Woolf, Virginia, 17

Wordsworth, William: "The Solitary Reaper," 154–55

Working class, 19, 28, 30, 37, 39–40,
43–48, 51–52, 147, 164, 183–84,
187, 196, 266, 281 n.37, 314 n.50;
class-consciousness in, 137; ethics of, 55; Jack London and, 34;
novels of, 29, 166; writer's affiliations with, 54. *See also* Labor

Works Progress Administration
(WPA), 5, 14, 28, 61, 63, 65, 68–
69, 92–94, 106, 129, 132, 209,
213, 215, 217, 227, 285 n.79,
318 n.39

Works Progress Administration Arts
Projects, 5, 6, 58–59, 68, 71, 138,
260, 286 n.89; Federal Music
Project of, 62; Federal Theater
Project of, 62, 68, 178, 185–86;
Federal Writers' Project of, 24,
27–28, 36, 42, 49, 52, 57–59,
62–63, 68–74, 120–21, 129,
146, 196, 203, 217, 234, 266,
287 n.93, 288 n.101, 290 n.114,
293 n.32, 320 n.62; termination
of, 202. *See also* Federal Arts
Projects

Wright, Richard, 2, 3, 11, 22, 37, 52,
62, 68, 70, 146, 207–8, 212, 215,
248–49, 268, 318 n.39, 320 n.62,
323 n.84, 324 n.89; *Black Boy*,
226; *Black Power*, 211; "Blueprint for Negro Writing," 251;
"How 'Bigger Was Born,'" 52,
208, 226; *Lawd Today*, 213, 246;
liberalism and, 22, 209–11, 217–
18, 255; *Native Son*, 3, 52, 98,
146, 208–11, 215–21, 225–27,
241, 252–55, 319 n.49, 325 n.91;
The Outsider, 11, 165, 203, 209–
12, 216–18, 250–51, 255,
319 n.39; *Savage Holiday*, 11,
221, 244, 325 n.90; *Twelve Million Black Voices*, 215–16; *Uncle
Tom's Children*, 251–52

Yeats, William Butler, 83–84, 98

Yerby, Frank, 62

Yezierska, Anzia, 62, 146

Young, Philip, 95

Zanuck, Darryl, 237

Zhdanov, Andrei, 36

Zukofsky, Louis, 47, 52

Michael Szalay is Assistant Professor of English at Fordham University.

• • •

Library of Congress Cataloging-in-Publication Data

Szalay, Michael
New deal modernism : American literature and the invention of the
welfare state / Michael Szalay.
p. cm. — (Post-contemporary interventions)
Includes bibliographical references and index.
ISBN 0-8223-2576-4 (cloth : alk. paper) — ISBN 0-8223-2562-4
(pbk. : alk. paper)
1. American literature — 20th century — History and criticism.
2. Modernism (Literature) — United States. 3. Roosevelt, Franklin D.
(Franklin Delano), 1882–1945 — Influence. 4. Politics and
literature — United States — History — 20th century. 5. Literature and
society — United States — History — 20th century. 6. Public welfare —
United States — History — 20th century. 7. Social problems in
literature. 8. New Deal, 1933–1939.
I. Title. II. Series.
PS228.M63 S93 2000
810.9′112 — dc21   00-029390

• • •